FOOTBALL
THE
COMPLETE
FACTS
STATS
AND
RECORDS

ISBN 1 85868 483 8

Printed and bound in Great Britain

FOOTBALL
THE
COMPLETE
FACTS
STATS
AND
RECORDS

Keir Radnedge

Contents

The Great Coaches

The Great Players

Contents

The Great Matches

The Famous Stadiums

The Great Countries

FIFA, the world governing body of association football, boasts more than 200 members. They are grouped into six regional confederations representing Europe (UEFA), South America (CONMEBOL), Central and North America (CONCACAF), Africa, Asia and Oceania.

Such is football's worldwide democracy that each country has one vote in FIFA's two-yearly congress – the same power belonging to both England and Ethiopia, Brazil and Botswana. International football is thus organised as a pyramid with the individual countries representing a third level of power – and with the clubs beneath them in the structure. Modern association football owed its creation to the English and it spread rapidly throughout the world thanks to British sailors, engineers and bankers but also thanks to students who travelled to England to study and took home with them a new-found love of what is now the world's greatest game. In each country, football developed along the same lines. Enthusiastic amateurs spread the word among their friends, they formed clubs and those clubs formed associations or federations and then knock-out cup competitions and league championships. As early as 1904 FIFA, the international federation of association football, was set up in Paris by delegates from Belgium, Denmark, France Holland, Spain, Sweden and Switzerland. FIFA was happy, in its early years, to accept the Olympic Games as a de facto world championship. After the first world war, however, it became clear to FIFA's French president, Jules Rimet, that the advance of professionalism demanded a world championship of its own. Thus the World Cup was born.

Argentina

Asociacion del Futbol Argentino

Founded:

1893

FIFA:

1912

World Cup:

1978, 1986

South American Championship:

1910, 1921, 1925, 1927, 1929, 1937, 1941, 1945, 1946, 1947, 1955, 1957, 1991, 1993*

Of all South American nations, Argentina are the most consistently successful.

Football was brought to Argentina by the British in the 1860s, and although, at first, it was exclusive to the British residents in Buenos Aires, by the turn of the century numerous clubs had been formed. The Argentine Football Association was founded in 1891 by an Englishman, Alexander Hutton, and a league was formed the same year. Although the championship was not a truly national competition, as it contained only clubs from Buenos Aires, La Plata, Rosario and Santa Fé, the intense rivalry of the clubs in Buenos Aires ensured that Argentina had a vibrant domestic scene from the outset.

In 1901 a representative side played neighbouring Uruguay, in the first international match to be staged outside Great Britain. The seeds were sown for a rivalry which has grown into one of the most enduring and intense derby matches in the world.

Professionalism was adopted in 1931, and River Plate and Boca Juniors soon emerged as dominant forces. River's side of the 1940s was the greatest of them all, containing a forward line of Munoz, Moreno, Pedernera, Labruna and Loustau which became known as La Maquina – the machine.

The national side were runners-up, to Uruguay, in the 1928 Olympics and met their deadly rivals again two years later in the 1930 World Cup Final. Although they lost 4–2 the impressive Argentine side was plundered by Italian and Spanish clubs – a draining process which continues to this day. To avoid a repeat of this poaching, a third-rate side went into the 1934 tournament, and Argentina did not make a serious attempt on the World Cup again until the 1950s.

Indeed, the 1950s saw the birth of an exceptional side, with another famous forward trio of Corbatta, Sivori and Cruz. They won the South American championship twice during the 1950s and then made an unsuccessful bid to host the 1958 World Cup. Little progress was made in the 1960s and 1970s, despite Independiente and Estudiantes dominating the Libertadores Cup, and Argentina had to wait until 1978 for their first success in the World Cup. On home soil, and with a side containing only one overseas-based player, Mario Kempes of Sevilla, Argentina deservedly won the tournament. They did so again in Mexico in 1986, when the side was led by Diego Maradona – who ranks as one of the greatest players the world has ever seen despite his drug abuse problems.

Although Argentina had two considerable advantages through playing at home – fanatical support and a repressive military regime – they were good enough to have won even if playing away. Kempes ended the tournament as top scorer with six goals, and Leopoldo Luque was a splendid foil for him, playing on bravely despite his brother's death in a road accident soon after the event began. Osvaldo Ardiles who was soon to join Tottenham in a ground-breaking over-the-ocean transfer deal, was a superb midfielder. Daniel Passarella a solid stopper. No team could live with the Argentines at that time, not even Holland, whose splendid Total Football proved a little too fragile in a bad-tempered final, settled 3–1 in extra time.

The team of eight years later were dominated by Maradona, but the part played by his illegal "Hand of God" goal in the defeat of England cannot be over-estimated. Without that infringement, ignored by the officials, Argentina may well have faltered. Striker Jorge Valdano was another excellent player, but the rest were mere journeymen

compared to Maradona, and the team almost wasted a two-goal lead when the Germans scored in quick succession, only to concede a winner to Jorge Burruchaga.

Argentina not only featured in the finals of three of the four World Cups from 1978 to 1990, they also won the first two South American Championships of the 1990s, and they continue to produce extremely gifted footballers. The captain of the 1978 World Cup winning team, Daniel Passarella, became national coach in 1995 and guided Argentina back to the 1998 World Cup finals.

France 98 proved to be a disappointment for the Argentines. Going into the tournament they were many people's favourites for the competition. With Gabriel Batistuta, Juan Veron and Ariel Ortega firing on all cylinders, Argentina powered their way through the group stages with wins over Japan, Jamaica and Croatia, and faced an impressive England side in the second round in what proved to be the game of the tournament. After trading two early penalties, they were victims of possibly the goal of the tournament by Michael Owen before levelling matters on the stroke of half-time through a well-worked free kick. They came through the penalty shoot-out despite being held to 2–2 by ten men through much of the second half. A quarter-final clash against Holland was their reward, but they went down 2–1 to a sensational Dennis Bergkamp goal.

Austria

Österreichischer Fussball-Bund

Founded:
1904

FIFA:
1905

Vienna arguably was the focal point of continental European football in the first half of the twentieth century, a situation which lasted until the 1960s. Britons living in Vienna provided Austrian football's early impetus and, as long ago as 1902, Austria trounced Hungary 5–0 at the Prater in what has become the world's second oldest regular international fixture after England vs. Scotland.

The inter-war period was Austria's most successful era, when the "Wunderteam" – led by Matthias Sindelar ("The Man of Paper") – swept all before them. In 30 matches from spring 1931 to summer 1934, the "Wunderteam" scored 101 goals, and the 1934 World Cup seemed to be at their mercy. But a defeat in the semi-final by the hosts Italy, on a quagmire of a pitch in Milan, ended their hopes. Austria's chances in the 1938 event were destroyed by the German occupation, and from 1938 "Austrian" football ceased to exist.

Regular Qualifiers

A new side came together in the 1950s, led by Ernst Ocwirck and Gerhard Hanappi, which looked set for World Cup success in 1954. But the Germans again spoiled the plan, winning the semi-final 6–1. A poor showing in 1958 in Sweden was followed by an inexorable decline, and despite qualifying for the 1978, 1982, 1990 and 1998 World Cup finals, Austria have continued to slide to the lower end of the middle-ranked nations in Europe.

For the national team, the lowest point was reached on September 12, 1991 when the minnows of the Faroe Islands – playing their first ever competitive match – won 1–0 in a European Championship qualifier. It was a humiliating result for Austria, a once great footballing nation, and a sign of how their football had suffered since the halcyon days of the 1930s.

But the country took stock and began the job of re-building both the pride and structure of the sport within Austria. They qualified for France and the 1998 World Cup, looking stronger than they had for a long time. They lost just one game on the way to the finals but disappointed once there, needing last-minute goals to draw their first two games and then being eliminated after losing to Italy, despite another goal in the last few seconds. Austria's long-awaited comeback to the world stage has been delayed again.

Belgium

Union Royale Belge des Sociétés de Football Association

Founded:

1895

FIFA:

1904 *

Belgian football has taken a long time to develop. With an association formed in 1895 and the second-oldest league outside Great Britain, it was natural for the Belgians to be a driving force behind the formation of FIFA and one of only four European sides to go to Uruguay for the first World Cup in 1930. But the strictly amateur nature of the domestic game hindered progress.

The yoke of amateurism was finally discarded in the 1972, with the introduction of full professionalism, and the national side immediately improved. From 1972 to 1984 Belgium reached the last eight of four successive European Championships, and in 1980 they appeared in the final, where they lost to West Germany by a goal scored three minutes from the end. The class of 1980 went on to represent Belgium for almost a decade and contained many of the country's most celebrated players, including goal-keeper Jean-Marie Pfaff, full-back Eric Gerets and forward Jan Ceulemans.

Their finest hour came at the 1986 World Cup finals, where they lost only to Argentina in the semi-finals. Players such as midfielder Enzo Scifo and goalkeeper Michel Preud'homme counted among the world's best but the lack of an outstanding marks-man has restricted Belgium to little more than respected makeweights at the major events.

In 1990, a last-minute goal by England's David Platt eliminated Belgium, somewhat unluckily, from the second round, and four years later, in the United States, they fell to Germany at the same stage, after taking great satisfacion from beating their age-old rivals, Holland, in the group stages with a goal from the versatile Philippe Albert.

A long row between Enzo Scifo and the national coach, Georges Leeskens, was eventually settled in time for the 1998 World Cup, which Belgium struggled to reach. They were second to Holland in their group, but managed to overcome the Republic of Ireland in a two-leg play-off. Once in the tournament proper, Belgium drew with Holland and Mexico before surprisingly being held to a draw against the unfancied South Koreans and thus failed to go through to the next stage.

All eyes will now focus on Euro 2000 which will see Belgium hosting the tournament along with Holland.

Brazil

Confederacao Brasileira de Futebol

Founded:
1914
FIFA:
1923
World Cup:
1958, 1962, 1970, 1994
South American Championship:
1919, 1922, 1949, 1989

Brazilian football has a romantic air about it that sets it apart from other nations. Between 1958 and 1970 they won the World Cup three times, with a team packed full of star players, including arguably the greatest footballer in history – Pele. Brazil remains the only country to have played in every World Cup finals tournament since 1930 and the only nation to have won the cup four times.

Brazilian football developed at the end of the nineteenth century, prompted by migrant British workers, and leagues were established in Rio de Janeiro and São Paulo by the turn of the century. The vast size of Brazil meant that a national league was impractical and until the 1970s these leagues dominated domestic football. The "classic" Rio derbies between Flamengo,

Fluminense, Botafogo and Vasco da Gama regularly attracted massive crowds to the 200,000-capacity Maracana Stadium.

The national team was a little slower out of the blocks, and their first real international was not played until 1914 with a visit to Buenos Aires. In 1916 Brazil entered the South American Championship but, perversely, this event has not been a rewarding one for the Brazilians, who have won it only four times – three of them on home soil.

The World Cup, however, is another matter. The first attempt on the trophy was made in 1930, when they went out in the first round. The 1934 campaign was equally bad, despite the presence of such fine players as Leonidas da Silva and Artur Friedenreich. In 1938, however, they showed the first signs of what was to come by reaching the semi-finals, where they lost to Italy.

Two Golden Decades

The golden age of Brazilian football was between 1950 and 1970, and it is the sides of this era that stick in the memory. In 1950 they were runners-up as Uruguay pipped them 2–1 for the title in the deciding match. Although they lost on that occasion, the final demonstrated just how popular the game was becoming in Brazil. The final was played at the Maracana Stadium in Rio de Janeiro and a record 200,000 fans crammed in to watch the contest.

Moving forward to 1954, with Nilton and Djalma Santos established at the back and Didi running the midfield, they reached the quarter-finals in Switzerland, where they lost to Hungary's "Magical Magyars".

In 1958 Brazil finally won the honour the nation's fans craved. With a forward line consisting of Garrincha, Vava, Zagalo and the 17-year-old Pele, they stormed to victory in Sweden, beating the hosts 5–2 in the final. In Chile in 1962, an almost identical team – minus the injured Pele – triumphed again, beating Czechoslovakia 3–1 in the final in Santiago.

In 1966, in England, the side was being rebuilt and Brazil fell in the first round. But the newcomers Tostao, Gerson and Jairzinho were present in Mexico four years later when Brazil clinched a hat-trick of World Cups, earning them the right to keep the Jules Rimet Trophy in perpetuity.

The 1970 side has been described as the best ever seen, and with some justification. The defence, marshalled by Carlos Alberto, was not all that strong, but this did not matter as the Brazilian approach at this time was all-out attack – and simply to score more goals than they conceded. This was football with a flourish and the global TV audience loved it. In attack, Pele was back to his best and he was superbly assisted by Jairzinho, Rivelinho and Tostao.

After 1970, it was 24 years before the national side again scaled such heights by winning the 1994 World Cup – albeit thanks to a penalty shoot-out after a disappointing 0–0 draw with that other great World Cup side, Italy.

Even though Brazil experienced a decline in playing standards in the years between their third and fourth World Cup triumphs, they certainly didn't disgrace themselves: fourth place in 1974, third place in 1978 and the quarter-final stage in 1986 is hardly the mark of a poor team. Arguably their best showing along the way, however, was in the 1982 World Cup, when a side containing Zico, Socrates, Junior and Falcao should have gone further than the second round in Spain, but were beaten in a thrilling match by eventual winners Italy.

International Domination

Ironically, in the 1994 qualifying matches, Brazil lost to Bolivia, their first defeat ever in a World Cup qualifier, and ultimately scrambled through in an unconvincing and uncharacteristic fashion. However, come the finals in the USA and Brazil were in imperious form as they reached the final against Italy and became the first side to win a World Cup final in a penalty shoot out, after a dour 0–0 draw after extra time.

Defending the title in France 98, Brazil were strong favourites to retain the trophy. Boasting the talent of Ronaldo, Denilson and Rivaldo they reached the final before succumbing 3–0 to an inspired French side.

Bulgaria

Bulgarski Futbolen Solus

Founded:
1923
FIFA:
1924

Bulgaria, like many Eastern Bloc countries, made little impact in international football until the Communists had taken over in 1944 – and completely reorganized the domestic game. Before 1944 football's development was hampered by the unstable political climate, but matters did improve after the First World War, when many clubs were formed – especially in Varna and the capital, Sofia.

The Communist reorganization, however, transformed Bulgarian football. A rigid style of passing play was imposed on the national side, merely requiring strong players to fit the pattern. The results were significant, making Bulgaria very difficult opponents and one of Europe's top sides during the 1960s and 1970s. But this system discouraged individual flair and flexibility – a point illustrated by Bulgaria's astonishingly poor record in the World Cup finals. Bulgaria qualified for five of the eight World Cup finals between 1962 and 1990, playing 16 matches … and did not win any of them! But this period did produce one of Bulgaria's

greatest players, Georgi Asparoukhov, who scored 19 goals in 50 games before dying, with team-mate Nikola Kotkov, in a 1971 car crash. This marked the end of one era and the start of a long period of transition from "state amateurism" to post-communist professionalism.

Bulgaria progressed beyond the group round of a World Cup for the first time in Mexico in 1986. They failed to do themselves justice, with lacklustre, unimaginative and ultra-cautious performances. But players such as goalkeeper Boris Mihaylov and forwards Hristo Stoichkov and Nasko Sirakov, then formed the backbone of the team which took the 1994 World Cup by storm.

They lost their first match 3–0 to Nigeria, recorded their long overdue first win by beating Greece 4–0, and then caused a tremendous surprise by defeating Argentina despite having a man sent off. True, Diego Maradona was ruled out of the match because he had failed a dope tesst, but even so the result was remarkable. Bulgaria followed with a win over Mexico on penalties and then the biggest surprise of all – a 2–1 defeat of Germany, even though they had scored first. Defeat by Italy in a reverse of that score was an anti-climax – as was the side's performance in Euro 96 and their 1998 World Cup campaign. They started with a 0–0 draw with Paraguay, lost 0–1 to Nigeria and were then crushed 6–1 by Spain, with coach Hristo Bonev resigning in disgust.

Cameroon

Féderation Camerounaise de Football

Founded:
 1960
FIFA:
 1962
African Nations Cup:
 1984, 1988

Of all the African nations to have reached the World Cup finals, Cameroon have made by far the biggest impact. In 1982, in Spain, they drew all three of their first round games – against Italy (eventual winners), Poland (third) and Peru – but went out at that stage. They qualified again in 1990, beat reigning champions Argentina in the opening match and reached the quarter-finals, losing narrowly to England. As a result of these performances FIFA agreed to grant Africa a third berth at the 1994 finals. This time, the "Indomitable Lions" were a major disappointment, torn apart by internal strife.

Cameroon's greatest player is undoubtedly striker Roger Milla, who played in the 1982, 1990 and 1994 World Cup teams. In 1994, when 42, he became the oldest player to appear in the finals. Although he played much of his club football in France, with Monaco and Bastia, Milla was voted African Footballer of the Year in 1976 and again in 1990, and delighted fans at Italia '90 with his goals and his celebratory wiggle which usually followed. Other Cameroon players to have won the award include Theophile Abega (1984), Thomas N'Kono (1979 and 1982) and Jean Onguene (1980). N'Kono is one of the greatest goalkeepers Africa has produced, and enjoyed a fine club career in Spain.

Cameroon also won the African Nations Cup twice, by beating Nigeria 3–1 in 1984 and again 1–0 in 1988, to confirm their status as the top side of the 1980s. Their clubs have also enjoyed considerable success in African competitions: with five wins in the Champions Cup and three in the Cup Winners' Cup.

Oryx Douala won the very first Champions Cup in 1964, followed by Canon Yaounde in 1971. Then came three wins in successive years by Canon Yaounde in 1978, Union Doula in 1979 and Canon Yaounde again a year later. In the Cup-winners' Cup, a Cameroon club – Tonnerre Yaounde – won the first version, in 1975, with Canon Yaounde following in 1979 and Union Doula in 1981.

The 1998 World Cup, however, was a big letdown, the team finishing bottom of their initial group after draws against Austria and Chile and a 3–0 defeat at the hands of Italy ending their World Cup dreams for another four years.

Chile

Federacion de Futbol de Chile

Founded:
1895

FIFA:
1912

Until Colo Colo's Libertadores Cup triumph in 1991, no Chilean side had ever won a major honour, and Chile have often been seen as the "nearly-men" of South American football. Colo Colo, Chilean nickname for a wildcat, were founded by five angry members of the old Magallanes FC. Even though Chilean football is generally held to lag far behind that of traditional giants Brazil, Argentina and Uruguay, Colo Colo have an enviable reputation throughout the continent. The club's vision has always stretched beyond the Andes. Such a tradition was laid down by David Orellano. He was a founder member of Colo Colo and one of the five Magallanes rebels who disagreed over the choice of a new club captain. The choice of the five fell upon Orellano and, within two years of Colo Colo's foundation, they had sent a team off to tour Spain.

Never Quite Made It

Chile qualified for five of the 11 post-war World Cups, but have only once progressed beyond the first round, in 1962, when they reached the semi-finals on home soil before losing to eventual winners Brazil. However, despite their sterling performances during that World Cup, what lingers most in the memory is the disgraceful group match with Italy that was more like a boxing match than a game of football. At one stage, police, officials and photographers wrestled on the pitch with players as order dissolved in a melée of bodies.

Chile's best performances in the South American Championship came in 1979 and 1987, when they were runners-up. Chile, like many of its neighbours, is continually drained of its best players by European clubs, and it is unlikely that the Chileans will ever be able to improve on their third place in the 1962 World Cup. The country continues, however, to turn up outstanding players and the strikeforce of Ivan Zamorano and new hero Marcello Salas – both players rated near the ten million-pound mark – proved lethal in the 1998 World Cup qualifiers – scoring 23 of Chile's 32 goals. Chile scraped through to World Cup qualification by coming fourth in the tough South American qualifying group. Despite being much fancied going into the tournament they could only muster three draws in the group stages to finish in second place and crashed out of the competition in the second round losing 4–1 to eventual finalists Brazil.

Colombia

Federation Columbiana de Futbol

Founded:
1924

FIFA:
1936

Colombia is only now emerging as a challenger to Argentina and Brazil after years of internal disputes, disruptions and turbulence. The most notorious came in 1950, shortly after professionalism was introduced, when a break-away league outside FIFA jurisdiction, the DiMayor, was formed and Colombian sides began importing players from all over South America and from Britain. The huge salaries on offer led to the four years of its existence being known as the "El Dorado" period. The bubble burst in 1954, when Colombia were readmitted to FIFA and the league collapsed, leaving many clubs in desperate financial trouble.

The national side made its debut as late as 1938, and results at first were poor. Between 1949 and 1957 no internationals were played at all, and thereafter outings were infrequent. It was a huge surprise, then, when Colombia qualified for the 1962 World Cup in Chile, although to do so they had only to beat Peru. However, the best they managed on their World Cup debut was a 4–4 draw with the USSR.

In 1965 another breakaway federation was formed and confusion reigned once more. FIFA had to intervene and effectively ran Colombian football up until 1971, when the present administration was installed. A new league structure was introduced in 1968, careful controls on the number of foreign imports were implemented, and the national side soon benefited.

In 1989 Nacional Medellin won the Libertadores Cup, the country's only victory, and a year later the national side, coached by Francisco Maturana, qualified for the 1990 World Cup finals.

But the best – and worst – followed. In the 1994 World Cup qualifiers, Argentina were thrashed 5–0 in Buenos Aires, which led a number of people to consider the Colombians a good bet to win the trophy, but their efforts foundered on poor morale, not helped by death threats against players and coach Maturana. Worst of all came after their surprise first-round elimination. Defender Andres Escobar – who had scored an own goal in the shock 2–1 defeat by the USA – was shot to death in Medellin. Drug and gambling cartels – believed to be behind the unsolved murder – still threaten to undermine all the good work achieved by outstanding players such as Carlos Valderrama, who was still in the team at the 1998 World Cup.

Croatia

Croatian Football Federation

Founded:
1991
FIFA:
1992

Croatia's qualification for the 1996 European Championship finals underlined their dramatic emergence as a major international football power. Clubs from Zagreb and Split had long been among the power centres of football in the former Yugoslavia. Croatia's independence revealed a rich depth of talent such as Zvonimir Boban, Robert Prosinecki and Davor Suker – all World Youth Cup-winners with Yugoslavia back in 1987. The players considered that national pride was worth at least one goal every game in Euro 96. They scored a notable 2–1 win over Italy in the qualifiers and ulitmately reached the quarter-finals before falling to Germany. After finishing in second place to Denmark in the World Cup qualifying group for the 1998 finals in France, they faced a potentially difficult hurdle in the play-offs with home and away ties against Ukraine. However, their quality shone through and their 3–1 aggregate victory took them to France.

Sporting success had brought fame to a little-known country struggling to become re-established after the break from Yugoslavia. Clubs in general struggled for support and sponsorship, but still the flow of individual talent refused to dry up, and the country's leaders – from President Franjo Tudjman downwards – were vociferous in their support for the game in general and for the national team in particular. The Croats also had a larger-than-life character in the squad's coach, Miroslav Blazic, who has been described as soccer's answer to Muhammed Ali because of some of the outrageous remarks he makes. "Pele was great on the field, but now he has shown his ignorance," was one comment after some criticism from Brazil and, "Our players are the best in the world," was his view after one hard-earned victory.

Blazic was so nearly proved right in France 98, however. His side finished second in their group with wins over Jamaica and Japan to face Romania, conquerers of England in the group stage, in the second round. A penalty by Suker was enough to see them into the quarter-finals where they would face three-time winners, Germany. Any doubters of Croatia's credentials as a true world force in football were silenced, as they crushed the Germans 3–0. Although losing to eventual champions France in the semi-finals by 2–1, Croatia had much to cheer, winning the play-off against Holland and having the tournament's leading goal-scorer in their midsts, as Davor Suker claimed the "Golden Boot".

Czech Republic

Cesko Moravsky Fotbalovy Svaz

Founded:
  1993
FIFA:
  1994
European Championship:
  1976
Olympics:
  1980 *(as Czechoslovakia)*

When the 1994 World Cup ended and Czechoslovakia ceased to exist as a football nation, the Czech Republic and Slovakia went their separate ways, each setting up a new association, league and national team. From the time Czechoslovakia came into existence in 1918, the Czechs were at the forefront of European football. They were runners-up in both the 1920 and 1964 Olympic Games, before finally winning the tournament in 1980, in Moscow. They were finalists at the 1934 World Cup with a side containing Antonin Puc, Frantisek Planicka, the finest pre-war goalkeeper, and Oldrich Nejedly.

The Communist take-over after the war led to the usual reorganization of the domestic game, which hindered rather than helped, because clubs such as Sparta and Slavia Prague had been doing very well as professional sides. The army team Dukla Prague rose to prominence and provided the basis of the 1960s Czech side which was among the best in the world. Josef Masopust, Czechoslovakia's most famous player, led the side to third place in the inaugural European Championship in 1960, and to the 1962 World Cup Final, which was lost 3–1 to Brazil.

Europe's Best

Czechoslovakia's biggest success came at the 1976 European Championship when, with stars such as goalkeeper Ivo Viktor, defender Anton Ondrus, Antonin Panenka, in midfield, and Zdenek Nehoda, in attack, they beat West Germany on penalties in the final after the Germans had equalized in the last minute of normal time.

The political split in 1994 affected Slovakia more than the Czech Republic, who qualified for Euro 96 and proved to be the most spirited of dark horses – beating Italy, Portugal and France and drawing with Russia en route to the final, where they lost 2–1 to Germany by a "Golden Goal" scored in extra time. As a follow-up, the team were expected to qualify for France '98, but failed to do so. They eventually came third in a tough qualifying group, with Spain and Yugoslavia ahead of them, despite leaking only six goals in their last ten group games.

Denmark

Dansk Boldspil-Union

Founded:
1889

FIFA:
1904

European Championship:
1992

Olympics:
1906

Denmark was one of the first countries in continental Europe to take up football and has some of the oldest clubs in the world. But their rigid adherence to the principle of amateurism meant that Denmark was left behind when most of the rest of Europe adopted professionalism.

As a strong "amateur" nation, Denmark has perhaps inevitably enjoyed its greatest success at the Olympics. Winners in 1906 and runners-up in 1908 and 1912, the Danes were a force to be reckoned with at this level and produced some outstanding players – notably Nils Middelboe, who played with great distinction for Chelsea.

A period of decline occurred during the inter-war years, but qualification for the 1948 and 1960 Olympics sparked hopes of a revival. But the amateur nature of the domestic game, together with a rule which barred foreign-based players from the national side, stifled progress. The 1970s prompted great changes for Danish soccer, though, as a flood of players – led by 1977 European Footballer of The Year Allan Simonsen – left Denmark to join clubs in Western Europe. The rule barring "exported" players such as Michael Laudrup, Preben Elkjaer, Jesper Olsen, Morten Olsen and Soren Lerby from the national side was lifted in 1976 and undoubtedly helped the national side develop. These players formed the nucleus of the 1980s "Dinamite" side which reached the 1984 European Championship semi-finals and the 1986 World Cup second round.

In the late 1980s the league was restructured, and a new generation of players – including Michael Laudrup's brother, Brian – emerged to propel Denmark to the dizzying heights of European Champions in 1992. That unexpected success in Sweden, clinched by a superb display against Germany in the final, was all the more remarkable as they were eleventh-hour replacements for the expelled Yugoslavs.

European success, combined with domestic restructuring, pushed Danish football into the European mainstream, with the clubs – particularly Brondby, OB Odense and FC Copenhagen – beginning to enjoy success in international competition as well as providing the backbone of the team which reached the quarter-finals of the 1998 World Cup.

England

The Football Association

Founded:
  1863
FIFA:
  1905–1920, 1924–1928, 1946
World Cup:
  1966
Olympics:
  1908, 1912 *(as Great Britain)*

England, as every schoolboy enthusiast knows, gave soccer to the world. Developed on the playing fields of England's great public schools in the middle of the nineteenth century, the game was first codified and organized in the 1860s, when the Football Association was formed – hence the name Association Football, and the nickname "soccer", to distinguish it from Rugby Football. The FA Cup was introduced in 1871, both the first and now the oldest surviving tournament in the world, and was fundamental in the development of the game – pitting the established amateur sides of the south against the burgeoning professional outfits of the north.

Early Internationals

A year later, the very first international match was played, between England and Scotland in Glasgow, and in 1888 the Football League was formed – to organize what was, by now, a largely professional game based mostly in the industrial north.

As the century closed, the British Championship, played between England, Scotland, Wales and Ireland, was the zenith of world football. Before the First World War, England and Scotland were well above the rest of the world and, as Great Britain, comfortably won Olympic gold in 1908 and 1912.

The FA joined FIFA in 1905, always took a disdainful attitude towards it, and withdrew in 1920, horrified at the prospect of having to play with wartime adversaries, and again in 1928 over the definition of the word amateur. It is doubtful whether they would have bothered to compete in the prewar World Cups anyway, such was the English view of their own superiority.

That view was unchanged after the humiliating 1–0 defeat by the United States in the 1950 World Cup which was dismissed as a fluke, even though England had a side containing such greats as Tom Finney and Billy Wright. However, in 1953, Hungary's "Magic Magyars" came to Wembley, led by the legendary Ferenc Puskas and finally destroyed English arrogance once and for all.

It was not merely the 6–3 scoreline, or the fact that this was England's first defeat by a non-British side at home, which changed attitudes: it was the manner of the defeat. The Hungarians were far superior technically and tactically. Further defeats at the 1954, 1958 and 1962 World Cup finals confirmed this and forced England to face the facts of the modern game, which had left them behind in the immediate post-war years.

The challenges presented by the new order were spectacularly answered in 1966, however, when England's "wingless wonders" won the World Cup on home soil, beating West Germany 4–2 in the Wembley final. Alf Ramsey, the stolid manager who led Ipswich to the Championship in 1962 during their first season in Division One, moulded his side around the outstanding talents of goalkeeper Gordon Banks, captain Bobby Moore, and the Charlton brothers Bobby and Jack. He created a system which worked with the players at his disposal, and instilled a team spirit and an understanding which no subsequent England side has matched.

European Club Victory

The 1966 success was the springboard from which English clubs launched an unprecedented assault on the three European competitions, winning trophy after trophy between 1964 and 1985. Conversely, the national side suffered. A defeat by West Germany in the quarter-final of the 1970 World Cup in Mexico marked the

beginning of the end of the Ramsey era, and failure to qualify for the 1974 and 1978 finals, despite an abundance of talented players, confirmed England's slump.

Following dismal performances at the 1988 and 1992 European Championship finals and, worse, the failure to qualify for the 1994 World Cup Finals, the structure of the English game came under scrutiny. Changes forced by the appalling loss of life at Bradford (1985) and Hillsborough (1989) led to a modernization of stadia, These moves, assisted by the influx of cash from a lucrative Sky TV contract, have drawn the crowds back to the game and, at the same time, seen an improvement in the fortunes of the national side.

Things began looking up in the mid-nineties, as British clubs again began to have more of an impact abroad. Arsenal won the 1994 European Cup-Winners Cup and Manchester United reached the semi-final of the Champions Cup in 1997.

The national side at last got its act together under the stewardship of Terry Venables during the 1996 European Championship. After destroying Holland 4–1 in their last group match, they saw off the Spanish before losing to their perennial foes, the Germans, in a nail-biting semi-final penalty shoot-out. The penalty jinx was to strike again in the 1998 World Cup, this time against Argentina, as England crashed out in the second round.

France

Fédération Française de Football

Founded:
1918
FIFA:
1904
World Cup:
1966
European Championship:
1984
Olympics:
1984

As England gave the game to the world, so the French organized it into a structured sport. The French were prime movers behind the creation of FIFA, UEFA, the World Cup, the European Championship and the European club cups, yet the 1984 European Championship and Olympic title are all they have to show for their skills in innovation and organization.

The FFF, formed in 1918, brought order to a chaotic domestic club scene which, at one stage, had five different bodies vying for control. Professionalism was accepted in 1932 and a league was set up. This helped the national side to improve on their previously poor results, but, despite this, the first three World Cups were disasters for the French. In the 1950s, Stade de Reims emerged as the best club side France had produced. They twice reached the European Cup Finals, losing both to Real Madrid, and the side contained Raymond Kopa and Just Fontaine – two great players and key members of the national side which finished third in the 1958 World Cup (Fontaine's 13 goals in those finals remain a record). But this success was not built on, and France qualified only once more before 1978.

In the late 1970s, Michel Platini arrived and transformed France into the most attractive side Europe had seen since the 1950s. Platini, a midfielder with immense skill, vision and grace, had a glorious club career with Juventus in Italy, and inspired France to reach the final stages of three World Cups (1978, 1982 and 1986). They put up their best World Cup performance in 1982 in Spain, when they were 3–1 up in the semi-final against West Germany in extra time . . . and lost on penalties. Platini's finest hours came in 1984, on French soil, when his nine goals in five games earned France the European Championship and confirmed him as the greatest player in French history. He later turned briefly to management and guided France, in 1992, to the first of two successive appearances at the European Championship finals.

International club success proved elusive until May 1993, when Marseille beat Milan 1–0 to win the Champions Cup. France went wild. But only briefly. Within a month Marseille had been engulfed by a match-fixing scandal which prevented them from defending the Cup, prompted their relegation and brought suspensions and legal action against the players and officials involved, including president Bernard Tapie. But Marseille's success was indicative of a general renaissance at club level. Paris Saint-Germain reached European club semi-finals in four straight seasons in the mid-1990s, and won the 1996 Cup-winners' Cup, while Bordeaux reached the 1996 UEFA Cup Final.

France were to host the 1998 World Cup finals – the second time that they were to host the competition after doing so in 1938 – and carried the weight of the nation's expectation.

They hosted the Tournoi in the summer of 1997 as a prelude to the World Cup with guests Brazil, England and Italy, but, despite all of their technical excellence, results under coach Aime Jacquet were not encouraging. They failed to win any of their three games and only a 2–2 draw against a weakened Italy saved them from bottom place. As Jacquet said, "Right now the World Cup looks like a huge mountain to climb. Fatigue played a significant part in our results. We conceded an 85th-minute goal against England and a last-minute equaliser to Italy. But when it comes to the World Cup finals, we will have more time to prepare – we will be refreshed."

The tournament started well for the French as they finished top of their group with wins over South Africa (3–0), Saudi Arabia (4–0) and Denmark (2–1). The only mar on the qualification was the sending off of the influential Zinedine Zidane for a cynical stamp in the game against Saudi Arabia. Fears grew in the French camp, as Zidane was the one player to ignite the creative force within the side, and following a two-match suspension would not appear again before the quarter-finals.

France were rescued in the second round with a "Golden Goal" – the first in World Cup history – from Laurent Blanc after a dour 0–0 performance against Paraguay. Another goalless performance against Italy saw the tournament's second penalty shoot out, and Di Biagio's penalty miss sent France through to a semi-final clash with Croatia. Two goals from Lilian Thuram, his first for the country, cancelled out the early goal from Suker and France were in to their first World Cup final.

The best was yet to come as villain turned hero. Two first-half headed goals from Zidane, followed by a last-minute strike from Arsenal's Emmanuel Petit, were enough to beat Brazil and send the French nation into a frenzy of euphoria, creating scenes throughout the nation reminiscent of their liberation after the Second World War. 850,000 crammed the Champs Elysées in celebration. France were the champions of the world.

Germany

Deutscher Fussball-Bund

Founded:
1900
FIFA:
1904–1946, 1950
World Cup:
1954, 1974, 1990
European Championship:
1972, 1980, 1996
Olympics:
1976 *(East Germany)*

Since the Second World War, Germany have enjoyed a record of success unparalleled in the history of the game. Yet Germany's pre-war record was quite poor, with third place at the 1934 World Cup the peak of their achievement. The war brought division and in 1948 East Germany, under the Soviets, formed its own association, league and national side. The East Germans, though, with their state-sponsored emphasis on individual rather than team sports, never matched the success of their countrymen on the other side of the Berlin Wall. Half a century of East German football produced only two successes of note: Olympic gold in Montreal in 1976 and a 1–0 victory over West Germany, in the only match ever played between the two, at the 1974 World Cup

finals.

But while the East floundered, the West flourished. Banished from FIFA in 1946, they were readmitted in 1950 as West Germany ... and won the World Cup just over four years later. That victory, engineered by coach Sepp Herberger, was all the more amazing because their Final opponents were the "Magic Magyars", whose 3–2 defeat was their second loss in five years!

From that initial breakthrough, the Germans pressed on to even greater heights of achievement. In the World Cup, they were semi-finalists in 1958, quarter-finalists in 1962 and runners-up in 1966. Full-time professionalism was introduced in 1963 and a decade later the Germans were unquestionably the world's best at both national and club levels.

The 1970s seemed to belong to Bayern Munich and West Germany. Bayern won a hat-trick of European Cups in 1974, 1975 and 1976, and provided the nucleus of the national side which won the European Championship in 1972, the World Cup in 1974, and after finishing second in 1976, the European Championship again in 1980. Goalkeeper Sepp Maier is remembered as the Germans' greatest No.1. Franz Beckenbauer single-handedly revolutionized the sweeper's role into one of attack as well as defence and was one of the finest defenders in the world; and Gerd Müller was the closest thing to a scoring machine yet seen. In 62 internationals, Müller scored an incredible 68 goals, most of them coming in competitive matches, not friendlies.

And the success story continues. The 1970s sides were replaced by new stars of the world game: Karl-Heinz Rummenigge, Lothar Matthäus, Rudi Völler, Jürgen Klinsmann, Thomas Hässler and Matthias Sammer. Following the World Cup success and German reunification in 1990, they capitalized on their new-found resources by securing victory in Euro 96, eliminating England on the way with a repeat of the 1990 World Cup penalty shoot-out victory. In the final they faced the Czech Republic, who themselves had dispatched Portugal and the much-fancied France along the way. The Czech Republic scored with a penalty in the 59th minute, but German fears of a repeat of the 1992 European Championship defeat were soon allayed when supersub Oliver Bierhoff came on to equalise with a thumping header within four minutes of his introduction by coach Berti Vogts. Four minutes into extra-time it was Bierhoff again who fired the Germans to victory firing home the "Golden Goal" to take the Germans to the title for the third time.

Then came France 98, in which Matthäus, recalled at 37 years of age after three years out because of injuries and disputes with colleagues, passed the record of 21 World Cup appearances first set by another German, Uwe Seller, in 1970.

Wins over the United States and Iran and a difficult draw with Yugoslavia – in which Vogts' team clambered back into the game after trailing 2–0 at half time – meant that the highly experienced German team topped their group only on goal difference. They went on to make heavy weather of what should have been an easy win against a lively Mexican team, falling behind to a goal by the pint-sized, blonde-haired striker Luis Hernandez. The ageing Klinsmann scored the equaliser and then Oliver Bierhoff once again proved his big-match-winning worth by scoring the winner – with yet another stunning header – only four minutes from time. The Germans earned themselves a quarter-final clash with surprise package Croatia. The last time the teams had met was at Euro 96, when the Germans had won the game after a controversial sending-off. The Croatians were out for revenge and that's just what they got. Robert Jarni scored on the stroke of half time, after 45 minutes of defensive play that had seen Germany fail to make the most of their few chances. Moments into the second half, Wörns was sent off and the Germans fell to pieces. The game ended 3–0 as Vlaovic and Suker added late goals. Had their finishing been more efficient, it could have been even more humiliating.

Following their exit from the tournament, the old guard of Klinsmann, Möller and Matthäus, amongst others, announced their retirement from international football.

Holland

Koninklijke Nederland Voetbalbond (KNVB)

Founded:
1889

FIFA:
1904

European Championship:
1988

The Dutch were early devotees of football, partly owing to the country's proximity to Britain, and were among the continent's leading amateur sides in the early 1900s. Indeed they reached the semi-finals of four consecutive Olympic Games from 1908 to 1924 . . . but lost them all. Third place in 1908 and 1912 was their best. The 1920s marked a move away from amateurism in other countries, and Dutch football entered a decline which lasted until the 1960s. Up to that decade, internationals were mostly played against European neighbours, especially Belgium, and first-round defeats in the 1934 and 1938 World Cups did little to encourage Holland to venture further afield.

The low point came just after the Second World War, when a dismal sequence of results, with just one victory in over five years, prompted modernization of the domestic game. So, in 1957, a national league was created and professionalism was introduced in an attempt to staunch the flow of Dutch players going abroad. The main beneficiaries of the reorganization were Ajax of Amsterdam, Feyenoord of Rotterdam and PSV Eindhoven – the "big three" who have dominated Dutch football ever since. The breakthrough came in 1970, when Feyenoord won the European Cup. It was the beginning of a golden era for Dutch football, in which Ajax won a hat-trick of European Cups (1971, 1972, 1973), Feyenoord and PSV both won the UEFA Cup, and Holland reached two consecutive World Cup Finals.

The generation of Dutch players which emerged in the 1970s was among the finest the modern game has seen. Ajax led the way, providing the backbone of the national side, with hugely talented players such as Johan Neeskens, Arie Haan, Ruud Krol, Wim Suurbier and, of course, Johan Cruyff, arguably the best player of his day. Along with the Feyenoord duo of Wim Van Hanegem and Wim Jansen, they formed the nucleus of a side which was unfortunate to lose the 1974 and 1978 World Cup Finals to the host nations, West Germany and Argentina respectively.

Coach Rinus Michels was the architect of the success with his "total football" system, which involved moulding highly skilled players into a team unit, with the emphasis on interchangeability and with every player totally comfortable in possession.

As the "total football" side broke up, the Dutch slipped into a malaise, failing to qualify for the 1982 and 1986 World Cup finals. But a revival was soon to follow, spearheaded by a new generation of players at Ajax and PSV. Ajax won the European Cup-winners' Cup in 1987 and completed a hat-trick of European successes when they won the UEFA Cup in 1992 (only the third side to complete this treble), while PSV won the European Cup in 1986. Ruud Gullit, Frank Rijkaard, Marco Van Basten and Ronald Koeman, once again under Rinus Michels' guidance, triumphed in the 1988 European Championship – Holland's only major success.

Although the Dutch domestic game operates a sort of conveyor-belt system for developing young talent. – the "big three" plunder the other clubs for the best players, and are then themselves plundered by clubs in Spain and, especially, Italy – any thoughts of this talent drain leading to a stagnation of the domestic game were dramatically misplaced in 1995 as Ajax went undefeated through the home league season and 11 European Cup games to win the trophy for the fourth time.

Observers from all over the world converged on Amsterdam to study Ajax's youth system which also provided Holland with their national team backbone at the 1996 European Championship finals.

Ajax slipped to fourth in 1997, but soared back to the top in 1998, scoring 112 goals in their 34 League games and providing a nucleus of players, both past and present, for another attempt on the World Cup.

With the likes of Bergkamp, the De Boers, Kluivert and Davids, expectation ran high for the Dutch as the tournament began – and, yet again, it was so near yet so far.

They finished top of their group, although only just. A goalless draw in the first game against old rivals Belgium was marred by the sending off of Patrick Kluivert. A 5–0 drubbing of South Korea paved the way for what should have been qualification to the second round as group winners and although that was the case they were made to sweat by Mexico who came from two goals down after 75 minutes to 2–2.

Two last-minute goals, one by Edgar Davids against Yugoslavia and the other, a "wonder goal" from Dennis Bergkamp against Argentina, were enough to take the Dutch into a semi-final against defending champions, Brazil.

An 87th-minute equaliser saw the game end 1–1 after Ronaldo had given the Brazilians the lead. But it was penalty-shoot-out heartbreak for the Dutch as Philip Cocu and Ronald De Boer both missed to send them packing.

All attention now shifts to Euro 2000, which the Dutch are hosting along with Belgium. All of Holland's fans will be hoping for a repeat of 1988 – their greatest footballing moment to date.

Hungary

Magyar Labdarugo Szovetseg

Founded:
1901
FIFA:
1906
Olympics:
1952, 1964, 1968

Just as Austria will always be renowned for the "Wunderteam" of the 1930s, so Hungary will be for the "Magic Magyars" side of the 1950s. This side was the finest the world had ever seen and had lost only one international in five years before, heartbreakingly, they failed in the 1954 World Cup Final. The forward line of Zoltan Czibor, Jozsef Toth, Nandor Hidegkuti, Sandor Kocsis and Ferenc Puskas – the greatest player of his era and still regarded as one of the best ever. The "Galloping Major", as Puskas was known, terrorized opposition defences the world over and scored 173 goals in this spell. In 1953, they became the first non-British side to beat England at home, winning 6–3 at Wembley, and shattering the aura of arrogance and invincibility that had enveloped the English for too long.

Chasing Success

Yet this was not the first outstanding side

Hungary had produced. Hungarian clubs, notably MTK Budapest, who won 10 consecutive titles (1914–25), dominated European football in the inter-war period, winning five Mitropa Cups in the 1930s. The national side reached the World Cup Final in 1938, where they were comfortably beaten 4–2 by the hosts Italy. The 1930s side contained such fine players as Gyorgy Sarosi and Gyula Zsengeller.

The Hungarian uprising of 1958 broke up the "Magic Magyars" side, but by the 1960s another had emerged. The new stars were Florian Albert and Ferenc Bene, who led Hungary to the 1962 and 1966 World Cup quarter-finals and Olympic gold in 1964 and 1968. The 1970s marked the beginning of an insipid decline for the national side, despite some notable successes for the clubs, particularly Ujpest, who won nine titles in 11 years. Failure to qualify for the 1970, 1974, 1990 and 1994 World Cup finals was matched by poor performances at the 1978, 1982, and 1986 tournaments, especially in Mexico in 1986 when they lost 6–0 to the Soviet Union.

The lowest point came, however, in a World Cup qualifier in June 1992 when Hungary lost 2–1 to unfancied Iceland... in Budapest of all places!

Hungary seemingly went close to qualification for France '98 when they earned a play-off place against Yugoslavia. Unfortunately they were beaten 12–1 on aggregate, including a humiliating 7–1 loss at home.

The Great Countries

Italy

Federazione Italiana Giuoco Calcio

Founded:
1898
FIFA:
1903
World Cup:
1934, 1938, 1982
European Championship:
1968
Olympics:
1936

The first 30 years of Italian football were chaotic and complicated, with various regional leagues and the industrial cities of the north – Milan and Turin – competing for power. But the Association finally settled in Rome, in 1929, and a national league was formed in 1930, providing the boost the game needed and leading Italy to unmatched success in the 1930s.

Under legendary coach Vittorio Pozzo, Italy lost only seven games during the decade, winning the World Cup in 1934 and 1938 and the 1936 Olympic title in between to confirm their superiority. The 1930s also saw the beginnings of a trend for Italian clubs to import foreign players to gain an advantage in the league. The best-known

stars of this era were Luisito Monti, born in Argentina, and Giuseppe Meazza.

After the war Torino were the dominant side, winning four consecutive titles, and providing virtually all of the national team. But, returning from Lisbon, their plane crashed into the Superga Hill outside Turin killing all on board, including ten internationals. Hardly surprisingly, this led to a decline for both Torino and Italy during the 1950s.

Many blamed the failure on the large number of foreign imports in the Italian game, which grew considerably in the 1950s – led by Milan with their Swedish "Gre-No-Li" trio of Gunnar Gren, Gunnar Nordahl and Nils Liedholm. Consequently, the importation of foreigners was banned in 1964. This hampered the clubs, who were making headway in Europe – Milan won the European Cup in 1963, Internazionale did so in 1964 and 1965 – but allowed a new generation of Italian players to develop, and they won the 1968 European Championship.

The 1970s, though, witnessed the rise of catenaccio, defensive, sterile football reflecting the attitude that not losing was more important than winning. For the clubs it was a lean time in Europe, but the national side did better, reaching the 1970 World Cup Final. The import ban was lifted in the early 1980s, and it was to be a decade of great successes for the clubs, who made full use of their foreign quota. Juventus, with French midfield genius Michel Platini, dominated the first half of the decade, while the national side, skippered by 40-year-old Dino Zoff, swept to victory at the 1982 World Cup in Spain. Then Milan – with a Dutch axis of Gullit-Rijkaard-Van Basten – dominated the second half, when Napoli, Internazionale and Sampdoria also tasted European success.

Juventus later became the dominant force again, winning the championship in 1990, 1995, 1997 and 1998 and reaching the European Champions Cup final three times in a row, although they won only the first, on penalties against Ajax in 1996 before losing to Borussia Dortmund and Real Madrid.

Italy today has the best league in the world, with the biggest stars, huge attendances and regular success in Europe. Arrigo Sacchi's attacking Milan side of the late 1980s and early 1990s has smashed catenaccio, one hopes for ever. The Serie A is now a hugely exciting league with many formidable teams. Even lesser clubs such as Parma have prospered, winning the European Cup-winners' Cup in 1993 and the UEFA Cup in 1995. The national side failed both to win the 1990 World Cup, in Italy, and to qualify for the 1992 European Championship. But a rebuilding programme halted the slide and, with Roberto Baggio leading the way, Italy reached the 1994 World Cup Final, where exhaustion as much as anything else cost them the game, albeit on penalties, against Brazil, where Roberto Baggio's miss cost them their fourth title and branded them as the first side to lose the World Cup final on penalties.

Things did not pick up for the Italians in Euro 96 as they failed to get through the group stages after they crashed to a shock defeat at the hands of the Czech Republic.

Qualification for France 98 was no easy matter either. A surprise draw against Georgia followed by a goalless draw against England in Rome confined the *azzurri* to a play-off against Russia – which they came through 2–1 thanks to a goal by Pierluigi Casiraghi after a 1–1 draw in Moscow.

France 98 proved to be a disappointment for the Italians. Comfortable qualification to the second round as group winners was assured with a 2–2 draw in their first game against Chile, followed by wins over Cameroon (3–0) and Austria (2–1).

Norway provided the next obstacle for the three-time winners, but they were pushed aside (1–0) with a goal by the in-form Christian Vieri, who finished the tournament as the second leading scorer with five goals.

The hosts lay in their path, and after a dour goalless draw, the nightmare of a penalty shoot-out defeat loomed yet again. Misses by both Albertini and Di Biagio confined the Italians to the same fate as 1994, but you can be sure that they will bounce back as major contenders for both Euro 2000 and the 2002 World Cup.

Mexico

Federacion Mexicana de Futbol Asociacion

Founded:
1927
FIFA:
1929
CONCACAF Championship:
1963, 1971, 1977, 1993

Mexico utterly dominate their Central American region, but this has hindered rather than helped their game. With no decent local opposition for the national side or the clubs, Mexico have enjoyed their greatest moments in the World Cup against opposition teams who can provide them with sterner tests than they are otherwise used to.

The federation was formed in 1927, and a trip to the Amsterdam Olympics a year later ended after just one match. Two years later they entered the World Cup and have qualified for all but four of the 16 finals tournaments, a statistic most other countries would be proud to have. It is a record which includes the 1990 finals in Italy, which they were barred from by FIFA for breaches of age regulations in a youth tournament.

Mexico's best World Cups were in 1970 and 1986, when they were hosts. They reached the quarter-finals of both and in 1986 were unlucky to lose on penalties to the eventual finalists, West Germany.

The Cartwheeling King

Star of the 1986 World Cup side was Hugo Sanchez, an agile forward who led Spanish giants Real Madrid to many honours in the 1980s. Famous for his exuberant, cartwheeling celebrations when he scored, Sanchez was Mexico's greatest player since Antonio Carbajal, the goalkeeper who created a unique record by playing in all five World Cup finals tournaments from 1950 to 1966. Mexico won the CONCACAF Championship four times, but were shocked in 1991 when the United States beat them in the semi-finals, though Mexico regained the upper hand in 1993 with a convincing display. Many believe Mexico would benefit from joining the South Americans, and in 1993 they, and the USA, were invited to take part in the South American Championship. Mexico embarrassed their hosts by reaching the final, losing narrowly to Argentina.

Mexico then qualified for the 1994 World Cup finals with comparative ease, only to lose to Bulgaria in a second round penalty shoot-out.

France 98 was a similar story as they progressed to the second round behind Holland, only to lose 2–1 to Germany after an 86th-minute winner in the second round.

Nigeria

Nigeria Football Association

Founded:
1945

FIFA:
1959

Olympic Games:
1996

African Nations Cup:
1980, 1994

Nigeria, with a huge population and over 500 registered clubs, emerged at last in the 1990s as one of the most powerful nations in Africa. Nigeria's youngsters had already proved well capable of winning trophies, and this continues to bode well for the future of the national side.

In 1985 Nigeria won the World Under-17 Championship, becoming the first African side to win a FIFA world tournament at any level, beating West Germany 2–0 in the final; in 1989, Nigeria were runners-up in the World Under-20 Youth Championship; and in 1993 the "Green Eaglets" won their second Under-17 title in only the event's fifth staging.

A World Cup breakthrough came in 1994 when Nigeria nearly sprang one of the greatest of all upsets. They topped their first-round group – ahead of Argentina, Bulgaria and Greece – and went within a couple of minutes of eliminating eventual finalists Italy in the second round.

Sadly, political problems then prevented Nigeria from defending their African Nations title in South Africa in 1996. But they more than atoned later in the year by becoming the first African nation to win the Olympic tournament. They did it the hard way too – beating favourites Brazil in the semi-final and Argentina in the final. Sadly their hero, forward Nwankwo Kanu, was forced out of the game for a spell shortly afterwards. He had just been sold by Ajax to Italy's Internazionale when a routine medical showed up a heart defect for which he underwent major surgery. Fortunately he recovered so well that he was able to take a place in the squad for the World Cup in France.

Nigeria were many neutral's choice to become the first African side to win the World Cup. They qualified easily for the finals, losing only one game in their last group stage. The Super Eagles started France 98 with a superb 3–2 win against a strong Spanish side, and the winner by Sunday Oliseh was seen by some as the goal of the tournament. They followed this up with a more sober 1–0 win against an ageing Bulgarian side, and, once qualification was assured, they lost to Paraguay. In the second round, the laid-back Eagles were knocked out, after being taken by surprise and hammered 4–1 by a stongly disciplined Danish

Portugal

Federacao Portuguesa De Futbol

Founded:
1914

FIFA:
1926

The Portuguese Football Association was founded in 1914 as the result of a merger between the associations of Lisbon and Oporto – the two cities which have utterly dominated domestic football. The Lisbon duo of Benfica and Sporting Lisbon, along with their rivals FC Porto from Oporto, are among the most famous names in world club football. The League Championship, set up in 1935, has only ever been won by these three, except in 1948 when Belenenses broke the monopoly.

Portugal's greatest era was in the 1960s, when Benfica won the European Cup twice (1961 and 1962) and reached a further three finals. The bulk of this Benfica side formed the nucleus of the national team which was then at its peak. The most famous of them was Eusebio, a strong, Mozambique-born striker who was arguably the best player of the 1966 World Cup. Fellow Mozambican Mario Coluna and Angola-born José Aguas were other "adopted" players who aug-

mented an impressive side which also included other Benfica players such as Costa Pereira, in goal, Germano, in defence, and Cavem and José Augusto raiding down the wings.

In those 1966 finals Eusebio scored nine goals, including four in a remarkable 5–3 quarter-final victory over North Korea – Portugal were three down after 22 minutes – as the Portuguese finished third. The national side had never scaled such heights before – this was their first appearance in the final stages of a World Cup – and they have never done so again. Their only other qualification was in 1986 when they finished bottom of their first-tound group, despite beating England in their opening match.

Portuguese clubs, though, staged a revival in the 1980s. Benfica reached the UEFA Cup Final in 1983, and in 1987 FC Porto became the third club side to win in Europe – Sporting had won the Cup-winners' Cup in 1964 – when they won the European Cup. Benfica also lost in European Cup finals in 1988 and 1990, while Portugal's youngsters won the World Youth Cup in 1989 and 1991and provided the nucleus of the side who reached the European Championship quarter-finals in 1996.

In 1998 Porto won the championship for the fourth year in a row, taking advantage of the financial crisis that had engulfed Benfica. And if Benfica suffer, then Portugal suffers too.

Romania

Federatia Romana de Fotbal

Founded:
  1908
FIFA:
  1930

Romania embraced football before most of her Balkan neighbours, mainly owing to the influence of the country's sovereign, King Carol, who was a soccer fanatic. He instigated the formation of a federation in 1908 and, having returned to power in 1930 after an abdication, he was determined that Romania should enter the first World Cup.

Romania duly made the long trip to South America and Uruguay, but were beaten by the hosts in the first round. They also entered the 1934 and 1938 tournaments, but could not progress beyond the first round, despite the presence of Iuliu Bodola, their top scorer to this day.

Bucharest Dominate

The Communists took over in 1944 and, as usual, reorganized the domestic game. Two of the clubs created in Bucharest, Steaua, the army team, and Dinamo, the police team, have dominated Romanian soccer ever since. After the war, the national side enjoyed a brief upsurge with qualification for the 1970 World Cup Finals, and a quarter-final finish in the 1976 European Championship. But, despite Anghel Iordanescu, one of the true greats of Romanian football, it was not until 1984 that they qualified for the finals of a major tournament again, the European Championship in France. Then their inexperience was cruelly exposed as they failed to register a win in their three group matches.

In the 1980s, under the direct influence of the brutal and ruthless Ceaucescu regime, Steaua and Dinamo dominated even more. In 1986 Steaua became the first team from behind the Iron Curtain to win the European Cup, beating the mighty Barcelona in a penalty shoot-out after the match had finished 0–0.

Despite the midfield inspiration of Gheorghe Hagi, they did not enjoy the best of luck at the World Cups of either 1990 or 1994. Both times Romania were eliminated after a second-round penalty shoot-out, first to the Republic of Ireland and then to the Swedes.

Euro 96 was a huge disappointment for the talented Romanians as they failed to qualify beyond the group stages.

After finishing top of their group at France 98 – defeating England 2–1 in the process – much was expected of the Romanians. They were confined to disappointment yet again, however, as they crashed to a 1–0 defeat by Croatia.

Russia

Russian Football Federation

Founded:

1922 *(as Soviet Union)*

FIFA:

1922 *(as Soviet Union)*

European Championship:

1960 *(as Soviet Union)*

Olympics:

1956, 1988 *(as Soviet Union)*

Russia's footballing history is inextricably entwined with that of the former Soviet Union, and it is under the banner of the latter that her greatest achievements have occurred down the years.

The Communists reorganized the structure of football methodically from top to bottom, with the emphasis on teamwork rather than individual flair. Moscow, then the Soviet capital, became the main football centre with five great workers' clubs: Dynamo (electrical trades), Spartak (producers' co-operatives), Torpedo (car manufacturers), Lokomitive (railways) and CSKA (the army).

In the 1950s the national side began to venture out to take on the rest of the world. They won a poorly-attended 1956 Olympic Games and then reached the quarter-finals of the 1958 World Cup at their first attempt. In 1960 they entered and won the first European Championship. This, however, remains the only major triumph that either the Soviet Union or Russia has ever had.

No Russian Success

The Soviet sides of 1986 and 1988 were arguably the best since the 1960s, but were composed of mainly Kiev Dynamo players. Indeed, it is a curious fact that despite Russia's dominance of Soviet football, the only Soviet sides to win European club competitions were not Russian. Kiev, in the Ukraine, won the Cup-winners' Cup in 1975 and again in 1986, and Tbilisi Dynamo, from Georgia, won the same tournament in 1981.

In September 1991, the Soviet Union began to disintegrate. The three Baltic states achieved independence and went their own way, quickly followed by the other 12 republics. The Soviets had qualified for the 1992 European Championship finals and took part under a "flag of convenience" name, the Commonwealth of Independent States – a television commentator's worst nightmare!

Russia picked up where the Soviet Union left off, entered the 1994 World Cup qualifying competition and qualified, with what proved misleading ease, from a very poor group. In the finals, Oleg Salenko scored a record five goals in a game against Cameroon, but they lost the other two games.

They went close to qualifying for France '98, but lost out to Italy in a two-legged play-off played in poor conditions.

Scotland

Scottish Football Association

Founded:
  1873
FIFA:
  1910–20, 1924–28, 1946

Scotland boasts a proud footballing heritage and, for such a small country, it has been a remarkable story. Founded in 1873, the Scottish FA still retains a permanent seat on the international board.

Scotland was also the venue for the world's first international match when, on November 30, 1872, Scotland and England drew 0–0. The Scotland vs. England rivalry has continued ever since, sharpened by the fact that many of England's most successful club sides have contained or been managed by Scots: Bill Shankly at Liverpool, Matt Busby at Manchester United, Alex Ferguson also at Manchester United and George Graham at Arsenal have been outstanding, while the players include Hughie Gallacher (Newcastle), Alex James (Arsenal), Alex Jackson (Huddersfield and Chelsea), Denis Law (Manchester United), Billy Bremner (Leeds), Kenny Dalglish (Liverpool) and literally hundreds more.

This continual draining of man-power would have withered many countries. But the Scottish League survives, thanks mainly to the two great Glasgow clubs, Celtic and Rangers. These two, representing the Catholic (Celtic) and Protestant (Rangers) halves of Scottish society, have dominated the domestic scene unlike any other country in Europe. Scottish club football was at its peak in the 1960s, with Celtic winning the European Cup in 1967 – the first British side to do so – and reaching the final again in 1970. Rangers won the 1972 European Cup-winners' Cup.

At the same time, the national side made steady progress. Having entered the World Cup for the first time in 1950, they then qualified for the finals in 1970, 1974, 1978, 1982, 1986 and 1990 and in 1998, but did not get beyond the first stage in any of them. In 1992 the Scots reached the European Championship finals for the first time, after seven attempts, and gave a good account of themselves. Scotland qualified again in 1996, but herein lies their problem. They seem capable of reaching finals tournaments, but are unable to survive the first round.

Domestically, the Glasgow monopoly was briefly threatened in the 1980s by Aberdeen (European Cup-winners' Cup winners in 1983) and Dundee United (UEFA finalists in 1987), but today Rangers are virtually all-powerful both on the pitch and financially, although in 1998 Celtic ended their rival's run of nine League titles.

Spain

Real Federacion Española de Futbol

Founded:

1913

FIFA:

1904

European Championship:

1964

Olympics:

1992

Spain's reputation as a world power in football is based largely on the exploits of her clubs, particularly Real Madrid and Barcelona, and the successes of the national side in the 1950s and 1960s. Football first got a foothold in the Basque country of Northern Spain, through migrant British workers, in the 1890s. Indeed, Spain's oldest club, Athletic Bilbao, still retain their English title. The game spread rapidly and was soon popular in Madrid, Barcelona and Valencia. The various regional organizations were brought together in 1913, when the Real Federacion Español de Futbol was formed. In 1920, the national side made its debut, with a 1–0 win over Denmark, and until the Civil War, Spain's record was quite good. They reached the quarter-finals of the 1928 Olympics, and the 1934 World Cup

finals – losing to Italy both times. Star of the side was goalkeeper Ricardo Zamora.

The Civil War and the Second World War halted internationals for almost a decade. But the domestic league grew stronger as the rivalry between Real Madrid, the "Royal" club, and Barcelona, the Catalan people's club, intensified. Barcelona had been a centre of resistance to Franco's fascists, and for the defeated and emasculated Catalan people, became their standard-bearers. This rivalry intensified in the 1950s, as both clubs began importing foreign talent. Real had Alfredo Di Stefano and Ferenc Puskas, while Barca had the Hungarian trio of Ladislav Kubala, Sandor Kocsis and Zoltan Czibor. Real Madrid won the first five European Cups (1956–60), heralding the 1960s as a decade of huge success at club and national level. Barcelona won the Fairs Cup, the former name of the UEFA Cup, in 1959, 1960 and again in 1966; Valencia won it in 1962 and 1963, Real Zaragoza in 1964. Meanwhile Atletico Madrid won the European Cup-winners' Cup in 1962, and Real Madrid won the European Cup again in 1966. There were also eight final defeats – shared among five clubs – in the three European competitions in this decade, a phenomenal record.

The national side qualified for the 1962 and 1966 World Cup finals and won the European Championship in 1964. A side containing Luis Suarez, possibly the greatest Spanish footballer ever, and one of the few

Spaniards to play in Italy (with Internazionale), beat the Soviet Union 2–1 in Madrid to clinch Spain's first major trophy. The 1970s, however, marked a decline at both levels. A ban on foreign imports, imposed in 1963, was lifted in 1973 in order to improve the national side. But it had the reverse effect. Spain failed to reach the 1970 and 1974 World Cup finals and, after Real's 1966 European Cup success, it was not until 1979 that European success returned, when Barcelona won the European Cup-winners' Cup. Spain hosted the 1982 World Cup, but failed miserably. They qualified again in 1986 and 1990 but could do no better than the quarter-finals in Mexico. But the clubs continued to do well. Real won two UEFA Cups in the 1980s, while Barcelona won the European Cup-winners' Cup in 1982 and 1989 and completed a hat-trick of European trophies by winning the European Cup in 1992 – seven years after losing a final to Steaua Bucharest by missing all four penalties they took in a shoot-out after a goalless draw.

When the national side failed to qualify for the 1992 European Championship finals, the question was raised again of whether Spanish clubs' liking for foreign imports was damaging the national side's chances. When the import ban was lifted in the early 1970s, many of the world's top stars moved to Spain, including Johan Cruyff, Johan Neeskens, Paul Breitner, Gunther Netzer and Johnny Rep. This influx coincided with a decline in the fortunes of the national team. Similarly, the 1980s saw top imports such as Diego Maradona, Bernd Schuster, Gary Lineker, Hugo Sanchez and Ronald Koeman playing in Spain while the national team stuttered.

However, the Under-23s success at the 1992 Barcelona Olympics and the continued successes of Barcelona and Real, domestically and in Europe, are reasons for hope. Several of the young Olympic victors were integrated into the full national side, which reached the quarter-finals of both the 1994 World Cup and the 1996 European Championship, being particularly unfortunate to go out to England in the latter event.

In 1998 Real won the European Cup for the seventh time, beating Juventus by the only goal scored by Yugoslav, Predrag Mijatovic. To emphasise the cosmopolitan nature of modern football, players of six other nationalities were represented in Real's starting line-up that evening, and the coach was a German, Jupp Heynkes. A month later, however, the Real success was not emulated by the Spanish national squad. They lost their opening game 3–2 to the highly entertaining Nigerians and followed up with a goalless draw against Paraguay. An emphatic 6–1 victory over Bulgaria was not enough as they were eliminated after the first stage of a World Cup where they had started among the favourites.

Sweden

Svensk Fotbollforblundet

Founded:
1904

FIFA:
1904

Olympics:
1948

Sweden have been Scandinavia's top national side since the 1920s, and have a deserved reputation for producing quality players. An Association was formed in 1904 and joined FIFA the same year.

Gothenburg was, and still is, the centre of Swedish domestic football and the National League, instituted in 1925, has been dominated by Gothenburg's clubs, Orgryte, IFK and GAIS, along with AIK and Djurgardens of Stockholm. Sweden's national side made their debut in 1908 and entered the first four Olympic tournaments – with mixed success. Sweden were at their best in the late 1940s when they boasted one of the most famous forward lines in history. Gunnar Gren, Gunnar Nordahl and Nils Liedholm – the "Gre-No-Li" trio – sparked Sweden to Olympic gold in 1948 and were promptly signed up by Milan, where they enjoyed great success. Swedes were regularly bought by European clubs but were then barred from the national side by the strictly-amateur rules of the association. Despite this handicap, Sweden finished third in the 1950 World Cup, with Nacka Skoglund the new star of his country.

The import ban was lifted in time for the 1958 World Cup Finals, which Sweden hosted, and with all their players available they reached the final, losing 5–2 to Brazil. A decline followed in the 1960s, but Sweden qualified for all three World Cup finals in the 1970s, with Bjorn Nordqvist clocking up a record 115 appearances between 1963 and 1978.

UEFA Cup Triumph

The clubs too began to make an impact, and Malmo reached the European Cup Final in 1979 where they lost to Nottingham Forest. IFK Gothenburg enjoyed the greatest success, though, winning the UEFA Cup in 1982 and 1987 – a feat made all the more remarkable as the team consisted of part-timers, because Sweden has not yet introduced full professionalism. Until it does, its top stars will continue to find football employment abroad.

Sweden's first appearance in the European Championship finals came in 1992, by virtue of being hosts, but they were beaten in the semi-finals by Germany. They followed up by finishing third in the 1994 World Cup and toppling Denmark as Scandinavia's best.

Uruguay

Asociacion Uruguaya de Futbol

Founded:
1900

FIFA:
1923

World Cup:
1930, 1950

South American Championship:
1916, 1917, 1920, 1923, 1924, 1926, 1935, 1942, 1956, 1959, 1967, 1983, 1987, 1995

Olympics:
1924, 1928

In the last decade before the Second World War, Uruguay were undoubtedly the best team in the world, effectively winning three World Championships. Today, Montevideo dominates the domestic scene and, as it is located just across the River Plate estuary from Buenos Aires, the two cities can rightly claim to be the centre of South American football. Montevideo's two great clubs, Peñarol and Nacional, have dominated Uruguayan football, winning more than 80 championships between them.

The national side dominated world football in the first half of this century, but has faded since the 1950s. Early successes in the South American Championship were followed by victories in the 1924 and 1928 Olympics. Two years later, as the host nation, Uruguay swept to victory in the first World Cup, defeating South American neighbours Argentina 4–2 in the final.

The side of the 1920s and 1930s contained many of Uruguay's all-time greats: skipper Jose Nasazzi, the midfield "Iron Curtain" of Jose Andrade, Lorenzo Fernandez and Alvarez Gestido, and outstanding forwards Hector Castro, Pedro Cea and Hector Scarone.

World Cup Glory

In 1950 Uruguay pulled off one of the biggest World Cup finals shocks in history, coming from a goal down to beat Brazil 2–1 in the deciding match in front of 200,000 seething Brazilian fans.

In Switzerland in 1954, the defence of their crown ended with a 4–2 semi-final defeat by favourites Hungary in one of the best World Cup games ever.

Since then, Uruguay have enjoyed regular success in the South American Championship, but in the World Cup they have failed to match their feats of the 1930s and 1950s.

With so many foreign-based players, Uruguay developed a schizophrenic approach to the World Cup and South American Championship, often entering wildly different teams for tournaments staged less than a year apart. This unpredictability was shown in 1995, when Uruguay won the Copa America, beating 1994 World Cup winners Brazil after a penalty shoot-out in the final.

USA

United States Soccer Federation

Founded:

1913

FIFA:

1913

CONCACAF Championship:

1991

The United States is viewed by many as a non-football country, yet US football has a long and interesting history. For example, the Oneida club of Boston was founded in 1862, making it the oldest outside England.

The national side entered the 1924 and 1928 Olympics and then travelled to Uruguay for the first World Cup in 1930 – where they reached the semi-finals. Four years later they were represented at the finals again, but lost to hosts Italy in the first round. In 1950 the US caused one of the biggest World Cup shocks ever when they beat England 1–0, with Haiti-born Joe Gaetjens scoring the winning goal. It would be 40 years before the US qualified for the World Cup finals again.

Apart from the victory over England, US soccer was long famed for one other reason – the North American Soccer League. Founded in 1967, the NASL featured corporate-backed teams which enabled the clubs to pay huge wages and attract top foreign stars. such as Pele, Franz Beckenbauer, Johan Cruyff and George Best, but the NASL collapsed in the late 1980s.

With Mexico suspended, the US qualified for the 1990 World Cup finals, but their international naivety was clearly shown, losing all three matches. FIFA, bidding to promote the game world-wide, selected the US to host the 1994 finals. No one doubted that they would be well organized, the fears were all about the hosts' quality of play.

But, under coach Bora Milutinovic, the team became hard to beat and, in 1991 they won the CONCACAF Championship – their only honour to date. The US – containing a number of players with experience of club football in Europe – then produced one of the shocks of the 1994 World Cup when they defeated dark horses Colombia in the group stage and lost only 1–0 to Brazil in the second round. The 1995 Copa America, under a new coach – Steve Sampson – proved this success was not a fluke, as the US reached the semi-finals after defeating Argentina 3–0.

Major League Soccer, the first outdoor professional league since the demise of NASL began play in 1996. Some of the glitz of the former league may have been missing, but MLS did have one big advantage: as well as stars from around the world, the league boasted famous internationals who were home-grown.

After qualifying for the final stages of France 98, the US were placed in a difficult group along with the likes of Yugoslavia, Iran and three-time winners, Germany. Three defeats, including a 2–1 defeat at the hands of Iran, will do little to encourage the growth of the game, however.

Yugoslavia

Fudbalski Savez Jugoslavije

Founded:
1919
FIFA:
1919
Olympics:
1960*

Yugoslavia were often called the Argentina of Europe for the way – before the civil war in the Balkans – in which they exported hundreds of fine players and coaches all over the world. This was the Yugoslavia who were World Cup semi-finalists in 1930 and again in 1962, but never really achieved as much as they should have, despite qualifying on six other occasions – 1950, 1954, 1958, 1974, 1982 and 1990 – and collecting the Olympic title in 1960.

At club level, too, the Yugoslavs did not often live up to the potential offered by so many players fine players. One victory in the old Fairs Cup, when Dynamo Zagreb beat Leeds 2–0 on aggregate in 1967, was followed by Red Star Belgrade's capture of the European Cup in 1991, when they beat Marseilles on penalties. But these are the only successes that they have achieved.

In 1991, however, the old nationalist tensions which have plagued the area for centuries erupted, and Yugoslavia violently disintegrated into several independent states. The former Yugoslavia's last international match was against Holland in the spring of 1992. Shortly afterwards, they were expelled from the European Championship finals on security grounds and barred from the 1994 World Cup and 1996 European Championship.

"New" Yugoslavia returned to international competition in the 1998 World Cup in which they reached the finals after thrashing Hungary in a play-off. Hopes of a speedy revival of football fortunes rested on the shoulders of Milan's Dejan Savicevic and Real Madrid's Predrag Mijatovic – scorer of seven goals in the two-leg World Cup play-off tie against Hungary.

Hopes were high after the group stage of the competition, and they could have been even higher had they not followed their opening 1–0 victory over Iran by surrendering a two-goal lead against Germany. A 1–0 victory over a stubborn United States team was not enough to see them win their group and they faced Holland in the second round.

The game appeared to be heading into extra time after Slobodan Komljenovic had equalised Dennis Bergkamp's earlier goal. However, a last-minute strike by Edgar Davids was enough to send the Yugoslavs crashing out. After years in the wilderness, however, they are back where they belong – performing on the world stage.

The Great Clubs

Professionalism swept through British football in the 1880s and western Europe in the late 1920s. The big clubs of Spain, Italy, France and Portugal were importing star foreigners by the turn of the 1930s, and it was not until the mid-1950s that Belgium, Holland and then Germany caught up with full-time professionalism.

When it did, the balance of the European game changed again. The great traditions of football have thus been kept alive, week in, week out, by the clubs. From Ajax in Holland to Vasco da Gama in Brazil, from Barcelona in Spain to Liverpool in England, they provide the first call of loyalty of the public. People who may never have attended a match in years still look out for the result of "their" club each week.

Evidence of the depths of loyalty which certain clubs can inspire is widely available – from the way Real Madrid's fans came up with the money to build the Estadio Bernabéu in the 1940s to the proud boast of Portugal's Benfica, having 122,000 members. Every club has its tales of the great days and the great victories. Some, like Manchester United, have been touched by tragedy. Others, like Marseille, with scandal. The greatest, clearly, are those who have repeatedly proved their power and strength by winning the continental cup competitions in Europe and South America. Soon, if FIFA has its way, their claims to pre-eminence will be tested by the leading clubs of Africa, Asia, Latin and North America and Oceania in a world club championship. Such a tournament, featuring the world's eight top clubs, could be launched as early as the summer of 1999 – as long as the game's rulers can adjust the international fixture calendars appropriately.

Ajax Amsterdam

Holland

Founded:
1900

Stadium:
Arena (50,000)

Colours:
Red and white broad stripes/white

League:
26

Cup:
12

World Club Cup:
1972, 1995

European Champions Cup:
1971, 1972, 1973, 1995

European Cup-winners' Cup:
1987

UEFA Cup:
1992

Super Cup:
1972, 1973, 1995

Ajax, on beating Torino in the 1992 UEFA Cup Final, became only the second team after Italy's Juventus to have won all three European trophies and a full house of all seven titles on offer to clubs. The achievement was popular, bearing in mind the entertainment and style the club had consistently provided. The first hints of glory to come were evident in 1966–67 when, under former Dutch international Rinus Michels, Ajax thrashed Liverpool 5–1 in a European Cup tie. Two years later, they became the first Dutch side to reach the European Cup Final, losing 4–1 to Milan. In 1971, Ajax were back, beating Panathinaikos 2–0 at Wembley. In the next two finals, they beat Inter 2–0, then Juventus 1–0, Johan Cruyff their inspiration.

Total Skill

Ajax's trademark was the "total football" system, taking advantage of a generation of skilled all-rounders whose versatility and footballing intelligence allowed bewildering changes of position. It was "The Whirl", as envisaged early in the 1950s by that football prophet, Willi Meisl. After the sale of Cruyff to Barcelona in 1973, Ajax fell away and it took his return, a decade later, as technical director, to propel them back to the peaks of the European game. Under Cruyff, the new generation took the Cup-winners Cup in 1987 – his pupil Marco Van Basten scoring the goal which beat Lokomotiv Leipzig in Athens. Cruyff's successor, Louis Van Gaal, secured the UEFA Cup five years later. Despite continuing to sell their best players, Ajax's 1994–95 squad was statistically their best ever, winning the League title without losing a game and the European Cup for the fourth time. Injuries foiled their bid for a fifth triumph the following season, when Ajax lost on penalties to Juventus in Rome.

Anderlecht

Brussels, Belgium

Founded:
1908

Stadium:
Constant Vanden Stock/Parc Astrid
(28,063)

Colours:
White with mauve/white

League:
23

Cup:
7

European Cup-winners' Cup:
1976, 1978

UEFA Cup:
1983

Super Cup:
1976, 1978

Anderlecht's international debut was not a happy one: they crashed 10–0 (12–0 on aggregate) to Manchester United in an early European Cup. Since then, however, the Royal Sporting Club have earned respect far and wide for their domestic domination and an international outlook which has brought success in both the European Cup-winners' Cup and the UEFA Cup. Much credit reflects on the coaching work of Englishman Bill Gormlie, a former Blackburn goalkeeper, who helped lay the foundations for success in the late 1940s and early 1950s. Equally important was the financial power of the millionaire brewer, Constant Vanden Stock. Before his takeover Anderlecht relied mainly on homegrown talent such as Paul Van Himst, the greatest Belgian footballer of all time.

International Selection

As Anderlecht's prestige grew, they were able to compete in the international transfer market. A significant coaching influence, in the early 1960s, was Frenchman Pierre Sinibaldi, who perfected a tactical formation which relied on a flat back four, the offside trap and possession football in midfield. It worked well against all opposition except British clubs, whose more direct style constantly caught the defenders on the turn. Thus, the first time Anderlecht reached a European final – the Fairs Cup in 1970 – they were beaten by Arsenal. European success, in the Cup-winners Cup in 1976 and 1978, had to await the more pragmatic coaching approach of Dutchman Wiel Corver and Belgian Raymond Goethals. Later, with Van Himst back as coach, Anderlecht won the UEFA Cup and in Enzo Scifo produced the finest Belgian player since Van Himst himself. The club's reputation nosedived in the late 1990s, however, when a match-fixing scandal surfaced concerning Anderlecht's UEFA Cup campaigns a decade earlier – most notably their semi-final victory over Nottingham Forest in 1984.

Arsenal

London, England

Founded:
1886

Stadium:
Highbury (38,500)

Colours:
Red/white

League:
11

Cup:
7

European Cup-winners' Cup:
1994

Fairs Cup:
1970

Arsenal, today a North London club, had their origins south of the Thames, at the Woolwich Arsenal. The club turned professional in 1891 and entered the Football League a year later, reaching the First Division in 1904 and the FA Cup semi-finals in 1906. After the First World War, they moved to Highbury, and appointed the legendary Herbert Chapman as manager in 1925.

Chapman had a flair for publicity, an innovative approach to tactics and a talent for motivation. He spent heavily but wisely on the likes of Charlie Buchan and Alex James, introduced the stopper centre-half and created the all-conquering outfit which won the League five times in the 1930s and the FA Cup twice. Arsenal won the League twice more and the FA Cup once in the first eight years after the war. A 17-year hiatus followed before the Gunners ended their longest trophy drought by winning the Fairs Cup in 1970.

Highbury Heroes

Suddenly, the jinx was broken. A year later manager Bertie Mee was celebrating an historic League and Cup double. His team mixed the volatile flair of Charlie George, determined leadership of Frank McLintock, rugged tackling of Peter Storey and creative class of George Graham. Graham later returned as manager, masterminding a string of successes in the League, League Cup, FA Cup and Cup-winners Cup, but his reign ended abruptly in 1995 amid controversy over transfer "bungs". Another Scotsman, Bruce Rioch, was hired for about a year, but he turned out to be only a stop-gap manager, filling in for a bigger name signing.

French coach Arsène Wenger, previously at Monaco and Grampus 8 in Japan, was hired in 1996 and rapidly transformed one of the most English of Premiership squads into a cosmopolitan double-winning mixture with the presence of Dutchmen Dennis Bergkamp and Marc Overmars and Frenchmen Patrick Vieira, Emmanuel Petit, Gilles Grimandi, Nicolas Anelka and Remi Garde.

Aston Villa

Birmingham, England

Founded:
  1874

Stadium:
  Villa Park (39,339)

Colours:
  Claret with blue sleeves/white

League:
  7

Cup:
  7

League Cup:
  5

European Champions Cup:
  1982

Aston Villa were one of the founders of the Football League back in the early days of organized football in the late 19th century. Those were also the club's greatest days because they won five of their championships and two of their FA Cups – including the double in 1896–97.

Honours have been gained in a rather more sporadic manner since then, though Villa did set the First Division scoring record with 128 goals in the 1930–31 season when they finished runners-up behind Herbert Chapman's Arsenal. Villa made history – for a brief time – when they won the FA Cup for a seventh time amid controversy in 1957. Villa beat Manchester United 2–1 at Wembley though United played much of the match with 10 men after goalkeeper Ray Wood was badly injured by a challenge from Villa's top-scoring outside left, Peter MacParland.

Villa's Greatest Achievements

At one stage in the succeeding decades, Villa suffered the indignity of relegation to the Third Division but regained their pride under the management of former wing-half Vic Crowe. Ron Saunders then took over and built the team which won the League in 1981, and his assistant and successor Tony Barton guided Villa to their greatest achievement when they beat Bayern Munich in Rotterdam to win the European Cup the following year. Peter Withe scored the only goal from close range in the Feyenoord stadium.

Villa used the income from their European runs to redevelop their home into one of the finest grounds in the Premier League while the team, simultaneously, underlined their competitive reputation with two League Cup successes in three seasons in the mid-1990s, thus equalling Liverpool's record of five victories in this competition.

And in 1997–98, the club showed signs of making an impact on the European scene once more, reaching the last eight of the UEFA Cup.

Atlético Madrid

Spain

Founded:
1903

Stadium:
Vicente Calderón/Manzanares
(62,000)

Colours:
Red and white stripes/blue

League:
9

Cup:
9

World Club Cup:
1974

European Cup-winners' Cup:
1962

Atlético Madrid have always existed in the shadow of neighbours Real, but they still rank among the Big Three of Spanish football and boast a proud record at international level. Not that life has always been easy. In the late 1930s, after the Spanish Civil War, it took a merger with the Air Force club to keep Atlético in business; in 1959, they just failed to reach the European Cup Final when Real beat them in a semi-final play-off; in the early 1960s they had to share Real's Estadio Bernabéu, because Atlético's Metropolitano had been sold to developers before the club's new stadium could be completed. European glory did come to Atlético in the shape of the Cup-winners Cup in 1962 and was a well-deserved prize for players such as inside-left Joaquín Peiro and his wing partner Enrique Collar. But it was not until the early 1970s that Atlético put together a comparable team, thanks to the purchases of Argentines Ruben Hugo Ayala and Ramon Heredia. In 1974, Atlético secured that elusive place in the European Cup Final. But, after taking the lead against Bayern Munich in extra time, Atlético conceded a last-kick equalizer.

One Team in Madrid

Consolation for their 4–0 defeat in the replay came with the opportunity to substitute for reluctant Bayern in the World Club Cup against Independiente of Argentina. By the time the tie came around, Atlético had appointed as coach Luis Aragones, the midfielder who had scored their goal in the European Cup Final against Bayern. Atletico duly beat Independiente 1–0 and were, for a year at least, on top of the world. In the late 1980s, the club was taken over by the extrovert builder Jesus Gíl. He pumped millions of pounds into the club but generated more bad publicity than good, hiring and firing coaches at a breathtaking rate. It all came together in dramatic fashion when Atlético won the league and cup double in 1996.

Atletico Nacional

Medellin, Colombia

Founded:
 1938
Stadium:
 Atanasio Giradot (35,000)
Colours:
 Green and white stripes/white
League:
 5
South American Club Cup:
 1989
European Champions Cup:
 1992
Inter-American Cup:
 1989

Atletico Nacional of Medellin are not the most famous club to come out of Colombia. That honour will always belong to Millonarios, who led the professional, pirate revolution in the early 1950s. But Nacional earned a place in history by becoming the first club to take the Copa Libertadores, the South American Club Cup, across the Andes to the western side of the continent. Nacional, who provided the base of the Colombian World Cup team in 1990, were in 1954 the first champions of Colombia after the rapproche-

ment with FIFA. Yet it was not until 1971 that they made their debut in the South American Club Cup under Argentine coach Osvaldo Zubeldia. He had earned a fearsome reputation as boss of the rugged Estudiantes de La Plata team which had dominated Argentine and South American club football in the late 1960s. However, without resorting to the cynicism which made Estudiantes hated, he turned Nacional into Colombian champions three times in the mid-1970s and early 1980s. Zubeldia was followed by Luis Cubilla, at whose suggestion, in 1986, Nacional appointed a former stalwart central defender, Francisco Maturana, as boss.

In 1987 and 1988 they finished championship runners-up and then, in 1989, seized the South American club crown by defeating Olimpia of Paraguay on penalties after a 2–2 draw on aggregate over two legs. Unfortunately, their preparations for the world club showdown with Milan were wrecked when the government halted the league season because of the increasing violence being engendered on the fringes of the game by the drug and betting cartels.

Nacional did not emerge with their reputation unscathed. It was not only that Medellin was the centre of the drugs trade; several Nacional players were friends of the notorious drugs baron Pablo Escobar. Indeed, when Escobar was eventually killed in 1993 by security forces, at his funeral the coffin was draped in a Nacional flag.

Barcelona

Spain

Founded:
1899

Stadium:
Nou Camp(115,000)

Colours:
Blue and red stripes/blue

League:
15

Cup:
24

European Champions Cup:
1992

European Cup-winners' Cup:
1979, 1982, 1989, 1997

Fairs Cup:
1958, 1960, 1966

Super Cup:
1992

Barcelona finally ended a duel with destiny when, in 1992, they beat Sampdoria 1–0 at Wembley to win the European Cup. It was a case of third time lucky, for the greatest prize in the European club game had twice eluded them at the final hurdle. Barcelona had been the first winners of the Inter-Cities Fairs Cup and had won the Cup-winners' Cup three times. But their European Cup campaigns seemed to have been jinxed. First, in 1961,

when Barcelona had apparently achieved the hard part by eliminating title-holders and bitter rivals Real Madrid, they lost to Benfica in the final, in Berne. Barcelona hit the woodwork three times, yet lost 3–2 against the run of play. Great players such as Luis Suarez, Ladislav Kubala, Sandor Kocsis and Zoltan Czibor had everything on their side except luck. History repeated itself in even more galling circumstances in 1986. Barcelona, coached by Terry Venables, faced Steaua Bucharest in Seville but lost on penalties after a goalless draw.

Second Generation

It took the return of 1970s inspiration Johan Cruyff, this time as coach, to steer a new generation of international stars – including Ronald Koeman, Hristo Stoichkov and Michael Laudrup – to victory long overdue for one of the world's biggest clubs. Barcelona's 1994 League title was their fourth in a row, the last three achieved in the closing moments of the final day, twice at the expense of Real Madrid.

Failure to win a trophy in 1995 or 1996, however, resulted in Cruyff's dismissal after eight years in charge. He was followed by Bobby Robson, whose recapture of the Cup-winners Cup and Spanish Cup could not save him from a move "upstairs" and replacement by another Dutchman, Louis Van Gaal. Another championship – the club's 15th – was followed by the Spanish Cup in 1998.

Bayern Munich

Germany

Founded:
1900
Stadium:
Olimpiastadion (69,261)
Colours:
All red
League:
14
Cup:
8
World Club Cup:
1976
European Champions Cup:
1974, 1975, 1976
European Cup-winners' Cup:
1967
UEFA Cup:
1996

Bayern are Germany's most glamorous club, even though high tax rates mean they have never been able to retain players tempted by the rich pickings of Italy. In the 1980s, Bayern became almost an Italian nursery as they lost Karl-Heinz Rummenigge, Andreas Brehme and Lothar Matthäus to Inter and Stefan Reuter and Jurgen Kohler to Juventus.

All this transfer activity underlines the fact that the Bayern success story is relatively recent.

Top Line-up
The identities of the men who secured all the glittering titles read like a *Who's Who* of the world game: Franz Beckenbauer, Gerd Müller, Sepp Maier, Paul Breitner, Rummenigge and Matthäus. The German championship was originally organized in regional leagues, with the winners playing off at the end of each season for the title: only once in the pre-war years did Bayern win all the way through. That was in 1932, when they defeated Eintracht Frankfurt 2–0. Not until 1957, and a 1–0 win over Fortuna Düsseldorf in the cup final, did Bayern have anything more to celebrate. Their record was so mediocre they were not included in the inaugural Bundesliga in 1963–64. But, a year later, Bayern won promotion; in 1966 they won the cup, and in 1967 secured the European Cup-winners' Cup. That was the team led by Beckenbauer as an attacking sweeper, with Maier in goal and Müller up front. All three starred in Bayern's European Cup hat-trick in the mid-1970s. In the 1980s, Bayern were twice European Cup runners-up, but it was not until Beckenbauer returned – as vice-president, coach, then president – that they triumphed again. Their 1996 UEFA Cup success made Bayern the fourth club to win all three European trophies.

Benfica

Lisbon, Portugal

Founded:
1904

Stadium:
Estádio do Benfica/Da Luz
(92,385)

Colours:
Red/white

League:
29

Cup:
26

European Champions Cup:
1961, 1962

Benfica are a national institution with their huge stadium – there was a 130,000 capacity before recent security constraints – and 122,000 membership. Living up to the standards of history is what Benfica believe they owe Cosme Damiao who, on February 28, 1904, organized the first recorded local game of *futebol* on a patch of Lisbon wasteland. The next day he formed his "team" into a club named Sport Lisboa and, two years later, was instrumental in arranging a merger with neighbours Sport Clube de Benfica.

In the early years, it was cycling which brought the club its first prizes. Following the launch of a Portuguese championship in the late 1920s, Benfica lorded it over Portuguese sport. In due course, Benfica set their sights on international glory and, in 1950, won the Latin Cup – a forerunner of the European Cup. English manager Ted Smith laid the foundations of a team which would dominate not only Portugal but then Europe.

Taking on All-comers

In 1954, Benfica followed the example being set in Spain and built a vast new stadium. An exiled Hungarian named Bela Guttman became coach, and his team filled the new stadium as Benfica broke Real Madrid's grip on the European Cup, sweeping to success in 1961 and 1962.

First they beat Barcelona, amid intense drama, by 3–2 in Berne, then Real Madrid 5–3 in Amsterdam. On both occasions Benfica were captained by their veteran centre-forward, José Aguas. They also introduced one of the most famous Portuguese footballers of all time in Eusebio (*see* page 104), greatest of the many fine players Benfica had discovered in the Portuguese colonies of Mozambique and Angola.

Benfica's boast of using only Portuguese (including colonial) players was scrapped in the mid-1970s, when the African colonies were cast adrift. Now they hunt Brazilians, Slavs and Danes with the rest – rewarded with nothing like the success of their earlier years.

Boca Juniors

Buenos Aires, Argentina

Founded:
1905

Stadium:
Bombonera (58,740)

Colours:
Blue with yellow hoop/blue

League:
19

World Club Cup:
1977

South American Club Cup:
1977, 1978

South American Supercup:
1989

Inter-American Cup:
1989

Boca are one of the two great clubs in the Argentine capital of Buenos Aires, along with rivals River Plate. They were founded by an Irishman named Patrick MacCarthy and a group of newly-arrived Italian immigrants. They joined the League in 1913 and were immediately caught up in a domestic football "war" which led to two championships being organized for most of the 1920s and early 1930s.

Boca stood astride the two eras. They won the final Argentine amateur championship in 1930 and the first unified professional one the following year. Two more titles followed in the next four years, thanks to some fine players, including the great Brazilian defender Domingos da Guia. In the 1940s and 1950s, Boca slipped into River Plate's shadow, re-emerging in 1963 when a team fired by the goals of José Sanfilippo reached the final of the South American Club Cup.

World Club Champions

Winning the title, however, would have to wait until the late 1970s. Then they reached the final three years in a row – beating Brazil's Cruzeiro in 1977 and Deportivo Cali of Colombia in 1978 before losing to Olimpia of Paraguay the following year.

Boca's rugged style, under Juan Carlos Lorenzo, proved controversial. Not one of the club's players figured in the squad which won the 1978 World Cup Final against Holland on home soil. But Boca had already secured their own world crown, defeating West Germany's Borussia Mönchengladbach in the World Club Cup in 1977.

Boca rebuilt their team around Diego Maradona in 1981, but they had managed to add few prizes to their trophy room when he rejoined them in 1995 – and none during his controversial two-year stay peppered with "retirements."

Borussia Dortmund

Germany

Founded:
1909
Stadium:
Westfalenstadion (42,800)
Colours:
Yellow/black
League:
5
Cup:
2
World Club Cup:
1997
European Champions Cup:
1997
Cup-winners Cup:
1966

Borussia Dortmund hold a particular place in history as the first German club to have won a European trophy. That was in 1966, when they beat Liverpool 2–1 after extra time in the final of the Cup-winners Cup at Hampden Park, Glasgow. Pride in that achievement extended almost to superstition when the members of that team were flown by Dortmund to the away leg of their 1993 UEFA Cup semi-final against French club Auxerre. The lucky charms paid off again, with Dortmund losing 2–0 but winning the penalty shoot-out 6–5. The magic failed temporarily when they lost the final against Juventus but they had their revenge four years later – beating Juventus 3–1 in the Champions League Final, in Munich.

Serious Success

The foundations had been in preparation for several years. Evidence was available when Dortmund finished runners-up in 1992 then in January 1993, when they paid £3 million to bring home outstanding sweeper Matthias Sammer from Inter. Sammer, a former East German international, had been sold to Inter only the previous summer, by Stuttgart. But he failed to adapt to football, life and the language in Italy and Dortmund's enterprise in bringing him home was rewarded with European and world club titles. Sammer himself was voted 1996 European Footballer of the Year.

Dortmund's home, the Westfalenstadion, was built for the 1974 World Cup and is one of the few modern German stadia created specifically for football. There is no athletics track surrounding the pitch and every survey among players finds Dortmund voted one of their favourite venues. Dortmund previously played in the 30,000-capacity Rote Erde stadium, part of a larger complex and which now sits in the shadow of the Westfalenstadion and is used for athletics and training.

Celtic

Glasgow, Scotland

Founded:
1888
Stadium:
Celtic Park (51,709)
Colours:
Green and white hoops/white
League:
35
Cup:
30
European Champions Cup:
1967

Celtic and rivals Rangers are Scottish football's greatest clubs, but it was Celtic who first extended that hunger for success into Europe when, in 1967, they became the first British club to win the European Cup. It was a measure of the way they swept all before them that season that they won every domestic competition as well: the League, the Cup and League Cup.

No other team in Europe had, until then, ended the season with a 100 per cent record in four major competitions. In winning the European Cup, Celtic refuted accusations – mostly from England – that their Scottish honours owed more to a lack of solid opposition than their own abilities. Celtic's 1967

team was shrewdly put together by manager Jock Stein, a former Celtic player. As well as new Scottish stars, he included veterans such as goalkeeper Ronnie Simpson and scheming inside-left Bertie Auld – the only two of the XI to have been with a club outside Scotland. In the Lisbon final, they beat former holders Inter 2–1.

On Top of Europe

Sadly, Celtic's golden touch did not survive long. A few months later they were beaten by Kiev Dynamo at the start of their European Cup defence, and were then dragged down to defeat and fisticuffs in the infamous World Club Cup battle with Racing of Argentina.

In 1970, Celtic returned to the European Cup Final, only to lose to Feyenoord in Milan; and, two years later, they lost only on penalties after two goalless draws in the semi-finals against Inter. More trouble lay ahead as Celtic proved unable to match Rangers' commercial and playing achievements in the late 1980s and slipped to the brink of bankruptcy before turning the corner after a boardroom revolution.

The subsequent appointment as manager of Wim Jansen, a Dutch World Cup hero of the 1970s, brought better days. Celtic just managed to end the domestic dominance of Rangers, who had triumphed in the Championship for nine successive seasons between 1989–97, thus equalling Celtic's record, but Jansen left the club after a dispute.

Colo Colo

Santiago, Chile

Founded:
1925

Stadium:
Colo Colo (50,000)

Colours:
White/black

League:
19

South American Club Cup:
1991

South American Recopa:
1991

Colo Colo, Chilean nickname for a wildcat, were founded by five angry members of the old Magallanes FC. Even though Chilean football is generally held to lag far behind that of traditional giants Brazil, Argentina and Uruguay, Colo Colo have an enviable reputation throughout the continent. The club's vision has always stretched beyond the Andes. Such a tradition was laid down by David Orellano. He was a founder member of Colo Colo and one of the five Magallanes rebels who disagreed over the selection of a club captain. The choice of the five fell upon Orellano and, within two years of Colo Colo's foundation, they had sent a team off to tour Spain and Portugal. In 1933 Colo

Colo were among the founders of a professional league; in 1941 they set another pioneering trend by introducing a foreign coach in the Hungarian, Ferenc Platko; and in 1948 they organized a South American club tournament which can now be seen as a forerunner of the Copa Libertadores, the official South American Club Cup launched in 1960.

Colo Colo are record league winners in Chile and the supreme transfer destination for most domestic players. Their greatest achievement in their first 50 years was in reaching the 1973 South American Club Cup Final. The teams drew 1–1 in Avellaneda and 0–0 in Santiago, and thus went on to a play-off in Montevideo, which Independiente won 2–1 in extra time. Colo Colo's consolation goal was scored by their most famous and popular player of the modern era, Carlos Caszely.

Then, in 1991, they became the first Chilean side to win the Libertadores and did so in fine style, winning all their seven home games, and drawing five and losing only two away. Their victims included Nacional of Uruguay, Boca Juniors of Argentina – the favourites – and the holders, Olimpia of Paraguay, in the final. Colo Colo forced a 0–0 draw in Asuncion, and then won 3–0 at home, with their last goal coming from Leonel Herrera, whose father had been in the losing Libertadores final side 18 years earlier.

Eintracht Frankfurt

Germany

Founded:
  1899
Stadium:
  Waldstadion (61,146)
Colours:
  Black and red stripes/black
League:
  1
Cup:
  4
UEFA Cup:
  1980

Eintracht Frankfurt occupy a very special place in football legend as the team Real Madrid beat in the European Cup Final at Hampden back in 1960. The score was 7–3 to Madrid, but Frankfurt were far from crushed and had proved their class by achieving a previously unknown feat, putting six goals past Glasgow Rangers – both home and away – in the semi-finals. Frankfurt's team was built on the midfield strength of Dieter Stinka and Jurgen Lindner, plus the creative talents of veteran inside-left Alfred Pfaff and right-winger Richard Kress. It may sound odd to suggest that everything after a

defeat was an anti-climax, but though Frankfurt were founder members of the West German Bundesliga in 1963, they have achieved comparatively little.

Boardroom problems in the mid-1980s dogged the club until the businessman Matthias Ohms took over and appointed Bernd Holzenbein, a World Cup winner in 1974 and an old Frankfurt favourite, as his executive vice-president. Holzenbein put Frankfurt back on a sound financial footing and bought stars such as midfielder Andy Möller (later sold to Juventus) and the brilliant Ghanaian striker, Anthony Yeboah. In 1992–93 they were pipped for the league title after the controversial mid-season departure of their charismatic Yugoslav coach, Dragoslav Stepanovic. His successor Jupp Heynckes did not last long either, after falling out with Yeboah, who was allowed to depart for English club Leeds, leaving Frankfurt to sink towards a first-ever relegation.

Frankfurt's one European success over the years was in winning the UEFA Cup in 1980. They beat their fellow Germans, Borussia Mönchengladbach, on the away goals rule in the Final, losing 3–2 away and then winning 1–0 back in the Waldstadion. Holzenbein had scored the all-important second away goal in the first leg.

At home, they have won the German Cup on four occasions – in 1974, 1975, 1981 and 1988.

* The Great Clubs

FC Porto

Oporto, Portugal

Founded:
1893

Stadium:
Das Antas (76,000)

Colours:
Blue and white stripes/white

League:
16

Cup:
11

World Club Cup:
1987

European Champions Cup:
1987

Super Cup:
1987

Porto were always considered to be number three in the Portuguese football hierarchy until their thrilling European Cup victory over Bayern Munich in Vienna, in 1987. Events then and since have ensured that, while their trophy count may not yet match those of Benfica and Sporting, Porto are clearly seen as an alternative centre of power in the domestic game.

Porto beat Bayern with the Polish goalkeeper Mlynarczyk, Brazilians Celso and Juary, and Algerian winger Rabah Madjer

supporting Portugal's own wonderboy, Paulo Futre. But that was entirely appropriate because, in the early 1930s, Porto had been pioneers in the international transfer market.

Importers of Talent

They began by bringing in two Yugoslavs, and that ambition was reflected in Porto's initial championship successes in 1938 and 1939. In those days, Porto's home was the old, rundown Campo da Constituição. Now, as befits a club with European Cup winning pedigree, home is the impressive 76,000-capacity Estádio das Antas.

Not only have Porto won the Champions Cup; they also finished runners-up to Juventus in the European Cup-winners' Cup in 1984. The creative force behind the club's progress in the 1980s was the late José Maria Pedroto. He led Porto to the cup in 1977 and league title in 1978 and 1979.

His work would be carried on by his pupil, former national team centre-forward Artur Jorge, who coached Porto to their 1987 European title and later took over the national side. Subsequently, under Brazilian Carlos Alberto da Silva, duly succeeded by Bobby Robson, Porto enhanced their standing as members of the European establishment when they reached the semi-finals of the Champions League in 1994 and the quarter-finals in 1997. Robson left Porto in 1996 after building a team which won a hat-trick of League titles.

Feyenoord

Rotterdam, Holland

Founded:
1908
Stadium:
De Kuyp (52,000)
Colours:
Red and white halves/black
League:
13
Cup:
10
World Club Cup:
1970
European Champions Cup:
1970
UEFA Cup:
1974

Feyenoord were founded by mining entrepreneur C. R. J. Kieboom. Their star player in the successful pre-war years was left-half Puck Van Heel, who appeared in the final tournaments of the 1934 and 1938 World Cups and set what was for many years a Dutch record of 64 international appearances. The post-war period was bleak until after the introduction of professionalism in the late 1950s. Then, Feyenoord entered their most glorious domestic era, winning the League six times in 13 years. Indeed, their

1965 and 1969 titles were half of League and Cup doubles. Stars included goalkeeper Eddie Pieters-Graafland, a then record £20,000 signing from Ajax, half-backs Reinier Kreyermaat, Hans Kraay and Jan Klaasens and, above all, outside-left Coen Moulijn. He was still a key figure when Feyenoord won the European Cup in 1970, along with Swedish striker Ove Kindvall and burly midfield general Wim Van Hanegem. Feyenoord's coach, for their extra time victory over Celtic in Milan, was Ernst Happel, the former Austrian international. Feyenoord – and not Ajax – were thus the first Dutch club to gain European success, and they went on to beat Estudiantes de La Plata of Argentina in the World Club Cup Final.

Ups and Downs

In 1974 Feyenoord added the UEFA Cup to their trophy room. But they gradually lost their grip on the Dutch game. Key players were sold to balance the books, among them Ruud Gullit, who Feyenoord discovered at Haarlem. He was sold to PSV Eindhoven and later moved to Milan and Chelsea. Not until the arrival as general manager of Wim Jansen, a former Feyenoord favourite who starred with Holland at the 1974 World Cup, did Feyenoord regain the title, in 1993. They appeared in the UEFA Champions League in 1997–98 but that was courtesy of a rule change to admit runners-up from Europe's top footballing leagues.

FK Austria

Vienna, Austria

Founded:
1911

Stadium:
Horr (10,500) / Prater (62,270)

Colours:
White with mauve/white

League:
21

Cup:
21

The history of the Fussball Klub Austria-Memphis began with a game of cricket. Just as the English exported their industrial know-how and educational skills around the world in the latter half of the nineteenth century, they also took with them their newly codified games and sports.

Thus the Vienna Cricket and Football Club was founded by the expatriate community in the 1890s. Cricket did not gain universal acceptance, but football was another matter, and November 15, 1894 was the date of the first proper football match ever staged in Austria. Vienna Cricket and Football Club beat 1st Vienna FC by 4–0 – and they have been winning matches and titles ever since.

Changing their name in 1925, FKA notched up many domestic honours in a list

which includes runners-up spot in the European Cup-winners' Cup in 1978, when a team inspired by midfield general Herbert Prohaska became the first Austrian side to reach a modern-day European final, only to lose 4–0 to Anderlecht of Belgium.

An appearance at the last stage of all was long overdue, because, in the late 1920s, FK Austria were one of the pioneers of European international club soccer when the Mitropa Cup drew clubs from Austria, Czechoslovakia, Hungary, Yugoslavia, Switzerland and Italy. FK Austria were triumphant in 1933 and 1936, inspired by the legendary centre-forward Matthias Sindelar.

Their delicate style of play, known as the "Vienna School", was modelled on the old Scottish close-passing game and had been taught them by Englishman Jimmy Hogan. His coaching genius contributed mightily to the development of the so-called "Wunderteam" which lost unluckily to England, by 4–3, at Stamford Bridge in 1932 and then reached the semi-finals of the 1934 World Cup, losing by the only goal to Italy, the eventual champions.

The backbone of the Wunderteam was provided by FK Austria. That tradition has been maintained ever since. Thus no fewer than six FKA stars travelled with the national squad to the 1990 World Cup Finals in Italy, where the team finished third in their group, behind Italy and Czechoslovakia.

Flamengo

Rio de Janeiro, Brazil

Founded:
1895 as sailing club;
1911 as football club

Stadium:
Gavea (20,000) and
Maracana (130,000)

Colours:
Black and red hoops/white

Rio state league:
22

Brazil championship (incl. Torneo Rio-São Paulo):
5

World Club Cup:
1981

South American Club Cup:
1981

Flamengo are the most popular club in Brazil, having been formed by dissident members of the Fluminense club but under the umbrella of the Flamengo sailing club – which now has more than 70,000 members. They first competed in the Rio league in 1912, winning the title two years later. In 1915, they regained the crown without losing a game. A string of great names have graced the red-and-black hoops over the years, among them defenders Domingos Da Guia and centre-forward Leonidas da Silva. Known as the "Black Diamond", Leonidas played for Flamengo from 1936 to 1942, inspiring two state championship triumphs and earning a worldwide reputation through his brilliance in the 1938 World Cup finals.

On Top of the World

Flamengo ran up a Rio state hat-trick in the mid-1950s with their team nicknamed "The Steamroller", but had to wait until 1981 for their greatest success. Then, riding high on the goals of a new hero, Zico – the so-called "White Pele" – they won the South American and World Club Cups. The former campaign was one of the most hostile in memory. Flamengo won a first-round play-off against Atletico Mineiro after their rival Brazilians had five players sent off, provoking referee José Roberto Wright to abandon the game. In the final, Flamengo beat Cobreloa of Chile in a play-off, in Uruguay, after the expulsion of five players. Fears about the outcome of Flamengo's world showdown against Liverpool proved unfounded. Zico was in a class of his own, creating the goals in a 3–0 win. The players dedicated the success to the memory of Claudio Coutinho, a former coach who had died in a skin-diving accident. In the mid-1990s, Flamengo sought to revive the glory days by twice bringing World Cup-winning striker Romario home from Spain – first from Barcelona and then from Valencia.

Fluminense

Rio de Janeiro, Brazil

Founded:
1902

Stadium:
Laranjeira (20,000) and
Maracana (130,000)

Colours:
Red, green and white
stripes/white

Rio state league:
27

Brazil championship (incl. Torneo Rio-São Paulo):
4

Fluminense have yet to win an international trophy, but that does not alter their status as one of South America's great clubs. "Flu" were founded in 1902 by an Englishman named Arthur Cox, and many of their first players were British residents.

The club's wealth and upper-class clientele resulted in the nickname "Po de Arroz" ("Face Powder", after the fashion of the time at the turn of the century). Today, the club's fans wear white powder on their faces as a sign of loyalty.

In 1905, "Flu" were founder members of the Rio de Janeiro league and of the Brazilian confederation; they won the first four Rio (Carioca) championships in 1906–09; and, in 1932, they became the first Brazilian club to go professional.

Superteam

By this time the "Flu-Fla" derby (against Flamengo) had been flourishing for 20 years, the first meeting between the clubs having taken place in 1912. In 1963, their clash drew an official crowd of 177,656 to the Maracana stadium in Rio, which remains a world record for a club game.

By 1930, Flu's stadium was the home of the national team and the club had launched a weekly newspaper, among other schemes. A few years later and Flu were ruling the roost with five Rio titles between 1936 and 1941. Star players were forwards Romeu, Carreiro and Tim – who coached Peru at the 1978 World Cup Finals.

In the early 1950s, Fluminense's star was the World Cup winning midfield general Didi. In the late 1960s and early 1970s the key player was another World Cup winner, Brazil's 1970 captain and right-back, Carlos Alberto Torres. In the 1980s, the mantle of inspiration-in-chief passed to the Paraguayan Romerito (Julio César Romero).

Fluminense collected a hat-trick of Rio titles in 1983, 1984 and 1985, with Romero their guiding light. He was rewarded by being nominated South American Footballer of the Year in 1985, and starred at the 1986 World Cup Finals in Mexico.

Hamburg

Germany

Founded:
1887

Stadium:
Volksparkstadion (61,234)

Colours:
White/red

League:
6

Cup:
3

European Cup:
1983

European Cup-winners' Cup:
1977

Hamburg can be considered by many to be the oldest league club in Germany, if one takes as their foundation date that of SC Germania, the oldest of three clubs which later amalgamated. The other two were Hamburger FC (1888) and FC Falke (1905). Hamburg's tradition, from that day to this, has been one of attacking football. The first major trophy could have been theirs in 1922. But when the championship play-off was abandoned because injury-hit Nürnberg had only seven men left on the pitch, Hamburg sportingly declined to accept the title. A year later Hamburg did win the championship,

and they did so again in 1928. They did not win it again until 1960, by which time they were being led by the greatest footballer in the club's history. Centre-forward Uwe Seeler, son of a former Hamburg player, was four times Hamburg's top scorer in the old regional league system, and after the creation of the Bundesliga was once the country's leading marksman. He also spearheaded Hamburg's thrilling 1960–61 European Cup campaign, in which they lost to Barcelona only in a play-off in the semi-finals.

Seeler went on to captain West Germany in their brave World Cup efforts of 1966 and 1970 – his international career lasted 17 years – but he had retired by the time Hamburg achieved a European breakthrough and won the Cup-winners' Cup in 1977. They beat holders Anderlecht 2–0 in a final which was the big-occasion debuts of two long-serving internationals, defender Manni Kaltz and midfield general Felix Magath.

Both were stalwarts of the side beaten by Nottingham Forest in the 1980 European Cup Final, when Englishman Kevin Keegan tried in vain to stimulate the Hamburg attack. Keegan had returned to England by the time Hamburg beat Juventus in Athens three years later.

After a decade in the doldrums, Seeler returned as president and Hamburg ended the 1995–96 German season in fifth position, their best placing for six years. 1998 saw a slip into mid-table obscurity.

Independiente

Avellaneda, Argentina

Founded:

1904

Stadium:

Cordero (55,000)

Colours:

Red/blue

League:

11

World Club Cup:

1973, 1984

South American Club Cup:

1964, 1965, 1972, 1973, 1974, 1975, 1984

Inter-American Cup:

1973, 1974, 1976

Independiente are perhaps the least familiar of international club football's great achievers, outside Argentina at least. This is because, despite two lengthy periods of command in South American club football, they won the world title only twice in five attempts, and that at a time when the competition's image was tarnished. Also, Independiente have always relied on team football rather than individual inspiration. One outstanding player who made his name with the club, however, was Raimundo Orsi. He was the left-winger who played for Argentina in the 1928 Olympics, signed for Juventus and then scored Italy's vital equaliser on their way to victory over Czechoslovakia in the 1934 World Cup Final.

Later, the Independiente fans had the great Paraguayan centre-forward, Arsenio Erico, to idolize. Erico had been the boyhood hero of Alfredo Di Stefano and, in 1937, set an Argentine First Division goalscoring record of 37 in a season.

Red Devils

Independiente did not regain prominence until the early 1960s, when coach Manuel Giudice imported an Italian-style *catenaccio* defence which secured the South American Club Cup in 1964 and 1965. Independiente were the first Argentine team to win the continent's top club prize. But in the World Club Cup Final they fell both years to the high priests of *catenaccio*, Inter of Italy.

In the 1970s, Independiente's Red Devils won the South American Club Cup four times in a row and collected the World Club Cup. It was an odd victory: European champions Hamburg declined to compete, so runners-up Juventus took their place – on condition that the final was a one-off match in Italy. Independiente not only agreed, they won it with a single goal from midfield general Ricardo Bochini.

In the late 1990s, Independiente sought to battle back out of a spell in the doldrums by signing Cesar Luis Menotti, Argentina's chain-smoking World Cup-winning coach of 1978.

Internazionale

Milan, Italy

Founded:
1908

Stadium:
Meazza (85,443)

Colours:
Blue and black stripes/black

League:
13

Cup:
3

World Club Cup:
1964, 1965

European Champions Cup:
1964, 1965

UEFA Cup:
1991, 1994, 1998

Internazionale, known as Inter, were founded out of an argument within the Milan club in the early years of the century. Some 45 members, led by Giovanni Paramithiotti, broke away in protest at the authoritarian way the powerful Camperio brothers were running the club. In the 1930s, fascist laws forced Internazionale into a name change to rid the club of the foreign associations of their title. So they took the name of their city's patron saint and became Ambrosiana. Under this name they led the way in continental club competition – being one of the leading lights in the pre-war Mitropa Cup.

European World-beaters

After the war, the club reverted to the Inter name and pioneered a tactical revolution. First manager Alfredo Foni, who had been a World Cup-winning full-back before the war, won the League twice by withdrawing outside-right Gino Armani into midfield; then Helenio Herrera conquered Italy, Europe and the world with *catenaccio*. Keeper Giuliano Sarti, sweeper Armando Picchi and man-marking backs Tarcisio Burgnich, Aristide Guarneri and Giacinto Facchetti were the foundation on which Spanish general Luis Suarez built the counter-attacking raids carried out by Brazilian Jair da Costa and Italian Sandro Mazzola.

Inter won the European and World Club Cups in 1964 and 1965 – beating Real Madrid and Benfica in Europe, and Argentina's Independiente twice for the world crown. But in 1966, Real Madrid toppled Inter in the European Cup semi-finals, Celtic repeated the trick a year later in a memorable Lisbon final, and Herrera was lured to Roma. Only when Lothar Matthäus drove them to the 1989 League title, followed by success in the 1991, 1994 and 1998 UEFA Cups, were Inter a force again.

Inter had spent some years in Milan's shadow, but returned to the limelight by paying £19.5 million for Brazilian Ronaldo.

Juventus

Turin, Italy

Founded:
1897

Stadium:
Delle Alpi (71,012)

Colours:
Black and white stripes/white

League:
24

Cup:
10

World Club Cup:
1985, 1996

European Champions Cup:
1985, 1996

European Cup-winners' Cup:
1984

UEFA Cup:
1977, 1990, 1993

Super Cup:
1984, 1996

Juventus were founded by a group of Italian students who decided to adopt red as the colour for their shirts. In 1903, however, one of the committee members was so impressed by Notts County's black-and-white stripes that he bought a set of shirts to take home to Turin. In the 1930s Juventus laid the foundations for their legend, winning the Italian league championship five times in a row. Simultaneously they also reached the semi finals of the Mitropa Cup on four occasion and supplied Italy's World Cup-winnin teams with five players in 1934 and three i 1938. Goalkeeper Gianpiero Combi, fro Juventus, was Italy's victorious captain i 1934, just as another Juventus goalkeepe Dino Zoff (*see* page 162), would be in 1982

Black and White

After the war, the Zebras (after the colours their shirts) scoured the world for talent match their import-led rivals. In 1971 the lost the Fairs Cup Final to Leeds on the awa goals rule, but in 1977 they beat Bilbao the UEFA Cup Final on the same regulatior

In 1982 no fewer than six Juventus play ers featured in Italy's World Cup winnin line-up, and Cabrini, Tardelli, Scirea, Genti and Paolo Rossi helped Juve win the 198 European Cup-winners' Cup and the 198 European Cup. Seeking new magic in th 1990s, Juventus paid huge fees for Rober Baggio and Gianluca Vialli. Both shared the 1995 league and cup double triumph b Baggio then left for Milan on the eve of season when Vialli led Juventus to victory the European Champions Cup final ov Ajax in Rome. They were runaway favourit to retain the Cup the next year but surprising slipshod work in defence led to defeat b Borussia Dortmund in the final, followed another upset against Real Madrid in 1998.

Kiev Dynamo

Ukraine

Founded:

1927

Stadium:

Republic (100,100)

Colours:

White/blue

League:

4 Ukraine, 13 Soviet

Cup:

2 Ukraine, 9 Soviet

European Cup-winners' Cup:

1975, 1986

Super Cup:

1975

Kiev were founder members of the Soviet top division, yet had to wait until 1961 before they became the first club outside Moscow to land the title. They achieved the league and cup double five years later and went on to a record-equalling hat-trick of league titles. Midfielders Iosif Sabo and Viktor Serebryanikov were key men, as too were forwards Valeri Porkuyan and Anatoli Bishovets. Porkuyan starred at the 1966 World Cup finals in England, and Bishovets did so four years later in Mexico.

Soviets in Europe

In 1975 Kiev became the first Soviet team to win a European trophy when they beat Ferencváros of Hungary 3–0 in the Cup-winners' Cup. Later that year, they clinched the league title for the seventh time in 14 seasons. It was then that the Soviet federation grew too demanding, saddling the Ukraine club en bloc with all the national team fixtures and, when the Olympic qualifying team began to falter, with their schedule too. It all proved too much. But that did not deter Kiev coach Valeri Lobanovsky from going back to square one and painstakingly developing another formidable team around record goal-scorer Oleg Blokhin.

In 1985, the renewed Kiev stormed to another league and cup double. A year later, Kiev charmed their way to the European Cup-winners' Cup, defeating Atlético Madrid 3–0 in the final.

Kiev were the richest and most powerful club in Ukraine on the collapse of the Soviet Union, but they failed to make this advantage count in their bid to conquer Europe and were dramatically expelled from the 1995–96 Champions League after officials were accused of trying to bribe a referee.

A three-year ban was later quashed by UEFA and Kiev took their chance, restoring veteran coach Valeri Lobanovsky as team manager and bringing through several talented new youngsters, headed by striker Andrei Shevchenko.

Liverpool

England

Founded:
1892

Stadium:
Anfield (41,000)

Colours:
All red

League:
18

FA Cup:
5

League Cup:
5

European Champions Cup:
1977, 1978, 1981, 1984

UEFA Cup:
1973, 1976

Super Cup:
1977

Liverpool: a name which says so much in pop music, in sport – specifically, in soccer. The Beatles may have split up and become part of the memorabilia of a major industrial centre, but the football club goes on, purveyor of dreams for the thousands who fill the seats and the millions on Merseyside who achieved international acclaim through their team.

For years, the proud boast of English football's hierarchy had been that such was the depth of talent, no one club could ever dominate the championship in the manner of Juventus in Italy, Real Madrid in Spain or Benfica in Portugal. Then, along came Bill Shankly. He was appointed manager of shabby, run-down, half-forgotten Liverpool in December, 1959. In two-and-a-half years he won promotion; the purchases of left-half Billy Stevenson and outside-left Peter Thompson, for a total of just £60,000, secured the Championship in 1964; and a year later they won the FA Cup. The next 20 years brought success on the greatest scale.

England's Most Successful Club

The secret was continuity. Shankly was succeeded by two of his former assistant coaches, Bob Paisley and Joe Fagan. A new player would be bought young and cheap, consigned to the reserves for a year to learn "the Liverpool way", then slotted in to replace one of the fading heroes.

Thus the generation of Emlyn Hughes, Ian St John, Roger Hunt and Ron Yeats gave way to the likes of Kevin Keegan and John Toshack, followed in turn by Alan Hansen, Kenny Dalglish and Graeme Souness, the last two of whom later took the manager's hotseat. Under Dalglish, Liverpool became only the third English club to achieve the League and Cup double this century in 1986 – a fine achievement tarnished by the disasters at Heysel in 1985 and Hillsborough four years later.

Manchester United

England

Founded:
1878

Stadium:
Old Trafford (55,000)

Colours:
Red/white

League:
11

FA Cup:
9

League Cup:
1

European Champions Cup:
1968

European Cup-winners' Cup:
1991

Super Cup:
1991

Manchester United were appropriate leaders of English re-entry into Europe in 1990, after the five-year Heysel disaster ban, because they had been the first English club to play in Europe in the mid-1950s when they reached the semi-finals of the European Cup in 1957 and 1958. On the latter occasion they lost to Milan with a makeshift side in the wake of the Munich air disaster in which eight players, including skipper Roger Byrne and the inspirational Duncan Edwards were killed.

Rebuilding Complete

United needed ten years to recover, in international terms. Thus it was in May 1968 that Busby's European quest was rewarded as United defeated Benfica 4–1 in extra time at Wembley. Bobby Charlton, a Munich survivor along with defender Bill Foulkes and Busby, scored twice to secure the club's most emotional triumph. Busby had been a Scotland international wing-half with Manchester City in the 1930s and took over United when war damage to Old Trafford meant playing home games at Maine Road.

Within three years, his side had beaten Blackpool in the 1948 FA Cup Final and created an entertaining, attacking style. In the 1960s, United had crowd-pullers such as Scotland's Denis Law and Northern Ireland's George Best. Later came England's long-serving skipper Bryan Robson, still there in 1993 when United, under Alex Ferguson, took the title for the first time in 26 years.

Robson left in 1994, when United became the fourth team this century to complete the double. They became the first club to repeat the feat in 1996, thanks to French genius Eric Cantona, wing wizard Ryan Giggs, Danish keeper Peter Schmeichel – and, above all, Ferguson's deft management.

Marseille

France

Founded:
1898

Stadium:
Vélodrome (46,000)

Colours:
All white

League:
9 (1993 title revoked)

Cup:
10

European Champions Cup:
1993

No French club had ever won the European Cup before Marseille; and nobody will ever forget what happened when they did. Millionaire entrepreneur Bernard Tapie, the club's high-profile president, had invested millions of pounds in pursuit of European glory. Unfortunately, some of the money had been used to try to fix matches along the road – if not in Europe, then in the French championship.

Barely had Marseille finished celebrating their Cup-winning 1–0 victory over Milan, in Munich, in May 1993, than it emerged midfielder Jean-Jacques Eydelie had passed cash to three players from Valenciennes to "go easy" on Marseille in a League fixture a

week earlier. Marseille were duly banned from their European defence in 1993–94, the French federation revoked their League title and they were subsequently penalised with enforced relegation. Bankruptcy, inevitably, followed but now they are once more challenging for the French title, led from the front by the enigmatic Italian striker Fabrizio Ravanelli.

Marseille's Rich Roots

Marseille's first championship had been celebrated back in 1929. Personalities in those days included Emmanuel Aznar (scorer of eight goals in a 20–2 league win over Avignon) and three English managers in Peter Farmer, Victor Gibson and Charlie Bell. After the war, Marseille collected the championship in 1948, but heavy expenditure on big-name foreigners such as Yugoslavia's Josip Skoblar, Swede Roger Magnusson and Brazil's Jairzinho and Paulo César drew only sporadic rewards. Marseille had slipped into the Second Division by the time ambitious businessman-turned-politician Tapie took over the helm in 1985.

Marseille immediately gained promotion and then, thanks to the skill of Jean-Pierre Papin and Chris Waddle, swept to four titles in succession. They also suffered a penalty shoot-out defeat by Red Star Belgrade in one of the most disappointing European Cup finals in 1991, before beating Milan to take the trophy two years later.

AC Milan

Italy

Founded:
  1899

Stadium:
  Meazza (85,443)

Colours:
  Red and black stripes/white

League:
  15

Cup:
  4

World Club Cup:
  1969, 1989, 1990

European Champions Cup:
  1963, 1969, 1989, 1990, 1994

European Cup-winners' Cup:
  1968, 1973

Super Cup:
  1989, 1990

AC Milan's domination of the European club game in the late 1980s and the early 1990s was achieved on a unique stage which would appear to represent the pattern of the future for a sport increasingly controlled by the intertwined commercial interests and demands of big business and television. In Milan's case, all these strands were in the hands of a puppet-master supreme in media magnate and then Prime Minister of Italy, Silvio Berlusconi. He had saved them from bankruptcy in 1986 by investing £20 million and turning Milan into a key player in his commercial empire. Milan had been one of the founders of the Italian championship back in 1898, but until the Second World War tended to be in the shadow of Inter.

Foreigners Help Out

After the war, Milan achieved spectacular success largely thanks to the Swedish inside-forward trio of Gunnar Gren, Gunnar Nordahl and Nils Liedholm. They also paid a then world record fee of £72,000 for Uruguay's Juan Schiaffino. They were dangerous rivals to Real Madrid in the new European Cup – losing narrowly to them in the 1956 semi-finals and only in extra time in the 1958 final. That was the year Milan's scouts first saw the teenage "Golden Boy" Gianni Rivera, whose inside-forward play and partnership with José Altafini inspired Milan to the 1963 European Cup triumph over Benfica. Rivera was Milan's figurehead as they won the European Cup again in 1969 and the Cup-winners' Cup in 1968 and 1973.

But even his charisma could not save the club from the scandals and financial disasters inflicted by a string of presidents. That was where Berlusconi came in, providing the cash and the men – Dutchmen Ruud Gullit and Marco Van Basten, Liberian George Weah and Yugoslavia's Dejan Savicevic – and turned Milan into a millionaires' club.

Millonarios

Bogotá, Colombia

Founded:
1938
Stadium:
El Campin – Estadio Distrital
Nemesio Camacho (57,000)
Colours:
Blue/white
League:
13

Millonarios remain a legendary name, if only because of the manner in which they led Colombia's fledgeling professional clubs into the El Dorado rebellion which lured star players from all over the world in the late 1940s and the early 1950s.

Many famous names in the game made their reputations there. The then club president, Alfonso Senior, later became president of the Colombian federation and a highly-respected FIFA delegate, while star player Alfredo Di Stefano used Millonarios as a springboard to European greatness with Real Madrid.

Blue Ballet

Taking massive advantage of a strike by players in both Argentina and Uruguay, Millonarios led the flight from FIFA and the chase for great players – not only Di Stefano but the acrobatic goalkeeper Julio Cozzi, attacking centre-half Nestor Rossi and attacking general Adolfo Pedernera. Nicknamed the "Blue Ballet", they dominated the pirate league and, when an amnesty was negotiated with FIFA, made lucrative "farewell" tours in Europe.

At the height of the rebel league's fame, there were more than 100 foreigners playing in Columbia, including Neil Franklin, who had left Stoke City – after winning 27 consecutive caps as England's centre-half – just before the 1950 World Cup, and who had gone to Millianarios to seek a promised fortune, which, despite the promises did not materialise. But Millianarios won the Columbian championship three years in a row from 1951, and then four times in succession from 1961, before losing ground to provincial rivals such as American Cali and Nacional Medellin.

Credit for the club's name goes to a journalist, Camacho Montayo. The club had been founded as an amateur side, Deportivo Municipal, in 1938. But as they pushed for a professional league, so Montayo wrote: "The Municipalistas have become the Millonarios." The name stuck. Millonarios remain a leading club but, despite appearing frequently in the South American Club Cup, the glory days of the 1950s and 1960s have never been repeated in this corner of the Colombian capital.

Moscow Dynamo

Russia

Founded:
   1923
Stadium:
   Dynamo (51,000)
Colours:
   White/blue
League:
   11 Soviet
Cup:
   6 Soviet

Dynamo are probably the most famous of all Russian clubs, having been the first Soviet side to venture out beyond the Iron Curtain in the 1940s and 1950s. Also, they were fortunate enough to possess, in goalkeeper Lev Yashin, one of the greatest personalities in the modern game – a show-stopper wherever he went.

East to West

Dynamo's origins go back to the beginning of soccer in Russia, introduced by the Charnock brothers at their cotton mills towards the end of the last century. The team won successive Moscow championships under the name Morozovsti and, following the Russian Revolution, were taken over first by the electrical trades union and then by the police. Thus the 1923 date marks the formal setting-up of Moscow Dynamo rather than the foundation of the original club.

Immediately after the end of the Second World War, Dynamo became a legend as a result of a four-match British tour in the winter of 1945. They drew 3–3 with Chelsea and 2–2 with Rangers, thrashed Cardiff 10–1 and beat a Arsenal, although reinforced by guest players, 4–3 in thick fog. Inside-forward Constantin Beskov later became national manager, but it was goalkeeper Alexei "Tiger" Khomich whose reputation lasted long after he had retired to become a sports press photographer.

He was succeeded in the team by an even greater goalkeeper in Yashin, who was to become the first Soviet player to be nominated as European Footballer of the Year. Given Dynamo's leadership, it was appropriate that, in 1972, they became the first Soviet side to reach a European final. But their 3–2 defeat by Rangers in Barcelona, when they almost managed to pull back a three-goal deficit, also stands as the high point of their modern achievement. Back home, Dynamo were pushed back down the ranks by regular title winners and neighbours Moscow Spartak, and even their status as second club in the city has in recent seasons come under threat from Lokomotiv, Torpedo and CSKA.

Moscow Spartak

Russia

Founded:
1922
Stadium:
Olympic-Lenin/Luzhniki
(102,000)
Colours:
Red and white/white
League:
6 Russia; 12 Soviet
Cup:
10 Soviet

Spartak, champions of Russia for all three seasons after the collapse of the Soviet Union, face an enormous challenge in the years ahead. They were a power in the land under the old system, but those were the days when players were not allowed to move abroad. Now Spartak must maintain their domestic command and compete effectively in Europe in an "open" transfer society.

That will be all the more challenging because Spartak had, for years, represented the official Communist Party line. They play their home matches in what was previously known as the Lenin stadium in the Luzhniki suburb, and their former heroes included such officially-approved characters as the 1950s top scorer Nikita Simonian (a club record-holder with 133 goals) and left-half Igor Netto (another club record-holder with 367 appearances). Spartak's best season in European competitions was 1990–91, when they beat the Italians of Napoli and Spanish giants Real Madrid to reach the semi-finals of the European Cup, before falling 5–1 on aggregate to Marseille.

In With The New

For years, the club had been ruled by the most respected members of the managerial old guard in veteran administrator Nikolai Starostin and former national coach Constantin Beskov. Starostin, a Spartak player in the club's formative days, stayed on after the political upheaval, but Beskov handed over the coaching mantle to his former pupil and international full-back, Oleg Romantsev.

Despite the loss of sweeper Vasili Kulkov and midfielders Igor Shalimov and Alexander Mostovoi, Romantsev kept Spartak on top of the table. The latest generation of heroes included left-back and skipper Viktor Onopko, versatile Igor Lediakhov and the young forward Mikhail Beschastnikh. Not only did Spartak mop up the 1992, 1993, 1994, 1996, 1997 and 1998 Russian League titles, they also won – in both 1993 and 1994 – the pre-season Commonwealth of Independent States Cup, contested by the champions of all the former Soviet states.

Nacional

Montevideo, Uruguay

Founded:
  1899
Stadium:
  Parque Central (20,000) and
  Centenario (73,609)
Colours:
  White/blue
League:
  36
World Club Cup:
  1971, 1980, 1988
South American Club Cup:
  1971, 1980, 1988
South American Recopa:
  1988
Inter-American Cup:
  1971

Nacional and Peñarol are the two great clubs of Uruguay and bitter rivals on the domestic and international stages. Nacional were formed from a merger of the Montevideo Football Club and the Uruguay Athletic Club, and in 1903 were chosen to line up as Uruguay's national team against Argentina in Buenos Aires. Nacional won 3–2 and have enjoyed the limelight ever since.

Peñarol won the first South American Club Cup in 1960, but Nacional soon set about catching up: runners-up three times in the 1960s, they first won the cup by defeating Estudiantes de La Plata in 1971. That led Nacional to the World Club Cup, where they beat Panathinaikos of Greece (European title-holders Ajax having refused to compete). The two decisive goals in Montevideo were scored by Nacional's former Argentine World Cup spearhead, Luis Artime. It was nine years before Nacional regained those crowns. They had a new centre-forward in Waldemar Victorino, who scored the only goal in the 1980 South American Club Cup triumph over Internacional of Brazil, and the lone strike which decided the world final against Nottingham Forest in Tokyo. By the time Nacional regained the crown in 1988, Victorino had left for Italy, just as so many Uruguayan stars before and since.

The Old Days

Back in the 1930s, Nacional sold centre-half Michele Andreolo to Italy, with which he won the 1938 World Cup. But Nacional quickly replaced him and, from 1939 to 1943, achieved what is nostalgically recalled as their Quinquenio de Oro: their golden five years. Nacional won the League in each of those seasons with a forward line built around the prolific Argentine marksman Atilio Garcia, who ended his career with 464 goals in 435 games. Under Scottish manager William Reasdale, Nacional also celebrated an 8–0 thrashing of the old enemy, Peñarol.

Peñarol

Montevideo, Uruguay

Founded:
1891

Stadium:
Las Acacias (15,000) and Centenario (73,609)

Colours:
Black and yellow stripes/black

League:
44

World Club Cup:
1961, 1966, 1982

South American Club Cup:
1960, 1961, 1966, 1982, 1987

Inter-American Cup:
1969

Peñarol were the first club to win the World Club Cup three times, but their success is no modern phenomenon. Peñarol have been the pre-eminent power in Uruguayan football since its earliest days, providing a host of outstanding players for Uruguay's 1930 and 1950 World Cup-winning teams.

Their own international awakening came in 1960, when Peñarol won the inaugural South American Club Cup (the Copa Libertadores). They were thrashed by the all-conquering Real Madrid in the World Club Cup, but made amends the following year

with a victory over Benfica, the first team to break Real Madrid's domination of European club football. It was no less than the talents of players such as William Martinez, centre-half Nestor Goncalves and striker Alberto Spencer deserved.

World Club Champions

Peñarol regained the world club crown in 1966, at the expense of Real Madrid, and again in 1982 when they beat Aston Villa in Tokyo. By now, Peñarol had unearthed another superstar in centre-forward Fernando Morena. He was the latest in a long line of great players, which included the nucleus of the Uruguayan national team who shocked Brazil by winning the 1950 World Cup.

Goalkeeper Roque Maspoli – later World Club Cup-winning coach in 1966 – captain and centre-half Obdulio Varela, right-winger Alcide Ghiggia, centre-forward Oscar Miguez, right-half Rodriguez Andrade and inside-right Juan Schiaffino all came from Peñarol, with Schiaffino going on to become one of the game's all-time greats.

Peñarol had been founded as the Central Uruguayan Railway Cricket Club in 1891, and changed their name in 1913 as the British influence waned. The railways sidings and offices were near the Italian Pignarolo district – named after the landowner Pedro Pignarolo – and so the Spanish style of the name was adopted for the club.

PSV

Eindhoven, Holland

Founded:
  1913
Stadium:
  Philips (30,000)
Colours:
  Red and white stripes/white
League:
  14
Cup:
  7
European Champions Cup:
  1988
UEFA Cup:
  1978

PSV equalled the achievements of Celtic (in 1967) and Ajax Amsterdam (in 1972) when they defeated Benfica in a penalty shoot-out to win the 1988 European Cup. Only those other two clubs had previously secured the treble of European Cup and domestic league and cup all in the same season. Remarkably, PSV achieved all they did despite having sold their finest player, Ruud Gullit, to Milan at the start of the season for a world record £5.7 million. The money was, however, invested wisely to secure some top players from Holland, Denmark and Belgium.

Such success was the reward for a long wait since PSV had been one of the invited entrants in the inaugural European Cup in 1955–56, when they crashed 1–0, 1–6 to Rapid Vienna in the first round. Surprisingly, considering PSV's position as the sports club of the giant Philips electronics corporation, they were long outshone by Ajax and Feyenoord. For years the Philips company took comparatively little interest in PSV, even though an estimated 40,000 of the 200,000 urban population of Eindhoven work directly or indirectly for the company. Only in the past decade have Philips become seriously involved with club policy and finance.

Advertising Deals

PSV had won the 1976 UEFA Cup without much fanfare. But 10 years later, realizing the potential to be reaped from soccer sponsorship, the company came up with the funds, and were duly rewarded two years later with the European Cup. In 1992, taking the process a stage further, the club changed its name in order to promote itself outside Holland as Philips SV (while domestic sponsorship regulations required it to stick with the PSV abbreviation in Holland).

Eindhoven finally broke Ajax's stranglehold on the Dutch league in 1997, falling just short of scoring 100 goals in their 34 games, but proved a huge disappointment in the following season's Champions League, going out at the group stage.

Rangers

Glasgow, Scotland

Founded:
1873

Stadium:
Ibrox Park (50,471)

Colours:
Blue/white

League:
47

Cup:
27

League cup:
19

European Cup-winners' Cup:
1972

Rangers are one half of the "Old Firm" – their rivalry with Celtic having dominated Scottish football for a century. Yet Rangers have never extended that power into Europe, their only prize from virtual non-stop international competition being the 1972 Cup-winners' Cup Final win over Moscow Dynamo. Not that Rangers' history is short on proud moments. One particularly glorious era was the 1920s, when Rangers' heroes included the legendary "Wee Blue Devil", Alan Morton.

Poor in Europe

In the 1960s, Rangers sustained some heavy European defeats at the hands of Eintracht Frankfurt, Tottenham and Real Madrid.

The start of the 1970s was a time of mixed emotions: 1971 brought the Ibrox disaster, when 66 fans died in a stairway crush at the end of a game against Celtic, which led to the introduction of the Safety of Sports Grounds Act in 1975. Then, a year later Rangers' European Cup-winners' Cup triumph was immediately followed by a European ban because of the way their celebrating fans ran amok in Barcelona.

The upturn began in November 1985 when Lawrence Marlboro bought control of the club. He brought in the former tough-tackling Liverpool midfielder Graeme Souness as player-manager. In 1988, David Murray bought Rangers, and Souness revolutionized their image by buying 18 English players and smashing the club's traditional Protestants-only ethic with his £1.5 million capture of Catholic and one-time Celtic favourite Mo Johnston, a move which proved deeply unpopular with certain sections of supporters.

Subsequent big-name signings such as Dane Brian Laudrup and Paul Gascoigne enabled Rangers to maintain their league title dominance for a remarkable nine seasons in a row between 1989-97 – equalling Celtic's record. Striker Ally McCoist capitalized by smashing the club record of 23 goals set 60 years earlier by the legendary Bob McPhail.

Rapid

Vienna, Austria

Founded:
1873

Stadium:
Hanappi (19,600)

Colours:
Green and white/green

League:
29

Cup:
13

Rapid were founded as the 1st Arbeiter-Fussballklub (First Workers Football Club) but, on changing their name, also set about refining the short-passing style of the "Vienna School" to such good effect that they won the championship eight times between 1912 and 1923. The success story did not end there. In 1930, Rapid became the first Austrian club to win the Mitropa Cup, defeating powerful Sparta Prague 2–0, 2–3 in the final. Several of Rapid's key players were members of the "Wunderteam", the national side who finished fourth in the 1934 World Cup under the captaincy of Rapid centre-half Pepe Smistik.

Politics and Football

Four years later, Austria was swallowed up into Greater Germany, and the Austrian league was incorporated into the Greater German championship. To the mischievous delight of their fans, and no doubt much of the rest of Europe, Rapid not only won the German Cup in 1938 (3–2 against FSV Frankfurt in the final) but also the German championship in 1941.

On a day which has entered football folk-lore, Rapid hit back from three goals down to defeat an outstanding Schalke side 4–3 before a 90,000 crowd in the Olympic stadium in Berlin. Their hero was centre-forward Franz "Bimbo" Binder, whose hat-trick was crowned by the winning goal when he hammered a free-kick through the defensive wall. Binder ended a great career with an astounding 1,006 goals and later became club coach.

Many of Rapid's old heroes returned as coaches, among them Karl Rappan (who developed the Swiss Bolt system), Edi Fruh-wirth and Karl Decker. Great players in the post-war years included wing-half Gerhard Hanappi – an architect by profession, who laid out the designs for the club's stadium, known locally as the Wiener – the tough defender Ernst Happel and another prolific goal-scoring centre-forward in Hans Krankl. He led Rapid's attack in 1985 in the first of their two defeats in the European Cup-Winners Cup Final, but had retired long before they fell to Paris Saint-Germain in the 1996 final.

Real Madrid

Spain

Founded:
1902

Stadium:
Santiago Bernabéu (105,000)

Colours:
All white

League:
28

Cup:
17

World Club Cup:
1966

European Champions Cup:
1956, 1957, 1958, 1959, 1960, 1966, 1998

UEFA Cup:
1985, 1986

What else is there left to say about Real Madrid? Seven times champions of Europe, 28 times champions of Spain – both record achievements. They have also won the World Club Cup, two UEFA Cups and 16 Spanish cups, which add up to a football honours degree for the club founded by students as Madrid FC. (The Real prefix, or Royal, was bestowed on the club by King Alfonso XIII.)

Madrid were not only among the founders of the domestic competitions: was also their president, Carlos Padros, wh attended on Spain's behalf the inaugura meeting of FIFA in Paris in 1904. In the lat 1920s, Real paid a then Spanish record fee £2,000 for Ricardo Zamora, still revered a the greatest-ever Spanish goalkeeper.

Rich History

The Civil War left Madrid's Chamartín sta dium in ruins. At the time, the club had n money, but boasted one of the greate visionaries in European football. He wa Santiago Bernabéu, a lawyer who had bee in turn, player, team manager and secretar and now club president. Bernabéu launche an audacious public appeal which raised th cash to build the wonderful stadium whi now bears his name. The huge crowds wh attended provided the cash to build the tea who dominated the first five years of th European Cup. Argentine-born strik Alfredo Di Stefano was the star of star though Bernabéu surrounded him with c leagues such as Hungary's Ferenc Puska France's Ramond Kopa and Brazil's Di Madrid won the European Cup again in 19 and the UEFA Cup twice in the 1980s, b later stars such as Pirri, Santillana, Juanit Hugo Sanchez, Emilio Butragueno and t latest hero, Raúl, would complain nothi they achieved – not even another Euro su cess in 1998 – would ever be enough. T 1960 team had been, if anything, too good

Red Star Belgrade

Yugoslavia

Founded:
  1945
Stadium:
  Crvena Zvezda (Red Star) (97,422)
Colours:
  Red and white stripes/white
League:
  20
Cup:
  15
World Club Cup:
  1991
European Champions Cup:
  1991

This may be the most schizophrenic club in the world. In Germany they are known as Roter Stern; in France as Etoile Rouge; in Spain as Estrella Roja; in Italy as Stella Rossa; in Serbo-Croat it's Fudbalski Klub Crvena Zvezda; in English, of course, Red Star Belgrade. Under whichever name, the 1991 European and world club champions stood revered as one of the pillars of the worldwide establishment until civil strife in the former Yugoslavia led to international suspension for both country and clubs. The consequences for Red Star were almost disastrous, because millions of pounds paid in transfer fees for their star players were suddenly frozen in banks around Europe.

Mass Exodus

Red Star were the last team to play Manchester United's "Busby Babes" before the Munich air crash and fought back from 3–0 down to draw 3–3, but lost on aggregate despite balletic goalkeeper Vladimir Beara, gypsy midfielder Dragoslav Sekularac and dynamic striker Bora Kostic (scorer of a club record 157 goals in 256 league games). All three later moved abroad, members of an ongoing exodus of more than 40 players including Dragan Dzajic (to Bastia), Dragan Stojkovic (to Marseille), Robert Prosinecki (to Real Madrid) and Darko Pancev (to Inter). This explains, perhaps, why Red Star, for all their talent, have only one win in the European Cup (the 1991 penalty shoot-out victory over Marseille in Bari), another win on penalties over Colo Colo in the World Club Cup later that year, and one runners-up spot in the UEFA Cup (beaten on away goals by Borussia Mönchengladbach in 1979).

Red Star were formally set up by students of Belgrade University after the war. They play their home matches in the so-called "Marakana", the first stadium in eastern Europe to host a mainstream European final, when Ajax beat Juventus to claim the 1973 European Cup.

River Plate

Buenos Aires, Argentina

Founded:
  1901
Stadium:
  Antonio Liberti/Monumental
  (76,000)
Colours:
  White with red sash/black
League:
  26
World Club Cup:
  1986
South American Club Cup:
  1986, 1996
Inter-American Cup:
  1986

River Plate are one of the two giants of Argentine football, Boca Juniors being the other. Traditionally the club from the rich side of Buenos Aires, River were founder members of the First Division in 1908, then took a leading role in the "war" which accompanied the introduction of professional football in the 1920s. Over the years River have fielded some wonderful teams. In the 1930s, they boasted Bernabe Ferreyra; in the late 1940s, their high-scoring forward line was so feared and admired they were nicknamed "La Maquina" (The Machine). The names of Munoz, Moreno, Peder-nera, Labruna and Loustau mean little outside Argentina today, but there they inspire awe as do the great Real Madrid side in Europe.

The greatest players

Later, River produced more great players: Alfredo Di Stefano, who would one day turn Real Madrid into possibly the greatest team of all time; Omar Sivori, who would form a wonderful partnership with John Charles after joining Juventus; and then 1978 World Cup winners Ubaldo Fillol, Daniel Passarella, Leopoldo Luque and Mario Kempes. In 1986, they were joined in River's Hall of Fame by the likes of goalkeeper Nery Pumpido, centre-back Oscar Ruggeri and schemer Norberto Alonso, after victory in the South American Club Cup provided River with formal confirmation of their lofty status. River really should have succeeded to the crown years earlier, but were unlucky runners-up in 1966 to Peñarol of Uruguay and in 1976 to Cruzeiro of Brazil. In 1986, they made no mistake, beating America of Colombia, then adding the World Club Cup by defeating Steaua of Romania 1–0 in Tokyo. One of their stars, midfielder Americo Gallego, later joined a triumvirate of coaches who all guided River to league championships – the others being Daniel Passarella and Ramon Angel Diaz.

Santos

ão Paulo, Brazil

ounded:
 1912

tadium:
 Vila Belmiro (20,000)

olours:
 All white

ão Paulo state league:
 15

**razil championship (incl. Torneo
io-São Paulo):**
 5

Vorld Club Cup:
 1962, 1963

outh American Club Cup:
 1962, 1963

he name of Santos will always be synony-
ous with that of Pele, who played all his
ainstream career there and returned as a
rector at the end of 1993 to try to help lift
s old club out of the depths of a severe
nancial and administrative crisis.

Santos had been founded by three mem-
rs of the Americano club, who stayed home
 the port of Santos when their club moved
 São Paulo. Santos joined the São Paulo
ate championship in 1916, became only the
cond Brazilian club to embrace profession-
ism in 1933, but did not hit the headlines

until the mid-1950s. Then, to organize a host
of talented youngsters, they signed the 1950
World Cup veteran, Jair da Rosa Pinto, and
discovered the 15-year-old Pele.

Pele's Home

To say that Santos were a one-man team, as it
often appeared from the publicity, would be
unfair. Santos harvested millions of pounds
from whistle-stop friendly match tours
around the world and reinvested heavily in
surrounding Pele with fine players: World
Cup winners in goalkeeper Gilmar, centre-
back Mauro and wing-half Zito; an outside-
left with a ferocious shot in Pepe; and the pre-
cocious young talents of right-winger Dorval,
schemer Mengalvio and centre-forward
Coutinho, Pele's so-called "twin" with whom
he established an almost telepathic relation-
ship on the pitch. Santos were more than a
football team; they were a touring circus.

The constant tours burned out many
youngsters before they had a chance to
establish themselves. But not before Santos
scaled the competitive heights as Pele led
them to the South American Club Cup and
the World Club Cup in both 1962 and 1963.

Independiente beat Santos in the 1964
South American Club Cup semi-finals, and
it was all over. Santos went on touring and
raking in cash, capitalizing on Pele's name
for as long as possible, but Pele's return did
not manage to inspire the sort of success
achieved in the 1960s.

São Paulo

Brazil

Founded:
1935
Stadium:
Morumbi (150,000)
Colours:
White with a red and black hoop/white
São Paulo state league:
17
Brazil championship (incl. Torneo Rio-São Paulo):
4
World Club Cup:
1992, 1993
South American Club Cup:
1992, 1993

São Paulo's victories over Barcelona and Milan in the 1992 and 1993 World Club Cups in Tokyo left no doubt about which was the finest club side in the world – for all the European hype which had surrounded the Italian champions. Those victories also underlined the depth of talent at São Paulo, bacause key midfielder Rai (younger brother of 1986 World Cup star Socrates), had gone to Paris Saint-Germain in 1993. They also enhanced the reputation of coach Tele Santana, Brazil's World Cup manager in 1982 and 1986, and one of the most eloquent and down-to-earth of football coaches.

São Paulo are, even so, comparative new-comers – founded in 1935, at a time when the likes of River Plate and Peñarol were already well-established powers in their own lands. The club was formed from a merger between CA Paulistano and AA Palmeiras. A leading light was Paulo Machado de Carvalho, who would later, as a senior administrator, contribute behind the scenes to Brazil's World Cup successes.

Strong start

Within a decade of being founded, São Paulo developed into the strongest team in the country, winning the state title five times in the 1940s. They imported Argentine inside-forward Antonio Sastre, and the continuing pressure of success led to the construction of the 150,000-capacity Morumbi stadium, the world's largest club-owned sports arena.

In the 1960s, São Paulo had to take a back seat to Santos. In 1974, they reached their first South American Club Cup Final (losing to Argentina's Independiente), but it was not until the arrival of Santana, in the late 1980s, that São Paulo emerged from the doldrums. Despite the continuing sale of star players – key defender Ricardo Rocha went to Real Madrid – São Paulo secured three state league titles in four years, used the cash to strengthen their squad and were rewarded with those recent World Club titles, becoming the first team to win in successive years.

Sparta Prague

Czech Republic

Founded:
1893

Stadium:
Letna (36,000)

Colours:
All red

League:
22

Cup:
9

Sparta are the most popular club in what is now the Czech Republic, as well as one of the oldest. They were founded as King's Vineyard in 1893, and took the name of Sparta, from one of the states of Ancient Greece, a year later.

They were one of Europe's great sides preceding the Second World War, winning the Mitropa Cup in the inaugural final in 1927 against Rapid Vienna. Victory over Ferençvaros of Hungary followed in 1935, and they were runners-up in 1936. Sparta's team then included the great inside-left, Oldrich Nejedly. He played a starring role in the 1934 World Cup, when Czechoslovakia finished runners-up. Again in 1962, when the Czechs next reached the World Cup Final, there were key places in the team for Sparta men such as right-winger Tomas Pospichal and schemer Andrzej Kvasnak.

All In The Name

Sparta suffered after the last war, and were forced to alter their name to Sparta Bratrstvi and then Spartak Sokolovo. But their loyal fans never called them anything but Sparta, and reality was recognized when the club's present title was adopted in 1965.

That same year they celebrated their first league title in more than a decade. Memories of the glory days of the Mitropa Cup were revived by the club's run to the European Cup-winners' Cup semi-finals in 1973 and by the impressive 1983–84 UEFA Cup campaign, during which they scored notable victories over Real Madrid and Poland's Widzew Lodz.

Sparta's continuing domination of the domestic game in the early 1990s was remarkable because, immediately after the World Cup finals, they lost a string of senior internationals, such as goalkeeper Jan Stejskal, defenders Julius Bielik and Michal Bilek, midfield general Ivan Hasek and striker Tomas Skuhravy, the second-top scorer at Italia '90 with five goals. But they were unable to come to grips with Europe's best, eliminated from their group, which contained holders Borussia Dortmund, in the 1997–98 Champions League.

Sporting Clube

Lisbon, Portugal

Founded:
1906
Stadium:
José Alvalade (70,000)
Colours:
Green and white hoops/white
League:
16
Cup:
16
European Cup-winners' Cup:
1964

Sporting Clube do Portugal last reached a European final back in 1964, when they won the Cup-winners' Cup. Now Benfica's deadly rivals – the grounds are barely a mile apart – dream of the day when they can bring those old heroes out of retirement obscurity to celebrate a European revival. The late 1980s and early 1990s brought Sporting the worst era in their history, an empty decade following the heady 1981–82 season in which they won the league and cup double under Englishman Malcolm Allison.

In 1992 the new president, José Sousa Cintra, brought in the former England man-

ager Bobby Robson – who had been successful at both club and international level – to try to recapture the Allison magic. Robson was given only 18 months, however, before former Portugal national coach Carlos Queiros, instead, was given the task of reviving the glories of the 1950s, when Sporting rivalled Benfica as the country's top club and took the championship seven times in eight years.

Single Trophy

En route to Sporting's sole European trophy, they beat APOEL Nicosia of Cyprus in the second round first leg by a European record 16–1. In the final against MTK Budapest in Brussels, Sporting went 1–0 down, recovered to lead 2–1, and went 3–2 behind before securing a 3–3 draw and a replay. That took place in Antwerp where a single goal after 20 minutes from Morais, direct from a corner, was enough to win the cup. Their back four of Morais, Batista, José Carlos and Hilario starred in the Portugal team which finished third in the 1966 World Cup finals in England.

The nearest Sporting have since gone to European success was in 1990–91, when they reached the UEFA Cup semi-finals before falling 0–0, 0–2 to eventual winners Inter. In the Portuguese league, they have recently failed to make any impact on Porto, who have marched off with the title every season since the 1993–94 triumph under Bobby Robson.

Steaua

Bucharest, Romania

Founded:
1947

Stadium:
Steaua (30,000)

Colours:
Red/blue

League:
18

Cup:
17

European Cup:
1986

Steaua – the word means "Star" – were one of the army clubs created in eastern Europe after the Communist takeovers of political power. Originally Steaua were known as CCA Bucharest, under which title they won the Romanian League championship three times in a row in the early 1950s. Later, renamed Steaua, they won the Romanian Cup five times in six seasons in the late 1960s and early 1970s.

In 1986 Steaua became the first eastern European team to win the European Cup when they beat Barcelona on penalties in Seville. Their penalty-stopping hero in the climactic minutes was Helmut Ducadam, whose career was ended prematurely by ill-

ness soon after. Steaua's power – including the right to sign any player they liked from any other Romanian club – was significantly reduced after the overthrow of the Communist dicatorship of the Ceausescu family.

Yet although the club now had to rely on time-honoured methods of recruitment, such as finding their own players instead of buying from rivals, Steaua continued to do well and won the Romanian championship five times in a row, 1994–98, without being able to achieve similar success in Europe. On their only other appearance in a Euro final, in 1989, a team comparing less facourably with that of three years earlier, lost 4–0 to a rampant AC Milan.

The 1986 squad was the "B" team – containing players such as Balint, Balan, Barbulescu and Belodedici, who set a record in 1991 by becoming the first player to win the European Champions Cup with two clubs when he helped Red Star Belgrade to beat Marseilles – on penalties.

Steaua still continue to supply a string of players to the national squad, notably Anghel Iordanescu, who later coached Romania in two World Cups, and Dan Petrescu, who played under Glenn Hoddle at Chelsea and later under the managership of former international stars Ruud Gullit and Gianluca Vialli and scored a last-gasp winner against Hoddle's England side in the 1998 World Cup tournament to secure victory for the Romanians.

Tottenham Hotspur

London, England

Founded:
1882

Stadium:
White Hart Lane (33,083)

Colours:
white/blue

League:
2

Cup:
8

European Cup-winners' Cup:
1963

UEFA Cup:
1972, 1984

Tottenham Hotspur are commonly considered one of the Big Five of English football but their achievements on the pitch in recent times hardly justify such status. Spurs do hold a place in British football history, however, having been the first English club in the 20th century to achieve the League and Cup double and following up by becoming the first British club to win a European trophy. That was the European Cup-winners' Cup, which Spurs won in 1963, thrashing holders Atlético Madrid 5–1 in Rotterdam.

The Professionals

Spurs were founded by a group of ex-grammar school boys who called the club Hotspur. The "Tottenham" label was added some years later to avoid confusion with a Hotspur club in nearby Wood Green. Spurs adopted professionalism in 1895, moved to their present home in 1899, won the Southern League championship in 1900 and, a year later, became the only non-league team ever to have won the FA Cup since the inception of the Football League.

Remarkably, Tottenham were not voted into the League until 1908, as replacements in the old Second Division for Stoke City.

The post-war years saw Spurs in the Second Division but, under the management of Arthur Rowe, they staged a memorable revival. The so-called "push and run" team won promotion in 1950 and the club's first league title a year later. Rowe's traditions of simple, effective football were taken to new heights when one of his players, Bill Nicholson, managed the so-called "Glory, Glory" team of the early 1960s.

This was Tottenham's greatest era, inspired by the leadership example of wing-halves Danny Blanchflower and Dave Mackay. The team was enhanced by the signing in 1962 of goal-poacher supreme Jimmy Greaves – a deal which set a big-spending reputation maintained with later captures such as Martin Peters, Martin Chivers, Argentina's Osvaldo Ardiles and Ricardo Villa and German captain Jürgen Klinsmann.

Vasco Da Gama

Rio de Janeiro, Brazil

Founded:

1898 as sailing club, 1915 as
football club

Stadium:

São Januario (50,000) and
Maracana (130,000)

Colours:

All white with black sash

Rio state league:

17

**Brazil championship (incl. Torneo
Rio-São Paulo):**

5

Like Flamengo, one of their long-time Rio
de Janeiro rivals, Vasco grew from a sailing
club – the impetus for football coming from
former members of a club called Luzitania
FC, who had been refused entry to the early
Rio de Janeiro state championship because
of their "Portuguese-only" policy. Transformed into Vasco da Gama, however, they
were elected to the championship in 1915
and had progressed to the top flight by 1923.
Support, both vocal and financial, has come
to the club over the years from the city's Portuguese community. In spite of their original
policies, Vasco quickly became noted for
their inclusion of mixed-race players at a
time, early in Brazilian football's development, when the game was riven by race and
class divisions. Vasco led the way, too, by
creating the São Januario stadium, which
was the first national stadium in Brazil and
hosted all major club and national team
matches before the building of the Maracana
in 1950.

Brazilian Skill Supply

In 1958 Vasco supplied Brazil's World Cup-
winning team with centre-back Luiz Bellini,
the captain, and centre-forward Vava. They
earned a long-awaited consolation for events
eight years earlier when no fewer than eight
Vasco players had figured in the Brazilian
squad which was pipped to the World Cup by
Uruguay. In the 1960s and 1970s Vasco figured, as ever, among the most powerful of
challengers to Fluminense and Flamengo.

Their 1997 national championship victory was remarkable in that both legs of the
play-off final against Palmeiras ended in
0–0 draws. Vasco took the title thanks to a
better record in tournament countback – and
despite having seen star marksman
Edmundo sent off no fewer than seven times
during the year. Edmundo was the latest in a
line of top forwards, including such World
Cup stars as Leonidas (1938), Ademir (1950)
and Romario, the star of the 1994 tournament who missed France 98 through injury.

The Great Coaches

Managers and coaches are either hero or scapegoat: one thing or the other. There is no in-between. He is responsible for choosing the team to represent a club, a city or a country. As Brazil's World Cup boss Mario Zagallo once said: "In my country we have millions of national managers and every one thinks he can do the job better than me. Maybe he or she can. But I am the one whose opinion matters – for the moment."

In the early days of association football, teams were chosen by committee. Later came the secretary-manager who was the club's administrator – a role which also included picking the team. That was the system which served British football largely through to the 1930s. But it did not last as long abroad. The reason was simple. The English took association football around the world, but the "new" countries needed to be taught the game and so the coach – the teacher, men such as the legendary Jimmy Hogan in Austria in the early decades of the 20th century – gained a greater power. He taught the game – the technique and the tactics – and therefore he assumed the right to pick the team.

In England the manager remained encumbered by working the transfer market, negotiating employees' terms and a myriad of other responsibilities now largely devolved upon the shoulders of a chief executive or managing director. But in the rest of the world the division of responsibility was made much earlier. Each system produced great individuals: coaches who could teach their players new skills and systems… and then motivate them to national and then international pre-eminence.

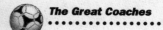

Sir Matt Busby

Manchester United manager 1945–71

Born: May 26, 1909

Died: January 20, 1994

Busby was a Scotland wing-half who played pre-war for Liverpool for four years and Manchester City for six years. He also earned one cap for Scotland in 1933. He took over United in 1945 when air raid damage had reduced Old Trafford to near-rubble. Such was his gift for management that, within three years, he had created the first of three memorable teams. His 1948 side won the FA Cup, his Busby Babes of the mid-1950s went twice to the Champions Cup semi-finals before being wrecked by the Munich air disaster, and his third team completed the European quest with victory over Benfica in 1968. Busby's love of entertaining football inspired some of British football's greatest talents – from Johnny Carey to Duncan Edwards, from Bobby Charlton to Denis Law and George Best. He was appointed to the Manchester United board in 1971 and became club President in 1982. He will be remembered as one of the most successful managers that the English game has ever known.

Hitting the target

- Busby was a hero on both sides of Manchester – first as a player for City then as manager of United.

- Eight of the so-called "Busby Babes" were killed at Munich, and Busby himself was seriously injured in the air crash in February 1958.

- After retiring as manager, Busby remained at Old Trafford as a director of United until his death.

Josef 'Sepp' Herberger

Germany manager 1936–63

Born: March 28, 1897

Died: April 28, 1977

Herberger was the founder of a German management dynasty. As a player, he was an inside-forward who played three times for Germany between 1921 and 1925, and he became assistant national manager to Dr Otto Nerz in 1932 and then succeeded him after what was seen as a disastrous defeat by Norway at the 1936 pre-war Berlin Olympics. Herberger travelled widely to keep abreast of the world game and astutely managed his players and tactics to maximum effect, above all at the 1954 World Cup.

There he took the bold step of fielding several reserves for a first-round match against Hungary. He was unfazed by the 8–3 defeat, knowing that his fresh "first team" could still reach the later stages and go on, as they did, to beat the Hungarians in the final. The Hungarian team had previously beaten England 6–3 at Wembley and 7–1 in Budapest and were probably the hottest ever favourites to win the World Cup.

Hitting the target ....

- Herberger was the second of only six German national team managers in 70 years.
- He played his football in the 1920s for two clubs, Waldhof and Mannheim, who later merged to form the present Bundesliga club, Waldhof-Mannheim.
- Playing his part in Germany's football dynasty, Herberger handed over on his retirement to assistant Helmut Schön.

Helenio Herrera

Coach of Red Star Paris, Stade Francais (France), Atlético Madrid, Valladolid, Sevilla (Spain), Belenenses (Portugal), Barcelona (Spain), Internazionale and Roma (Italy); also Spanish and Italian national teams

Born: April 17, 1916

Died: November 9, 1997

Herrera was one of the world's most innovative and single-minded coaches. Born in Argentina, brought up in Morocco, Herrera was a player in France, and experimented at Barcelona in the 1950s by using inside-forwards at wing-half to turn "easy" matches into goal sprees. His attacking tactics proved ineffective at Inter so Herrera developed, instead, the most ruthlessly disciplined *catenaccio*. Herrera demanded total obedience, insisting that his players place their hands on the ball and swear loyalty to each other before going out for a match. Stars who baulked at such rituals were sold, however popular or successful. This ruthless method of dealing with players obviously worked, because under Herrera, Inter won the World Club and Champions Cups twice each. Herrera's career went into decline after he moved to Roma.

Hitting the target ....

- Herrera started his playing career as centre-forward as a teenager in Morocco – but made the grade as a full-back in France.

- So demanding was Herrera as a coach that he was nicknamed "Slave Driver" by many of his players.

- Great players who fell out with Herrera included Hungary's Ladislav Kubala and the Italo-Argentinian Antonio Valentin Angelillo.

Hugo Meisl

Austria manager and general secretary 1906–37

Born: November 16, 1881

Died: February 17, 1937

Meisl was the errant son of a Viennese banking family who was too infatuated with football in Central Europe in the early years of the century to want to enter the business. Meisl was playing inside-forward for FK Austria when he met the English coach, Jimmy Hogan, whom he persuaded to go and work in Vienna. Later Meisl became involved with neighbours Admira and then became secretary of the Austrian federation. Simultaneously he was also national manager, and his partnership with Hogan led to the rise of the legendary Austrian "Wunderteam" of the 1920s and early 1930s. Among other feats, his team beat Scotland 5–0, Germany 6–0 and lost only 4–3 to England at Stamford Bridge. Meisl, Vittorio Pozzo from Italy and Herbert Chapman from England were the three most dominant figures in pre-war football. Meisl is known as the 'Father of Austrian Football' and influential in the early days of FIFA, the game's administrative body.

Hitting the target

- Meisl's first involvement in football was arranging summer tours in Austria in the early 1900s by clubs such as Manchester United, Everton and Tottenham.
- FIFA Congress took place in Vienna in 1908 at Meisl's invitation to mark the 60th anniversary of Emperor Franz Josef.
- Meisl tried to sell Austria's star goalkeeper, Rudi Hiden, to Arsenal in 1930… but he could not get a work permit.

Marinus 'Rinus' Michels

Coach of Ajax Amsterdam (Holland), Barcelona (Spain), Los Angeles Aztecs (USA), Bayer Leverkusen (Germany); also Holland national team

Born: February 9, 1928

Michels, a Dutch international centre-forward in the early 1950s, led a revolution in the late 1960s when he developed the "total football" philosophy at Ajax. Much of Michels's coaching career linked with the presence, as leader on the pitch, of Johan Cruyff. Michels went to Barcelona after winning the Champions Cup with Ajax in 1971, went back to Ajax to sign Cruyff, and the pair were partners again when Holland finished runners-up at the 1974 World Cup. "Iron Rinus" was never afraid to take tactical risks, such as when he guided Holland to European Championship success in 1988 by using Ruud Gullit as a static, right-side attacker. Nor was Michels ever afraid of stating his opinions, however blunt.

Hitting the target

- In 1969, under Michels' management, Ajax became the first Dutch team to reach the Champions Cup Final.

- Michels had two spells in charge at Barcelona, but the nearest he got to winning the Champions Cup was the semi-finals in 1975.

- In the 1980s Michels was granted a special permit to coach in the Bundesliga because of his international record – even though he did not hold the German coaching certificate.

Vittorio Pozzo

Italy Manager 1932–48

Born: March 12, 1885

Died: December 21, 1968

Pozzo was a giant figure in Italian football history. He "found" football when he came to England as a student before the First World War. His admiration for Manchester United, their centre-half Charlie Roberts and football in general led to his refusing family orders to come home until he was sent a return ticket. In 1912 Pozzo managed Italy's team at the Olympic Games in Stockholm, where he met Hugo Meisl. He later became an admirer of Herbert Chapman. At club level Pozzo was long associated with Torino and he was manager, director and psychologist of the Italian team which won the World Cup in 1934 and 1938 and the Olympic Games tournament in 1936.

Hitting the target ....

- Under Pozzo, Italy lost only seven matches during the 1930s.

- Legend has it that before the 1938 World Cup Final against Hungary, the players received a telegram from fascist dictator Benito Mussolini, warning them: "Win or die!"

- Of the 1938 World Cup winners, Pozzo had retained only inside forwards Meazza and Ferrari from the triumphant 1934 team.

Sir Alf Ramsey

England manager 1963–74

Born: January 22, 1920

Ramsey earned a knighthood for managing England to World Cup victory over West Germany at Wembley in 1966, the peak of a double international career as both player and administrator. As a player, Ramsey was a creative and intelligent right-back with Southampton and Tottenham and an integral member of Spurs' push-and-run team which won the Second and First Division titles in successive seasons in 1950 and 1951. He joined the side in May 194 and became a regular choice in the same position for the English national team as well. On retiring in 1955, Ramsey became manager of Ipswich and his success in taking the East Anglian club from the Third Division to the First Division title in just seven years earned his appointment in 1963 as England's first "proper" manager with sole responsibility for team selection. He was England's most successful manager – his team famously won the World Cup in 1966 and lost only 17 matches out of the 113 in which he was in charge. He was dismissed after the World Cup qualifying failure against Poland in 1974 and returned to management briefly with Birmingham City before retiring.

Hitting the target

- Ramsey won his 32nd and last cap at right–back when Hungary became the first foreign side to beat England at Wembley, 6–3 in 1953.

- One of Ramsey's Ipswich successors, Bobby Robson, also followed him as an England manager.

- Ramsey later had a brief spell back in management – as caretaker boss of Birmingham City.

Tele Santana

Coach of Atletico Mineiro, Gremio, Flamengo, Fluminense, Palmeiras (Brazil), Al Ahly (Saudi Arabia), Sao Paulo FC (Brazil); also Brazil national team

Born: July 25, 1933

Santana was an outside-right with South American club side Fluminense in the early 1950s but never good enough to challenge Julinho or Garrincha in Brazil's World Cup teams. Instead, he reached the World Cup finals in both 1982 and 1986 as manager of Brazil. Santana's insistence on attacking football was criticised as naive after Brazil's failures in, respectively, the second round and quarter-finals. But Santana had the last laugh when he won the World Club Cup twice as boss of São Paulo in 1992 and 1993. Simultaneously, Santana was not afraid to pinpoint high levels of corruption in the Brazilian game, as well as poor refereeing, for the failure to regain World Cup supremacy in the 1980s and early 1990s.

Hitting the target

- Santana once played at West Ham – for Fluminense in a friendly in 1952.
- Attacking brothers Socrates and Rai both owed promotion to stardom to Santana – Socrates with Brazil, Rai with São Paulo.
- Santana became, in 1980, Brazil's first full-time manager; previous bosses had also held club jobs simultaneously.

 **The Great Coaches**

Helmut Schön

West Germany manager 1963–78

Born: September 15, 1915

Died: February 23, 1996

Schön scored 17 goals in 16 internationals for Germany between 1937 and 1941, when he was a star inside-forward with the famous Dresden SC. After the war he played on in Berlin for a while and then stepped up to become national coach to the briefly independent federation of the Saar. In 1955 Schön was appointed number two to Sepp Herberger as manager of West Germany and succeeded him, with enormous success, in 1963. Schön took West Germany to the World Cup runners-up spot in 1966 (losing to England at Wembley), third place in 1970 (West Germany lost to Italy after taking the game to gripping extra time) and finally to victory in 1974 (Johan Cruyff's Holland were unable to win, despite being favourites with their 'Total Football' playing style). Under Schön, Germany were also European Champions in 1972 (beating the Soviet Union 3–0 in the final) and runners-up in 1976 (losing only to Czechoslovakia in a penalty shoot-out after extra time.)

Hitting the target

- Schön lost potentially the best years of his playing career during the Second World War.
- Away from football Schön was never happier than living a quiet family life – and walking his beloved dogs.
- Just as Schön took over from Herberger, so he handed over in due course to his own assistant, Jupp Derwall.

Gustav Sebes

Hungary manager 1949–56

Born: June 21, 1906

Died: January 30, 1986

Sebes was a successful player in the 1920s with Vasas and MTK Budapest, but is best-known for the creation of the "Magic Magyars" of the late 1940s and 1950s. The Communist take-over allowed the Hungarian federation to transfer Hungary's top players into the two top clubs, Honved and Red Banner (formerly MTK), and Sebes fused their talents for the national team, built around the tactic of the withdrawn centre-forward. Hungary won the 1952 Olympic title but lost the 1954 World Cup Final, against all the odds, to West Germany. Sebes resigned following the loss of many star players who fled abroad after the 1956 Revolution.

Hitting the target ....

- Sebes played as a wing-half in the 1920s in both Hungary and France.
- He won only one cap himself for Hungary – in a 3–2 win over Germany in Budapest in 1936.
- In the late 1950s Sebes became a vice-president of newly-formed European confederation, UEFA.
- Honved were considered to be the best club side in Europe, if not the world, in the late 1940s

Bill Shankly

Manager of Carlisle, Grimsby, Workington, Huddersfield and Liverpool

Born: September 2, 1913

Died: September 29, 1981

Shankly played for Carlisle and then Preston North End in the 1930s, winning the FA Cup in 1938 and playing for Scotland five times in the 1938–39 season. He returned to Carlisle in the late 1940s, to begin his managerial career. After spells at Grimsby, Workington and Huddersfield, he took over a faded Liverpool in the Second Division in December 1959, and there was no stopping either him or the club once promotion had been achieved in 1962. Shankly's dry humour struck a chord with Anfield fans. He brought them the League, FA Cup and League again in successive seasons, signed some of the club's greatest servants and laid foundations for further success both on and off the pitch. "His" Liverpool also won the FA Cup and UEFA Cup in 1974, and the year after he was awarded an OBE. Shankly had an eye for youthful talent – which he squirrelled away in the reserves until they were ready – and for managerial expertise. Later Liverpool managers Bob Paisley, Joe Fagan and Roy Evans came out of Shankly's fabled "boot room."

Hitting the target

- Shankly played in two FA Cup finals – for Preston in 1937 and 1938, collecting a winners' medal in the latter.

- The most famous protégé from Shankly's time at Huddersfield was a great fellow Scot, Denis Law.

- Shankly was famous for one-liners such as the reputed: "Some people say football is a matter of life and death. They're wrong. It's more important than that."

Giovanni Trapattoni

Coach of Milan, Juventus, Internazionale, Bayern Munich, Cagliari and Bayern Munich

Born: March 17, 1939

Trapattoni was a wing-half in the late 1950s and early 1960s whose sure tackling and football brain earned him a reputation as the only man who could play Pele out of a game by fair means rather than foul. After winning two Champions Cups with club side Milan, Trapattoni retired to a post on the youth coaching staff. In time he became first-team caretaker before moving to Juventus with whom he became the most successful club coach of all time. Inside eight years, Trapattoni guided Juve to the World Club Cup, Champions Cup, European Cup-Winners Cup, UEFA Cup, European Super Cup, seven Italian championships and two national cups. Late in his career he took a major gamble by moving to Bayern Munich in Germany and was quickly rewarded with league title success in 1997 and the German Cup a year later, before returning to Italy and joining Fiorentina.

Hitting the target ....

- Trapattoni won the European Champions Cup with Milan in 1963 and 1969.
- Trapattoni's collection of 14 major honours at Juventus is a record for an Italian manager.
- Franz Beckenbauer appointed him at Bayern Munich because "German footballers need to improve their defensive skills."

The Great Players

Football is a team game, but if that were the beginning and end of it then few people would cross the street to watch. It's the great players – the individuals with crowd-pleasing flair, style and personality – who provide the addictive allure which draws fans back, week in, week out. But all the great players down the years have been so different.

South America has produced players with a unique explosive talent – the likes of Brazil's Pele and Argentina's Diego Maradona. Europe, by contrast, has boasted players with a professional consistency of high standard such as Ferenc Puskas and Franz Beckenbauer. A majority of the greatest players have honed their skills by moving around the world – leaving their home country for the technical challenge offered abroad. Many more exported players have failed than have succeeded, whether in Italy, Spain or England. But the greatest players have imposed themselves across all borders, styles and competitions.

Down the years the game has changed. As Franz Beckenbauer once said: "In the old days a player had time to stop a ball, look around, decide what to do and then do it. Nowadays the ball arrives just a split second ahead of two opponents determined to stop you playing." But Beckenbauer, like all the superstars, believes that great ability will always triumph. Thus the great players of yesteryear would be great today, given all the advantages of the modern game's physical conditioning. Just as well for the World Cup, however, that they have been spread out down the years.

Osvaldo Ardiles

1952 Born on August 3 in Cordoba.

1969 Turned professional with Huracan of Buenos Aires.

1978 Key midfielder in Argentina's World Cup-winning side who beat Holland 3–1 in a passionate final under the management of Cesar Luis Menotti. Then transferred, sensationally, to Tottenham Hotspur (*see* page 70) for £300,000 in July of that year – along with Argentina team-mate Ricardo Villa.

1981 Ardiles achieved career ambition of winning the FA Cup, as Tottenham beat Manchester City 3–2 in a replay after the original match had ended all-square at 1–1.

1982 Ardiles returned to South America as a dispute over the Falkland Islands between Britain and Argentina escalated into full-scale war. By doing so he was denied the opportunity to win a second consecutive FA Cup winners' medal as Spurs beat QPR.

1982 Ardiles played in his second World Cup but Argentina failed to make the semi-finals. After a short and unhappy spell in France, he returned to Tottenham in December.

1983 A broken shin in only his fourth game back ruled him out for 10 months.

1984 Won the UEFA Cup with Tottenham in a thrilling penalty shoot-out victory over Belgian club Anderlecht.

1987 Made up for the disappointment of 1982 by appearing in the FA Cup final against Coventry City. For the first time in their history, Tottenham lost in an FA Cup final.

1988 Terry Venables arrived as manager at White Hart Lane, Ardiles was loaned to Blackburn in March before joining QPR on a free transfer in the summer.

1989 Became manager of Swindon Town.

1991 Took over the manager's chair at Newcastle United.

1993 Returned to Tottenham as manager under the chairmanship of Alan Sugar in succession to Terry Venables.

1994 Sacked as Tottenham manager and went to work in Mexico.

1997 Off to yet another country – coaching in Japan.

Roberto Baggio

1967 Born on February 18 in Caldogno.

1983 Made his league debut with local club Vicenza in the Italian third division aged only 15.

1985 Transferred to Fiorentina.

1988 Made his international debut for Italy.

1989 In his fifth and final season at the club, Baggio scored 17 goals in 32 league games and led Fiorentina to the semi-finals of the UEFA Cup where they lost to Juventus.

1990 Was sold by Fiorentina, despite three days of fans' protests on the streets of Florence that needed the intervention of riot police, to Juventus for a world record £8 million. Helped justify his fee with a marvellous solo goal against Czechoslovakia in the World Cup finals in 1990.

1991 In a match against Fiorentina, Baggio was substituted after he refused to take a penalty against his old club. He left the pitch wearing a Fiorentina scarf.

1993 Won the UEFA Cup with Juventus, topped a century of Italian league goals and was voted FIFA World Footballer of the Year and European Footballer of the Year.

1994 Played a starring role as Italy progressed to their first World Cup Final appearance since 1982. He scored the 88th-minute equaliser that saved Italy from humiliation against Nigeria in the Second Phase, then scored the winner from the penalty spot. In an absorbing semi-final with Bulgaria, Baggio scored another brace to take them through to the final and a clash with Brazil. The match failed to live up to expectations and, for the first time in World Cup history, the final was decided by a penalty shoot-out. Baggio missed the decisive kick and Brazil were crowned champions.

1995 Won the Italian league with Juventus – then transferred to Milan after failing to agree terms for a new contract.

1996 Won the Italian league with Milan, only the third player in Italian history to win the championship with different clubs in successive seasons.

1997 Failed to impress with Milan and transferred to Bologna.

1998 A surprise choice for the World Cup.

Gordon Banks

1937 Born on December 20 in Sheffield.

1955 Turned professional with Chesterfield.

1959 Transferred to Leicester City.

1961 FA Cup runner-up against Tottenham's double-winning side.

1963 Experienced an unhappy afternoon in his second FA Cup appearance as Manchester United beat Leicester 3–1. Banks was held responsible for two of the United goals.

1963 Made his England debut against Scotland in rather inauspicious circumstances as the Scots won 2–1 at Wembley, their first victory in London for 12 years.

1964 A winner at last with Leicester as they beat Banks' future club Stoke City 4–3 on aggregate in the League Cup Final.

1966 Member of the England team which won the World Cup beating West Germany 4–2 in a thrilling final. In the semi-final against Portugal, the great Eusebio scored from the penalty spot to bring to an end Banks' record of seven consecutive clean sheets.

1967 Sold to Stoke City for a British goalkeeping record fee of £65,000.

1970 Illness caused Banks to miss, crucially, England's 3–2 World Cup quarter-final defeat by West Germany in Leon, Mexico. His absence encouraged the Germans, who fought back from 2–0 down to win through to the semi-final. In a group match against Brazil, Banks made what many still believe to be the greatest save the world has ever seen. A Pele header was destined for the bottom corner, but as the great man wheeled away to celebrate, Banks somehow managed to turn it round the post.

1970 Awarded the MBE for services to football.

1972 Won the prestigious Footballer of the Year award and the League Cup with Stoke.

1972 Won his 73rd and last cap in the 1–0 defeat of Scotland. Despite his advanced age of 34, Banks had just signed a new six-year contract with Stoke when he was involved in a serious car accident and lost the sight of one eye. Although his international career was over he did continue to play in the short-lived North American Soccer League.

Francesco 'Franco' Baresi

1960 Born on May 8 in Taravagliato.

1974 Along with his elder brother Giuseppe, Baresi attended trials with Internazionale in Milan. Big brother was accepted, but Baresi junior was rejected as being too frail. A week later he joined AC Milan.

1977 Turned professional with Milan, to whom he stayed loyal for the rest of his career. Was then an attacking midfielder but was soon switched to sweeper with considerable success.

1978 Made his league debut still aged only 18.

1979 Installed as first-choice sweeper and played a large part in helping AC win the Italian Championship.

1980 Personal and team fortunes took a dive when Baresi suffered from a blood disorder and Milan were relegated to the Second Division following a betting scandal.

1982 Member of Italy's World Cup-winning squad in Spain, though he did not play in any of their matches in the finals. Made his national team debut in a 0–0 draw against Romania in Florence.

1988 Won the Italian league with Milan – the first of his five national championships.

1989 Won the European Champions Cup and the World Club title, the start of Milan's nine international club honours in the Sacchi–Capello era.

1990 Steered Milan to their second consecutive "double" – a Champions Cup triumph against Benfica and a 3–0 thrashing of Olimpia in the World Club Championship.

1990 Cornerstone of the Italian national side who beat England 2–1 in the Third Place Play-off at the World Cup finals in Italy.

1994 Suspension ruled him out of Milan's magnificent Champions Cup Final victory against Barcelona.

1994 World Cup runner-up as sweeper in the Italian side beaten on penalties by Brazil.

1997 Retired after 20 years with the one club.

Franz Beckenbauer

1945 Born on September 11 in Munich.

1955 Began playing for the schoolboy team, FC 1906 Munich.

1959 Joined Bayern Munich youth section.

1962 Gave up a job as a trainee insurance salesman to sign full-time with Bayern.

1964 Made his Bayern debut in a 4–0 win away to St Pauli in Hamburg.

1965 Made his national team debut in a 2–1 World Cup qualifying win in Sweden.

1966 Starred in midfield, on the losing side, for West Germany in the 4–2 World Cup Final defeat by England at Wembley.

1967 Captained Bayern Munich (*see* page 38), from sweeper, to victory over Rangers in the European Cup-Winners' Cup Final.

1970 Took part in his second World Cup tournament, and scored the goal that sparked the German revival against England in the quarter-final. They lost to Italy in the semis.

1972 Captained West Germany to European Championship victory over the Soviet Union in Brussels. Won the European Footballer of the Year award.

1974 Captained Bayern Munich to victory in the European Cup Final and then West Germany to victory in the World Cup Final against Holland.

1976 Collected his second European Footballer of the Year award.

1976 Completed a record 103 appearances for West Germany before transferring to New York Cosmos in the North American Soccer League. During his time in the USA, Beckenbauer won the NASL Soccer Bowl in 1977, 1978 and 1980.

1984 Appointed national manager of West Germany in succession to Jupp Derwall.

1986 Guided an average side to the World Cup Final, where they lost 3–2 to Argentina.

1990 Became the first man to captain and then manage a World Cup-winning team when West Germany beat Argentina 1–0 in Rome.

1993 After a short spell as coach of Olympique Marseille, returned to Bayern as executive vice-president.

1994 Took over as coach and guided Bayern to the league title.

Dennis Bergkamp

1969 Born on May 10 in Amsterdam. He was named after his father's favourite footballer, Scotland star Denis Law. His name had two 'Ns' because the registrar said 'Denis' was too much like the girl's name 'Denise'.

1984 Hailed by the Dutch media as a star of the future after outstanding displays in the Ajax youth squad.

1986 Promoted to the first team at 17 and praised as a "new Cruyff" or a "new Van Basten."

1987 Appeared as substitute as Ajax beat Lokomotiv Leipzig 1–0 in Athens to win the European Cup-Winners Cup under the management of Cruyff.

1992 Leading role as Ajax won the UEFA Cup, defeating Torino of Italy on the away goals rule in the final. Then starred for Holland at the European Championship finals in Sweden, despite the semi-final upset by Denmark.

1993 Transferred to Internazionale of Italy, who beat off competition from Barcelona and Juventus. In 103 matches for Ajax he had scored 103 goals.

1994 Found a new role with Holland at the World Cup finals in the United States, playing behind the main striker, and turned on a match-winning performance against the Irish Republic.

1995 Could not adjust to life or lifestyle in Italy. Having scored only 11 goals in 52 matches he was sold by Inter to Arsenal for a club record £7.5 million.

1996 Helped Arsenal to third in the English Premiership with a total of 12 goals.

1997 Scored a hat-trick against Wales in a World Cup Qualifier – Holland qualified at the top of their group. Bergkamp closed in on the Dutch all-time national scoring record held by 1970s star Johan Neeskens.

1997 Started the season in outstanding form for Arsenal and became the first player to win the top three goals in the BBC's *Match of the Day* 'Goal of the Month' competition.

1998 Won a League championship medal, but missed Arsenal's FA Cup final victory through injury.

George Best

1946 Born on May 22 in Northern Ireland.

1961 Joined Manchester United as an amateur, aged 15.

1963 Signed as a professional for Manchester United (*see* page 51) on his 17th birthday and made his Football League debut in a 1–0 win over West Bromwich Albion at Old Trafford in September.

1964 Made his debut for Northern Ireland in a 3–2 win over Wales at Swansea.

1965 Won his first league championship.

1966 Scored two majestic goals in what was perhaps the greatest match of his career, a 5–1 win away to Benfica in the Champions Cup quarter-finals. After his display, the Portuguese nicknamed him "El Beatle", a tribute to British soccer's first superstar.

1967 Scored twice in Manchester United's 4–1 victory over Benfica in the European Champions Cup Final at Wembley.

1968 Voted domestic Footballer of the Year and then European Footballer of the Year.

1970 Suspended for four weeks and fined £100 for bringing the game into disrepute after knocking the ball out of referee Jack Taylor's hands following the Manchester City vs. United League Cup semi-final... then marked his first game after suspension by scoring six times in United's 8–2 win over Northampton Town in the FA Cup fifth round.

1972 Announced he was quitting the game a week after he'd failed to show for a Northern Ireland match. He flew off to Spain for a holiday.

1974 Made his last appearance for United, in a 3–0 defeat by Queens Park Rangers, after a succession of retirements and comebacks.

1976 Scored within 71 seconds of his debut for Fulham. A month later he became one of the first players to be shown a red card – a recent introduction into the English league – for using foul language.

1978 Won the last of his 37 international caps against Holland. After his spell at Fulham, Best moved to Hibernian in Scotland and finished his career with Tampa Bay Rowdies in the ill-fated NASL.

Danny Blanchflower

1926 Born on February 10 in Belfast.

1945 Joined Irish side Glentoran, who were managed at the time by former Spurs player Frank Grice. He played once for Swindon Town during the war years.

1949 Transferred to English football with Barnsley for £6,500, later moving on to Aston Villa in 1951.

1949 Made his international debut against Scotland in October.

1954 Transferred to Tottenham Hotspur (*see* page 70) for £30,000.

1955 Played for Great Britain in a match against a Europe XI.

1957 Captained Northern Ireland to their shock, first-ever victory over England at Wembley.

1958 Blanchflower's year started disastrously when brother Jackie was badly injured in Manchester United's Munich air crash. Despite the absence of his brother from the team, Danny led Northern Ireland to the quarter-finals of the World Cup.

1958 Won the Footballer of the Year award.

1961 Inspirational captain and right-half of Tottenham Hotspur's League and FA Cup double-winning side – the first club to achieve this feat in the 20th century. Won his second Footballer of the Year award.

1962 Captained Spurs to victory in the 3–1 FA Cup win against Burnley.

1963 Captain of Tottenham as they became the first British side to win a European club trophy, beating Atlético Madrid 5–1 in the Cup-Winners Cup Final in Rotterdam.

1963 Won the last of his 63 Northern Irish caps, against Poland.

1964 Troubled by a knee injury, Blanchflower retired from playing in June.

1965 Adapted to life after Spurs by becoming a successful and much-respected football journalist.

1978 Became manager of Chelsea in December but left the following year.

1993 Died in London in December aged 67.

Billy Bremner

1942 Born on December 9 in Stirling.

1960 Made his debut for Leeds United as a right-winger aged only 17. One of his team-mates was Don Revie, a man nearly twice his age and who would later become Bremner's manager at Leeds.

1965 Won the first of his 54 caps for Scotland in a 0–0 draw with Spain at Hampden Park.

1965 Scored Leeds' only goal as they went down 2–1 to Liverpool in the FA Cup Final.

1967 Tasted defeat again as Leeds lost 2–0 on aggregate to Dinamo Zagreb in the final of the Inter-Cities Fairs Cup.

1968 After 50 years of famine, Leeds won two trophies within six months. Arsenal were beaten 1–0 in the League Cup and then Ferençvaros were defeated by the same scoreline in the Inter-Cities Fairs Cup.

1969 Bremner scored six league goals as he helped Leeds win their first ever Championship.

1970 Won the Footballer of the Year award – some compensation for second place in the League and in the FA Cup final.

1972 Leeds defeated holders Arsenal 1–0 in the FA Cup Final.

1974 Bremner collected his second Championship medal in a season in which he scored nine league goals.

1974 Played in all three of Scotland's matches at the World Cup finals in West Germany.

1975 Unlucky to be refused a "goal" for a controversial offside as Leeds lost 2–0 to Bayern Munich in the European Champions Cup Final in Paris.

1976 Played in his last league match for Leeds before he joined nearby Hull City. Bremner had scored 90 goals in 587 league appearances for Leeds.

1985 Returned to Leeds as manager but found the club in disarray.

1988 Despite having reached the semi-final of the 1987 FA Cup, Bremner was sacked early in the 1988–89 season.

1997 Leeds, Scotland and soccer fans around the world mourn Bremner's untimely death.

Eric Cantona

1966 Born on May 24 in Paris.

1983 Made his French league debut for Auxerre.

1987 Played his first match for France, against West Germany.

1988 Achieved his first major transfer, joining Marseille for £2 million from Auxerre.

1990 Helped Montpellier win the French Cup.

1990 Banned from the national team for a year for insulting manager Henri Michel.

1991 Ended a further odyssey via Bordeaux, Montpellier and Nimes by quitting the game after a shouting match with a disciplinary panel.

1992 Tempted by the offer of a trial with Sheffield Wednesday, Cantona arrived in England but found himself bought by Leeds United for £900,000.

1992 A cult figure with his new club and won the league title with Leeds.

1992 Cantona became the target for Manchester United (*see* page 51) and Leeds were shocked when he was transferred for £1.2 million at the end of 1992.

1993 Cantona was instrumental as United won the Championship for the first time since 1967 and the era of Matt Busby and Bobby Charlton.

1994 Again Cantona was the man running the show as United became only the fourth club this century to win the League and Cup "double".

1995 An astonishing attack on a hooligan fan at Crystal Palace stunned the football world and cost him a seven-month ban from football and a community service sentence from the courts.

1996 Voted Footballer of the Year and then, as captain, sealed United's second and historic "double" when he scored the winning goal in the FA Cup Final against Liverpool. Despite his weekly displays in England, his past behaviour in France led to his omission from their Euro 96 squad.

1997 Manchester United won the league again, but despite having scored 11 goals Cantona stunned the world when he announced his retirement during the close season, aged only 31, to pursue a career as an actor.

Bobby Charlton

1937 Born October 11 in Ashington, County Durham.

1954 Signed as a professional for Manchester United, one of the most exciting of the so-called "Busby Babes".

1957 Played in the FA Cup Final at 19 but was on the losing side against Aston Villa.

1958 A year of tragedy and triumph for Charlton. In February he was lucky to escape with his life from the wreckage of Manchester United's plane which had crashed in thick snow at Munich airport. Eight of the "Babes" were killed and manager Busby was in hospital for months. Charlton recovered with such speed that he played in United's 2–0 defeat against Bolton in the FA Cup Final a few months later. The same year he won the first of 106 England caps when he played against Scotland in a 4–0 victory.

1963 Played in his third FA Cup Final, and was at last on the winning side as United beat Leicester City 3–1.

1965 Won the Championship with United, a feat they repeated in 1967.

1966 Took a starring role for England in the World Cup triumph – including scoring their magnificent first goal in the finals, against Mexico. Won both the European Footballer of the Year and English Footballer of the Year awards.

1968 Scored two goals as captain in inspiring United to victory over Benfica at Wembley in the European Champions Cup Final. Charlton and Bill Foulkes were the only two of the 1968 team who had survived the Munich air disaster. Signed an eight-year contract with Manchester United that was the longest-ever in English football.

1970 Won his 106th and last cap for England in the 3–2 defeat by West Germany in the World Cup quarter-finals in Leon. His record of 49 goals for England has yet to be beaten.

1972 Retired as a player at United, having scored 198 goals for them in 606 league appearances. He became briefly player-manager at Preston North End before subsequently returning to Old Trafford as a director.

1994 Received a knighthood.

Johan Cruyff

1947 Born on April 25 in Amsterdam.

1959 Enrolled by his mother in the Ajax youth section.

1963 Signed his first Ajax (*see* page 32) contract at 16 on the recommendation of English coach Vic Buckingham, then marked his debut with a goal.

1966 Made his debut for Holland in a 2–2 draw against Hungary, the first of his 48 internationals, and scored a last-minute equaliser.

1969 Made his first European Cup final appearance with Ajax, but Milan won 4–1 in Madrid.

1971 Won the first of three successive European Cups, helping Ajax defeat Panathinaikos of Greece at Wembley. He was also voted European Footballer of the Year.

1973 Sold by Ajax to Barcelona for a then world record transfer fee of £922,000.

1974 Captained and inspired Holland to reach the 1974 World Cup Final in Munich, where they lost 2–1 to hosts West Germany. The thrilling Dutch style of play, labelled "Total Football" won Cruyff and his team-mates countless admirers. Won the European Footballer of the Year award for the third time, the first player to achieve such a distinction.

1978 Retired from the national team before the World Cup finals in Argentina, and left Barcelona to play in America with Los Angeles Aztecs and Washington Diplomats.

1981 Returned to Europe to play for minor club Levante in Spain, then to Holland with Ajax and, finally, Feyenoord.

1984 Went back to Ajax, this time as technical director.

1987 Guided Ajax to victory in the European Cup-Winners Cup as a parting gift before being appointed coach to Barcelona.

1992 Managed Barcelona to their long-awaited victory in the European Cup Final, where they beat Sampdoria 1–0 at Wembley.

1996 Left Barcelona after a record nine years in charge, including four consecutive league championships.

Kenny Dalglish

1951 Born on March 4 in Glasgow.

1967 Joined Celtic just as the senior team were winning the European Champions Cup against Internazionale in Lisbon.

1971 Made the first of his record 102 appearances for Scotland, as a substitute against Belgium.

1977 Joined Liverpool (*see* page 50) for £400,000 as replacement for Hamburg-bound Kevin Keegan after winning six League titles, four cups and one League Cup while with Celtic, and scoring 112 league goals.

1978 Scored Liverpool's winner against Club Brugge in the European Champions Cup Final at Wembley.

1985 Was appointed player-manager of Liverpool, in succession to Joe Fagan, on the eve of the tragic Champions Cup Final against Juventus in Brussels, when 39 died after crowd trouble.

1986 Made history as the only player-manager ever to have won the League and FA Cup double.

1987 Made his last appearance for Scotland in a 0–0 draw with Luxembourg. With 30 goals he equalled Denis Law's record.

1989 Manager of Liverpool on the club's disastrous day, when 89 fans died in a crush at the FA Cup semi-final against Nottingham Forest at Hillsborough, Sheffield.

1989 Made his last league appearance for Liverpool having scored 118 goals, becoming the only player to have scored 100 League goals for one club in both England and Scotland.

1990 Resigned as manager of Liverpool in the middle of an FA Cup sequence against Everton, largely as a result of the stress of helping Liverpool, both football club and city, cope with the aftermath of Hillsborough.

1991 Returned to football as manager of Blackburn Rovers.

1995 Thanks to the millions of owner Jack Walker, Dalglish's big-spending style took Blackburn to victory in the Premiership – then moved up to an uncertain role as director of football.

1996 Quit Blackburn before the start of the season.

1997 Returned to management as successor to Kevin Keegan at ambitious, big-spending Newcastle United.

Billy 'Dixie' Dean

1907 Born on January 22 in Birkenhead, Cheshire.

1924 Signed professional for Tranmere Rovers and broke his skull in a road accident early on in his career.

1925 Joined Everton, where he remained until 1938.

1927 Began his international career as England centre-forward against Scotland with a dream sequence by scoring 2, 3, 2, 2 and 3 goals in successive games. Two of the goals came in the 2–1 win against Scotland at Hampden Park, England's first success in Glasgow since 1904.

1928 Completed his record season in which he scored 60 League goals for Everton in only 39 league matches, finishing with two, four and three to overhaul George Camsell's 59 for Middlesbrough. He also scored 22 goals in other competitions to bring his total for the season to 82. Perhaps not surprisingly, Everton were crowned champions.

1932 Won another Championship medal with Everton.

1933 Played his last game for England against Northern Ireland – having scored 18 goals in 16 appearances – as well as 47 in 18 other representative matches.

1933 For the first time numbered shirts were worn in an FA Cup Final and Dean scored one of Everton's three goals as Manchester City were beaten 3–0.

1936 Passed Derby County's Steve Bloomer's pre-war record of 352 goals and finished the season with 375.

1938 Transferred to Notts County but played only a handful of games before he moved to Ireland and Sligo Rovers. Helped Rovers to the final of the Irish Cup.

1939 Retired from football having scored 379 English league goals in 437 matches, including 34 hat-tricks.

1964 Retired from his job as a licensee in Chester. A belated testimonial match at Everton drew a 40,000 crowd.

1980 Fittingly, Dean died at Goodison Park after collapsing while watching Everton play Liverpool.

Frank de Boer

1970 Born on May 15 1970 in Hoorn, Holland.

1980 Played for junior club De Zouaven.

1982 Joined Amsterdam Ajax youth with brother Ronald.

1988 Made his league debut for Ajax at the start of the 1988–89 season after turning professional in the summer.

1992 Gained a UEFA Cup winners medal with Ajax after drawing 2–2 on aggregate with Torino but winning because of the away goals rule.

1992 Made his debut for Holland and helped them reach the semi-final of the European Championships before they lost against Denmark in a penalty shoot-out.

1994 Played in the World Cup Finals in the USA, when Holland lost 3–2 to Brazil in the quarter-finals.

1995 A member of the Ajax team which beat AC Milan 1–0 in Vienna to win the European Champions' Cup. Also went on to win the European Super Cup, defeating Real Zaragoza 5–1 on aggregate.

1996 Collected a losers' medal in the European Champions Cup defeat against Juventus. The final went to penalties but de Boer had already gone off with an injury.

1996 Forced to miss Holland's disappointing European Championships campaign because of the injury sustained in the Champions Cup Final.

1997 Won his 50th cap for Holland as they successfully qualified for the 1998 World Cup Finals. Scored two goals in the 4–0 defeat of San Marino and another as Wales were thrashed 7–1.

1998 Played in his second World Cup.

Didier Deschamps

1968 Born on October 15 in France.

1986 Made his league debut for Nantes.

1989 Made his debut for France against Yugoslavia.

1990 Won the French league championship with Marseille.

1991 Appeared in the first of four European Champions Cup finals and was a loser as Marseille lost on penalties to Red Star Belgrade.

1992 Collected a second championship medal with Marseille.

1993 Captain of the Marseille side which beat AC Milan 1–0 in Munich. Unfortunately, Marseille were later stripped of the title because of allegations of corruption involving club president Bernard Tapie.

1994 Moved to Italian club Juventus in July.

1995 Found success immediately as he picked up the Italian league and cup double with Juventus.

1994 Narrowly missed out on a treble when Juventus lost 1–0 to Parma in the final of the UEFA Cup.

1996 Won a European Champions Cup winners' medal when Juventus beat Ajax in a penalty shoot-out.

1996 Steered France to the semi-final of the European Championships, where they lost on a penalty shoot-out to the Czech Republic. Won his 50th cap during the championships.

1997 Member of the Juventus side which lost 3–1 to Borussia Dortmund in the final of the Champions Cup.

1998 On the losing side in another Champions League final, against Real Madrid. Appeared for hosts France in the 1998 World Cup finals, leading his side to the final and raising the trophy as France are crowned world champions.

Alfredo Di Stefano

1926 Born Alfredo Stefano Di Stefano Lauhle on July 4 in Barracas, Argentina.

1940 Hinted at things to come by scoring a hat-trick in 20 minutes for his first youth team, Los Cardales.

1942 Left Los Cardales after a row with the coach, to join his father's old club, River Plate.

1943 Made his debut for River Plate, playing as a right-winger, aged 17, against Buenos Aires rivals San Lorenzo.

1944 Transferred on loan to Huracan, for whom he scored the winner in a league game against River Plate.

1946 Returned to River Plate (*see* page 65) to succeed the great Adolfo Pedernera at centre-forward in an attack nicknamed La Maquina (the Machine).

1947 Already an international, won the South American Championship with Argentina.

1949 Lured away, during the famous Argentine players' strike, to play in a pirate league outside of FIFA's jurisdiction in Colombia for Millonarios of Bogota.

1953 Moved to Spain where he joined Real Madrid.

1956 Inspired Madrid to the first of five successive European Cup victories and topped the Spanish League scoring tables for five of the six seasons between 1954–59, with a record 49 goals in 58 European Cup matches.

1956 Won the first of his 31 caps for Spain (*see* page 27), for whom he scored 23 goals. Also won seven caps for Argentina and three for Colombia.

1960 Scored a hat-trick in Real's legendary 7–3 victory over Eintracht Frankfurt in the European Cup final at Hampden Park, Glasgow.

1963 Kidnapped – and later released unharmed – while on tour with Real in Venezuela.

1964 Left Madrid for one last season as a player with Español of Barcelona, before becoming coach for Elche.

1968 Returned to Argentina to coach and revived the fortunes of Boca Juniors.

1970 Took up a coaching position with Valencia in Spain and led them to their first league title in 24 years.

Duncan Edwards

1936 Born on October 1 in Dudley.

1950 Made his England representative debut, playing for the under-14s against Ireland at Oldham.

1952 Signed for Manchester United.

1953 Made his league debut at 16 years 185 days in a 4–1 home defeat by Cardiff City but was soon labelled one of the "Busby's Babes" in recognition of manager Matt Busby's young side.

1955 Became England's youngest international this century when he made his senior debut in a 7–2 win over Scotland aged only 18 years and 183 days – the first of 18 full internationals in which he scored six goals. Edwards also played for England Youth, England Under-23, England B and the Football League.

1956 Played a large part in helping Manchester United win the Championship title. Established himself as one of the world's best players with a supreme display in Berlin as England trounced West Germany 3–1. Edwards scored the first goal and earned the nickname "Boom-Boom" for the power of his shooting.

1957 FA Cup Final runner-up with Manchester United against Aston Villa, but won his second Championship title. The club made their first venture into European football, reaching the semi-final of the European Cup before losing 3–5 on aggregate to eventual winners Real Madrid.

1958 Scored United's first goal away at Arsenal in what is considered one of the greatest ever matches in the English league. United lead 3–0 at half-time, but Arsenal rallied and drew level. United came back and scored two more goals, Arsenal got a fourth but lost 5–4.

1958 Travelled to Belgrade for the European Cup quarter-final with Red Star. United drew 3–3 to secure their place in the semi-final. On the return flight, the plane stopped to re-fuel at Munich. As it attempted to take off in heavy snow it crashed, killing eight of the players. Edwards was critically injured and died in hospital two weeks later.

Eusebio

1942 Born Eusebio Da Silva Ferreira on January 25 in Lourenco Marques, Mozambique.

1952 Joined the youth teams of Sporting (Lourenzo Marques), a nursery team for the Portuguese giants of the same name.

1961 Sporting tried to bring Eusebio to Lisbon, but he was "kidnapped" on arrival by Benfica. In the autumn, with barely a dozen league games to his name, he made his debut for Portugal against England at Wembley and played so well he was already being talked of as a new star.

1961 Between 1961 and 1973, Eusebio won the Portuguese League seven times and he was the top scorer in the league in seven of these years; also won the Portuguese Cup five times.

1962 Scored two thundering goals as Benfica beat Real Madrid 5–3 in a classic European Cup Final in Amsterdam. He was also a runner-up three times with Benfica in this competition, in 1963, 1965 and 1968.

1963 Scored a cracking consolation goal for Benfica against AC Milan in a 2–1 European Cup Final defeat at Wembley.

1965 Voted European Footballer of the Year.

1966 Crowned top scorer with nine goals as Portugal finished third in the World Cup finals in England, where he was nicknamed the "new Pele" and the "Black Panther." In all, he scored 38 goals in 46 internationals.

1974 Having scored 316 league goals in 294 matches he left Benfica and travelled to North America to take part in the new NASL. Started with Boston Minutemen, then moved to Toronto Metros and finished with Las Vegas Quicksilver.

1977 Returned to Benfica as coach.

1992 A statue in his honour was unveiled at the entrance to Benfica's Estadio da Luz (*see* page 192) in Lisbon and a film about his life was released entitled *Sua Majestade o Rei* – His Majesty the King.

Giacinto Facchetti

1942 Born on July 18 in Treviglio.

1956 Joined youth system of local club CS Trevigliese, where he started out as a centre-forward.

1960 Signed professional for Internazionale, his only senior club, where master coach Helenio Herrera (*see* page 76) converted him to full-back.

1961 Made his league debut in a 2–0 away win over Roma.

1963 Won the first of four league championships with Inter and made his Italy debut in a 1–0 win over Turkey in Istanbul.

1964 Won the European Champions Cup with Inter against Real Madrid in Vienna and then the World Club Cup against Independiente of Argentina – in a play-off in, ironically, Madrid.

1965 Won both European and World club cups for a second successive year.

1966 Scored 10 goals in 1965–66 season, a record for a full-back in Serie A. Became captain of the national side in his 25th international.

1968 Became a European champion at national team level when Italy defeated Yugoslavia after a replay in the European Nations Final in Rome.

1970 World Cup runner-up as captain of Italy against Brazil in Mexico City.

1971 Converted from left-back to sweeper. His 59 goals in 476 games for Inter were a record for an Italian full-back.

1971 Became the most capped Italian player of all time when he passed Umberto Caligaris's previous record of 59 appearances in September of this year.

1972 Surprisingly dropped by Italy, but returned to play in the 1974 World Cup finals in West Germany.

1977 Played his last international for Italy in a 2–0 defeat by England at Wembley in a World Cup qualifier – but Italy still qualified for the finals. Injury prevented Facchetti from playing in the finals in Argentina – or adding to his then record total of 94 caps.

Tom Finney

1922 Born on April 5 in Preston.

1938 Signed for Preston North End, his local, and only, senior club.

1941 Played for Preston in the 1941 wartime FA Cup Final.

1942 Served in North Africa with the British Eighth Army.

1946 Eight years after signing for Preston he made his first league appearance for them.

1946 One month later he played for England against Scotland – although caps weren't awarded for the match.

1947 Won the first of his 76 caps, against Wales, in a career notable for ongoing controversy over whether he, or Stanley Matthews, was the better right-winger. He won 40 caps at outside-right, 33 at outside-left and three as a centre-forward.

1950 Played in England's first World Cup finals but it ended in disaster when they lost to the USA 1–0.

1954 Went closest to a major club honour when Preston lost 3–2 to West Bromwich Albion in the FA Cup final. Voted English Footballer of the Year.

1954 Second World Cup finals appearance as England reached the quarter-final stage.

1957 Won the Footballer of the Year award for a second time.

1958 A key veteran member of the England team which reached the 1958 World Cup finals – his finals – but were eliminated in a first-round play-off by the Soviet Union, with Finney missing through injury.

1959 Played his last international for England against the Soviet Union, 13 years after first appearing for his country, and his English record of 30 international goals stood until broken by Bobby Charlton

1960 Played last of his 433 league matches for Preston, for whom he scored 187 goals.

1975 Elected president of Preston North End.

1998 Awarded a knighthood in the New Year Honours List. Still with Preston – as club president.

Just Fontaine

1933 Born on August 18 in Marrekech.

1953 Brought up in Morocco, but turned professional in France with Nice.

1954 Helped Nice to win the French Cup.

1956 Won French league honours with Nice before being transferred to Reims as replacement for Real Madrid-bound centre-forward Raymond Kopa. Made his debut for France.

1958 Won the French league and cup with Reims.

1958 Injury to Reims team-mate René Bliard opened the door for Fontaine to lead the French attack at the World Cup finals in Sweden despite having played only once more since his debut in 1956. He scored 13 goals during the finals, a record which still stands, including a hat-trick in France's opening game against Paraguay and four in the 6–3 win over West Germany, to secure third place for his country. A semi-final defeat by eventual winners Brazil had ended France's hopes of winning the cup.

1960 Broke a leg in March of this year in a league game. The break proved so bad that it was feared he may never play again.

1961 Suffered an extraordinary stroke of ill-luck when, on one of his first games back from his broken leg, he broke the same for a second time.

1962 Forced to retire after failing to recover fully from his double leg fracture. French football was plunged into despair at the announcement. Fontaine's record of twice being top league scorer and totalling 27 goals in 20 internationals was testimony to his greatness as a striker.

1963 Became the first president of the French Professional Footballers' Union.

1967 Appointed director of the French national team but didn't hold the position for long.

The Great Players

Paul Gascoigne

1967 Born on May 27 in Gateshead.

1983 Joined Newcastle United as an apprentice.

1985 Made his first-team debut for Newcastle a month before he turned professional.

1987 Made his debut for England Under-21s.

1988 Transferred to Tottenham for £2 million in July and made his full England debut a month later when he went on as a sub against Denmark. Also voted Young Player of the Year.

1990 Suddenly achieved international superstar status with his displays at the World Cup finals, culminating in his tearful exit from the semi-final against West Germany.

1990 Won the BBC's Sports Personality of the Year.

1991 Won an FA Cup-winner's medal even though he was on a stretcher at the time, having incurred a career-threatening cruciate ligament injury early in the game with a rash challenge on Nottingham Forest defender Gary Charles.

1992 Sold to Lazio for a reduced fee of £5.5 million, a year later than planned because of his knee injury. Made his first appearance for England for over a year.

1995 Returned to British football with Rangers, after playing only 42 league games in his three seasons with Lazio – missing a significant chunk because of a leg fracture suffered in training.

1996 Won his first-ever league championship medal in his first season with Rangers and was voted Footballer of the Year in Scotland.

1996 Embroiled in trouble with the media for drunken antics on a short tour to the Far East, "Gazza" responded in stunning fashion when he scored a magnificent goal against Scotland in the European Championships and helped England to the semi-finals.

1997 Won a second Championship medal with Rangers and played a large part in steering England to the 1998 World Cup finals, but was controversially left out of the squad soon after joining Middlesbrough.

Jimmy Greaves

1940 Born on February 20 in London.

1957 Made his first-team debut with Chelsea and reached a century of goals within 133 appearances.

1959 Scored on his debut for England in a 1–4 defeat against Peru.

1961 Joined Milan for £80,000 in June after scoring a remarkable 124 goals in 157 league games for Chelsea including a club record 41 in the 1960–61 season. Never adjusted to the lifestyle or discipline of Italian football, though he scored nine goals in the first 10 games of what was ultimately a league championship-winning season. Sold back to English football in December with Tottenham Hotspur – though manager Bill Nicholson insisted on paying £99,999 so Greaves would not be saddled with the label of the first £100,000 footballer!

1962 Won the FA Cup with Tottenham (*see* page 70).

1963 Scored twice for Tottenham in the 5–1 win over Atlético Madrid which made them the first British club to lift a European trophy, the Cup-winners Cup. Also scored what was then a Tottenham club record 37 league goals in the 1962–63 season.

1966 Hit the lowest point of his career when he was injured in the first round of the World Cup finals against France and failed to regain his place from Geoff Hurst for the Final.

1967 His last club triumph – winning the FA Cup with Tottenham. In the first all-London final, Spurs beat Chelsea 2–1 and Greaves and captain Dave Mackay were the only two survivors from the 1962 triumph.

1967 Won the last of his 57 caps, against Austria. Scored a total of 44 goals for England.

1970 Transferred to West Ham United as part of the £200,000 deal which took Martin Peters to Tottenham.

1971 Retired at "only" 31 after totalling 357 League goals, all in the top division. Now a popular television soccer analyst.

John Greig

1942 Born on September 11 in Edinburgh.

1960 Moved from junior club Whitburn to Rangers – his only senior club, whom he continued serving in managerial and administrative capacities long after his retirement.

1962 Established himself as Rangers right-half, though it was subsequently in the centre of defence that he made most of his record 496 league appearances for the club.

1964 Won the first of his 44 caps for Scotland in a 1–0 defeat of England at Hampden Park. Voted Scottish Player of the Year.

1966 Voted Scottish Footballer of the Year for a second time.

1967 Senior member of the Rangers side beaten after extra time by Bayern Munich in the European Cup-winners Cup Final in Nuremberg. To compound matters for Greig and the Rangers team, Celtic succeeded where they failed and became the first British side to win the European Cup.

1971 Endured the horror of witnessing 66 people crushed to death during the New Year's Day Old Firm clash at Ibrox.

1972 Won that elusive European medal and became the only Rangers skipper to lift a European trophy when Rangers defeated Moscow Dynamo 3–2 in the final of the Cup-winners' Cup in Barcelona's Nou Camp stadium.

1976 Five years after his last cap, Greig was recalled by Scotland for one more appearance, against Denmark. It was his last international.

1977 Awarded the MBE.

1978 Stopped playing and became manager of Rangers. His managerial career started in blazing fashion, winning both the League Cup and the Scottish Cup and enjoying a good run in Europe.

1983 Resigned as manager of the club, despite winning four trophies in five seasons, ending an association with Rangers that had begun 23 years earlier.

Ruud Gullit

1962 Born on September 1 in Surinam.

1978 Discovered by a Welsh coach, Barry Hughes, who signed him for Haarlem.

1980 Joined Feyenoord, playing sweeper, but subsequently converted to forward after moving to PSV Eindhoven.

1981 Won the first of his 65 caps on his 19th birthday, in a 2–1 defeat by Switzerland.

1985 Moved to PSV Eindhoven.

1987 Sold to Milan for a world record £5.5 million and helped inspire their first league championship victory in nine years. Won his first World Footballer of the Year award and voted European Player of the Year.

1988 A few weeks after winning the Italian league, Gullit captained Holland to European Championship glory in Munich – scoring the first of their two goals in the Final victory over the Soviet Union.

1989 Scored two goals in Milan's 4–0 thrashing of Steaua Bucharest in the European Champions Cup Final in Barcelona's Nou Camp. Voted World Footballer of the Year for the second time.

1990 Came back from a serious knee injury to win a second Champions Cup-winners medal as Milan beat Benfica 1–0 in Vienna.

1993 Joined Sampdoria and made his last appearance for Holland.

1995 Left Italy, after restless and unsatisfactory spells with Sampdoria, Milan again and then Sampdoria again, to start a new career in England with Chelsea under the managership of Glenn Hoddle.

1996 Appointed player-manager of Chelsea after Hoddle's departure to become manager of England.

1997 Became the first continental coach to land an English prize as Chelsea beat Middlesbrough 2–0 to win the FA Cup.

1998 Controversially sacked and replaced by Gianluca Vialli.

Gheorghe Hagi

1965 Born on February 5 in Constanta.

1980 Played first-team football for local club FC Constanta as well as making his debut for Romania's youth team.

1982 By now an established league player, at 17, with Sportul Studentesc of Bucharest.

1983 Made his debut for the Romanian senior team against Norway, aged 18.

1984 Was a member of Romania's team at the European Championship finals in France, but the team failed to spark and they returned home having failed to win any of their three pool matches.

1985 Hailed as the league leading marksman after scoring 20 goals in the 1984–85 season from his position as an attacking midfielder. By this time he had already developed a reputation for his skill with free kicks and penalties.

1986 Became top league scorer again, this time with 31 goals after scoring six in one match, and was "stolen" by Steaua Bucharest without a transfer fee – an escapade approved by the ruling Ceaucescu family, who were Steaua supporters and directors.

1990 Starred for Romania as they reached the second round of the World Cup finals before losing to the Republic of Ireland in a penalty shoot-out. Was later transferred to Spain with Real Madrid.

1992 Fell out with Madrid's other star players and was sold to Italian club Brescia, who already had two other Romanian players and a Romanian coach in Mircea Lucescu.

1994 Hailed as one of the great stars at the World Cup finals, where Romania were eliminated once again after a penalty shoot-out, this time against Sweden, in the quarter-finals. On returning to Europe, Hagi was transferred back to Spanish football, with Barcelona.

1996 Failed to impress Johan Cruyff and was sold off yet again, this time to top Turkish club Galatasaray. Played in a disappointing European Championship campaign for Romania.

1998 Played in his third World Cup.

Helmut Haller

1939 Born on July 21 in Augsburg.

1957 Turned semi-professional with local club BC Augsburg.

1958 Made his senior national team debut at inside-right for West Germany in a 1–1 draw with Denmark in Copenhagen – the Germans' first match since their 6–3 defeat by France in the World Cup third place match. Haller was injured, however, and had to be substituted by Hans Cieslarczyk.

1961 Transferred to Italian club Bologna.

1963 Haller's attacking partnership with Danish striker Harald Nielsen inspired Bologna to their first league championship in more than 20 years – they beat Inter 1–0 in a title play-off in Rome after both clubs finished level on points.

1966 Was one of the most influential players at the World Cup finals – even before he pounced on a mistake by Ray Wilson to shoot West Germany into a 1–0 lead against England in the Final at Wembley. Unfortunately for Haller, England came back to win 4–2.

1968 Left Bologna after six seasons to join Juventus, with whom he won two league championships – in 1972 and 1973.

1970 Played his 33rd and last international for West Germany in the struggling 2–1 win over Morocco in Leon at the World Cup finals. He was dropped immediately after the match and therefore had to watch from the sidelines as West Germany avenged their 1966 World Cup Final defeat to England by knocking the holders out in a gripping quarter-final encounter. The Germans went out 4–3 in the semi-finals to the Italians, but claimed third place after beating Uruguay in the decider.

1973 Haller went close to a European club medal, when he appeared as a substitute in Juventus' 1–0 Champions Cup Final defeat by Ajax in Belgrade.

Johnny Haynes

1934 Born on October 17 in London.

1950 Joined Fulham as a schoolboy.

1952 Turned professional with his only English club, Fulham, after playing for England at youth and schools levels.

1955 Won the first of 56 caps, against Northern Ireland and, in the process, became the first English player to be capped at all five international levels – Schoolboy, Youth, Under-23, "B" and Full.

1960 Appointed captain of England in succession to Ronnie Clayton.

1961 Became English football's first £100-a-week footballer after the abolition of the maximum wage. Key man in midfield for England after manager Walter Winterbottom switched to the 4–2–4 system with Haynes partnered in the engine room by Bobby Robson. In successive games, England won 5–2, 9–0, 4–2, 5–1, 9–3 and 8–0. The 9–3 result was a thrashing of Scotland at Wembley in 1961, perhaps the best performance of Haynes's England era.

1962 Captained England in the World Cup in Chile. After a win, a draw and a defeat in the pool matches, his appearance against Brazil in the 3–1 quarter-final defeat turned out to be his last because of injuries suffered in a serious car crash that August which sidelined him for a year. He captained his country on 22 occasions during his 56 caps and scored 18 goals.

1963 Haynes decided to stay with Fulham despite a record-breaking bid from Tottenham Hotspur, then the strongest team in England.

1969 Retired from English football still with Fulham and after scoring 145 goals in 594 league games.

1970 Ended his playing career in South Africa, winning a championship medal with Durban City.

Glenn Hoddle

1957 Born on 27 October in Hayes, England.

1975 Having been spotted playing a junior cup final, Hoddle made his league debut for Spurs.

1979 Scored on his debut for England against Bulgaria.

1981 Won an FA Cup winners' medal against Manchester City.

1982 Won a second FA Cup winners' medal and scored the winning goal against QPR from the penalty spot.

1982 Made two appearances for England in the World Cup Finals.

1986 Reached the World Cup quarter-finals before losing to Argentina.

1987 Appeared in his third FA Cup final with Spurs but picked up a losers' medal after a 3–2 defeat against Coventry City.

1987 After 590 appearances for Spurs he moved to French side Monaco for £750,000.

1988 Won a championship medal with his new club and was voted best foreign player in France.

1988 Won the last of his 53 caps, against the USSR, during the European Championships.

1990 Bought up his contract with Monaco after a serious knee injury and returned to England and Chelsea.

1991 Joined Swindon Town as player-manager and won promotion to the Premier League.

1993 Joined Chelsea as player-manager.

1994 Brought himself on as a substitute during the FA Cup final, his sixth including two replays, but Manchester United beat Chelsea 4–0.

1996 Took over from Terry Venables as coach of the England team

1997 England won 'Le Tournoi' trophy, a competition involving France, Italy and Brazil.

1998 Guided England to the 1998 World Cup Finals in France.

Geoff Hurst

1941 Born on December 8 in Ashton, Lancashire.

1959 Signed for West Ham, as a wing-half or inside-forward, but was converted into a striker by manager Ron Greenwood and scored 180 goals in 409 league starts – ultimate reward for his decision to pursue football instead of a cricket career.

1964 Scored a strangely premonitory in-off-the-crossbar goal as West Ham beat Preston 3–2 in the FA Cup Final.

1965 Led West Ham's attack in their 2–0 win over TSV 1860 Munich in the European Cup-winners Cup Final.

1966 Made his senior debut for England against Scotland, having previously played for his country at youth and under-23 level. Considered a reserve in the squad for the World Cup finals but was brought in for the quarter-final against Argentina after Jimmy Greaves was injured playing against France. Hurst scored the winner against Argentina, set up one of Bobby Charlton's goals in the semi-final victory over Portugal… and then scored the historic hat-trick in the 4–2 victory over West Germany in the Final.

1970 Played in the World Cup Finals in Mexico and this time lost out to the Germans as England lost 3–2 in the quarter-finals.

1972 Transferred from West Ham to Stoke City after 13 seasons with the London club. In that time he scored 180 goals in 410 league matches. Played his last match for England against West Germany. He scored 24 goals in 49 appearances.

1975 Moved on from Stoke to West Bromwich Albion. After retiring he tried his hand at management in the League with Chelsea but, after his dismissal 18 months later, went out of football and into the insurance business.

1996 Was one of the "front men" for the 1996 European Championship promotional campaign and then for the bid to bring the 2006 World Cup finals to England.

1998 Became Sir Geoffrey – just in time for the World Cup!

Jairzinho

1944 Born on December 25 in Rio de Janeiro, full name Jair Ventura Filho.

1959 Moved from his home town to sign professional with Botafogo at 15 and play outside-right as deputy to the great Garrincha.

1963 Won a gold medal at the 1963 Pan American Games.

1964 First capped by Brazil.

1966 Played in the same squad as Garrincha, his hero, at the World Cup finals in England, but had only three games.

1970 Made history by scoring in every game in every round of the World Cup finals on Brazil's way to their ultimate 4–1 victory over Italy in the Final. Jairzinho scored seven goals, including two in Brazil's opening win over Czechoslovakia and one in the climactic defeat of Italy.

1971 Broke a leg and spent several months on the sidelines.

1972 Transferred to Europe to play for Marseille but returned home within a year after disciplinary problems.

1974 Played in his third World Cup, but this year it was the turn of Holland to play the beautiful football and they knocked Brazil out in the second round. Retired shortly afterwards having scored a total of 37 goals in 87 appearances for Brazil.

1976 Re-emerged as a veteran hero with Cruzeiro of Belo Horizonte in their run to the final of the South American Club Cup, the Copa Libertadores. In the final Cruzeiro beat River Plate 4–1 in the first leg but lost 2–1 away in the return. Jairzinho missed the play-off, which Cruzeiro won 3–2 in Santiago, because of injury. He was back for the World Club Cup final but Cruzeiro lost 0–2, 0–0 against European champions Bayern Munich of West Germany.

1991 Jairzinho re-emerged into the international headlines after discovering a talented youngster named Ronaldo. Subsequently Jairzinho was appointed coach to his old club Cruzeiro.

Pat Jennings

1945 Born on June 12 in County Down, Northern Ireland.

1961 Made his debut in goal for his home-town team, Newry.

1963 Moved to England with Watford, for whom he played 48 matches.

1964 Transferred to Tottenham Hotspur as successor to double-winning Scotland keeper Bill Brown. Won his first Northern Irish cap, against Wales.

1967 FA Cup-winner with Tottenham Hotspur, then scored a goal with a clearance from hand during the Charity Shield against Manchester United.

1971 Won the first of three cup medals in consecutive years. This year it was the League Cup, followed by the UEFA Cup in 1972 and ending with another League Cup triumph in 1973.

1973 Voted Footballer of the Year.

1977 Surprisingly released by Spurs after playing 472 league matches in 12 years and snapped up for a paltry £40,000 by North London neighbours Arsenal – with whom he extended his career by a further seven years and 237 league games.

1979 FA Cup-winner with Arsenal having finished on the losing side the previous season – and before picking up a further loser's medal in 1980.

1982 Played in Northern Ireland's World Cup campaign as they topped their group, which included a controversial 1–0 defeat of hosts Spain. They eventually lost 4–1 to France in the second round.

1985 Earned a reputed £100,000 from his testimonial game between Spurs and Arsenal. Having not played a senior club match for nearly a year, Jennings performed heroically as his saves booked Northern Ireland a place in the 1986 World Cup.

1986 Bowed out of football in a big way by winning his 119th cap on his 41st birthday – in a World Cup finals defeat against Brazil in Guadalajara, Mexico.

1993 Returned to football as goalkeeping coach with Tottenham.

Jimmy Johnstone

1944 Born on September 30 in Glasgow.

1964 Made his Scotland debut against Wales – the first of his 23 caps. He almost certainly would have won more caps but for an aversion to flying which he overcame, to some extent, only later in his career. He scored four goals for his country.

1965 Career really took off at Celtic after the managerial takeover by Jock Stein which started with Scottish Cup success. Went on to win 16 medals with the club – one European Cup, eight league, three Scottish Cup, four League Cup.

1966 Retained that title and won his first league championship with Celtic.

1967 One of the heroes of Celtic's 2–1 comeback victory over Internazionale in the European Champions Cup Final in Lisbon, when Johnstone became one of the few right-wingers to give Giacinto Facchetti a tough time. This was the end of the season in which Celtic achieved a unique quartet of trophies – also winning the Scottish league, the League Cup and the Scottish FA Cup.

1970 A night of unbridled passion and raw emotion as the kings of Scottish football, Celtic, faced their English counterparts, Leeds United, in the semi-final of the European Cup. In front of 134,000 fans at Hampden Park, Johnstone reigned supreme as he tormented the Leeds defence. Celtic won 2–1 (3–1 on aggregate), but lost 2–1 to Feyenoord in the final.

1972 Celtic reached their eighth consecutive League Cup Final, against lowly Partick Thistle, but were stunned 4–1 in an amazing match. To compound Johnstone's misery he was taken off injured.

1974 Celtic won the league championship for the ninth consecutive season; they also won the Scottish Cup.

1975 Won the last of his 23 caps in the 1–1 draw with Spain in a European Championship qualifier.

Kevin Keegan

1951 Born on February 14 in Yorkshire.

1968 Turned professional with Scunthorpe United.

1971 Cost Liverpool a bargain £35,000 when he signed from Scunthorpe as an orthodox outside-right. Proved an overnight success at Anfield, later as a free-ranging attacking raider.

1973 Won the first of his three league championships with Liverpool, the others coming in 1976 and 1977. Made his debut for England against Wales in a 3–0 victory.

1976 Won the UEFA Cup against Club Brugge.

1977 Inspired Liverpool to their first European Champions Cup victory, a 3–1 win over Borussia Mönchengladbach in the Olympic stadium in Rome. Immediately after the final he transferred to Hamburg for £440,000.

1978 Voted European Footballer of the Year.

1979 Retained that title and won the German championship with Hamburg.

1980 Collected a European Champions Cup runner-up medal after Hamburg lost 1–0 to Nottingham Forest in the Bernabéu stadium in Madrid.

1980 Returned to England with Southampton.

1982 Keegan's only World Cup opportunity was sadly wasted because of a back injury which prevented his appearing until just a substitute's second-half role in England's last match, a 0–0 draw against Spain in the second round. It turned out to be the last of his 63 caps.

1982 Moved to Newcastle for two seasons and proved a huge hit with the fans.

1984 Announced his retirement from the game.

1992 Returned to Newcastle, this time as manager, and guided them to promotion.

1997 Quit as Newcastle manager shortly before the club's flotation on the stock market. At the end of the year he was appointed Director of Football at Fulham with the aim of guiding the club back to the top flight.

Mario Kempes

1952 Born on July 15 in Bellville, Argentina.

1967 Turned professional with home-town club Instituto de Cordoba.

1970 Transferred to Rosario Central.

1974 Made his senior national team debut for Argentina and was hailed as one of the outstanding young players on view at the World Cup finals in West Germany, where Argentina reached the second round before losing to Holland 4–1 and South American rivals Brazil.

1976 Sold by Rosario Central to Valencia of Spain, where he developed into such a devastating hammer of opposing defences that he was the only foreign-based player recalled to join the hosts' World Cup squad under Cesar Luis Menotti in 1978.

1978 Voted Player of the Tournament in recognition of top-scoring with six goals as Argentina won the World Cup for the first time. Kempes had scored the first goal of the final after 38 minutes, but the Dutch equalised eight minutes from the end of normal time and the match went into extra time. Again it was Kempes who broke the deadlock and it was his deft one-two with Bertoni that made the scoreline 3–1 and ensured that the World Cup went to Argentina for the first time. Kempes was rewarded with the South American Player of the Year award.

1980 Won his one and only European club trophy when Valencia defeated English club Arsenal on penalties to win the European Cup-winners' Cup in the Heysel stadium in Brussels.

1981 Left Spain to return to Argentina, where he joined River Plate.

1982 Recalled by Argentina for the 1982 World Cup finals in Spain but this time could not work the same magic, failing to co-ordinate effectively with the new Argentinian hero Diego Maradona, and Argentina drifted out in the second round. When he retired shortly afterwards, Kempes had scored 20 goals in 43 internationals.

Jürgen Klinsmann

1964 Born on July 30 in Boblingen, Germany.

1972 Started with TB Gingen before moving to SC Geislingen and then Stuttgart Kickers, also making his debut for the German national youth team.

1984 Joined VfB Stuttgart and was, in his first season, the club's second-highest scorer with 15 goals. Made his debut for Germany at under-21 level.

1986 Became only the 11th player in Bundesliga history to score five goals in a match.

1987 Made his full international debut in a 1–1 draw with Brazil.

1988 Was the Bundesliga's top scorer with 19 goals. Made a big international impression during the European Championship finals in West Germany. Also a member of the bronze-medal winning team at the Seoul Olympic Games. Voted German Footballer of the Year.

1989 Helped Stuttgart reach the UEFA Cup final, in which they lost to Napoli. Then made his first move abroad, to Italy and Internazionale.

1990 Made a fine start in Serie A, scoring 13 times in his first season. Then enjoyed his greatest triumph as West Germany won the World Cup.

1992 Member of the German team surprisingly beaten in the European Championship Final by Denmark. Left Inter to play for Monaco.

1994 Enjoyed a major personal success at the World Cup finals even though Germany lost in the quarter-finals – then transferred, surprisingly, to Tottenham Hotspur.

1995 Voted Footballer of the Year. Also captained the German national team for first time, against Spain, before leaving Tottenham to join Bayern Munich.

1996 Returned to England to captain Germany to victory in the European Championship as well as scoring 15 goals in Bayern Munich's UEFA Cup triumph – an individual record for a player in a European season.

1997 Won his long-awaited league championship medal in Germany with Bayern, then returned to Italy with Sampdoria… before returning to England with Tottenham to help them in avoid relegation.

1998 Led the Germany team to the quarter-finals of France 98.

Ronald Koeman

1963 Born on March 21 in Holland

1980 Made his debut in defence for his father's old club, FC Groningen

1981 Scored 15 goals in his first full season with Groningen

1983 Transferred to Ajax Amsterdam

1986 Transferred to PSV Eindhoven

1987 Scored 21 goals for Eindhoven

1988 Won the European Champions Cup after a penalty shoot-out against Benfica.
Completed a stunning treble with Eindhoven by winning the Dutch league and cup.

1988 Along with brother Erwin, was a member of the Dutch side which won the 1988
European Championships. Scored a penalty in the 2–1 defeat of West Germany in the
semi-final.

1989 Moved to Spanish giants Barcelona

1990 Played for Holland in the World Cup finals, but they lost to West Germany in the
second round.

1991 Scored for Barcelona but was a loser in the 2–1 defeat against Manchester United in
the European Cup-winners' Cup final.

1992 Scored the free-kick that beat Sampdoria 1–0 in the final of the European
Champions' Cup at Wembley.

1992 A member of the Dutch side that lost in a penalty shoot-out to Denmark in the semi-
final of the European Championship.

1993 Scored a crucial free-kick against England in a World Cup qualifier, to send Holland
through to the 1994 World Cup.

1994 Appeared in his second World Cup finals, but Holland lost 3–2 to eventual winners
Brazil in the quarter-finals.

1995 Returned to Holland to play for Feyenoord and scored 10 goals in his first season.

Michael Laudrup

1964 Born on June 15 in Copenhagen.

1978 Joined youth section at Brondby.

1981 Made league debut aged 17 for KB Copenhagen before moving back to Brondby.

1982 Brilliant as a new kid on the block with Brondbyernes and was duly voted Footballer of the Year. Made his national team debut against Norway on his 18th birthday.

1984 Transferred by Brondby, where his father was youth coach, to Juventus – despite rival bids from the likes of Liverpool, Ajax and Anderlecht. Juventus loaned Laudrup out to Lazio.

1985 Recalled by Juventus as replacement for Zbigniew Boniek and helped them win the World Club Cup. Voted Denmark's Footballer of the Year for a second time.

1986 Starred at the World Cup finals in Mexico, above all inspiring Denmark's 6–1 thrashing of Uruguay in the Neza stadium in Mexico City.

1989 Grew tired of the disciplines of Italian football and transferred to Barcelona – winning the league championship with them for four successive years from 1991 to 1994.

1992 Missed Denmark's shock European Championship win after falling out with coach Richard Moller Nielsen over team selection and tactics.

1994 Omitted from Barcelona's team beaten by AC Milan in the European Champions Cup Final. Transferred to Barcelona's great rivals, Real Madrid, and returned to the Danish national team after making his peace with Moller Nielsen.

1995 Demonstrated his winning class by leading Real Madrid to their first league championship in five years.

1996 Captained Denmark at the finals of the European Championship and then moved on yet again, this time to Vissel Kobe in Japan – which was expected to mean the end of his national team career.

1997 Insisted on continuing to play for Denmark and returned to Europe to pick up his top level club career with Ajax Amsterdam.

Denis Law

1940 Born on February 22 in Aberdeen, Scotland, in the same week as another goalscorer supreme, Jimmy Greaves.

1955 Joined Huddersfield Town as a teenager, later coming under the guidance of a fellow Scot, manager Bill Shankly.

1959 Made his international debut for Scotland against Wales aged 18, the first of 55 caps and 30 goals – a Scottish international record until equalled by Kenny Dalglish.

1960 Sold to Manchester City for a British record £55,000.

1961 Sold to Italian club Torino for £100,000, then a world record, and including a £10,000 signing-on fee, but never settled in Italy despite achieving considerable popularity. Later that year he returned to Manchester, joining Matt Busby's United and raising the world record transfer fee to £115,000.

1963 Scored the first goal in helping Manchester United beat Leicester City 3–1 to win the FA Cup final, and scored for the Rest of the World against England on the same Wembley pitch.

1964 Chosen as European Footballer of the Year.

1965 Helped United to win the League Championship.

1967 Another Championship winners' medal, despite recurring injuries.

1968 Missed United's European Cup triumph against Benfica through knee trouble.

1973 Returned to Manchester City.

1974 Played his 452nd and last league game, scoring the City winner that condemned bitter derby rivals United to the Second Division. He scored more than 250 club goals during his league career.

1974 Played in his 55th and last international, against Zaire, in the 1974 World Cup finals, his only appearance in the competition.

Tommy Lawton

1919 Born on October 6 in Bolton, England.

1935 Joined Burnley as an amateur after scoring 570 goals in three seasons as a schooboy.

1936 Made his senior debut four days after his 17th birthday, against Tottenham, and became the youngest player in the Football League to score a hat-trick.

1937 Bought by Everton as a replacement for the great Dixie Dean for £6,500, a record for a teenager.

1938 First Division top scorer with 28 goals.

1939 Top again with 34 as Everton won the Championship, and at least one in all his first six internationals. A penalty on his debut, against Wales, made him England's youngest-ever scorer, at 19 years and 17 days – a record that stood until 1998.

1946 Resumed career after 24 goals in 23 wartime internationals. Sold to Chelsea.

1947 Scored 28 First Division goals, a club best.

1948 Joined Notts County, then in Division Three South, for £20,000 (a 25 per cent increase on the previous record). Won his last four caps with Notts, and ended his England career against Denmark with a 0–0 draw, having scored 22 goals in 23 full internationals.

1950 Shot Notts County to promotion with 31 goals.

1951 Became player-manager of Brentford.

1953 Reverted to player only, in order to have a final fling with Arsenal.

1955 Retired after 390 League games, 231 goals and not a single booking.

1956 Player-manager of non-league Kettering.

1958 A brief spell back at Notts County, as manager.

1972 Testimonial match at Everton raised £6,300.

1997 Died from pneumonia, aged 77.

otetotetN

otN

etN

etNN

etNN

etN

etN

Gary Lineker

1960 Born on November 30 in Leicester, England.

1977 Signed for Leicester City.

1979 January 1 marked the first of his career total of 430 Football League games.

1980 Helped City to promotion from Division Two.

1984 First of his 80 caps, as a substitute away to Scotland.

1985 First of his 48 England goals, against Eire at Wembley. Sold to Everton for £1.1 million.

1986 Footballer of the Year but a losing FA Cup Finalist despite scoring the first goal, against Liverpool. Then scored six in the World Cup finals, the highest ever by a British player, and was sold to Barcelona for £2.75 million.

1987 Scored all four for Barcelona against Real Madrid.

1988 Helped his club to win the Spanish Cup.

1989 In the Barcelona team which won the Cup-winners Cup, beating Sampdoria in the final. Sold to Tottenham for £1.2 million.

1990 Top First Division scorer for the third time with a third club – Leicester, Everton and now Spurs. Another four goals in Italia 90, making him one of only nine players to reach double figures in World Cup finals. Unable to prevent England losing to West Germany in a semi-final penalty shoot-out.

1991 Missed an FA Cup Final penalty (saved by Forest's Crossley) and had a goal disallowed, but finished a winner, 2–1.

1992 Lineker, without a goal in five games, was controversially taken off by coach Graham Taylor during the sixth, thus ending his career one short of Bobby Charlton's England scoring record. Voted Footballer of the Year for the second time.

1994 Went to Nagoya Grampus Eight in a "missionary" move to Japan that was badly hampered by a persistent toe injury.

1996 Retired from soccer and became a media figure.

Ally McCoist

1962 Born on September 24 in Glasgow.

1978 Left local minor football for Perth, and joined St Johnstone.

1979 Made senior debut and in his first season he played nine games plus six as substitute, all without scoring.

1981 Remarkable improvement led to his transfer to Sunderland for £300,000, but he struggled again.

1983 After 56 appearances and only eight goals, the first of them against Forest's Peter Shilton, he gladly returned to Scotland, to join Rangers (*see* page 61) (despite coming from a largely pro-Celtic family), and scored in the first minute of his debut – against Celtic! – and helped them to an incredible list of trophies. Possibly the best £180,000 they ever spent.

1986 Won his first Scotland cap, against Holland.

1992 Voted Scotland Player of the Year and won Europe's "Golden Boot" award for leading goalscorer with 34 goals.

1993 League Cup and Championship secured. Broke a leg in a World Cup qualifier against Portugal and missed another Scottish Cup Final victory.

1994 League Cup, Championship.

1995 Championship.

1996 After a 28-month absence from the national team, McCoist marked his return with a winner against Greece.

1996 Scorer of Scotland's only goal in Euro 96. Broke Scotland's post-war scoring record, 264, and won an eighth Championship, but missed another Scottish Cup through injury.

1997 Part of a Rangers team that equalled Celtic's record of winning nine Scottish Championship titles in a row.

1998 Began the year with 58 caps and 19 goals, but was left out of the World Cup party and joined the BBC commentary team.

Paul McGrath

1959 Born on December 4 in London.

1982 Signed for Manchester United in April after being spotted playing for junior Dublin side St. Patricks.

1985 Made his international debut for Republic of Ireland in a 2–1 defeat by Italy, playing in central midfield despite playing for his club in defence.

1985 Won a FA Cup winners' medal with Manchester United in a 1–0 victory against Everton

1988 Represented Republic of Ireland when they reached the European Championships for the first time in their history. Played in the 1–0 defeat of England.

1989 Transferred from Manchester United to Aston Villa for £400,000 after making 163 League injuries in a seven-year spell marred by knee injuries.

1990 Republic of Ireland reached the finals of the World Cup for the first time and McGrath played a central role in helping his country to the quarter-finals. He appeared in all of their five matches.

1994 Played in Aston Villa's 3–1 defeat of Manchester United in the League Cup Final.

1994 Played in all four of the Republic's matches during the World Cup Finals.

1996 Won a second League Cup winners' medal when Aston Villa beat Leeds 3–0.

1996 Transferred from Aston Villa to Derby County for £100,000 after making 252 league appearances for Villa.

1997 Made the last of his record 83 appearances for the Republic of Ireland, aged 37, in a 0–0 draw with Wales.

Billy McNeill

1940 Born March 2, Blantyre, Scotland.

1957 Signed professional forms for Celtic on his 17th birthday, although he had gone to a rugby-playing school in Hereford.

1959 Made the first of more than 600 senior appearances for his club, as a splendid central defender and skipper.

1961 Won his first cap – in the infamous 9–3 defeat by England – but survived the repercussions and made at least one appearance for his country for 11 successive seasons, gaining 29 caps in all.

1965 Voted Scotland's Footballer of the Year, and helped Celtic to win the Scottish Cup after an 11-year gap.

1966 League Cup, Championship.

1967 Captained Celtic to victory in every competition they entered – Scottish Cup, League Cup, Championship, and the European Cup. Celtic became the first British side to win the competition, with a torrid 2–1 victory against Inter Milan.

1968 League Cup, Championship.

1969 European Cup runner-up, Scottish Cup, League Cup, Championship.

1972 Made his last appearance for Scotland – like his debut it was against England, and although the Scots lost, it was only 1–0, an improvement on his debut result!

1974 Scottish Cup, Championship – his ninth in a row. In those nine years he appeared in 282 League games out of a possible 306, more than any other Celtic player.

1975 Retired after winning both domestic cups yet again. His final total: European Cup 1, Championship 9, Scottish Cup 7, League Cup 6, plus numerous second places.

1983 Became manager of Manchester City.

1986 Left City and became manager of Aston Villa.

1987 Villa were relegated and McNeill was sacked after only eight months in the job. He also had two spells as manager of his old club.

Sepp Maier

1944 Born on February 28 in Haar, Germany.

1960 Started making a name for himself as a teenage goalkeeper with regional league TSV
Haar. Impressed Bayern officials even though he was the goalkeeper on the wrong
end of Haar's 8–1 defeat in a junior league match!

1964 Turned professional with Bayern Munich.

1966 Made his debut for West Germany in a 4–0 win over the Republic of Ireland in
Dublin on the eve of the World Cup finals – for which he was the Germans' third-
choice keeper. That was the first of his 95 caps.

1967 Helped Bayern win the European Cup-winners Cup in extra time against Rangers in
Nuremberg.

1972 Collected another continental title, winning the European Championship with West
Germany.

1973 Won his first league championship with Bayern, despite being an object of fun for his
trademark long, baggy shorts.

1974 Reached the pinnacle of his career – winning the European Champions Cup on the
first of three occasions with Bayern and then the World Cup with West Germany in
his home stadium in Munich against Holland. Maier was the first goalkeeper ever
beaten by a penalty (from Johan Neeskens) in a World Cup final. That was in the first
minute, but Germany recovered to win 2–1.

1975 Invested much of his earnings in a centre specialising in what he called his "real
favourite sport" – tennis. Voted Footballer of the Year.

1976 Became a double world champion when Bayern defeated Cruzeiro of Brazil to win the
World Club Cup. Suffered one of only a few career setbacks when West Germany lost a
penalty shoot-out to Czechoslovakia in the European Championship Final in Belgrade.

1977 Voted Footballer of the Year twice in succession – in both 1977 and 1978. Forced by
injury to retire having played 473 league matches, including a record run of 422
consecutive games.

Paolo Maldini

1968 Born on June 26 in Milan.

1982 Joined Milan's youth system under the coaching direction of his father, Cesare
Maldini, a former Milan captain, Italian international – and future national team
manager.

1985 Made his Milan league debut in January in a 1–1 draw away to Udinese, at the age of
16 – sensational in Italian football.

1988 Won the first of five league championships with Milan under the managerial
guidance of one of his greatest fans, Arrigo Sacchi – who would later appoint
Maldini as national team captain. Also made his senior national team debut for Italy
in a 1–1 draw against Yugoslavia in Split.

1989 Won the first of three European Champions Cups (the other were in 1990 and 1994)
4–0 over Steaua Bucharest in Barcelona.

1990 Member of the Italian side which beat England 2–1 to finish third at the World Cup
staged on Italian soil, having lost to Argentina in the semi-final.

1994 One of the heroes of Milan's outstanding 4–0 thrashing of Spanish giants Barcelona
in the European Champions Cup Final in Athens – a particularly notable performance
because Maldini had to play in the centre of defence due to the absence through
suspension of regular skipper and Italian clubmate Franco Baresi. Was then one of
the heroes of Italy's run to the World Cup final, where his duel with Brazil's raiding
full-back Cafu was one of the highlights of the match (which Italy lost on penalties).
Was then voted World Player of the Year by the London magazine, *World Soccer*.

1996 Captained Italy during their disappointing European Championship performance in
England.

1997 Helped Italy beat Russia in the World Cup qualifiers play-off to secure their place in
the 1998 Finals.

1998 Led Italy to the quarter-finals of the 1998 World Cup finals, where they suffered
penalty-shoot-out heartache going out to eventual winners, France.

Diego Maradona

1960 Born on October 30 in Lanus, Buenos Aires.

1976 Made his league debut at 15 for Argentinos Juniors.

1977 Made his international debut at 16 for Argentina (*see* page 10) in a friendly against Hungary.

1978 Fell out with national coach Cesar Menotti after he being overlooked for the Argentine squad which won the World Cup in front of their home crowd.

1980 Sold to Boca Juniors for £1 million, a record for a teenager.

1982 Sold to Barcelona for another world record £3 million, then out of the game for four months after a reckless tackle by Bilbao's notorious defender, Andoni Goicochea.

1984 Sold to Napoli for a third world record, now £5 million.

1986 Inspired Argentina to victory at the World Cup finals in Mexico: was unanimous choice as Player of the Tournament, but made himself the most umpopular man in England with his "Hand of God" goal against England in the quarter-final.

1987 Led Napoli to their first-ever Italian league title plus victory in the Italian cup.

1988 Won his only European prize as Napoli beat Stuttgart in the UEFA Cup Final.

1990 Despite a collection of injuries, Maradona led Argentina back to the World Cup Final, where they were defeated 1–0 by West Germany.

1991 Failed a dope test and was banned for 15 months.

1992 Made a disappointing comeback with Sevilla in Spain.

1993 Sacked by Sevilla, Maradona began a second comeback in Argentina with Newells Old Boys.

1994 Banned again, for 15 months, after a positive drugs test during the World Cup.

1995 Returned briefly to playing with Boca Juniors after coaching stints with Deportivo Mandiyu and Racing Avellaneda.

1996 Retired again.

1997 Tried another brief comeback with Boca.

Lothar Matthäus

1961 Born on March 21 in Erlangen, Germany.

1977 Left school and studied interior design and decorating before deciding on a life in football.

1978 Turned professional with Borussia Mönchengladbach.

1980 Was a substitute for the West German side who won the 1980 European Championship – making his national team debut against Holland – the first of a national record 122 caps. Scored for Monchengladbach in their UEFA Cup Final defeat.

1984 Joined Bayern Munich for a then domestic record of £650,000.

1986 Established himself in the national side after scoring a magnificent winner against Morocco in the World Cup second round on the way to defeat by Argentina in the Final – where his task, despite a broken wrist, was to mark Diego Maradona.

1988 Moved to Italy with Internazionale for £2.4 million.

1990 Matthaus's career reached its zenith when he was not only West Germany's World Cup-winning captain in Rome, but was also voted Player of the Tournament by the world's media. Duly voted World, European and German Footballer of the Year.

1991 Won the UEFA Cup with Inter Milan and scored a penalty.

1992 Missed the European Championship finals – in which Germany lost to Denmark in the Final – because of a serious knee injury. Subsequently returned from Internazionale to Bayern Munich.

1993 Restored to the German side.

1996 Led Bayern from both midfield and sweeper roles to victory in the UEFA Cup.

1996 Missed the European Championships because of injury.

1997 German league champion with Bayern for the third time.

1998 Picked for the World Cup squad at the age of 37 and broke the record of 21 appearances in the final stages.

Stanley Matthews

1915 Born on February 1 in Hanley, Stoke-on-Trent.

1932 Turned professional with local club Stoke City and played his first league game for them aged only 17.

1933 Won Division Two honours with Stoke, something he repeated 30 years later.

1935 Made his debut for England in a 4–0 win over Wales in Cardiff.

1946 Sold to Blackpool for £11,500.

1948 Played a key role in one of England's greatest victories, by 4–0 over Italy in Turin, and was voted Footballer of the Year, the first time the award was made.

1953 Sealed his place among football's legends by inspiring Blackpool's FA Cup Final comeback against Bolton which came to be known as the "Matthews Final". Blackpool were 3–2 down with only three minutes remaining, and it seemed that Matthews was destined never to win the major domestic English honour, but he inspired his side as Blackpool to score twice and snatch a 4–3 victory.

1955 One of his many summer exhibition tours took him to Mozambique, where among the ball boys mesmerized at a match in Lourenzo Marques was Eusebio.

1956 Won the inaugural European Footballer of the Year award.

1957 Played the last of 84 games for England (including wartime internationals) aged 41 in a 4–1 World Cup qualifying victory over Denmark in Copenhagen. He won 54 official caps and scored 11 goals, including three in a 5–4 win over Czechoslovakia.

1961 Returned to Stoke for a mere £2,800 and, despite his 46 years, inspired their successful campaign to get back into the First Division.

1963 Won the Player of the Year award for the second time.

1965 After becoming the oldest player to appear in the First Division (a record that seems destined to remain unbroken), when he played for Stoke against Fulham aged 50 years and five days, he retired from the game a short while later, after a star-spangled Farewell Match at Stoke's Victoria Ground featuring the likes of Di Stefano, Puskas and Yashin. Was knighted for his services to soccer the same year.

Joe Mercer

1914 Born August 14, Ellesmere Port, Cheshire.

1932 Signed for Everton as a 16-year-old.

1939 Won First Division Championship. Also made his debut for England against
Scotland. Won four more caps that season but didn't play again after the war.

1946 Returned to Everton after serving as a physical training instructor during World War
Two and played 25 non-cap internationals for England. Troubled by a knee injury, and
transferred to Arsenal, where a career that appeared to be over got better as the years
passed.

1948 An inspirational skipper as Arsenal won the Championship.

1950 In tandem with manager Tom Whittaker, Mercer led Arsenal to a 2–0 FA Cup victory
over Liverpool. Voted Footballer of the Year.

1952 Perhaps his finest performance, as injury-battered Gunners held Newcastle in the FA
Cup final until a late, lone goal denied them victory

1953 His third Championship.

1954 Career ended by a broken leg in his 40th year.

1955 Became manager of Sheffield United.

1958 Took over at Aston Villa, helping them to promotion and the League Cup.

1964 Retired through ill-health but later joined Manchester City as manager, with Malcolm
Allison as coach. In 1967 they won promotion to Division One and the following
year won the Championship.

1969 Won FA Cup, thus completing the Double Double of both Cup and League as both
player and manager.

1970 Won Cup-winners Cup.

1972 Retired again.

1974 Had a seven-match spell as England's caretaker manager – won three, drew three, lost
one.

1990 Died on his beloved Merseyside, on his 76th birthday.

Roger Milla

1952 Born on May 20 in Yaoundé, real name Roger Albert Miller.

1967 Began making a teenage name for himself for Leopard of Douala, then transferred to Tonnerre Yaoundé.

1976 Voted African Footballer of the Year for the first time. Moved to French football with Valenciennes.

1980 Won his first European club prize by helping Monaco triumph in the French cup. Was then transferred to the Corsican club, Bastia.

1981 Proved a lucky mascot by winning the French cup again, this time with Bastia. Later moved on to Saint-Etienne and Montpellier.

1982 First appeared at the World Cup finals, leading Cameroon's attack in Spain. They were eliminated in the first round on goal difference in a group which included Poland, Peru and Italy – the prospective champions with whom Cameroon finished level on points!

1984 Won the African Nations Cup with Cameroon, beating Nigeria 3–1 in the Final.

1986 Runner-up in the African Nations Cup, Cameroon having lost on penalties in the Final against hosts Egypt in Cairo.

1990 One of the stars of the World Cup finals, after being persuaded out of retirement to return to the national team. Milla scored both Cameroon's goals in their 2–1 win over Romania in the first round, then the extra-time winner against Colombia in the second round after a blunder by South American keeper Rene Higuita. Delighted crowds with his celebratory dances around the corner flags. Duly voted African Footballer of the Year again, the first player to win the award twice.

1994 Persuaded out of retirement once again for the World Cup and became, at the age of 42, the oldest player ever to appear in the finals at USA'94. Also became the oldest to score a goal in the finals when he struck Cameroon's consolation in their 6–1 thrashing by Russia.

Bobby Moore

1941 Born April 12, Barking, England.

1958 Signed for his local team, West Ham, and went on to make 642 appearances in competitive matches – the club record.

1962 After playing for England Youth (winning a record 18 caps) and Under-23s, he won the first of his 108 international caps.

1964 Captained West Ham when they beat Preston North End in the last minute to take the FA Cup. Voted Footballer of the Year.

1965 Led the Hammers to another victory in a Wembley final, 2–0 against Munich 1860 in the European Cup–Winners' Cup.

1966 Moore's – and England's – finest hour-and-a-hal as he led his country to World Cup glory on home soil. In a pulsating final, Moore received the cup from the Queen after England win 4–2. Another Cup final, this time for West Ham, ended in a defeat against West Bromwich in the two-leg League Cup.

1970 Defeat by Germany in the World Cup quarter-final in Mexico, with Moore as calm as ever despite having being under arrest in Colombia, falsely accused of stealing a bracelet.

1973 His last cap (and his 90th as captain).

1974 Transferred to Fulham.

1975 Final Wembley appearance as Fulham are beaten 2–0 by his old club West Ham in the FA Cup Final.

1977 Retired after 150 games for Fulham, giving him a career total of exactly 900 for two clubs and his country. Later played briefly in the USA.

1984 Began a two-year spell as Southend manager.

1993 Died aged 53 in London after a courageous fight against cancer. Footballing stars from all around the world attended his funeral.

Stan Mortensen

1921 Born May 26 in South Shields.

1940 Joined the RAF as a wireless operator on the outbreak of World War Two, and was the only survivor when his bomber plane crashed.

1943 Having scored dozens of wartime goals he was an England reserve against Wales at Wembley, then played for the Welsh because they did not have a substitute of their own.

1947 Scored four against Portugal in Lisbon on his full international debut for England.

1948 Scored Blackpool's second goal in the FA Cup Final, but they lost 4–2 to Manchester United.

1950 Had the dubious honour of representing England in their first ever World Cup Finals. Tipped as pre-match favourites, England were dumped out of the tournament when they lost 1–0 to the USA and to Spain.

1951 Another Final, another defeat, this time 2–0 by Newcastle. Morty, ever the sportsman, shook Milburn's hand after his second goal.

1953 A FA Cup winners' medal at last, and he became the first man to score a hat-trick in a Wembley final. Despite Mortensen's goals which win Blackpool the cup 4–3 against Bolton, the final is rather unfairly called the "Matthews Final" in tribute to Mortensen's teammate Stanley Matthews. Later that year Morty scored his 23rd and last goal in his 25th international, the infamous 6–3 defeat by Hungary.

1955 Left Blackpool after 197 League goals, all in the top division, and 30 in the Cup. Joined Hull.

1957 Moved to Southport, later playing non-league with Bath and Lancaster.

1967 Began a two-year spell as Blackpool manager.

1989 Made a Freeman of Blackpool, where he had been prominent in civic affairs, and had auctioned his medals to help his old club through a tough spell.

1991 Died just before his 70th birthday. More than 700 people attended his funeral.

Alan Morton

1893 Born April 24 in Airdrie, Scotland.

1913 Joined Queens Park, playing as an amateur against professional opponents in Scotland's top division. He was naturally right-footed, but operated at outside-left and earned fame as "The Wee Blue Devil", a nickname given to him by an admiring English journalist.

1920 Capped twice at full international level, first against Wales in a 1–1 draw at Cardiff and then in a 3–0 thrashing of Northern Ireland. He then turned professional for Rangers. He was the first signing made by Will Struth, who was to manage the club for 34 years.

1921 Won the first of his Championship titles with Rangers.

1928 Although Morton stood a mere 5ft 4ins, was a mining engineer by profession and trained only in the evenings, his career lasted 20 years. The highlight was the 1928 5–1 win over England by the team who became known as the Wembley Wizards. Three of Scotland's goals were as a direct result of Morton's inch-perfect crosses.

1928 One of the great days in Rangers' history as Celtic were thrashed 4–0 in the final of the Scottish FA Cup. A crowd of 118,000 was present to see this fifth 'Old Firm' Cup final.

1930 Won the Scottish Cup for the second time against Partick.

1932 Won the last of his 31 caps aged 39 in a 3–1 win against France.

1933 Retired from playing after 495 games for Rangers, all in the first team, and 115 goals. During his time at Ibrox the club had won the Championship nine times and the Cup three times, and they achieved further glories during the next 30 years ,which he spent as one of their directors until he stepped down in 1968.

1971 Died peacefully in Glasgow at the age of 78.

Gerd Müller

1945 Born on November 3 in Zinsen, Bavaria.

1964 Joined Bayern from TSV Nordlingen at the insistence of president Wilhelm
Neudecker. Coach Tschik Cajkovski was not impressed, saying: "I can't put that little
elephant in among my string of thoroughbreds." But once he had done so, Bayern
never looked back. He went on to score well over 600 goals, including a record 365
in the Bundesliga.

1966 Müller shot Bayern to his first major trophy, the West German cup, with a 4–2
victory over Meideriecher SV. Made his senior national team debut in a 2–0 win over
Turkey in Ankara. Went on to score an astonishing 68 goals in 62 internationals for
West Germany.

1967 Won the European Cup-winners Cup with an extra-time victory over Rangers in
Nuremberg. Was voted Footballer of the Year for the first time – collecting the award
again in 1969. Was joint league top scorer with 28 goals, also collecting this accolade
in 1960, in 1970, in 1972, in 1973, in 1974 (jointly) and in 1978.

1969 Won the first of his five league championships with Bayern.

1970 A sensation at the World Cup finals in Mexico, being top scorer with 10 goals
including two in the remarkable semi-final defeat by Italy. His goals earned him
selection as European Footballer of the Year.

1974 Retired from the national team after scoring his most famous goal – the one with
which West Germany beat Holland in the 1974 World Cup Final in his home club
stadium in Munich. That same year Muller also helped Bayern Munich win the first
of three successive European Champions Cups – scoring twice in the 4–0 replay win
over Atletico Madrid.

1976 Became a double world champion as Bayern defeated Cruzeiro of Brazil to land the
World Club Cup. Later emigrated to the United States, where he played for Fort
Lauderdale in the North American Soccer League.

1995 Returned to Germany to take up a role on the Bayern Munich coaching staff.

Johan Neeskens

1951 Born on September 15. in Heemstede, Holland.

1968 Made his name in midfield with Haarlem – where Ruud Gullit would later begin his career, too.

1971 Helped Ajax win the first of their three European Champions Cups in a 2-0 victory over Panathinaikos at Wembley.

1972 Won the Champions Cup again, now firmly entrenched in midfield alongside Arie Haan, in a 2–0 win over Internazionale in Rotterdam.

1973 Completed the Champions Cup hat-trick – at the age of 22 – with Ajax's 1–0 win over Juventus in Belgrade.

1974 Starred for Holland as the midfield enforcer of the team who reached the World Cup Final before losing 2–1 to hosts West Germany in Munich. Under coach Rinus Michels, Neeskens was one of the key components in the "Total Football" Holland were encouraged to play. The concept of thrilled the world and deserved better than t lose out to the more pragmatic and dour approach of the Germans. Neeskens scored the most memorable of his 17 goals in 49 internationals when he earned a place in history by converting the first-ever World Cup Final penalty within the first two minutes of the match.

1975 Followed former Ajax team-mate Johan Cruyff to Barcelona.

1978 Won his only Spanish club trophy – the cup.

1978 Appeared in his second World Cup Finals, but again emerged a loser as Holland were beaten 3–1 by the host nation, Argentina.

1979 Key man in midfield as Barcelona won the European Cup-winners Cup – beating Fortuna Dusseldorf 4–3 after extra time in Basle.

1981 Wound down his career in the North American Soccer League, although he later tried an ill-fated comeback in Switzerland.

Gunter Netzer

1944 Born on September 14.

1961 Joined his only senior German club, Borussia Möenchengladbach, where he became the key midfield general in the side built by master-coach Hennes Weisweiler.

1965 Won the first of his 37 West German caps, against Austria.

1970 Won his first domestic honour as Borussia took the league championship.

1971 Won his second championship medal with Borussia.

1972 Seen at his very best in West Germany's successful European Nations Championship campaign. Having ousted Wolfgang Overath in midfield, Netzer forged an inspired creative partnership with Franz Beckenbauer which reached a peak when West Germany defeated the Soviet Union 3–0 in the Final in Brussels. On the way to the final, West Germany beat England in the quarter-final and the Belgians 2–1 in the semi-final.

1973 Was a West German cup-winner with Borussia and was voted Footballer of the Year for the second successive time.

1974 Lost his place in the national team to Overath as his team-mates went on to beat Holland 2–1 in the final – his only appearance in the World Cup finals being in the shock 1–0 defeat by East Germany in Hamburg in the first round. Transferred to Spain with Real Madrid.

1975 Won the first of two successive Spanish league championships with Real Madrid, who also won the Spanish cup in 1975.

1977 Left Spain for one last playing season with Grasshopper in Switzerland.

1978 Retired from playing and returned to German football as general manager of Hamburg, overseeing their 1979 league title win and run to the 1980 European Champions Cup Final (where they lost 1–0 to Nottingham Forest in Netzer's old "home" at the Real Madrid stadium).

Wolfgang Overath

1943 Born on September 29, 1943.

1961 Turned professional – part-time at first – with Köln.

1963 Key young member of the Köln side which won the first Bundesliga championship – scoring 83 goals in 409 league games with his only club up until his retirement in 1977.

1963 Made his senior national team debut for West Germany in a 3–0 win over Turkey in Frankfurt. Overath entered the game late on as a second-half substitute for Timo Konietzka.

1966 Now a fixture in midfield but unable to spark West Germany as they finished World Cup runners-up to England in a 4–2 thriller at Wembley.

1970 Avenged England's 1966 World Cup triumph by helping to beat them in the quarter-final, and then scored the goal with which West Germany secured third place at the World Cup finals, defeating Uruguay 1–0 in the semi-final losers' play-off.

1971 Dropped from the national team in favour of Gunter Netzer after a disappointing 0–0 draw at home to Poland in Hamburg in the European Championship qualifying competition.

1974 Timing his return to form to perfection, he regained his place in the West German team from Netzer in time to help guide his country to a 2–1 World Cup victory over the Dutch in front of a delirious home crowd. By doing so, Overath thus became one of the handful of players in history to have finished winner, runner-up and placed third in the World Cup. He had achieved just about every honour in world football he retired from the national team after the World Cup Final victory over Holland, having scored 17 goals in 81 internationals.

1978 Honoured with selection for the World XI which played Brazil in Rio de Janeiro.

Pele

1940 Born on October 21 in Tres Coracoes. Universally known as Pele, but full name is Edson Arantes do Nascimento.

1950 Began playing with local club Bauru, where his father was a coach.

1956 Transferred to big-city club Santos and made his league debut at 15.

1957 Made his debut for Brazil, aged only 16, against Argentina and scored.

1958 Became the youngest-ever World Cup winner, scoring two goals in the final as Brazil beat Sweden 5–2. In the semi-final Pele had scored a hat-trick in the 5–2 demolition of France.

1962 Brazil won the World Cup for a second time but Pele missed the final win against Czechoslovakia because of injury in the first round. But he compensated for the disappointment by winning the World Club Cup with Santos.

1963 Won the World Club Championship for a second time with Santos.

1970 Inspired Brazil to complete their historic World Cup hat-trick in Mexico. Pele sparked Brazil's rampage that destroyed Italy in the final with the opening goal, his fourth of the tournament. The final scoreline of 4–1 proved to the world that this Brazilian team was the best the world had ever seen.

1971 Won the last of his 111 international caps having scored 97 goals in that time (77 goals from 92 matches on a stricter international definition).

1974 Retired from the game.

1975 Ended an 18-month retirement to play for Cosmos of New York in the dramatic, short-lived North American Soccer League.

1977 Retired again after lifting Cosmos to their third NASL championship. This time it was permanent and Pele could look back on a career in which he had scored 1281 goals in 1363 matches.

1982 Presented with FIFA's Gold Medal Award for outstanding service to the worldwide game.

1994 Appointed Brazil's Minister for Sport.

Michel Platini

1955 Born on June 21 in Joeuf, France.

1972 Joined Nancy from AS Joeuf.

1976 First appeared on the international stage at the 1976 Olympic Games in Montreal.

1978 His first World Cup, in Argentina, where Platini gave an indication of the great things to come.

1979 Moved to St Etienne.

1982 Inspired France to fourth place at the World Cup when he was man of the match in the dramatic semi-final defeat by West Germany in Seville. After the finals Platini was sold to Juventus.

1983 The first of three seasons in which he was the Italian league's top scorer. Was also voted European Footballer of the Year and subsequently became the only player to win the accolade three years in a row.

1984 The greatest year of his career. Platini was captain and nine-goal top scorer as hosts France won the European Championship. He scored the first goal in the 2–0 victory over Spain in the final at Parc des Princes in Paris.

1985 Converted the penalty kick which brought Juventus their long-awaited European Champions Cup victory over Liverpool (albeit overshadowed by the Heysel tragedy).

1987 Shocked French and Italian football by retiring while still comparatively young to concentrate on commercial interests and TV work. He had scored 348 goals in 648 matches, including 41 from 72 international appearances.

1990 Persuaded back into football as national manager and guided France to the finals of the 1992 European Championship. France disappointed, and Platini left the job to become joint head of the team set up by the French federation to organize the 1998 World Cup finals.

1996 Turned down the official proposal that the new World Cup stadium in Paris should be named after him. It thus became, instead, the Stade de France.

Ferenc Puskas

1927 Born on April 2 in Budapest.

1943 Made his debut for his father's old club, Kispest.

1945 Played his first international for Hungary against Austria aged only 18. He went on to play 84 times for Hungary and scored a record 83 goals.

1948 Transferred with the entire Kispest playing staff to the new army club, Honved, and top-scored with 50 goals in the League championship. Because of his army connections he became known as the "Galloping Major".

1952 Captained Hungary to victory over Yugoslavia in the final of the Olympic Games soccer tournament in Helsinki.

1953 Earned a place in history by inspiring Hungary's historic 6–3 victory over England at Wembley.

1954 Played despite injury, amid controversy, in the World Cup Final which Hungary lost 3–2 to West Germany in Berne – their first defeat for four years.

1956 Stayed in western Europe when the Hungarian Revolution broke out while Honved were abroad to play a European Cup tie against Bilbao.

1958 Signed for Real Madrid by his old manager at Honved, Emil Oestreicher. For the Spanish club, he scored an amazing 35 goals in 39 European matches.

1960 Scored four goals for Madrid in their famous 7–3 demolition of Eintracht Frankfurt in the European Cup Final at Hampden Park, Glasgow.

1962 Played in the World Cup finals in Chile, this time for his adopted country of Spain.

1966 Retired and turned to coaching.

1971 Achieved his greatest success as a trainer, guiding outsiders Panathinaikos of Athens to the European Cup Final (they lost 2–0 to Ajax at Wembley).

1993 Appointed, briefly, as caretaker-manager of Hungary during the 1994 World Cup qualifiers.

Frank Rijkaard

1962 Born on September 30 in Surinam.

1979 Turned professional with Ajax under the management of Johan Cruyff.

1981 Made his senior national team debut for Holland against Switzerland despite protests from Ajax that he should not have been picked because at the age of 18 he was too young.

1987 Won the European Cup-winners Cup with Ajax, was then appointed captain after the departure for Milan of Marco Van Basten... and fell out with manager Cruyff.

1988 After hardly playing for Ajax in the first half of the 1987–88 season, Rijkaard was sold to Sporting of Lisbon in the spring – and then sold on to Milan in the summer. In between he was a key man in the centre of defence as Holland won the European Championship in West Germany in blissful style, avenging their 1974 defeat in the World Cup Final by the Germans by beating them 2–1 in the semi-final, before defeating the Soviet Union 2-0 in the final in Munich.

1989 Milan coach Arrigo Sacchi described Rijkaard as: "So good I don't know which position to use him in." In fact he played midfield for Milan as they won the Champions Cup, beating Steaua Bucharest 4-0 in the final in Barcelona, the biggest winning margin in a Final since 1974.

1990 Won a second successive Champions Cup with Milan, this time beating Benfica 1–0 in Vienna.

1990 Experienced a miserable World Cup in Italy; Holland slumped and Rijkaard was sent off against Germany.

1993 Played virtually his last game for Milan in the 1–0 defeat by Marseille in the European Champions Cup Final in Munich. Afterwards Rijkaard returned to Holland with Ajax.

1995 Played his last game against Milan, helping Ajax beat them 1–0 in the Champions Cup Final in Vienna – thus joining the handful of players who have won the competition with different clubs. Retired at the season's end.

Bryan Robson

1957 Born January 11, Chester-le-Street.

1975 Joined West Bromwich from local amateur football in the North-East, making his senior debut at 18. Despite two broken legs and numerous other injuries, he went on to become an outstanding midfielder, with a strong tackle, excellent passing ability and a spirit that adversity never quenched.

1980 The first of 90 England caps (65 as captain, and 26 goals).

1981 Joined his former manager, Ron Atkinson, at Manchester United, for £1.5 million – then the British record fee.

1982 Scored in the first minute of England's first match in the World Cup Finals (a goal often wrongly credited as being the fastest in the tournament's history).

1983 The first of three FA Cup-winning appearances as United captain (followed by 1985 and 1990).

1984 Scored a hat-trick against Turkey, becoming the first England skipper to get three in a match for 75 years.

1986 Dislocated a shoulder in a friendly before the World Cup, then did it again in the second of England's games in the tournament. The team reached the quarter-final, but lost to Argentina.

1990 Another injury kept Robson out of the later stages of the World Cup, in which his team reached the semi-final before losing to West Germany.

1991 Captained the United team to victory in the European Cup–Winners' Cup, beating Barcelona.

1993 Club captain as United ended a 25-year gap by winning the Championship, although he made only five full appearances.

1994 Appointed player-manager of Middlesbrough,

1995 Boro promoted to the Premiership as champions of the new First Division.

1997 Boro relegated, despite Robson's huge spending on transfers. They also reached the League Cup and FA Cup Finals for the first time, and lost both.

Romario

1966 Born on January 29 1966 in Rio de Janeiro. Full name Romario Da Souza Faria.

1983 Joined Olario Juniors.

1985 Scored four goals against Vasco da Gama and impressed so much they signed him.

1988 Finished top scorer at the Seoul Olympics with seven goals.

1989 Having scored 73 goals for Vasco da Garma in 123 matches he moved to Dutch side PSV Eindhoven.

1990 Travelled to the World Cup in Italy with the Brazilian squad but played only 65 minute after criticizing selection policies. Manager Carlos Alberto Parreira was so incensed by his outbursts he later banned him from the Brazilian squad for the 1994 qualifying games.

1991 A broken leg sidelined him for much of the year.

1993 After a turbulent spell at PSV where he often fell out with team-mates and complained about the weather he was bought by Johan Cruyff, manager of Barcelona, for £3 million. He had scored 125 goals for PSV. Scored a hat-trick in his first game for his new club.

1993 Brought back into the Brazilian side to face Uruguay in the vital match that would decide who qualified for USA 1994. Romario scored the two goals that won the match for Brazil 2–0.

1994 Showed his true colours with some masterful displays during the 1994 World Cup in the USA. He scored five goals in the tournament, including the 81st-minute winner against Sweden in the semi-final that sent Brazil through to the final, where they beat Italy.

1995 Returned to Brazil to play for Flamengo.

1997 A regular once again in the Brazilian side, Romario scored the winner against England during Le Tournoi competition in France.

1998 Was selected for the 1998 World Cup but had to pull out through injury.

Ronaldo

1976 Born Ronaldo Luiz Nazario da Lima on September 22 in Belo Horizonte, Brazil.

1989 Scored eight goals in 12 matches for junior club Social Ramos in Rio before being spotted by former Brazilian legend Jairzinho.

1990 Moved to Sao Cristovao and scored 36 goals in 54 matches over the next two seasons.

1993 Having been rejected by Brazilian giants Flamengo, he joined Cruzeiro and scored 58 goals in 60 matches.

1994 Made his international debut for Brazil against Argentina. Travelled with the national squad to the World Cup Finals but didn't play.

1994 Moved to Europe to join PSV Eindhoven and scored 35 goals in his first season.

1995 Runner-up with Brazil in the Copa América.

1996 Won the Dutch Cup with PSV.

1996 Voted World Footballer of the Year.

1996 Won an Olympic bronze medal with the Brazilian side.

1996 Moved to Barcelona for £13 million at the start of the season having scored 55 goals for PSV in just 56 matches.

1997 Scored the penalty that won Barcelona the European Cup-Winners Cup. Also collected a winners' medal in the Spanish Cup.

1997 Voted World Footballer of the Year for the second consecutive year.

1997 After negotiations with Barcelona broke down, he moved to Internazionale of Milan for a record £19.5 million in June, having scored 47 goals for Barcelona in only 49 matches.

1998 Was highly impressive for Brazil scoring four goals in the World Cup and helping them to the final – his performance there was surrounded in controversy as post-match reports suggested that he had suffered a fit the evening before.

Paolo Rossi

1956 Born on September 23 in Prato, Italy.

1972 Moved from Prato to the Juventus youth system but they gave him away to Como on a free transfer in 1975 after operations on both knees.

1976 Signed for Lanerossi Vicenza in Serie B and his 21 goals in 36 games shot them to promotion.

1977 Made his Serie A debut with Juventus.

1978 Emerged from the league shadows to star for Italy at the World Cup finals, scoring in the victories over France, Hungary and then, in the second round, Austria.

1979 Perugia paid a world record £3.5million to sign Rossi from relegation-bound Vicenza.

1980 Perugia were relegated and Rossi was suspended for two years after being convicted of alleged involvement in a betting-and-bribes scandal.

1981 Juventus bought Rossi from Perugia for £650,000 while he was still in the middle of his suspension.

1982 Was only three matches out of his ban when Italy took him to the World Cup finals, where he top-scored with six goals and collected a winners' medal from the Final victory over West Germany in Madrid, where he opened the scoring. His finest hour, however, came in the the thrilling quarter-final win over favourites Brazil where he scored a stunning hat-trick as Brazil crashed out 3–2. Voted European Footballer of the Year and World Footballer of the Year.

1984 Helped Juventus win the Cup-Winners' Cup with a 2–1 defeat of Porto.

1985 Won the European Champions Cup with Juventus against Liverpool at the Heysel stadium in Brussels, a match marred by the deaths of Juventus fans caused by crowd trouble.

1986 Starred for Juventus with the World Club Cup then retired, aged 29, because of recurring knee trouble. He had scored 20 goals in 48 internationals for Italy.

Karl-Heinz Rummenigge

1955 Born on September 25 in Lippstadt.

1974 Gave up his job as a bank clerk when Bayern Munich paid Lippstadt just £4,500 for their young, blond right-winger.

1976 Rummenigge collected his only Champions Cup winners medal as Bayern beat St. Etienne 1–0 in Glasgow. Later he also won the World Club Cup with Bayern against Cruzeiro of Brazil. Made his West German national team debut versus Wales, the first of 95 international appearances which also brought 45 goals.

1978 Shot to international stardom at the World Cup finals in Argentina, scoring twice in a 6–0 win over Mexico and once in a 3–2 defeat by Austria.

1980 Key influence in West Germany's European Championship victory – as well as providing the corner from which Horst Hrubesch headed the injury-time winner in the final against Belgium in Rome.

1981 Elected European Footballer of the Year for the second successive season.

1982 As captain of Germany he carried a leg injury throughout the World Cup finals in which he eventually finished as a runner-up to Italy. In the semi-finals, it was the introduction of substitute Rummenigge in extra time which was crucial to Germany's recovery from 3-1 down to 3-3 against France – and then winning on penalties.

1984 Bayern sold Rummenigge to Internazionale of Italy, a decade after he joined them, for more than £2 million.

1986 Finished a World Cup runner-up again, this time in a 3–2 defeat by a Diego Maradona-inspired Argentina.

1987 Moved from Inter to Servette Geneva in Switzerland.

1989 Retired and moved into television commentating.

Ian Rush

1961 Born October 20, Flint, Wales.

1978 Joined Chester and made his debut at 17.

1980 Cost Liverpool a £300,000 fee when still only 19, but went on to repay it many times over with his splendid scoring record and general all-round usefulness. In the same year he won the first of 73 Welsh caps.

1981 Gained his first medal League Cup final replay against West Ham.

1982 Won the League Cup and the Championship.

1983 A third League Cup and a second Championship.

1984 League Cup No. 4 ,Championship No. 3, a European Cup, 48 goals in all games, and Footballer of the Year..

1986 A fourth Championship and a first FA Cup, Rush scoring twice against Everton.

1987 On the losing side in the League Cup final against Arsenal – the first time Liverpool had lost after a Rush goal in 140 games: won 118, drawn 21. Went to Juventus for £3.2 million, but did not settle in Italy.

1988 Rejoined Liverpool for £2.8 million.

1989 Ill for part of the season, but returned in triumph as a substitute in the FA Cup final and scored twice – against Everton again.

1990 Rush's fifth Championship medal.

1992 A fifth FA Cup Final goal, against Sunderland, and a third victory.

1995 A record fifth League Cup final win, this time as captain against Bolton.

1996 His Liverpool career ended with him as the club's highest scorer in history, as well as being the top scorer in the FA Cup competition and in FA Cup finals this century, joint top for the League Cup, and top for Wales. Went to Leeds but scored only three goals in almost a full season, often being used in midfield.

1997 Another surprise transfer, this time joining old pal Kenny Dalglish at Newcastle.

Peter Schmeichel

1963 Born November 18 in Gladsaxe, Denmark.

1975 Joined local club Gladsaxe Hero.

1984 Moved to Hvidovre and made his debut for Denmark Under-21s.

1987 Transferred to Brondby and capped for Denmark in the 5–0 win against Greece.

1988 Helped Brondby to win the Danish Championship and kept goal for his country in the Olympic qualifying tournament.

1989 Another winner in his home country, this time in the Danish Cup.

1991 Manchester United signed him in a bargain £500,000 deal and he made his debut in August in a 2–0 win over Notts County.

1992 Helped Denmark to their surprise victory in the European Championship, making vital saves against Holland in the semi-final and Denmark in the final. Denmark had only entered the tournament at the last minute after Yugoslavia were banned because of the political unrest in their country.

1993 United won the first of the new Premiership titles, and their first Championship title since 1967, and much of it was due to the acrobatics and skill of Schmeichel's goalkeeping.

1994 By this time he was perhaps the world's best goalkeeper, helping United to the Championship-and-Cup double, only the fourth club this century to achieve such a feat.

1995 A loser in the FA Cup Final to Everton, and a runners-up medal in the Premiership.

1996 A star again as United did the double for the second time in three years, an achievement unmatched in English soccer. Represented Denmark in the European Championships, but no repeat of the 1992 success. Passed 85 caps for his country.

1997 A fourth Championship in only five seasons, and a semi-final place in the European Cup. Even in his mid-thirties, Schmeichel was still in superb form as he approached 250 appearances for United.

1998 Helped Denmark qualify for the 1998 World Cup.

Vicenzo 'Enzo' Scifo

1966 Born on February 19 in Le Louviere, Belgium, the third son of Sicilian parents.

1973 Played for a local club when aged seven, alongside his elder brother.

1982 Made his debut for Anderlecht aged 17 and was an instant goalscoring success.

1983 Came to the attention of the Italian national coach, but Enzo took up Belgian citizenship and signed a new contratc with Anderlecht.

1984 Collected a UEFA Cup loser's medal when Anderlecht lost to Tottenham Hotspur in penalty shoot-out.

1984 Made his international debut for Belgium and played in the European Championships.

1985 Won the Belgian league and cup double.

1986 Won a second consecutive championship medal with Anderlecht.

1986 Played a starring role for Belgium when they made their best-ever showing at the World Cup Finals – fourth place after losing to eventual winners Argentina in the semi-finals.

1987 Won the Belgium Cup with Anderlecht before moving to Italy and Internazionale Milan for a season.

1988 Loaned from Inter to French club Bordeaux.

1989 Loaned again to another French side, Auxerre.

1990 Resurrected his career with an accomplished performance for Belgium in the 1990 World Cup Finals.

1990 Moved back to Italy and Torino, whom he helped to the 1992 UEFA Cup Final.

1993 Torino forced to sell Enzo to Monaco because of financial problems.

1994 Appeared in his third World Cup finals

1998 Having rejoined Anderlecht, he was chosen for his fourth World Cup.

David Seaman

1963 Born on 19 September in Rotherham, England.

1982 Joined Peterborough United for £4,000 after serving his apprenticeship at Leeds.

1984 Transferred to Birmingham City for £100,000.

1986 Moved to Queens Park Rangers for £225,000.

1988 Made his debut for England in a 1–1 draw with Saudi Arabia.

1990 Moved to Arsenal for £1,300,000, a then record for an English goalkeeper.

1991 Won a championship winners' medal with his new club having kept 29 clean sheets in his first 50 matches.

1993 Won FA Cup and League Cup winners' medal, as Arsenal beat Sheffield Wednesday in both finals.

1994 A member of the Arsenal side that beat Parma 1–0 in the final of the European Cup-Winners' Cup.

1995 Came to Arsenal's rescue in a penalty shoot-out against Sampdoria in the semi-finals of the Cup-Winners' Cup. Arsenal played Real Zaragoza in the final but a lucky strike from Nayim defeated the holders.

1996 Performed heroics in the England goal during the European Championships, particularly in the quarter-final penalty shoot-out with Spain. Couldn't prevent Germany from winning their semi-final clash.

1997 Troubled by a rib injury but still kept 13 clean sheets out of 28 matches.

1997 A member of the England team that drew 0–0 with Italy in Rome and secured their place in the 1998 World Cup Finals. It was his 38th cap.

1998 A broken finger sidelined him for much of the season but he played in his second winning FA Cup final, for Arsenal against Newcastle, and in the World Cup.

Uwe Seeler

1936 Born on November 5 in Hamburg.

1952 Joined his father's old club, Hamburg, at the age of 15.

1954 The West German national squad was badly hit by illness so the young Seeler was called up for his international debut against France as substitute for Termath. He was only 17. His first international start was in the subsequent 3–1 defeat by England at Wembley. In all, he scored 43 goals in 72 internationals.

1958 Played in the first of his four World Cup finals as West Germany made it to the semi-finals before losing 1–0 to hosts Sweden.

1960 Won his only German league championship, with Hamburg. Was voted the first German Footballer of the Year. Collected the honour again in 1964 and 1970.

1961 Narrowly failed to reach the European Champions Cup Final when Hamburg lost in a semi-final play-off to Barcelona.

1963 Won the German cup with Hamburg.

1964 Top scorer with 30 goals in the first-ever unified Bundesliga championship.

1966 Seeler captained West Germany in their World Cup Final defeat against England at Wembley – 12 years after first appearing on that ground.

1968 Captained Hamburg in the final of the European Cup-Winners Cup against AC Milan.

1970 Gained a measure of revenge against England by scoring a remarkable back-headed goal when Germany won 3–2 in extra time in the dramatic quarter-final. Seeler and Pele are the only men to have scored in four World Cups. The third-place match against Uruguay was Seeler's last for his country and his 21st – then a record – in the World Cup finals.

1971 Seeler retired after playing for Hamburg throughout his career from 1952, loyally rejecting a string of offers from Italy and Spain.

1996 Returned to Hamburg as club president.

Alan Shearer

1970 Born August 13 in Newcastle.

1986 Joined Southampton from minor soccer in the North-East.

1988 Went on as a substitute in March for his Southampton debut against Chelsea. Made his full debut a few games later, against Arsenal, aged 17 years and 240 days, and scored a hat-trick – the youngest First Division player ever to do so in his first full game.

1991 Made England Under–21 debut and scored 13 goals in his 11 internationals.

1992 Made his senior international debut, and scored a brilliant goal against France, but a knee injury kept him out of the England team in the 1992 European Championships. In the same year he joined Blackburn for £3.3 million, then a British record fee, after scoring a moderate 23 goals in 118 matches for Southampton.

1993 After suffering a serious knee injury on Boxing Day 1992, Shearer was out of action for eight months. In the 1993–94 season, however, he hit 31 goals in 40 matches.

1995 His goals helped Blackburn win the Premiership title for the first time since 1914. Shearer was voted Player of the Year.

1996 Scored 31 League goals, becoming only the second player ever to pass 30 in the top division in each of three successive seasons (David Halliday did it it four seasons running for Sunderland in the 1920s). First player to reach 100 goals in the Premiership.

1996 After sensational form in the European Championships – he finished top scorer with five goals – where England reached the semi-final, he was sold to Newcastle for £15 million, almost double the existing British transfer record.

1997 Scored 25 goals in 31 League games for his new club and took his England record to 16 goals in 35 appearances. In a pre-season friendly he suffered an horrific ankle injury that threatened his career.

1998 Returned to action after a lengthy spell out and immediately showed much of his old form. He led England to the second round of the 1998 World Cup finals.

Peter Shilton

1949 Born 18 September in Leicester.

1965 Made his Football League debut for Leicester as a 16-year-old.

1969 Played in his one and only FA Cup Final, a 1–0 defeat for Leicester against Manchester City.

1971 Made his England debut against East Germany at Wembley.

1974 Joined Stoke City and spent three seasons with the club.

1977 Transferred to Nottingham Forest, where he came under the command of Brian Clough at the peak of his managerial powers. With Forest he won the European Champions Cup in 1979 and 1980, the League title in 1978 and the League Cup in 1979.

1982 Played in the World Cup in Spain where he made five appearances, the first of 17 World Cup matches. England remained unbeaten throughout the tournament and in his five matches Shilton let in only one goal. Transferred from Nottingham Forest to Southampton.

1986 Played in all five of England's World Cup matches and again limited the opposition scoring opportunities; three goals in five games, but England lost controversially to Argentina and Maradona's "Hand of God" in the quarter-finals.

1987 On the move again, this time to Derby County.

1990 Made his 125th and last appearance – an English record – in the third/fourth play-off match in the World Cup. In the semi-final against Germany he had been beaten by only a looping deflection off one of his own players to beat him. England finished fourth, their best result for 24 years. During those 125 appearances, Shilton conceded a mere 80 goals.

1992 Became player-manager of Plymouth Argyle.

1996 After further spells with Bolton and West Ham, Shilton played in his 1000th league match on 22 December at the age of 47. Shilton kept a clean sheet as Third Division Leyton Orient won 2–0 against Brighton.

Graeme Souness

1953 Born 6 May in Edinburgh.

1969 Having played for Scotland Schools, Souness joined Tottenham Hotspur as an apprentice.

1970 Turned professional but first-team chances were limited and made only one appearance, as a sub in the 1971 UEFA Cup.

1973 Joined Middlesbrough for £32,000.

1974 Made his Scotland debut against East Germany – the first of 54 caps.

1978 Transferred to Liverpool, where he made a total of 352 appearances and scored 56 goals. He won just about every major club honour available including five Football League titles, four League Cups and three European Cups.

1984 Moved to Italian club Sampdoria.

1986 Returned to Scotland in April to become Rangers' new player-manager. In his first full season, his new club won the Scottish League title and Cup. In the next five years he continued to win a host of trophies for Rangers including the championship title in 1988–89, 1989–90 and 1990–91 (the last being achieved shortly after his departure). The structure set in place at the club continued long after his departure and Rangers won their ninth consecutive title in 1997.

1990 Caused controversy when he signed Mo Johnston, the first high-profile Catholic to join Rangers.

1991 Stunned Rangers when he quit to become manager of Liverpool.

1992 Despite having undergone extensive heart surgery only weeks before, Souness was present to see Liverpool beat Sunderland to lift the FA Cup.

1994 After continued criticism, Souness resigned as manager of the club in January.

1995 Became manager of Turkish side Galatasaray.

1996 Appointed manager of Southampton.

1997 Resigned as manager of Southampton to take up an appointment with Torino, but soon left to join Benfica in Portugal.

Hristo Stoichkov

1966 Born on August 2 in Plovdiv.

1985 Suspended by the Bulgarian federation after becoming involved in player mayhem during the domestic cup final between Stoichkov's CSKA Sofia and old rivals Levski.

1987 Won his first international cap against Belgium.

1989 Won the first of four consecutive Bulgarian Footballer of the Year awards.

1990 Bought by Barcelona from CSKA after winning three league titles for a Bulgarian record £2 million in 1990, on the specific personal recommendation of coach Johan Cruyff. Shared the "Golden Boot" award for Europe's leading scorer with Mexico and Real Madrid star Hugo Sanchez, who also scored 39 goals in the season.

1992 Helped Barcelona achieve their dream by winning the European Champions Cup. Stoichkov nearly did not play against Sampdoria at Wembley after falling out with Cruyff over a transfer offer from Napoli. The match went to extra time but the Spanish club emerged 1–0 winners.

1993 Furious when voted only runner-up to Roberto Baggio in the European Footballer of the Year poll.

1994 Was the inspiration from an attacking midfield role in Bulgaria's best-ever fourth-place finish at the World Cup finals. They had started terribly with a shock 3–0 defeat by Nigeria but Stoichkov was in inspirational form. He finished the World Cup joint top scorer with six goals – and thus earned the European Footballer of the Year prize.

1996 Captained Bulgaria to first-round elimination at a disappointing European Championships, and then boycotted the national team after falling out with the federation over various issues.

1997 Made peace with new national coach Hristo Bonev in time to return to duty.

1998 World Cup campaign is a disaster for Stoichkov and Bulgaria.

Carlos Valderrama

1961 Born on September 2 in Santa Marta, Columbia.

1977 Joined local club Santa Marta.

1987 Starred for Colombia at the Copa America finals in Argentina and was then voted South American Footballer of the Year.

1988 Moved to Europe with Montpellier.

1990 Won the French cup with Montpellier, led Colombia to the second round of the World Cup finals after a solid first round draw with eventual winners West Germany. In the next round they lost to the surprise package of the tournament, Cameroon. Then transferred to Spain with Valladolid, under the managership of Colombian boss Pacho Maturana.

1992 Returned home to Colombia and rediscovered his old form with Atletico Junior of Barranquilla and then Nacional of Medellin.

1993 Inspired Colombia to a sensational 5–0 win over Argentina in Buenos Aires in the World Cup qualifying competition and was duly voted South American Footballer of the Year for the second time.

1994 One of the few Colombian players to have done themselves justice in a disappointing – and ultimately tragic – first-round failure at the World Cup finals. Touted as one of the pre-tournament favourites, Colombia sank without trace, losing first to Romania and then the USA. In the game against the United States, centre-back Andres Escobar had inadvertently scored an own goal. A few days after returning home, he was shot dead.

1997 Became the first Colombian player to reach a century of international appearances, in a World Cup qualifying match.

1998 Colombia qualified for the 1998 World Cup in France where the priority wasn't football but to honour the memory of former team-mate Escobar.

The Great Players

Marco Van Basten

1964 Born on October 31 in Utrecht.

1980 Signed by Ajax after being spotted during the club's annual youth talent "gala."

1983 Hit the international headlines for the first time as centre-forward with Holland at the World Youth Cup finals.

1986 Won the Golden Boot for the top league marksman in Europe thanks to his 37 goals for Ajax in the 1985–86 season.

1987 Captained Ajax to victory in the European Cup-winners Cup Final victory over Lokomotiv Leipzig, and scored the winning goal. Then, having scored 128 league goals in Holland, he was sold for a bargain £1.5 million to Milan.

1988 Van Basten's attacking partnership with fellow Dutchman Ruud Gullit helped inspire Milan to their first league title win in nine years – and then brought Holland European Championship victory over the Soviet Union. Holland won the final 2–0 in Munich and Van Basten's goal, an exquisite volley from wide out – Holland's second – was hailed as one of the greatest in international history. Voted European Footballer of the Year.

1989 Won the European Footballer of the Year award for a second time and scored twice as Milan beat Steaua Bucharest 4–0 in the final of the European Champions Cup.

1990 Van Basten and Holland experienced World Cup misery as they crashed out in the second round phase, losing 2-1 to West Germany.

1992 Voted World and European Footballer of the Year. Rejected medical advice to cut short his career after suffering a string of serious ankle injuries, only to miss a decisive penalty in the European Championship semi-final shoot-out against Denmark after he had performed brilliantly in normal time. In 58 appearances for his country he scored 24 goals.

1993 Made a brave comeback for Milan in the European Champions Cup Final but they lost 1–0 to Marseille in Munich – and that proved to be his last game.

Gianluca Vialli

1964 Born on July 9 in Cremona, Italy.

1980 Made the first of 105 appearances for Cremonese.

1984 Transferred to Serie A side Sampdoria.

1985 Made his debut for Italy in a 1–0 defeat by Poland.

1985 Won the Italian Cup

1988 Won a second Italian Cup winners' medal.

1989 Won the Italian Cup for a third time and picked up a losers' medal against Barcelona in the final of the European Cup-Winners' Cup.

1990 Scored twice for Sampdoria in the 2–0 defeat of Anderlecht in the European Cup-winners' Cup.

1991 Won the league title with Sampdoria.

1992 Made the last of his 59 appearances for Italy against Malta.

1992 Moved to from Sampdoria having scored 85 league goals in 223 appearances.

1993 Collected a UEFA Cup winner's medal with a 6–1 aggregate win over Borussia Dortmund.

1995 Part of the Juventus side which won the Italian league and cup double.

1995 Scored the Juventus goal in the 2–1 defeat by Parma in the final of the UEFA Cup.

1996 Completed a full set of European medals when Juventus defeated Ajax in the final of the Champions Cup.

1996 Joined Chelsea from Juventus on a free transfer.

1997 Went on as a sub during the FA Cup Final against Middlesbrough and picked up a winner's medal in the 2–0 victory.

1998 Replaced Ruud Gullit as manager of Chelsea.

1998 Left himself out of the starting line-up in the Coca-Cola Cup Final against Middlesbrough at the end of March. Chelsea won 2–0 and Vialli collected the trophy. He also took the Cup-winners' Cup after his team beat Stuttgart.

George Weah

1966 Born on October 1 in Monrovia, Liberia.

1988 Taken to French club Monaco by manager Arsène Wenger after being spotted playing for Cameroon side Tonerre Yaounde.

1989 Struggled early on his career as civil war raged in his homeland, but developed an understanding with team-mate Glenn Hoddle that gave him confidence.

1989 Won the first of three African Footballer of the Year awards.

1991 Won the French league title with Monaco.

1992 Collected a European Cup-Winners' Cup losers' medal with Monaco, defeated 2–0 by Werder Bremen in the final.

1992 Moved to Paris Saint-Germain.

1993 Won the French cup with Paris Saint-Germain.

1995 Transferred to AC Milan for what turned out to be a bargain £3.5 million after the Milan staff had seen him in action for the Paris club when the two sides met in the Champions Cup.

1994 Voted African Footballer of the Year

1995 Awarded European Footballer of the Year after rules were relaxed to allow a player of any nationality to win, and picked up his third African Footballer of the Year award.

1996 Voted FIFA World Footballer of the Year and dedicated the award to his former Monaco manager Arsène Wenger.

1997 Despite scoring a superb solo goal to give Liberia a 1–0 win against Egypt in a World Cup qualification match, his country didn't make it through to France 98.

1998 Christened the "Light of Liberia" for his hard work in helping the people his country recover from war.

Billy Wright

1924 Born on February 6 in Shropshire.

1940 Signed by the legendary Major Buckley for his only club, Wolverhampton Wanderers, even though Buckley thought he was probably too small to make the grade.

1946 Made his England debut against Northern Ireland – the first of Wright's then-record 105 caps. Of those, 51 were won at right-half, 46 at centre-half and eight at left-half. He captained England in 90 of his 105 matches.

1949 Captained Wolves to a 3–1 victory against Leicester City in the FA Cup Final.

1950 Played at wing-half and then centre-half, being a key member of the first England side to appear at the World Cup finals, in Brazil in 1950. Unfortunately, it was not a memorable experience as England lost 1–0 to the USA and to Spain, and crashed out. Also played in the finals in Switzerland in 1954 and in Sweden in 1958.

1952 Voted Footballer of the Year.

1954 Led Wolves to the club's first League Championship title.

1958 Collected another Championship title with Wolves.

1959 Won his 100th cap against Scotland and his third championship title with Wolves before he retired prior to the start of the following season after being omitted by Wolves manager Stan Cullis for a pre-season warm-up match. He had played in 490 league matches for the club, and a grand total of 541 peacetime appearances.

1959 Played his 105th and last international, against the USA. He missed only three of England's first 108 matches after the Second World War. Awarded the CBE for services to football.

1962 Wright moved into management with Arsenal.

1966 Parted company with Arsenal and moved into television as a match analyst and executive with independent television in the Midlands.

1990 Made a director at Wolves.

1994 Died at the age of 70.

Lev Yashin

1929 Born Lev Ivanovich Yashin on October 22 in Moscow.

1946 Joined Moscow Dynamo as an ice hockey goaltender.

1951 Made his first-team debut for Moscow Dynamo. He went on to win the Russian League five times with Dynamo.

1953 Finally took over as Dynamo's first-choice keeper after "Tiger" Khomich suffered a long-term injury.

1954 Made his Soviet Union senior debut in a 3–2 win over Sweden.

1956 Goalkeeper with the Soviet side that won the Olympic Games gold medal in Melbourne.

1960 Star of the Soviet side that won the inaugural European Nations Championship, beating Yugoslavia in the final in Paris.

1962 Played in his second World Cup Finals in Chile but under-performed in the USSR's shock defeat against the hosts in the quarter-final.

1963 Became the only goalkeeper to win the European Footballer of the Year presented by Paris magazine *France Football*. Played for FIFA's World XI at Wembley in a match to mark the centenary of the Football Association.

1966 Played in his third successive World Cup finals – this time in England – helping the Soviet Union to a best-ever fourth place after losing 2–1 to West Germany in the semi-final.

1967 Won the last of his 78 caps for the USSR.

1968 Awarded the Order of Lenin by the Soviet government.

1971 Such was Yashin's fame and reputation that Pele, Eusebio, Bobby Charlton and Franz Beckenbauer were among world superstars who flew to Moscow to play in his farewell match. He was appointed manager of Dynamo the next day as a reward for services rendered.

1990 Died tragically from cancer in Moscow and was mourned throughout the world.

Zico

1953 Born on March 3 in Rio de Janeiro (as Artur Antunes Coimbra) but nicknamed Zico from an early age.

1968 Youngest of three professional football brothers, and at first considered too lightweight when he signed for Flamengo. Special diets and weight training were prescribed.

1975 Scored with one of his speciality free-kicks on his Brazil debut against Uruguay. He went on to score 66 goals in 88 internationals.

1977 Won his first South American Footballer of the Year award.

1978 Went to the World Cup finals hailed as the "white Pele" but proved a flop after squabbling over tactics with coach Claudio Coutinho, and Brazil had to watch rivals Argentina win the cup.

1981 Inspired Flamengo to victory over Cobreloa in the South American Club Cup final then to a memorable 3–0 win over European champions Liverpool in the World Club Cup final in Tokyo.

1981 Voted South American Footballer of the Year for the second time.

1982 Probably Zico's best personal World Cup – even though Brazil were surprisingly eliminated in the second round by a Paolo Rossi-inspired Italy. Won the South American Footballer of the Year award for the third time. Moved from Flamengo to Italian club Udinese.

1985 Transferred back to Flamengo.

1986 Plagued by injury during the World Cup Finals in Mexico, and never fulfilled his potential. He played in the thrilling quarter-final clash with France, but at one apiece after extra time, Zico missed his spot kick in the penalty shoot-out and Brazil were eliminated.

1992 Retired from playing and was appointed Brazil's Sports Minister.

1993 Returned to playing for Kashima Antlers to help launch the new J-League in Japan.

Dino Zoff

1942 Born on February 28 in Mariano del Friuli, Italy.

1967 Transferred to Napoli after graduating through Udinese and Mantova.

1968 Made his debut for Italy in a 2–0 win over Bulgaria in April and then held the job to
help Italy win the European Championship for the first time, in a replay win over
Yugoslavia in Rome.

1972 Hit the big-time aged 30 when he transferred to Italian giants Juventus, with whom
he won the UEFA Cup in 1977 as well as five Italian league titles and two Italian cup
wins.

1974 Set a world record of 1,143 international minutes (12 matches) without conceding a
goal – until he was beaten by Haiti's Emmanuel Sanon in Italy's first match at the
World Cup finals in West Germany. The goals conceded against Poland and
Argentina meant Italy were knocked out at the first hurdle.

1978 A better World Cup for Zoff and Italy as they reached the third-place decider before
losing 2–1 to Brazil.

1982 Emulated Juventus' pre-war keeper Gianpiero Combi by captaining Italy to World
Cup victory over West Germany in Spain. The Final was the 106th cap of Zoff's
career.

1983 Retired after playing a record-breaking112 internationals in a career that spanned
three decades, and having made 570 First Division and 74 Second Division
appearances in the Italian league.

1988 Appointed coach to Juventus.

1990 Zoff guided Juventus to success in the 1990 UEFA Cup when they beat Fiorentina
3–0 on aggregate.

1992 Left Juventus for Rome club Lazio, where he subsequently rose from coach to
executive director.

Andoni Zubizarreta

1961 Born on October 23 in Bilbao.

1981 Discovered by Athletic Bilbao while playing for minor regional club Alaves in the heart of his native Basque region.

1984 Played for Spain when they lost to England in the Under–21 European Championship.

1985 Made the first of a record 100-plus international appearances for Spain after appearing as a second-half substitute for Luis Arconada in a 3–1 victory against Finland.

1985 Won the Zamora Trophy – in honour of Spain's goalkeeper in the 1930s – for the best Spanish goalkeeper.

1986 Sold by Bilbao to Barcelona for a then world record fee for a goalkeeper of £1.2 million – the first goalkeeper to be transferred for over £1 million. Played in his first World Cup Finals as Spain lost to Belgium on a penalty shoot-out in the quarter-finals.

1990 A disappointing World Cup for Spain ended in the second round, when they lost 2–1 to Yugoslavia after extra time.

1992 Kept goal in the Barcelona side which achieved the club's long-overdue ambition of winning the European Champions Cup, in a 1–0 extra-time defeat of Sampdoria at Wembley.

1993 Overtook Jose Camacho's record of 81 international appearances for Spain in a World Cup qualifier against the Republic of Ireland in Dublin.

1994 Joined Valencia, reviving his career after being released on a free transfer by Barcelona, who were seeking scapegoats after their 4–0 defeat by Milan in the Champions Cup Final. Played in his third World Cup as Spain lost to Italy in the quarter-finals.

1997 Played regularly for Spain as they qualified comfortably for France 98.

1998 Appeared in his fourth World Cup.

The Great Matches

The prospect of great players scoring great goals on the great occasions is the lure which fills the stadia. Often, the big match will not live up to its billing. The passes are wasted, the shots fly wide. But once every so often a game unfolds which features all the disparate elements which make soccer such great theatre. Cup finals lend themselves easily to such a status. It's sudden death for one team or the other, the outcome resting on one man's mistake or another man's flash of genius.

That's why the 1994 World Cup Final remains in the memory: not because of the quality of the football – two tired teams could produce precious little – but because of the dramatic penalty failures of Franco Baresi and Roberto Baggio in the decisive shoot-out after extra time. Thus it is no accident that the World Cup and the European Cup have produced probably a greater share of great games than other competitions. It is logical that the greatest players produce the greatest football – and they are brought into conflict in the greatest competitions. Real Madrid's 7–3 defeat of Eintracht Frankfurt in the 1960 Champions Cup Final remains popularly established as the greatest game of all. Great players such as Alfredo Di Stefano and Ferenc Puskas reached the peak of their careers. Those fans with longer memories might argue for Hungary's 4–2 defeat of Uruguay in the 1954 World Cup semi-final. Those whose football memories rest largely on the projection of the age of colour television might well opt for Italy's thrill-a-minute 4–3 victory over West Germany in the 1970 World Cup semi-finals. That was simply... great.

White Horse Cup Final 1923

April 28, 1923
Wembley, London,
FA Cup Final

Bolton Wanderers 2
(Jack 3, Smith, J.R., 55)
West Ham United 0

Half Time:
1–0.
Attendance:
126,047 (officially, though many thousands more forced their way in)
Referee:
D. D. H. Asson (West Bromwich)
Bolton:
Pym, Haworth, Finney, Nuttall, Seddon, Jennings, Butler, Jack, Smith, J.R., Smith, J., Vizard.
West Ham:
Hufton, Henderson, Young, Bishop, Kay, Tresadern, Richards, Brown, Watson, Moore, Ruffell.

King George V was there, and somehow a match was laid on for him which, through good fortune and the crowd's good sense, was not the tragedy it might have turned out. Otherwise, the first event staged at the now historic Wembley Stadium might well have been the last. Such was the over-crowding that there could have been a disaster beyond even the awful proportions of Heysel or Hillsborough. Thanks to the self-discipline of the fans in a less impatient age, and to the police – led by Constable George Scorey on his legendary white horse, Billy – the Cup Final took place, starting almost an hour late. The match was not ticket-only, and nobody had anticipated such an enormous turn-out at the new stadium, built as part of the complex to house the Empire Exhibition. The ground was estimated to have a capacity of 125,000, but the combination of a fine spring day, the new arena and the appearance of a London club in the Final (even if a Second Division club) led to an estimated 250,000 trying to gain admittance – and mostly succeeding.

Many who had bought seats were unable to claim them in the crush. Some of the Bolton directors, travelling separately from the team, did not see a ball kicked, but the match went on and football entered the mass consciousness.

The first goal, by David Jack, came as an opponent was trying to climb back out of the crowd next to the touchline; and the second, by the Scot, Jack R. Smith, was thought by some observers to have rebounded from a post, but had in fact bounced back from the wall of spectators pressed against the back of the netting.

Uruguay vs. Argentina 1930

July 30, 1930
Centenario, Montevideo
World Cup Final

Uruguay 4

(Dorado 12, Cea 57, Iriarte 68, Castro 90)

Argentina 2

(Peucelle 20, Stabile 37)

Half Time:

1–2.

Attendance:

93,000

Referee:

J. Langenus (Belgium)

Uruguay:

Ballesteros, Nasazzi, Mascharoni, Andrade, Fernandez, Gestido, Dorado, Scarone, Castro, Cea, Iriarte.

Argentina:

Botasso, Della Torre, Paternoster, Evaristo, Monti, Suarez, Peucelle, Varallo, Stabile, Ferreira, Evaristo.

Few newspapers outside South America and Central Europe bothered to report the match. The Belgian referee John Langenus wore a tie and plus-fours, and several players covered their heads with handkerchiefs to keep the sun at bay. What little film survives shows a near laughable standard of goalkeeping and defensive technique. Yet this game went into history simply because it could not be repeated. The first World Cup was over, and international football now had a standard to surpass.

Soccer statesmen Guérin from France and Hirschman from Holland had mooted the idea of a World Cup and brought it to fruition, even though only 13 nations turned up, including a mere four from Europe. Uruguay, celebrating 100 years of independence, guaranteed to refund all expenses of the other competing nations, just managed to get a new stadium built in time, and fittingly reached the final. There were no seeds, just four groups, each of which sent one team to the semi-finals, where Yugoslavia and the United States both lost 6–1. So the final pitted hosts against neighbours, with thousands crossing the River Plate to play their part in a deafening climax to the fledgeling tournament.

The Uruguayans took the lead, fell behind, then went ahead again at 3–2 before striker Guillermo Stabile hit their crossbar. Castro, who had lost part of an arm in childhood, then headed the goal which clinched Uruguay's victory, to be greeted by a national holiday in his country… and bricks through the windows of the Uruguayan Embassy in Buenos Aires.

Germany vs. England 1938

May 14, 1938
Olympic Stadium, Berlin
Friendly International

Germany 3
(Gauchel 20, Gellesch 42, Pesser 70)

England 6
(Bastin 12, Robinson 26, 50, Broome 36, Matthews 39, Goulden 72)

Half Time:
2–4

Attendance:
103,000

Referee:
J. Langenus (Belgium)

Germany:
Jakob, Janes, Muenzenberg, Kupfer, Goldbrunner, Kitzinger, Lehner, Gellesch, Gauchel, Szepan, Pesser.

England:
Woodley, Sproston, Hapgood, Willingham, Young, Welsh, Matthews, Robinson, Broome, Goulden, Bastin.

One of England's most effective displays followed a shameful incident brought about by political pressures of the era. In an effort to placate Hitler, still furious at the way the majority of his athletes had been humbled in the same stadium at the 1936 Olympics, the England team were ordered to join the Germans in giving the Nazi salute as the German national anthem was played. The instruction came from the British Ambassador, Sir Neville Henderson, supported by Stanley Rous (later Sir Stanley), then FA secretary. The players, unwilling to make a fuss, reluctantly got on with it, then showed their feelings by beating a very good German team out of sight. Stanley Matthews said later that he and his team-mates had been inspired by hearing – despite the roars of the German fans – "a few piping voices from behind one goal shouting: Let'em have it, England." Don Welsh, one of two men making their England debut, was to say later: "You couldn't have asked for a greater team performance than this. Only when the heat got to us in the second half did we have to slow down a bit. I honestly thought we could have scored ten." Jackie Robinson, only 20, was a perfect partner for Matthews, and little Len Goulden hit a tremendous 30-yard goal to add to his all-round industry. The other debutant, Frank Broome, also scored. An unsung hero in defence was wing-half Ken Willingham, who barely allowed the German star, Fritz Szepan (nicknamed Saucepan by England's players), a kick.

Brazil vs. Uruguay 1950

July 16, 1950
Maracana, Rio de Janeiro
World Cup final pool

Brazil 1

(Friaca 47)

Uruguay 2

(Schiaffino 66, Ghiggia 79)

Half Time:

0–0

Attendance:

199,000

Referee:

G. Reader (England)

Brazil:

Barbosa, Da Costa, Juvenal, Bauer, Alvim, Bigode, Friaca, Zizinho, Ademir, Jair, Chico.

Uruguay:

Maspoli, Gonzales, Tejera, Gambetta, Varela, Andrade, Ghiggia, Perez, Miguez, Schiaffino, Moran.

Figures for the attendance vary from source to source, but this was certainly the highest at any soccer match since Wembley 1923. The first post-war World Cup, played without a knockout final stage, provided what was in effect a final and established the tournament as the leading worldwide soccer competition. Even England were in it this time, having snubbed the three pre-war events. They failed miserably, however, struggling to beat Chile, then losing to the United States and Spain. So the Spaniards went through to the final pool, with Brazil, Uruguay and Sweden, and the fixtures worked out perfectly.

Brazil, overwhelming favourites, beat Sweden 7–1 and Spain 6–1. Uruguay trailed both Spain and Sweden 2–1, but drew the first game and won the second. So they had to beat Brazil at the enormous newly-built Maracana, while Brazil needed only to draw. Coach Flavio Costa seemed the only Brazilian unsure of victory, but his warnings about previous encounters in which Uruguay had disturbed Brazil went unheeded.

Even after winger Friaca hit their 22nd goal in six games, Brazil kept pressing forward: Costa later protested that he had ordered men back into defence, but his words had gone either unheard or unheeded. Uruguay, remarkably calm amid the crescendo, equalized through Schiaffino. Then Ghiggia slipped through on the right and shot between Barbosa and his near, left-hand post: not a great goal, but an historic one. Uruguay's inspiration was their attacking centre-half and skipper Obdulio Varela. After listening to manager Juan Lopez's gloomy team-talk, he told his players: "Forget all that. Keep your heads and your positions – and we can win this."

Blackpool vs. Bolton 1953

May 2, 1953
Wembley, London,
FA Cup Final

Blackpool 4
 (Mortensen 35, 68, 89, Perry 90)

Bolton Wanderers 3
 (Lofthouse 2, Moir 41, Bell 55)

Half Time:
 1–2

Attendance:
 100,000

Referee:
 M. Griffiths (Wales)

Blackpool:
 Farm, Shimwell, Garrett, Fenton, Johnston, Robinson, Matthews, Taylor, Mortensen, Mudie, Perry.

Bolton:
 Hanson, Ball, Banks, Wheeler, Barrass, Bell, Holden, Moir, Lofthouse, Hassall, Langton.

Stanley Matthews, at 38, stood football on its head. He gained a Cup-winners' medal after being on the losing side twice, he played a barely credible part in his team's winning rally from two down (the first of only two such recoveries in Wembley history) and he persuaded the hidebound FA to add him to their party to go to South America a few days later, after they had left him out on the grounds of his age.

Blackpool's victory now appears to have been achieved by fate as much as their footballing ability: in Coronation Year, with Everest climbed, the Ashes regained and Gordon Richards winning his first Derby, how could unfancied, homespun Bolton have won the Cup?

But they very nearly did, in a game of remarkable drama, poor goalkeeping – the first, third, fifth and sixth goals ought to have been stopped – and tactical naivety. In the last half-hour, Bolton kept both goalscorer Eric Bell, limping badly from a first-half injury, and Ralph Banks, also hobbling on bravely, on their left (this was 13 years before substitutes). That was also Blackpool's right, the flank which Fenton and Taylor ensured was stuffed full of passes for the shuffling, mesmerizing genius that was Matthews.

In the incredible final moments, after the other Stanley, Mortensen, completed his hat-trick (still the only one in a Wembley FA Cup Final) with a free-kick, and Matthews had made the winner for Perry, the scoreboard momentarily showed the score as 4–4. Even today, when the talk is of cup finals, 1953 is usually No. 1.

England vs. Hungary 1953

November 25, 1953
Wembley, London
Friendly International

England 3
   (Sewell 15, Mortensen 37, Ramsey 62 pen)
Hungary 6
   (Hidegkuti 1, 20, 56, Puskas 22, 29,
   Bozsik 65)
Half Time:
   2–4
Attendance:
   100,000
Referee:
   L. Horn (Holland)
England:
   Merrick, Ramsey, Eckersley, Wright,
   Johnston, Dickinson, Matthews, Taylor,
   Mortensen, Sewell, Robb.
Hungary:
   Grosics (Geller 74), Buzansky, Lantos,
   Bozsik, Lorant, Zakarias, Budai, Kocsis,
   Hidegkuti, Puskas, Czibor.

Why were England so confident? Did they not know that Hungary went to Wembley having won 25 and drawn six of their previous 32 games, and having scored in every match they had played for six seasons? Yet England, fielding two debutants in a team averaging more than 30 years of age, still looked on the match as something of a training spin, fooled by a xenophobic Press which had little or no direct knowledge of Ferenc Puskas and his colleagues. "This will be easy," said one England player as the teams walked out, "they've all got carpet slippers on."

Indeed, Hungary's footwear did look like slippers compared with England's thunderous boots, but they could smack the ball pretty hard when they needed to, as Nandor Hidegkuti did in the opening seconds, from 20 angled yards, his shot arrow-straight past goalkeeper Gil Merrick.

The Hungarians played in tight little triangles, then suddenly opened up with a raking pass of 30, 40, 50 yards or more to a sprinting colleague. They gave the impression that they could always score a goal if they really needed to – and skipper Puskas scored one marvellous individual goal which is still considered one of the greatest of all time.

The defeat, clear and unequivocal, was England's first by a continental invader. That was not in itself important, but the manner and margin of the massacre forced a furious tactical rethink in succeeding seasons. So great a rethink that it is fair to consider whether, without the shock treatment administered by Puskas and Co., England would have won the World Cup 13 years later.

Brazil vs. Hungary 1954

June 27, 1954
Wankdorf, Berne
World Cup quarter-final

Brazil 2

(D. Santos 18 pen, Julinho 65)

Hungary 4

(Hidegkuti 4, Kocsis 7, 90, Lantos 55 pen)

Half Time:

1–2

Attendance:

40,000

Referee:

A. Ellis (England)

Brazil:

Castilho, Santos, D., Santos, N., Brandaozinho, Bauer, Pinheiro, Julinho, Didi, Humberto, Indio, Maurinho.

Hungary:

Grosics, Buzansky, Lantos, Bozsik, Lorant, Zakarias, Toth, M., Kocsis, Hidegkuti, Czibor, Toth, J.

This violent clash between two outstanding teams had a cleansing effect on soccer for a short time. The appalling scenes and continuing controversy served to warn players and officials that football could go close to anarchy unless all concerned showed some respect for the traditions of the game as well as for its rules.

Hungary's part in this disgrace made a lot of people glad when they eventually lost the final, although victory in the world championship would have been a fitting reward for a team of majestic power. Some of the blame must attach to referee Ellis, who sent off three players but never had the match under control.

Hungary, 2–0 up within eight minutes, showed unseemly arrogance, and a wild tackle cost them a penalty, halving their lead. When another penalty enabled them to go two up again, after most people felt that Kocsis had committed the foul, Brazil lost their heads.

Offence followed offence on both sides of Julinho's second goal for Brazil, until Ellis eventually sent off Bozsik (a member of the Hungarian Parliament) and Nilton Santos for fighting, followed by Humberto for a deliberate kick. Kocsis headed a clinching goal in the last seconds, but the violence spilled over into the dressing-rooms, and Ellis needed an armed guard.

FIFA abstained from punitive action, but the Hungarian authorities threatened all sorts of sanctions if there was any repetition. In the semi-final, three days later, Hungary – with nine of their quarter-finalists in action again – played superbly, and cleanly, to beat Uruguay 4–2. The lesson had been learned.

West Germany vs. Hungary 1954

July 4, 1954
Wankdorf, Berne
World Cup Final

West Germany 3
(Morlock 10, Rahn 18, 82)
Hungary 2
(Puskas 6, Czibor 8)
Half Time:
2–2
Attendance:
60,000
Referee:
W. Ling (England)
West Germany
Turek, Posipal, Kohlmeyer, Eckel,
Liebrich, Mai, Rahn, Morlock, Walter O.,
Walter F., Schaefer.
Hungary:
Grosics, Buzansky, Lantos, Bozsik,
Lorant, Zakarias, Czibor, Kocsis,
Hidegkuti, Puskas, Toth, J.

German fortitude overtook Hungarian class in a thrilling final, played with great speed and skill despite steady rain. The match was perhaps the first major indication that West Germany's well-organized methods could prove too much for technically superior opposition. Germany have been a force in virtually every World Cup since, whereas Hungary have rarely approached the heights of the Puskas era.

The game also showed the benefit of tactical awareness. German coach Sepp Herberger had fielded only six of his eventual finalists in an earlier group game, which Hungary won 8–3, gambling on doing well in the play-off against Turkey that this defeat would bring. Sure enough, the Turks were beaten 7–2, and Germany went into the quarter-finals and then on to eventual victory.

Ironically, Puskas could be held responsible for his team's defeat. He had been injured in the qualifying game against the Germans a fortnight earlier and had not played since. Although he said he was fit, and scored the first goal, he was nowhere near 100 per cent. The offside decision by linesman Mervyn Griffith that prevented what would have been his late equaliser was another decisive blow. Two early goals took Hungary's total for the tournament to 27, still the record for all finals, but two defensive errors enabled Germany to level with only 18 minutes gone. More than another hour passed before the powerful Rahn – a late addition to the squad after his international career had seemed over – shot Germany's third. Hungary had lost for the first time in 32 games, and the Germans had outsmarted the rest.

Real Madrid vs. Reims 1956

May 13, 1956
Parc des Princes, Paris
European Cup Final

Real Madrid 4
(Di Stefano 15, Rial 30, 80, Marquitos 72)
Reims 3
(Leblond 4, Templin 11, Hidalgo 63)
Half Time:
2–2
Attendance:
38,238
Referee:
A. Ellis (England)
Real Madrid:
Alonso, Atienza, Lesmes, Munoz, Marquitos, Zarraga, Joseito, Marsal, Di Stefano, Rial, Gento.
Reims:
Jacquet, Zimny, Giraudo, Leblond, Jonquet, Siatka, Hidalgo, Glovacki, Kopa, Bliard, Templin.

The European Champions Club Cup at last struggled into life, having been conceived and forced through a difficult birth by Gabriel Hanot, a former French international full back and by now the editor of the influential daily newspaper, *L'Equipe*. Only 16 clubs were invited to compete – not all of them national champions: Hibernian, who reached the semi-finals, had finished only fifth in Scotland the previous season.

England, still insular, did not take part, Chelsea meekly complying with a Football League ruling that a European tournament would complicate the fixture list. Attack was the order of the day, or night, in those earlier, more innocent times. The 29 games contained 127 goals (an average of 4.37 per match), with Real scoring 20 and Reims 18, while attendances averaged 31,000. The tournament was a winner, beyond any shadow of doubt.

So too were Real, inspired off the field by far-seeing president Santiago Bernabéu and on it by Alfredo Di Stefano, arriving from Argentina via a brief stop in Colombia's rebel, unrecognized league. Real's exploits over this and the next few seasons established them at the top of the Spanish and European trees, proving the wisdom of Bernabéu's expenditure on a ground capable of holding 125,000. Reims scored two early goals and – under Raymond Kopa's direction – Real had arranged to sign him immediately afterwards – took the lead again later. But Real, on a then huge bonus of £400 each, battled on to earn the first of their five successive European victories. A great team had arrived.

Brazil vs. Sweden 1958

June 29, 1958
Rasunda, Stockholm,
World Cup Final

Brazil 5

(Vava 9, 30, Pele 55, 90, Zagalo 68)

Sweden 2

(Liedholm 4, Simonsson 80)

Half Time:

2–1

Attendance:

49,737

Referee:

M. Guigue (France)

Brazil:

Gilmar, Santos, D., Santos, N., Zito, Bellini, Orlando, Garrincha, Didi, Vava, Pele, Zagalo.

Sweden:

Svensson, Bergmark, Axbom, Borjesson, Gustavsson, Parling, Hamrin, Gren, Simonsson, Liedholm, Skoglund.

Brazil's victory over the host nation in Stockholm proved to a vast audience – thanks to the spread of television – that South Americans can, after all, travel well. The team deservedly went into history as one of the greatest ever, after wonderful performances in the semi-final (5–2 against France) and the final, when they overcame an early deficit with unstoppable power.

Manager Vicente Feola had restored Didi, thought by some to be too old at 30, and preferred Vava to 19-year-old Mazzola as striker. These changes worked well, as did Feola's decision to bring back Djalma Santos in defence after Di Sordi had played all the previous games in the final stages. Santos, thought Feola, had the pace necessary to deal with brilliant Swedish left-winger Lennart Skoglund – and so it proved.

Perhaps the most crucial decision in Brazil's path to glory, however, was made by the players and their insistence that Feola find a place for Garrincha on the right wing. Feola somewhat reluctantly agreed – and Garrincha, often tantalisingly inconsistent, responded superbly. His speed left the Swedes for dead to make two goals for Vava, and Pele conjured a magical third, controlling a long cross from Mario Zagalo on one thigh, flicking the ball over his head, whirling and shooting, all in a fraction of a second.

After adding the final goal, Pele dissolved in tears of joy on the shoulders of veteran goalkeeper Gilmar. Pele, perhaps the greatest player ever, had made a worldwide mark on the sport he would later describe as "the beautiful game". At 17 he was the youngest ever winner of a competition he would still be dominating 12 years later.

Real Madrid vs. Eintracht Frankfurt 1960

May 18, 1960
Hampden Park, Glasgow
European Cup Final

Real Madrid 7
  (Di Stefano 27, 30, 73, Puskas 36, 48 pen, 58, 63)
Eintracht Frankfurt 3
  (Kress 18, Stein 72, 80)
Half Time:
  3–1
Attendance:
  127,621
Referee:
  A. Mowat (Scotland)
Real Madrid:
  Dominguez, Marquitos, Pachin, Vidal, Santamaria, Zarraga, Canario, Del Sol, Di Stefano, Puskas, Gento.
Eintracht Frankfurt:
  Loy, Lutz, Hofer, Weilbacher, Eigenbrodt, Stinka, Kress, Lindner, Stein, Pfaff, Meier.

Real Madrid's fifth successive European Cup was achieved by their greatest performance in front of yet another great crowd. In their seven matches they scored 31 goals and were watched by 524,097 people – an average of nearly 75,000 per game. In the semi-final, Real beat Barcelona 3–1 home and away, after Barça had crushed Wolves, the English champions, 9–2 on aggregate. In the other semi-final, Eintracht performed the barely credible feat of twice scoring six goals against Rangers, but in the final they conceded hat-tricks to Di Stefano and Puskas in a wonderful performance watched by a crowd so big that only one larger attendance has been recorded in Britain since. Hardly any left early, even though the Germans were a beaten team well before the end. The fans stayed to bay a seemingly never-ending roar of tribute to one of the finest displays ever put on by any team, anywhere. The Scots were quick to appreciate their good fortune.

Real were now under their fourth coach in five years, wing-half Miguel Munoz from their 1956 team having taken over. His two signings, Del Sol and Pachin, augmented an already illustrious squad, with the Uruguayan Santamaria a rock in defence, Gento a rapier on the left, and – towering above all – Di Stefano and Puskas, creators and finishers of a standard rarely seen before or since. Yet not even Real could win everything. Although they went on to beat Peñarol 5–1 in the first (unofficial) club championship, they were only runners-up in their domestic league and cup.

Benfica vs. Barcelona 1961

May 31, 1961
Wankdorf, Berne
European Cup Final

Benfica 3

 (Aguas 30, Ramallets 31 (o.g.), Coluna 55)

Barcelona 2

 (Kocsis 20, Czibor 79)

Half Time:

 2–1

Attendance:

 33,000

Referee:

 G. Dienst (Switzerland)

Benfica:

Costa Pereira, Mario Joao, Angelo, Neto, Germano, Cruz, José Augusto, Santana, Aguas, Coluna, Cavem.

Barcelona:

Ramallets, Foncho, Gracia, Verges, Garay, Gensana, Kubala, Kocsis, Evaristo, Suarez, Czibor.

A curious match which showed a corporate se and some individual falls. Benfica, little known outside Portugal and rank outsiders beforehand, took the European Cup and began a parade of domestic success that brought 12 championships in the next 16 seasons, all in bunches of three: 1963–64–65, 1967–68–69, 1971–72–73 and 1975–76–77. And the Hungarian link with European Cup finals was now almost severed. Kocsis and Czibor, who both scored for Barcelona, had been on the losing side – beaten by the same score on the same ground – in the 1954 World Cup Final. They were virtually the last link with the marvellous Magyar team, though Puskas was to have the final word with a hat-trick for Real in the European Cup Final a year later. Another Hungarian, Kubala – who played for three countries – was a third key figure for Barça, but their downfall was due to a home-bred player.

Their international keeper Ramallets missed a cross and let in Aguas for Benfica's equalizer. A minute later, he fumbled a backheader by Gensana and allowed the ball to cross the line before knocking it back. Even Coluna's thunderous, long-range third might have been saved had he reacted more quickly.

Those errors sapped Barça's confidence, but they battled on, hitting the woodwork three times, four if Kubala's shot that came out after striking both posts is counted twice. Benfica, however fortunate with their goals, were a good, adventurous side and held out calmly even after conceding a late second. Kocsis and Czibor left the field in tears... the Wankdorf stadium having robbed them again, as in 1954.

The Great Matches

Celtic vs. Internazionale 1967

May 25, 1967
National Stadium, Lisbon
European Cup Final

Celtic 2
(Gemmell 73, Chalmers 85)
Internazionale 1
(Mazzola 8 pen)
Half Time:
0–1
Attendance:
45,000
Referee:
H. Tschenscher (W Germany)
Celtic:
Simpson, Craig, Gemmell, Murdoch, McNeill, Clark, Johnstone, Wallace, Chalmers, Auld, Lennox.
Internazionale:
Sarti, Burgnich, Facchetti, Bedin, Guarneri, Picchi, Domenghini, Mazzola, Cappellini, Bicicli, Corso.

Celtic, one of Scotland's big two clubs, were minnows in the mainstream of Europe, despite frequent forays. Only two of their team on this balmy night in Portugal, before a frenzied crowd of adoring travellers, had any experience of the game outside their native land. Bertie Auld spent a none-too-productive spell at Birmingham, and Ronnie Simpson had left Newcastle more than a decade earlier (and now, at 37, was Scottish Footballer of the Year). The rest were a mixture of Glasgow lads and small-fee bargains recruited by Jock Stein, a manager adept at making the whole much greater than the sum of the parts – nowadays he would have a degree in Human Resources.

Inter, European champions in 1965, returned to the final with the help of a 'deal' that would not now be allowed: after two draws with CSKA Sofia, Inter won the right to stage the play-off in Bologna – virtually a home game – simply by promising the impoverished Bulgarians 75 per cent of the takings. When Inter won through by a lone goal, many neutrals turned against them: certainly Celtic had incredible support in a comparatively small crowd at Lisbon, where they won the right to be called Lions.

Inter were also hampered by the absence through injury of their Spanish playmaker, Luis Suarez, upon whom their counter-attacking tactic depended. Even though the Scots trailed for more than an hour, their faith in hard work and uncomplicated, attacking football paid off with two goals. So bargain-basement Celtic won every tournament they contested that season, while big-money Inter did not win anything. Delightful irony, but how things have changed

Manchester United vs. Benfica 1968

May 29, 1968
Wembley, London
European Cup Final

Manchester United 4

(Charlton 53, 104, Best 91, Kidd 95)

Benfica 1

(Graça 85). After extra time.

Half Time: **90 minutes:**

0–0   1–1

Attendance:

100,000

Referee:

C. Lo Bello (Italy)

Manchester United:

Stepney, Brennan, Dunne, Crerand, Foulkes, Stiles, Best, Kidd, Charlton, Sadler, Aston.

Benfica:

Henrique, Adolfo, Cruz, Graça, Humberto, Jacinto, José Augusto, Eusebio, Torres, Coluna, Simoes.

One shot, one save… so much glorious English football history might never have happened. Eusebio, the mainspring of a fine Benfica side, had a chance to win the game, moments after Graça's late equalizer of a rare Bobby Charlton headed goal had sent United reeling. A thunderous right-foot shot from 18 yards after he had been put through the middle brought an instinctive save from Alex Stepney and a rueful clap from Eusebio: did he realize, even then, that a more delicate placing could have won the cup for his own team?

In extra time, United regained their poise and power, with a glorious solo goal by George Best just a minute into the deciding half-hour being followed by two others, one from Brian Kidd, on his 19th birthday, who headed the ball in at the second attempt after the goalkeeper had parried his first header, pushing it back out to him, and the other by skipper Charlton, one of the World Cup winners on the same pitch two years earlier.

So United, the third fine team assembled by manager Matt Busby in 20 years, became the first English club to annex Europe's leading trophy. The early post-war United were too soon for Europe: the mid-1950s Busby Babes reached the semi-finals in 1957, losing to Real Madrid, and the patched-up, post-Munich side suffered an inevitable defeat against Milan in 1958.

Thus a decade passed after Munich before Busby's third great team , with Charlton and Foulkes the survivors of the crash, swept to their majestic triumph. In so doing, they gave extra heart to other English clubs who had faltered on Europe's threshold: in the next decade, nine English clubs reached various finals on the Continent.

The Great Matches

Italy vs. West Germany 1970

June 17, 1970
Azteca, Mexico City
World Cup semi-final

Italy 4
(Boninsegna 7, Burgnich 97, Riva 103, Rivera 111)
West Germany 3
(Schnellinger 90, Müller 95, 110) aet
Half Time: 90 Minutes:

1–0   1–1

Attendance:

80,000

Referee:

A. Yamasaki (Mexico)

Italy:

Albertosi, Burgnich, Cera, Bertini, Facchetti, Rosato (Poletti), Domenghini, Mazzola (Rivera), De Sisti, Boninsegna, Riva.

West Germany:

Maier, Vogts, Beckenbauer, Schulz, Schnellinger, Grabowski, Patzke (Held), Overath, Seeler, Müller, Löhr (Libuda).

Six goals in 21 minutes made this one of the most exciting matches in the history of the World Cup or any other competition. Sadly, such are the demands of modern tournament structures, both teams ended up as losers. Three days earlier, in a thrilling quarter-final, Germany had played extra time before beating England 3–2, and coach Helmut Schön blamed defeat by Italy on the draining effects of that match. Four days later, an unchanged Italian side crashed 4–1 in the final, and although there was no mistaking Brazil's right to the Jules Rimet Trophy, equally there was no doubting the fact that the Italians, in turn, had not fully recovered from their exertions against the Germans.

Players, no matter how fit, need ample time to recuperate from two tense, testing hours in the Mexican sun. Schön, usually a master at tactical substitution, was caught out this time and forced to leave Beckenbauer on the field after he had dislocated a shoulder – bravery unquestioned but ability impaired. The gallant Beckenbauer played for an hour, including extra time, with the shoulder strapped.

Germany could not afford such luxuries. Italy led for nearly all normal time, after Boninsegna's early snap shot, but Schnellinger, playing in his fourth World Cup, equalized in injury time – only seconds from defeat. That began a remarkable scoring burst, with Germany leading 2–1, Italy going 3–2 ahead, the Germans levelling – Müller's 10th goal of the tournament – and Rivera carefully rolling in what proved to be the decider, from the restart.

Italy vs. Brazil 1982

July 5, 1982
Sarria, Barcelona
World Cup Group C

Italy 3

(Rossi 5, 25, 75)

Brazil 2

(Socrates 12, Falcao 68)

Half Time:

2–1

Attendance:

44,000

Referee:

A Klein (Israel)

Italy:

Zoff, Gentile, Collovati (Bergomi), Scirea, Cabrini, Tardelli (Marini), Antognoni, Oriali, Graziani, Conti, Rossi.

Brazil:

Waldir Peres, Leandro, Oscar, Luisinho, Junior, Toninho Cerezo, Socrates, Zico, Falcao, Serginho (Paulo Isidoro), Eder.

On the morning of April 29, 1982, Paolo Rossi returned from suspension, having been banned for three years – later reduced to two – for allegedly accepting a bribe and helping

'fix' a match in the Italian league. Some 11 weeks later, Rossi was the hero of all Italy. He scored three goals in this vital group qualifying match to eliminate the favourites, Brazil, two in the semi-final against Poland, and one in the final, when Italy beat West Germany 3–1. His six goals made him the tournament's leading marksman and completed a remarkable comeback for one of the most effective strikers of his generation.

Rossi was still only 24, and Juventus had such faith in him that they paid Perugia £600,000 to buy him while he had a year of the ban to run. He had always protested his innocence – and his demonic efforts to regain match fitness, plus his finishing, took Italy to a merited success after they had managed only three draws in their initial qualifying group.

Brazil began against Italy needing only a draw to reach the semi-finals, and should have achieved it with some ease. But their two brilliant goals encouraged them to keep on attacking and their over-stretched defence made too many errors against a forward in such inspired mood as Rossi, the man who came back, and perhaps the best team in the competition were out.

The consolation of the finest goal of the game, however, went to Brazilian midfielder Paulo Roberto Falcao – driving a thunderous shot past Dino Zoff for the equalizer at 2-2 after his team-mates' dummy runs pulled the Italian defence all over the place and left Zoff and the goal at his mercy.

The Great Matches

West Germany vs. France 1982

**July 8, 1982
Sanchez Pizjuan, Seville
World Cup semi-final**

West Germany 3
(Littbarski 18, Rummenigge 102, Fischer 107)
France 3
(Platini 27 pen, Trésor 92, Giresse 98) aet

Half Time: 90 Minutes: Penalties:
1–1   1–1   5–4

Attendance:
63,000

Referee:
C. Corver (Holland)

West Germany:
Schumacher, Kaltz, Forster, K.-H.,
Stielike, Briegel (Rummenigge), Forster,
B., Dremmler, Breitner, Littbarski, Magath
(Hrubesch), Fischer.

France:
Ettori, Amoros, Janvion, Bossis, Tigana,
Trésor, Genghini (Battiston, Lopez),
Giresse, Platini, Rocheteau, Six.

The first World Cup finals match to be decided

on penalties was resolved because indomitable German spirit proved just too much for French skill. But West Germany were lucky to go through after an appalling foul by goalkeeper Harald Schumacher on French substitute Patrick Battiston. Schumacher's headlong charge left Battiston unconscious for several minutes. A penalty? A sending-off? Not even a booking. The referee, in his wisdom, allowed Schumacher to remain, staring cold-eyed as Battiston was carried away.

France recovered so well after a poor opening that they might well have won inside 90 minutes. Then two quick goals in extra time seemed to have made them safe, and delighted all neutrals. Yet the Germans again showing remarkable spirit in adversity pulled the game round.

Karl-Heinz Rummenigge, their captain went on as a substitute, although far from fit and scored almost at once. Then, with Rummenigge this time the creator, an overhead hook from centre-forward Klaus Fischer levelled the scores.

Even then France should have won. They won the toss to decide who took the first penalty of the shoot-out, which usually prove a mental advantage, and when Uli Stielike missed Germany's third attempt, France led 3–2. But Six failed and, after West Germany had levelled at 4–4, Schumacher made himself even less popular with the world at large by parrying a weak effort from Maxime Bossis. Hrubesch promptly hit the winner.

214

West Germany vs. England 1990

July 4, 1990
Delle Alpe, Turin
World Cup semi-final

West Germany 1
(Brehme 59)
England 1
(Lineker 80) aet

Half Time:	90 Minutes:	Penalties:
0–0	1–1	4–3

Attendance:
62,628
Referee:
J R Wright (Brazil)
West Germany:
Illgner, Brehme, Kohler, Augenthaler, Buchwald, Berthold, Matthäus, Hässler (Reuter), Thom, Völler (Riedle), Klinsmann.
England:
Shilton, Wright, Parker, Butcher (Steven), Walker, Pearce, Beardsley, Platt, Gascoigne, Waddle, Lineker.

Two of soccer's oldest rivals served up a magnificent match, sadly decided by what was then FIFA's only solution to draws after 120 minutes: penalties. England went so very, very close to reaching the final for only the second time. Despite all the trials and tribulations besetting their manager, Bobby Robson, and despite the lack of class players – in the English game at large, let alone in the squad – there was only the merest fraction between the teams at the end. The splendid spirit in which the match was contested was another bonus. So, on a more personal level, was the flood of tears released by the England enigma, Paul Gascoigne, which made him a media and public darling overnight and earned him a wallet of gold to go with his later-revealed feet of clay.

This was a night with many heroes, perhaps none more so than the referee, Jose Roberto Wright, who let the game run without the nit-picking fussiness of so many other officials. The Germans, often wanting to referee as well as play, were none too keen on Wright's firm hand, but that suited England perfectly and helped them to play above themselves. Only a freak goal by Andy Brehme, deflected high over Peter Shilton by Paul Parker's attempted interception, put Germany in front. The indomitable Gary Lineker pounced on a half-chance to level and from then on penalties seemed the only solution. The Germans scored all the four they needed to take whereas Stuart Pearce and Chris Waddle missed England's last two. No arguing with that – only with the system.

The Great Matches

Denmark vs. Germany 1992

June 26, 1992
Ullevi, Gothenburg
European Championship Final

Denmark 2
(Jensen 18, Vilfort 78)
Germany 0

Half Time:
1–0

Attendance:
37,800

Referee:
B. Galler (Switzerland)

Denmark:
Schmeichel, Piechnik, Olsen L., Nielsen, Sivebaek (Christiansen 68), Vilfort, Jensen, Larsen, Christofte, Laudrup B., Povlsen.

Germany:
Illgner, Reuter, Kohler, Helmer, Buchwald, Brehme, Hässler, Effenberg (Thom 80), Sammer (Doll 46), Klinsmann, Riedle.

Germany or Holland seemed the likely winners of the ninth European Championship. France and perhaps even England looked likely to have a good run. As for Denmark, they had not even qualified for the finals and got in only when war-ravaged Yugoslavia had to withdraw after topping their qualifying group, a point ahead of the Danes.

When Denmark began by drawing with England and losing to Sweden they seemed lost beyond retrieval. Many of the players had been on holiday and out of training when the call came for them to sweat off the pounds and make the trip to Sweden. Manager Richard Moller Nielsen was in the middle of decorating his kitchen and most of the fine team from the 1980s were no longer in the reckoning – Michael Laudrup having squabbled with Moller Nielsen – while several of the squad were injured during the event. Despite all that, the Danes showed spirit and considerable skill and discipline. A late goal against France made them second in their group and meant a semi-final against the Dutch, who snatched a late equalizer but lost on penalties – the decisive kick being wasted by Marco Van Basten, of all people.

So Denmark went through to meet Germany in what was expected to be a one-sided final – except that nobody had told the Danes. From Schmeichel to Povlsen, they all played their parts to perfection on an evening when little the Germans did went right. Vilfort, who scored the conclusive goal (did he handle the ball first?) had just returned to the squad after going home because of his daughter's illness. Hans Christian Andersen could not have written a finer fairytale.

England vs. Germany 1996

June 30, 1996
Wembley, London, European Championship semi-final

England 1
(Shearer 2)
Germany 1
(Kuntz 16) After golden goal extra-time

Half Time:	Full Time:	Penalties:
1–1	1–1	5–6

Attendance:
75,862
Referee:
S. Puhl (Hungary)
England:
Seaman, Southgate, Adams, Pearce, Anderton, Platt, Ince, Gascoigne, McManaman, Sheringham, Shearer.
Germany:
Köpke, Reuter, Babbel, Sammer, Helmer (Bode 95), Ziege, Scholl (Hässler 76), Eilts, Möller, Freund (Strunz 104), Kuntz.

Germany won the European Championship for a record third time but hosts England were indirect winners as well for the staging of the most prestigious European event, mixing drama on the pitch with enthusiastic, welcoming support off it as well as a national team which rose to the occasion in magnificent style to reach the semi-finals.

As in the 1990 World Cup, England and Germany could only then be separated by a penalty shoot-out after a night of exciting intensity which a 76,000 crowd at Wembley and 26 million domestic television viewers will never forget.

England had a magnificent start, Shearer heading home in the second minute. Germany, with only one fit striker, responded with courage and invention and that lone raider, Stefan Kuntz, equalized in the 16th minute.

The game was an emotional roller-coaster and produced one of the most thrilling extra time spectacles Wembley has witnessed thanks to the introduction of the golden goal rule. Darren Anderton was an inch from the vital goal when he hit a post, then Germany thought they had it as Kuntz headed past Seaman, only for referee Sandor Puhl to penalize the German for pushing.

And so to penalties. Both teams converted their five regulation efforts. Then Gareth Southgate ran up, only to push his kick low into the grateful arms of German keeper Andy Köpke. Andy Möller ran up for Germany… and shot them into the final. German coach Berti Vogts had plainly written the script, saying later: "I told my players in which order they would take the penalties – and I told Möller he would shoot the winner."

The Famous Stadiums

A football stadium is a simple thing: a mixture of concrete, steel, stone and plastic which serves a similarly simple purpose: to allow thousands of like-minded people to watch 22 men play football. Yet the great stadia of the world have long since taken on personalities of their own – the power of their presence offering strength and confidence to the footballers who call the ground "home."

Real Madrid, for instance, were never beaten at the mighty Bernabéu stadium in the first seven dominant years of their command of European club football. But even Madrid were set on the defensive by the challenge of playing in Barcelona's Nou Camp or the Meazza stadium at San Siro, Milan – a ground whose terraces rise like the steepest, noisiest cliffs above the tempestuous football sea at their feet. The stadia of different countries offer contrasts. England boasts the most recently redeveloped stadia in Europe, although Italy, Spain and Germany have grounds with bigger capacities. Most capital cities possess a proud, monolithic structure to show off their football prowess. Many of these stadia serve a dual purpose, possessing the pitch-side facilities for other sports. Thus Rome, Berlin and Moscow have all played host to the Olympic Games as well as top-level international football. One stadium has played host twice to the World Cup Final itself – the Azteca in Mexico City, lately renamed in memory of top local soccer director, Guillermo Canedo. The Maracana in Rio, which once welcomed 200,000 at the 1950 World Cup, has had its capacity cut for security reasons. But it is still Brazil's home – and playing there or in any one of these other great stadia remains a status symbol among footballers the world over.

Nou Camp

Barcelona, Spain

Capacity:
115,000
Opened:
1957
Club:
FC Barcelona
Hosted:
1982 World Cup Opening Match (Belgium 1, Argentina 0); 1992 Olympic Final (Spain 3, Poland 2); 1989 European Cup Final (Milan 4, Steaua Bucharest 0); 1982 European Cup-winners' Cup Final (Barcelona 2, Standard Liège 1)

Higher and higher, bigger and better could be the motto of Barcelona's towering and breathtaking Nou Camp, "the new ground", which opened its doors on September 24, 1957 and was financed to the tune of 66 million pesetas by club members. In Europe today only Benfica's Estadio da Luz can claim to be larger. Sport, it has been said, is the acceptable substitute for war, and Barcelona, the football team (*see* page 37) has always been a vehicle for the fervent nationalism of Catalonia. The rivalry with Madrid is intense, and the Nou Camp's continual improvements and expansion have much to do with the desire to outdo Real's Bernabéu stadium.

Barcelona, formed in 1899, outgrew their old Les Corts ground in the 1940s and moved to the new stadium, in an area of allotments to the west, in 1957. When Nou Camp was inaugurated with a match against Legia Warsaw, plans had already been laid to increase capacity to 150,000.

An indoor sports hall, connected to Nou Camp by a concourse, was opened in 1971 and houses the club's basketball, handball and volleyball teams. Ice hockey is held in the adjacent Ice Palace. Even more remarkably, there is a walkway over a road leading to another football stadium, the 16,500 capacity Mini Estad, opened in 1982 and used by Barcelona's nursery team in the Spanish Second Division as well as by the club's top amateur side.

Capacity increase

The first major redevelopment of the main stadium was in the early 1980s, when the addition of a third tier increased capacity to 120,000 in time for Nou Camp to host the opening ceremony of the 1982 World Cup. When the old ground was opened in 1922, "Barça" had a membership of 5,000. When Pope John Paul II visited Nou Camp in World Cup year he was enrolled as member no. 108,000. Since then membership has passed 110,000, making Barcelona the largest club in the world. The work never stops. For the 1992 Olympic Games in Barcelona, two more tiers were installed above the previous roof line, with a suspended cantilevered roof soaring overhead.

Olympia-stadion

Berlin, Germany

Capacity:

76,006

Opened:

1936

Clubs:

Hertha BSC, Blau-Weiss 90

Hosted:

1936 Olympic Final (Italy 2, Austria 1);
1974 World Cup group matches

Berlin's historic – or notorious – stadium may be considered not so much a theatre of dreams, more a monument to the nightmarish world of Adolf Hitler and his national socialism. It was here that Hitler opened the 1936 Olympics, a giant propaganda exercise, to Wagnerian strains before an ecstatic 100,000 crowd. And it was here, much to his chagrin, that the black American athlete Jesse Owens won four gold medals to challenge the myth of Aryan superiority. Two years later the England team played Germany and avenged the politically-engineered demand that they give the Nazi salute by winning 6–3 (see page 168).

The Olympiapark, of which the Olympiastadion is the neo-classical centre-piece, had its origins before the First World War because Germany had been chosen to stage the Games in 1916. The unused facilities, adjacent to the Grunewald racecourse, were taken over when Hitler came to power in 1933. His grand plan involved the 86,000-capacity stadium on a 131-hectare sports field which also included hockey, riding and swimming stadia plus an open-air amphitheatre. These were all linked to the vast Maifeld, used by the Nazis for mass rallies.

East vs. West

The stadium suffered from Allied bombing but was repaired by the mid-1960s, when Hertha Berlin drew 70,000 crowds in the early years of the Bundesliga, the new national championship of West Germany. The stadium was renovated for the 1974 World Cup, when it staged three group matches. The use of the Olympiastadion in the first place had caused political tension between East and West, and its incorporation in the World Cup programme at all was a triumph for German football chief Hermann Neuberger.

The unique political problems of Berlin meant that the stadium was underused for years. It was the home of both Hertha and Blau-Weiss Berlin but that meant mainly Second Division football. Now, since reunification, the Olympiastadion has regained its status as a focal point for German football and it is once again the home of the German cup final.

Monumental

Buenos Aires, Argentina

Capacity:

76,000

Opened:

1938

Club:

River Plate

Hosted:

1978 World Cup Final (Argentina 3, Holland 1 aet); 1946, 1959 and 1987 South American Championships

There were many misgivings about holding the 1978 World Cup in Argentina, not the least of which concerned the political climate. Ultimately, the ruling military junta invested huge sums in the renovation of the Monumental, which had been the home of the national side and of one of the world's great clubs, River Plate (*see* page 65). Several of River's own players, including skipper Daniel Passarella (Argentina's manager for the 1998 World Cup in France), goalkeeper Ubaldo Fillol and forwards Leopoldo Luque and Oscar Ortiz, featured in the side which defeated the Netherlands 3–1 in the final amid a paper snowstorm which tumbled down the Monumental and set the scene for the coming 90 minutes.

Work had begun on the Monumental on September 27, 1936 and it was ready for the River team to move in by May 1938. The dressing-rooms and offices were of a standard then unique in South America, while the three-sided horseshoe had an original capacity of 100,000, with the potential of a third tier which would lift it to 150,000. That third tier was never needed.

The opening game, a 3–1 win over the Uruguayan champions Peñarol, was watched by a crowd of 70,000. But the stadium itself was not completed, even in its initial phase, for many years, until 1957, when River invested much of the then world record fee of £97,000 they had received from Italy's Juventus for their inside-forward Omar Sivori.

Another World Cup?

Apart from the 1978 World Cup, the Monumental has staged to many internationals and South American club ties, as well as key games when Argentina have taken their turn to host the Copa America (the South American Championship).

Major redevelopment work has been under consideration for some time, to assist crowd control after increasing problems of hooliganism in Argentine soccer but also because the Monumental will be the centre-piece of the projected bid to host the World Cup once again.

Hampden Park

Glasgow, Scotland

Capacity:
50,000

Opened:
1903

Club:
Queen's Park

Hosted:
1960 European Cup Final (Real Madrid 7, Eintracht Frankfurt 3), 1976 (Bayern Munich 1, Saint-Etienne 0); 1961 European Cup-winners' Cup (Fiorentina 2, Rangers 0), 1962 (Atlético Madrid 1, Fiorentina 1, replay in Stuttgart), 1966 (Borussia Dortmund 2, Liverpool 1); 1989 World Under-17 Championship Final (Saudi Arabia 1, Scotland 1 aet: Saudi Arabia 5-4 on pens).

As early as 1908, Glasgow had three of the largest grounds in the world: Ibrox, home of Protestant Rangers, Celtic Park, home of Catholic Celtic, and Hampden, owned by amateurs Queens Park. Hampden was already the national stadium, never more vibrant than when hosting games against the old enemy England, whom Scotland had met in the first-ever international in

1872. It was the largest stadium in the world until Maracana opened in 1950 and still holds several attendance records. In 1937, 149,415 paid to see the Scots beat England, a record for a match in Europe. A week later, a European club record 147,365 saw Celtic beat Aberdeen for the Scottish Cup.

Ten-goal Final

In 1960, 135,000 watched Real Madrid trounce Eintracht Frankfurt 7–3 in the European Cup Final (*see* page 176). That record was bettered five years later, when 136,505 saw Celtic's semi-final with Leeds in the same competition. Since then there has been major redevelopment. First came a £3 million refurbishment in 1975 then, a £12 million remodelling in the early 1990s. Hampden was shut again after the 1996 Scottish Cup Final for the construction of an 18,000-capacity new South Stand. Considering all the work carried out, it is remarkable that Hampden has not staged a European club final for more than 20 years.

While it remains easily the most famous soccer stadium in Scotland, Hampden has faced a challenge from the major redevelopment projects undertaken at both of Glasgow's other big grounds.

It remains, fortunately, the one stadium in the city where fans of both the Old Firm clubs can meet on neutral territory.

Estádio Da Luz

Lisbon, Portugal

Capacity:
  130,000
Opened:
  1954
Club:
  Benfica
Hosted:
  1991 World Youth Cup Final (Portugal 0, Brazil 0: Portugal 4–2 on pens); 1967 European Cup Final (Celtic 2, Internazionale 1); 1992 European Cup-Winners' Cup Final (Werder Bremen 2, Monaco 0)

Although the 'Stadium of Light' is one of the most evocatively named arenas in the world, it takes its name not from the power of its floodlighting but from the nearby Lisbon district of Luz. Yet one of the most dazzling players in history, the 'Black Pearl' Eusebio, led Benfica to unparalleled heights here during the 1960s and 1970s, 1961 and 1962, when 14 league titles, two European Cup wins (1960 and 1961) and three more final appearances established Benfica among the aristocracy of European football.

In 1992, a statue of their greatest son, Eusebio, was unveiled to celebrate his fiftieth birthday, before a match with old British rivals Manchester United, and this now greets visitors as they arrive at the entrance of the stadium.

Porto Keep Winning

Benfica, or Sport Lisboa Benfica as they are officially named, were formed in 1908, and by the 1950s had long outgrown their fifth ground at Campo Grande. Plans for the 60,000 capacity Estádio da Luz were drawn up by a former Benfica athlete in 1951 and the original two–tiered stadium was opened in 1954. Porto won the inaugural game 3–0, and Portugal's first floodlit game, again won by Porto, took place four years later. By 1960 a third tier had been added to increase the capacity to 75,000, and by the late 1970s the Estádio Da Luz, all white and bright, seated 130,000, and was legendary throughout Europe.

The stadium has only ever been filled to that full capacity on one occasion, however, when Portugal defeated Brazil in a penalty shoot-out in the 1991 World Youth Cup final. UEFA restrictions on standing and security, introduced in the wake of various crowd disasters around the world, meant reducing the available matchday capacity to its current limit, which is around the 92,000 mark.

Wembley Stadium

London, England

Capacity:
80,000

Opened:
1923

Club:
None

Hosted:
1948 Olympic Final (Sweden 3, Yugoslavia 1); 1966 World Cup Final (England 4, West Germany 2 aet); 1996 European Championship; 1963 European Cup Final (Milan 2, Benfica 1), 1968 (Manchester United 4, Benfica 1 aet), 1971 (Ajax 2, Panathinaikos 0), 1978 (Liverpool 1, Brugge 0), 1992 (Barcelona 1, Sampdoria 0 aet); 1965 Cup-Winners Cup Final (West Ham 2, Munich 1860 0); 1993 (Parma 3, Antwerp 1)

Wembley may be the ageing grande dame of stadia but, steeped in history and with its distinctive twin towers, it remains the Mecca of English football and is revered by players and fans throughout the world. Wembley is synonymous with England internationals, the FA Cup Final and the epic World Cup Final of 1966.

Unusually for a major stadium, Wembley is privately owned and financed by its staging of major soccer, greyhound racing, rugby league, showpiece American football games, and ancillary sporting activities at the nearby 9,000-seater Arena. In the 1920s the green fields of Wembley Park were chosen as the site for the 1923 Empire Exhibition. The then Empire Stadium was built between January 22 and April 23. It was hailed as the largest monumental building of reinforced concrete in the world, and a troop of soldiers marched up and down the terracing in a unique safety check.

A crowd of "only" 53,000 had turned up for the 1922 FA Cup Final at Stamford Bridge, and the authorities were concerned that Bolton and West Ham might not fill the new 126,000-capacity ground the following year. But on April 28 more than 200,000 people besieged Wembley, and that Bolton were eventually able to defeat West Ham 2–0 was due in no small part to the good nature of the crowd in the presence of King George V and a celebrated policeman on his white horse (*see* page 166). The Wembley legend was born.

Wembley has moved with the times. The surrounding exhibition centre was redeveloped while the stadium was remodelled in the 1980s. Adapting to all-seater demands meant a capacity reduction from 100,000. The addition of an Olympic Gallery beneath the roof edge kept an 80,000 level at which Wembley took centre stage in England's hosting of the 1996 European Championship.

Santiago Bernabéu

Madrid, Spain

Capacity:
105,000

Opened:
1947

Club:
Real Madrid

Hosted:
1982 World Cup Final (Italy 3, West Germany 2); 1964 European Championship Final (Spain 2, Soviet Union 1); 1957 European Cup Final (Real Madrid 2, Fiorentina 0), 1969 (Milan 4, Ajax 1), 1980 (Nottingham Forest 1, Hamburg 0).

It is thanks to the visionary foresight of long-time president Santiago Bernabéu that Real Madrid (*see* page 63) boast an imposing edifice on Madrid's most prestigious street, the Castellana, housing one of the world's foremost clubs and a trophy room bulging with silverware and displaying more than 5,000 items. The ground, which began life as Nuevo Chamartin Stadium in 1944 on five hectares of prime land, was Bernabéu's brainchild. He was a lawyer who had been, in turn, player, captain, club secretary, coach and then, from 1942, president. The old stadium had been ravaged during the Spanish Civil War of the 1930s and Bernabéu decided that a super new stadium was needed if the club were to raise the funds needed to build a super new team. Real Madrid, who now include the King and Queen of Spain and International Olympic Committee President Juan Antonio Samaranch among their members, raised an astonishing 41 million pesetas by public subscription to finance the land purchase and first stage of building. The stadium was opened, with a 75,000 capacity, for a testimonial for veteran player Jesus Alonso against Portuguese club Belenenses of Lisbon in December, 1947.

In the 1950s the finance raised by Real's dominance of the fledgeling European Cup enabled capacity within the distinctive white towers to be extended to 125,000. The name Estadio Santiago Bernabéu was adopted in 1955 and the floodlights were switched on in 1957 for the European Cup Final.

Bernabéu, who died in 1978, had plans for another new stadium north of the city but for once did not get his way and, instead, Spain's hosting of the 1982 World Cup led to more improvements to the original stadium. A total of 345,000 people watched three group matches and an outstanding World Cup Final in a stadium offering 30,200 seats and standing room for 60,000. Ten years on, the improvements continue. A third tier has been completed and further remodelling has increased the seating to 65,000 within a total capacity of 105,000.

Estadio Guillermo Canedo

Mexico City, Mexico

Capacity:
110,000
Opened:
1960
Club:
America (but others for big matches)
Hosted:
1968 Olympic Final (Hungary 4, Bulgaria 1); 1970 World Cup Final (Brazil 4, Italy 1); 1986 World Cup Final (Argentina 3, West Germany 2)

Better know as the Azteca, the pride and joy of Mexican football has been the venue for some of the most memorable World Cup matches in history. It is also one of the most enjoyable, passionate and colourful stadiums in which to watch a game since, because lower tier is only 30 feet from the pitch, thus providing fans there with a sense of immediacy, while those in the upper tier benefit from the steep, cliff-like design. Azteca was the first stadium to stage two World Cup Final matches and the 1970 tournament also produced an incredible semi-final between West Germany and Italy. The drama was won 4–3 by the talented Italians who were, in turn, swept aside 4–1 in the final by a Brazilian side rated as the finest to take the field in the history of the competition.

A second World Cup

Some 16 years later Mexico stepped in at short notice to beat the United States and Canada to the right to host the finals after Colombia pulled out. In the final Argentina, led by Diego Maradona at the height of his creative footballing powers, lifted the crown for a second time, against West Germany.

The stadium, built on scrubland to the south-west of the sprawling mass which is Mexico City, required 100,000 tons of concrete, four times more than was used to build Wembley Stadium in London. It was planned for the 1968 Olympics and opened in June 1966 with a match betweeen Mexico and Turin, but the first major internationals came during the 1968 Games. Since then, club sides America, Atlante, Necaxa and Cruz Azul have all used the the three-tiered Azteca for important games.

In 1997 the stadium was renamed in memory of the late Guillermo Canedo, who had been Mexico's top football official for more than 20 years – as well as a vice-president of FIFA. Will their be a third World Cup in Mexico? It seems unlikely, but there are many worse places for a major tournament. And the crowd is virtually guaranteed – big.

Giuseppe Meazza

Milan, Italy

Capacity:

83,107

Opened:

1926

Club:

Milan, Internazionale

Hosted:

1965 European Cup Final (Internazionale 1, Benfica 0), 1970 (Feyenoord 2, Celtic 1 aet); 1990 World Cup opening and group matches.

Fantastic is a much misused word, but it seems appropriate to describe the home of two of Europe's leading clubs in the city which can claim to be the continent's premier soccer centre. The cylindrical towers which allowed builders to construct a third tier and roof in advance of the 1992 World Cup have become just as much a trademark as the ramp system which gave access to the original two tiers of what used to be known as the San Siro. The cost of the remodelling came close to £50 million – even before the extra expense of sorting out problems with the pitch caused by shutting out both light and breeze.

San Siro, named after the suburb, was originally the home of Milan, formed in 1899 by an Englishman, Alfred Edwards. They outgrew their original ground in the mid-1920s, and the site of their new stadium was bought by their president, Piero Pirelli of tyre fame. It was Inter of all teams who ruined the opening party at the 35,000 capacity Stadio Calcistico San Siro by beating their rivals 6–3 in a local derby in September 1926.

The stadium grows

The stadium was bought from Milan by the local council and was gradually enlarged until a 65,000 crowd was able to watch Italy play their Axis partners, Germany, in 1940. Inter had outgrown their own Stadio Arena by 1947; but the proposed groundshare needed an even larger stadium. San Siro reopened in 1955 with an increased capacity of 82,000, as the home ground for two teams who have been bettered in domestic football by Juventus and Torino but are second to none in European success.

San Siro was renamed Stadio Giuseppe Meazza in 1979 to honour the memory of one of the only two players to appear in both Italy's 1934 and 1938 World Cup-winning sides. Meazza had been hero-worshipped while playing for both Milan clubs, and scored more than 300 goals in club matches plus 33 – then a record – in international matches.

Centenario

Montevideo, Uruguay

Capacity:
 76,609
Opened:
 1930
Club:
 Peñarol, Nacional
Hosted:
 1930 World Cup Final (Uruguay 4,
 Argentina 2); 1942, 1956, 1967, 1983 and
 1995 South American Championships

Centenario holds a special place in football history, having been the stage for the first World Cup Final in 1930 when Uruguay, then Olympic champions and enjoying their golden age in international football, defeated Argentina, their old rivals from across the River Plate, by 4–2 after being 2–1 down at half-time. But it was a close call for Montevideo's magnificent new stadium, which was being built especially for the fledgeling world championship and to celebrate 100 years of the country's independence. Work continued throughout the first days of the tournament to have it ready for the final, but in the end a fine stadium, with a capacity of 93,000, was erected in just over six months on land taken from two adjoining parks. Eight of the 16 games in 1930 were staged

there, with the others being staged on club grounds.

It has since become the regular venue for internationals, the South American Championship (the world's longest-running international competition since the demise of the British Home Championship in 1984), the World Club Championship, the South American club championship (Copa Libertadores), Supercopa and Recopa. Uruguay's most recent international success came in the 1995 South American Championship, when Brazil were beaten on penalties at the Centenario, after a 1–1 draw.

Peñarol and Nacional dominate

Football in Uruguay is really all about football in Montevideo and Centenario is home to two of the leading clubs, Peñarol and Nacional, who dominated the Copa Libertadores in its early years. From 1960, when Peñarol defeated Olimpia of Paraguay 1–0 in the Centenario and 2–1 on aggregate, they and Nacional were involved in 10 of the first 11 finals, and in 1968 the stadium was full to see Estudiantes beat Palmeiras 2–0 in a final play-off.

Peñarol entertained Real Madrid in the first World Club Championship in 1960, but were held to a goalless draw and lost 5–0 away. They took their revenge by beating Benfica the following season in a play-off, and Real, by 2–0 both home and away, in 1966.

Luzhniki

Moscow, Russia

Capacity:
100,000
Opened:
1956
Club:
Spartak Moscow
Hosted:
1980 Olympic Final (Czechoslovakia 1, East Germany 0)

A statue of Vladimir Ilyich Lenin, the now discredited father of the Russian Revolution, for years welcomed the visitor to the Centralny Stadion Lenina on the banks of the Moscow River, which is the site of possibly the largest and most popular sports complex in the world. There are 140 separate sports centres, including a Palace of Sports, an open-air swimming centre, a multi-purpose hall, 22 smaller halls, 11 football pitches, four athletics tracks, three skating rinks and 55 tennis courts.

Many countries cannot offer as much. The all-seater football stadium plays host to the capital's most popular club, Spartak, as well as games which involve the Russian international team. It is built on the site of the old Red Stadium where Spartak, then called Moscow Sports Club, were founded in 1922. They adopted the present name in 1935 after affiliating to the trade unions for producers' co-operatives.

The new stadium opened in 1956 with the first All Union Spartakia, which brought together 34,000 athletes to celebrate Communist sport. But the history of the Luzhniki is darkened by one of soccer's major disasters: in October 1982, Spartak were playing Haarlem of Holland in the second round of the UEFA Cup. Most of the crowd were leaving just before the end when Spartak scored their second goal. As fans tried to get back up the icy steps a fatal crush occurred. The Soviet people only learned of the tragedy almost seven years later, and then the official death toll was way below the 340 estimated at the time.

The stadium was closed for much of 1996 and 1997 for major redevelopment. The first major international it should have staged was then Russia versus Italy play-off first leg in the 1998 World Cup qualifying competition.

Unfortunately, the new pitch had deteriorated so rapidly that the game had to be switched to the Dynamo stadium, where the capacity is little more than half that of the Luzhniki – the switch also proved unfortunate for the Russians who lost the tie 2–1 on aggregate and missed out on France 98. Spartak now play some home games at the Lokomojiv stadium, to save wear on their own pitch.

Olympia-stadion

Munich, Germany

Capacity:
74,000

Opened:
1972

Club:
Bayern Munich

Hosted:
1972 Olympic Final (Poland 2, Hungary 1); 1974 World Cup Final (West Germany 2, Holland 1); 1988 European Championship Final (Holland 2, Soviet Union 0); 1979 European Cup Final (Nottingham Forest 1, Malmo 0), 1993 (Marseille 1, Milan 0), 1997 (Borussia Dortmund 3, Juventus 1)

Descriptions of the individualistic Olympiastadion vary from a futuristic Bedouin tent to a steel and glass spider's web – although the desert analogy can feel rather tenuous in the depths of a Bavarian winter on the site of the airfield to which Neville Chamberlain flew in 1938 for his infamous ("Peace in our time") meeting with Hitler. The tragic shadow of history fell across the stadium again at the end of the 1972 Olympics for which it had been built, when Arab terrorists took hostage and murdered some of the Israeli athletes competing at the Games.

The bill for Behnisch and Otto's staggering creation at the centre of the green and pleasant Olympiapark came to 137 million marks, but this proved to be money well spent. The Park has become Germany's leading tourist attraction and a stunning venue for major events.

Bayern make strides in Europe

Bayern Munich, about to establish themselves as European giants with players such as Franz Beckenbauer, Paul Breitner and Gerd Müller, moved into the new stadium in 1972, two seasons before they lifted the first of their three successive European Champions Cups. Müller had helped to celebrate the opening by scoring all four goals in West Germany's 4–1 win over the Soviet Union in 1972. Two years later the stocky striker's place in soccer's hall of fame was assured by his winning goal against Holland – who had gone ahead in the first two minutes – in the 1974 World Cup Final in front of his home fans.

The Dutch took happier memories away from the 1988 European Championship Final when they overcame the Soviets 2–0. Most recently Borussia Dortmund, taking advantage of playing what was virtually a home fixture, surprised the favourites Juventus by defeating them 3–1 in the Champions Cup Final in 1997.

San Paolo

Naples, Italy

Capacity:
65,102

Opened:
1960

Club:
Napoli

Hosted:
1968 European Championship semi-final
(Italy 2, Soviet Union 1); 1980 European
Championship finals venue; 1990 World
Cup semi-final (Italy 1, Argentina 1:
Argentina 4–3 on pens)

Regarded purely as a stadium, the concrete
bowl of San Paolo, complete with roof since
the 1990 World Cup, is unremarkable. But
on match days it is transformed into a
vibrant, uninhibited place by the local *tifosi*,
some of the most colourful, eccentric and
volatile fans (hence the moat and fences) in
the world.

San Paolo represents the third home for
Napoli, a club formed in 1904 with the help
of English sailors and looked upon with
some disdain by the more sophisticated clubs
of Turin and Milan, though one of them,
Juventus, deigned to come south to play the
first match in the new stadium in the
Olympic year of 1960.

Napoli, despite the largesse of millionaire president and shipping owner Achille
Lauro, had little success until the arrival of
the Argentine superstar Diego Maradona in
the mid-1980s. He filled San Paolo as it had
never been filled before. The size of the stadium enabled Napoli to sell 70,000 season
tickets, an Italian record, and thus not only
pay Barcelona the then world record transfer
fee of £5 million for Maradona, but afford
his wages and bring in other superstars, such
as Brazil's Careca, into the bargain.

Sadly, the club has later become
embroiled in controversy, first over links
with the Camorra (the local version of the
Mafia) and then over the misuse and misap-
propriation of funds set aside for development work in and around the stadium for the
1990 World Cup. Long-serving club president Corrado Ferlaino was forced to step
down at one stage but he later took command
again – only to be assailed by a consortium
seeking to bring back Maradona as chief
executive cum player-coach.

Maradona had played twice on the club's
ground in the World Cup, against the Soviet
Union and Cameroon, in the first round.
Cameroon appeared their against Columbia
and England as well, and the fifth match of
the tournament at Sao Paolo was a semi-
final, in which Diego and company eliminated Italy on penalties, before going on to
lose the World Cup Final to Germany in the
match played at Rome.

Parc des Princes

Paris, France

Capacity:
48,700

Opened:
1887 (rebuilt 1932, 1972)

Club:
Paris Saint-Germain, Racing Club

Hosted:
1984 European Championship Final
(France 2, Spain 0); 1956 European Cup
Final (Real Madrid 4, Reims 3), 1975
(Bayern Munich 2, Leeds 0), 1981 (Liver-
pool 1, Real Madrid 0); 1978 European
Cup-winners' Cup Final (Anderlecht 4,
FK Austria 0); 1994 European Cup-win-
ners' Cup Final (Zaragoza 2, Arsenal 1)

The award of the 1998 World Cup to France
has spelled the beginning of the end of Parc des
Princes as a major soccer venue. The all-con-
crete near-50,000 capacity stadium designed
by Roger Taillibert for soccer and rugby union
in the early 1970s fails to meet FIFA's minimum capacity of 80,000 for a final, and the
French government has spent £300 million on
a new, 80,000-capacity stadium in the northern
suburb of St Denis.

Parc des Princes lies in the south-west

and, as the name suggests, before the Revolution it was a pleasure ground for royalty.
The stadium began life as a velodrome at the
end of the last century and, until 1967, was
the finish for the Tour de France.

When professional football was introduced
in 1932 the Parc became home to Racing Club
de France, but they had only limited success
and Stade Colombes remained the favourite
ground for internationals and the 1938 World
Cup. Until the current stadium was built, one
of the biggest soccer matches staged was the
first European Cup Final in 1956, when a sell-
out 38,000 crowd saw Real Madrid beat Stade
Reims 4–3. Paris, sad to say, is the great capital
under-achiever in soccer terms.

The creation of the Périphérique, the Paris
ring road, led to the new two-tiered state-of-
the-art stadium being built. It was the first in
Europe with integral floodlighting and closed-
circuit television. Problems with the pitch
dogged its early years, but these ills were cured
by the time the Parc was needed to host three
group matches and the final of the 1984 European Championship, won in style by France's
finest-ever team, led by Michel Platini.

Racing Club went out of professional
soccer business in 1964, and Paris Saint-
Germain, an amalgamation of Paris FC and
Saint-Germain, moved into the new stadium
in 1973. They drew 20,000 crowds, became
only the second Paris club to win the Championship, and dominated the domestic game
in the mid-1990s.

Rose Bowl

Pasadena, United States

Capacity:

102,083

Opened:

1922

Hosted:

1984 Olympic Final (France 2, Brazil 0);
1994 World Cup Final (Brazil 0, Italy 0 –
Brazil win 3–2 on penalties).

The Rose Bowl, synonymous with American football, came into its own as a soccer venue at the 1994 World Cup, when it served as a home from home for the United States. The stadium, far better equipped for the occasion than the more famous Los Angeles Coliseum, held three matches in the opening round, including the hosts' 2–1 victory over Colombia.

Later it staged one second-round match (Romania 3 Argentina 2), a semi-final (Brazil 1 Sweden 0), the third-place match (Sweden 4 Bulgaria 0) and the final itself. That brought Pasadena a place in soccer history as venue for the only World Cup Final ever decided in a penalty shoot-out, with Brazil defeating Italy after Franco Baresi and Roberto Baggio missed decisive kicks.

Those critics who claimed that the USA was no place to hold a World Cup had to think again when total attendances topped 3.5 million, more than a million better than the previous best. Pasadena's seven games drew 610,000 fans – nearly 86,000 per game!

Crowd puller

The rose-covered stadium, based in the leafy city of Pasadena seven miles northwest of downtown Los Angeles, cut its teeth on soccer in the 1984 Olympics, when the tournament drew massive crowds. Yugoslavia versus Italy was attended by 100,374 spectators. France's semi-final against Yugoslavia attracted 97,451, and 101,799 watched France defeat Brazil in the final. That topped the record attendance for gridiron football's Superbowl XVII in 1983, when 101,063 had turned up to see Washington Redskins defeat Miami Dolphins.

The Rose Bowl has hosted five Super Bowls but is best known as the home of UCLA and the annual Rose Bowl game on New Year's Day.

It has also become home of Los Angeles Galaxy, the club set up as the local entrant into Major League Soccer, the new professional championship set up in the wake of the success of the 1994 World Cup finals. Drawing heavily on the enthusiasm for soccer among the local Latin American element, Galaxy regularly draw crowds of more than 30,000 for their big games.

Mario Filho/ Maracana

o de Janeiro, Brazil

pacity:
20,000

ened:
950

b:
otofago, Vasco da Gama, Flamengo,
luminense

sted:
950 World Cup Final (Uruguay 2, Brazil
); 1989 South American Championship

at Wembley is to the old world, Maracana
o the new. This architectural marvel is the
est stadium in the world and the spiritual
ne to Brazil's second religion, football.
wever, it has spent much of the last few
rs out of commission while work has
n carried out to renovate a bowl which
started, literally, to fall apart.

Maracana, which takes its name from the
e river that runs close by, was begun out-
e the city in 1948 in preparation for the
0 World Cup, but was not   completed
il 1965. What has become Brazil's
onal stadium was originally intended to

replace Vasco da Gama's club ground and
was built and is still owned by the city, being
formally named after the mayor, Mario
Filho, who carried the project through. It was
officially opened in June 1950 with a game
beween Rio and São Paulo, the first goal
being scored, appropriately, by Didi. a
Brazilian legend.

The first great matches were staged in
the fourth World Cup, which culminated in
the hosts losing to old rivals Uruguay before
a world record crowd of 199,850. Like Hampden Park in Glasgow, Maracana sets and
holds attendance records. In 1963, 177,656
watched a league match between Flamengo
and and Fluminense, a world club record
attendance. Internationals have drawn
crowds of 180,000, and league matches in
the 1980s were watched regularly by
130,000. Santos even flew north to use
Maracana for their World Club Cup Final
ties against Benfica and Milan in 1962 and
1963.

The stadium is oval in shape and topped
by a breathtaking cantilevered roof, while a
moat separates the fans from the pitch. Like
Wembley and Olympiastadion in Munich,
Maracana has become a major tourist attraction and is held in such esteem that several
smaller versions have been built throughout
Brazil. Next to the stadium is Maracanaz-
inho, a scaled-down indoor version which
stages boxing, tennis, music festivals and
concerts.

Olimpico

Rome, Italy

Capacity:
60,000

Opened:
1953

Club:
Roma, Lazio

Hosted:
1960 Olympic Final (Yugoslavia 3, Denmark 1); 1990 World Cup Final (West Germany 1, Argentina 0); 1968 European Championship Final (Italy 1, Yugoslavia 1; replay, Italy 2, Yugoslavia 0), 1980 (West Germany 2, Belgium 1); 1977 European Cup Final (Liverpool 3, Borussia Mönchengladbach 1), 1984 (Liverpool 1, Roma 1: Liverpool 4–2 on pens) 1996 (Juventus 1, Ajax 1: Juventus 4–2 on pens)

Benito Mussolini was bad news for Italy. But allegedly he did make the trains run on time, and left the beautiful Foro Italico sports complex at the foot of Monte Mario as a legacy. His original plan was to stage the 1944 Olympics there, much as Hitler used Berlin for propaganda purposes in 1936. Then the Second World War intervened. The stadium was originally called Stadio dei Cipressi, but was inaugurated in 1953 as the Olimpico by the legendary Hungarian team, who beat Italy 3–0 in front of an 80,000 crowd. The stadium became the focal point of the 1960 Olympic Games, a home to both Roma and Lazio, and the scene of a home triumph in the 1968 European Championship, when Italy overcame Yugoslavia in a replay.

All roads led to Rome for Liverpool in 1977, when they turned the stadium into a sea of red, before, during and after celebrating the first of their four European Cup triumphs. Estimates vary, but it seems likelt that more than 20,000 Liverpool supporters made the journey, many of them by rail or raod. They returned for the 1984 Final to beat Roma, playing on their own ground but unable to take advantage. Liverpool eventually won on penalties.

To allow the stadium to stage the 1990 World Cup, individual seating had to be increased to 80,000 and a roof added to give two-thirds cover. Only in Italy could the wrangling and talking have gone on until May 1988. A year later the roof design was ditched, costs had risen to £75 million, and the odds shifted against the stadium being ready.

FIFA's threat to move the final to Milan eventually saw to it that this beautiful venue was ready for West Germany's revenge over Argentina: a gracious setting for what proved to be an uninspiring contest, won by a late penalty.

Morumbi

São Paulo, Brazil

Capacity:

150,000

Opened:

1978

Club:

São Paulo FC, Corinthians

Hosted:

1992 Copa Libertadores (South American club championship) Final 2nd leg (São Paulo 1, Newells Old Boys 0: agg 2–1)

The rivalry between Rio de Janeiro and São Paulo provides much of the dynamic rivalry which fires domestic football within Brazil. Fans from the respective cities consider "their" state championships – the Carioca and the Paulista – as the best and most important, and fail to understand why players from the other city should ever be preferred to any of their favourites for the national team.

They are equally partisan about their stadia. Just as Rio de Janeiro has Maracana as venue for the 1950 World Cup Final and host to a world record soccer attendance – São Paulo football centres on the magnificent Morumbi.

The name is that of a suburb of São Paulo, and the stadium is formally entitled the Estadio Cicero Pompeu de Toledo – explaining, perhaps, why it is generally known by the much shorter name 'barrio'.

Morumbi is effectively Brazil's biggest stadium, because a failure to maintain Maracana has led to its capacity being steadily reduced for security and safety reasons. Other 100,000–plus stadia include Castelao at Fortaleza and Mineirao at Belo Horizonte.

The first big game

The first major fixture to be staged at Morumbi was in the South American Championship in 1979, when Brazil beat Bolivia 2–0 on their way to the semi-finals and a surprise defeat by Paraguay.

São Paulo FC and Corinthians both play all their big games in Morumbi, though Corinthians did have to move out briefly for a South American club tie in 1993, when the date clashed with a pop concert. International club matches, such as ties in the three South American club tournaments, are guaranteed to draw big crowds but domestic matches are not such crowd-pullers. In particular, the problems associated with the organization of the Brazilian national championship have meant that even Morumbi has seen only four-figure crowds on occasion – underlining the frequently heard public and media criticism about a surfeit of football in Brazil.

National Olympic Stadium

Tokyo, Japan

Capacity:
62,000
Opened:
1972
Club:
None
Hosted:
1979 World Youth Cup Final (Argentina 3, Soviet Union 1); World Club Cup finals (every year since 1980)

Soccer is the 1990s growth sport in Japan, so the stadium built to host the 1964 Olympics naturally served as the home of the national team and launched the successful professional J-League in 1993. Japan's appetite for big-time soccer was whetted in 1980, when Tokyo became the permanent home of the World Club Cup Final under the terms of a sponsorship arrangement with Toyota.

This previously two-leg affair between the European and South American Club Champions had become progressively discredited since its inception in 1960, often degenerating into violence. But the deci sion to change the format to a one-off game in front of an excitable but well-behave Japanese crowd, beginning with Naciona of Uruguay's 1–0 defeat of Nottingham Forest in 1980, has transformed it into popular fixture in the international calen dar early each December.

The stadium proved one of the points o weakness, however, in the Japanese bid t gain the right to host the 2002 World Cu finals. The city of Tokyo and the govern ment failed to agree on how best to shar funding for redevelopment work whic would have been necessary to bring it up t World Cup standard. That meant that Japa did not have an obvious capital city mai venue in their World Cup proposals despite the state-of-the-art construction c a new stadium in the nearby port of Yoko hama. In due course South Korea mad excellent propaganda use of the presence i Seoul of their Olympic stadium – and tha certainly helped them catch the Japanese i the bid process.

Ultimately, of course, FIFA decided tha the 2002 finals should be co-hosted though it still seems there may be no plac in the tournament for the stadium whic has played such a key role in soccer deve opment in Japan, and could do even more i it was made available for more matche instead of the yearly handful it current stages.

Ernst-Happel-Stadion

Vienna, Austria

Capacity:
62,958

Opened:
1931

Club:
No permanent club

Hosted:
1964 European Cup Final (Internazionale 3, Real Madrid 1), 1987 (Porto 2, Bayern Munich 1), 1990 (Milan 1, Benfica 0), 1995 (Ajax 1, Milan 0); 1970 European Cup-winners' Cup Final (Manchester City 2, Gornik Zarbrze 1)

Long known as the Prater, the Ernst Happel stadium gained its new name in memory of the late Austrian international defender and coach. It overlooks the pleasure grounds forever associated with Orson Welles and *The Third Man*, but Austrian fans associate it more with the Hugo Meisl "Wunderteam" of the 1930s, which counted England among its victims in 1936. The stadium was used as a troop headquarters during the latter stages of the Second World War and suffered severe bomb damage. This was rapidly repaired and the Prater regularly welcomed capacity 70,000 crowds throughout the 1950s and early 1960s.

It has been transformed in recent years into one of Europe's leading venues, the original open two-tiered amphitheatre topped by a remarkable roof which was erected in 10 months during 1985 at a cost of £17.5 million. The original 60,000-capacity stadium, a legacy of the socialist-controlled city administration, opened in July 1931 with a match appropriately between two workers teams, and hosted athletics championships and the long forgotten Workers Olympiad.

After the Anschluss, the stadium became an army barracks, and staged wartime internationals while serving as a staging post for Austrian Jews on their way to concentration camps. Though badly damaged by Allied troops, the stadium was quickly restored after the war. Rapid (*see* page 62) played Real Madrid under floodlights in 1955 and a record 90,593 watched Austria play Spain in 1960. In the 1970s, the provision of an all-weather track cut capacity to 72,000.

No club has used it permanently for league matches since FK Austria moved out in 1982. But Rapid, FK Austria and even Casino Salzburg have all used it intermittently for European cup-ties.

The Statistics

Statistics are what make the football world go round. Who won what when and who scored the winning goal? From Amsterdam to Athens and Seoul to São Paulo, football fans are always on a quest to discover yet more information about the world's most 'beautiful game'.

The international programme has grown in piecemeal fashion since the first match between Scotland and England in 1872. Now there are myriad tournaments, ranging from the World Cup, the planet's most popular sporting event, to the well-established club competitions such as the European Champions Cup and the South American Copa Libertadores. All results and statistics, from all the major competitions, are covered in comprehensive detail.

Key: WCQ = World Cup Qualifier

WCF = World Cup Final

ECQ = European Championship Qualifier

ECF = European Championship Finals

UT = Umbro Tournament

TdF = Tournoi de France

* = after extra time

The World Cup

1930 World Cup

Pool 1

France	4	Mexico	1
Argentina	1	France	0
Chile	3	Mexico	0
Chile	1	France	0
Argentina	6	Mexico	3
Argentina	3	Chile	1

Teams	P	W	D	L	F	A	Pts
Argentina	3	3	0	0	10	4	6
Chile	3	2	0	1	5	3	4
France	3	1	0	2	4	3	2
Mexico	3	0	0	3	4	13	0

Pool 2

Yugoslavia	2	Brazil	1
Yugoslavia	4	Bolivia	0
Brazil	4	Bolivia	0

Teams	P	W	D	L	F	A	Pts
Yugoslavia	2	2	0	0	6	1	4
Brazil	2	1	0	1	5	2	2
Bolivia	2	0	0	2	0	8	0

Pool 3

Romania	3	Peru	1
Uruguay	1	Peru	0
Uruguay	4	Romania	0

Teams	P	W	D	L	F	A	Pts
Uruguay	2	2	0	0	5	0	4
Romania	2	1	0	1	3	5	2
Peru	2	0	0	2	1	4	0

Pool 4

USA	3	Belgium	0
USA	3	Paraguay	0
Paraguay	1	Belgium	0

Teams	P	W	D	L	F	A	Pts
USA	2	2	0	0	6	0	4
Paraguay	2	1	0	1	1	3	2
Belgium	2	0	0	2	0	4	0

Semi-finals

Argentina	6	USA	1
Uruguay	6	Yugoslavia	1

Leading scorers:

8 Stabile (Argentina); 5 Cea (Uruguay).

Final

Uruguay	(1)4	Argentina	(2)2
Dorado, Cea,		*Peucelle,*	
Iriarte, Castro		*Stabile*	

Uruguay:

Ballesteros, Nasazzi (capt.), Mascheroni, Andrade, Fernandez, Gestido, Dorado, Scarone, Castro, Cea, Iriarte.

Argentina:

Botasso, Della Torre, Paternoster, Evaristo J., Monti, Suarez, Peucelle, Varallo, Stabile, Ferreira (capt.), Evaristo M.

1934 World Cup

First round

Italy	7	USA	1
Czech.	2	Romania	1
Germany	5	Belgium	2
Austria	3	France	2*
Spain	3	Brazil	1
Switzerland	3	Holland	2
Sweden	3	Argentina	2
Hungary	4	Egypt	2

Second round

Germany	2	Sweden	1
Austria	2	Hungary	1
Italy	1	Spain	1*
Italy	1	Spain	0
Czech.	3	Switzerland	2

Semi-finals

Czech.	3	Germany	1
Italy	1	Austria	0

Third place match

Germany	3	Austria	2

Final

Italy	(0)2	Czech.	(0)1*
Orsi, Schiavio		*Puc*	

Italy:
Combi (capt.), Monzeglio, Allemandi, Ferraris IV,
Monti, Bertolini, Guaita, Meazza, Schiavio, Ferrari,
Orsi.

Czechoslovakia:
Planicka (capt.), Zenisek, Ctyroky, Kostalek, Cambal,
Kreil, Junek, Svoboda, Sobotka, Nejedly, Puc.

Leading scorers:
4 Nejedly (Czechoslovakia),
Schiavio (Italy), Conen (Germany).

1938 World Cup

First round

Switzerland	1	Germany	1*
Switzerland	4	Germany	2 (r)
Cuba	3	Romania	3*
Cuba	2	Romania	1 (r)
Hungary	6	Dutch E. Indies	0
France	3	Belgium	1
Czech.	3	Holland	0*
Brazil	6	Poland	5*
Italy	2	Norway	1*

Second round

Sweden	8	Cuba	0
Hungary	2	Switzerland	0
Italy	3	France	1
Brazil	1	Czech.	1*
Brazil	2	Czech.	1*

Semi-finals

Italy	2	Brazil	1
Hungary	5	Sweden	1

Third place match

Brazil	4	Sweden	2

Final

Italy	(3)4	Hungary	(1)2
Colaussi (2),		*Titkos, Sarosi*	
Piola (2)			

Italy:
Olivieri, Foni, Rava, Serantoni, Andreolo, Locatelli,
Biavati, Meazza (capt.), Piola, Ferrari, Colaussi.

Hungary:
Szabo, Polgar, Biro, Szalay, Szucs, Lazar, Sas, Vincze,
Sarosi (capt.), Szengeller, Titkos.

Leading scorers
8 Leonidas (Brazil); 7 Szengeller (Hungary); 5 Piola
(Italy).

1950 World Cup

Pool 1

Brazil	4	Mexico	0
Yugoslavia	3	Switzerland	0
Yugoslavia	4	Mexico	1
Brazil	2	Switzerland	2
Brazil	2	Yugoslavia	0
Switzerland	2	Mexico	1

Teams	P	W	D	L	F	A	Pts
Brazil	3	2	1	0	8	2	5
Yugoslavia	3	2	0	1	7	3	4
Switzerland	3	1	1	1	4	6	3
Mexico	3	0	0	3	2	10	0

Pool 2

Spain	3	USA	1
England	2	Chile	0
USA	1	England	0
Spain	2	Chile	0
Spain	1	England	0
Chile	5	USA	2

Teams	P	W	D	L	F	A	Pts
Spain	3	3	0	0	6	1	6
England	3	1	0	2	2	2	2
Chile	3	1	0	2	5	6	2
USA	3	1	0	2	4	8	2

Pool 3

Sweden	3	Italy	2
Sweden	2	Paraguay	2
Italy	2	Paraguay	0

Teams	P	W	D	L	F	A	Pts
Sweden	2	1	1	0	5	4	3
Italy	2	1	0	1	4	3	2
Paraguay	2	0	1	1	2	4	1

Pool 4

| Uruguay | 8 | Bolivia | 0 |

Teams	P	W	D	L	F	A	Pts
Uruguay	1	1	0	0	8	0	2
Bolivia	1	0	0	1	0	8	0

Final pool

Uruguay	2	Spain	2
Brazil	7	Sweden	1
Uruguay	3	Sweden	2
Brazil	6	Spain	1
Sweden	3	Spain	1
Uruguay	2	Brazil	1

Teams	P	W	D	L	F	A	Pts
Uruguay	3	2	1	0	7	5	5
Brazil	3	2	0	1	14	4	4
Sweden	3	1	0	2	6	11	2
Spain	3	0	1	2	4	11	1

Leading scorers:

9 Ademir (Brazil); 6 Schiaffino (Uruguay); 5 Zarra (Spain).

Deciding match

Uruguay	(0)2	Brazil	(0)1
Schiaffino,		Friaca	
Ghiggia			

Uruguay:

Maspoli, Gonzales, M., Tejera, Gambetta, Varela, Andrade, Ghiggia, Perez, Miguez, Schiaffino, Moran.

Brazil:

Barbosa, Augusto, Juvenal, Bauer, Danilo, Bigode, Friaca, Zizinho, Ademir, Jair, Chico.

1954 World Cup

Pool 1

Yugoslavia	1	France	0
Brazil	5	Mexico	0
France	3	Mexico	2
Brazil	1	Yugoslavia	1

Teams	P	W	D	L	F	A	Pts
Brazil	2	1	1	0	6	1	3
Yugoslavia	2	1	1	0	2	1	3
France	2	1	0	1	3	3	2
Mexico	2	0	0	2	2	8	0

Pool 2

Hungary	9	Korea	0
W. Germany	4	Turkey	1
Hungary	8	W. Germany	3
Turkey	7	Korea	0

Teams	P	W	D	L	F	A	Pts
Hungary	2	2	0	0	17	3	4
W. Germany	2	1	0	1	7	9	2
Turkey	2	1	0	1	8	4	2
Korea	2	0	0	2	0	16	0

Play-off

W. Germany	7	Turkey	2

Pool 3

Austria	1	Scotland	0
Uruguay	2	Czech.	0
Austria	5	Czech.	0
Uruguay	7	Scotland	0

Teams	P	W	D	L	F	A	Pts
Uruguay	2	2	0	0	9	0	4
Austria	2	2	0	0	6	0	4
Czech.	2	0	0	2	0	7	0
Scotland	2	0	0	2	0	8	0

Pool 4

England	4	Belgium	4
England	2	Switzerland	0
Switzerland	2	Italy	1
Italy	4	Belgium	1

Teams	P	W	D	L	F	A	Pts
England	2	1	1	0	6	4	3
Italy	2	1	0	1	5	3	2
Switzerland	2	1	0	1	2	3	2
Belgium	2	0	1	1	5	8	1

Play-off

Switzerland	4	Italy	1

Quarter-finals

W. Germany	2	Yugoslavia	0
Hungary	4	Brazil	2
Austria	7	Switzerland	5
Uruguay	4	England	2

Semi-finals

W. Germany	6	Austria	1
Hungary	4	Uruguay	2

Third-place match

Austria	3	Uruguay	1

Final

W. Germany	(2)3	Hungary	(2)2
Morlock,		*Puskas, Czibor*	
Rahn (2)			

Leading scorers

11 Kocsis (Hungary); 8 Morlock (W. Germany); 6 Probst (Austria), Hügi (Switzerland).

West Germany:

Turek, Posipal, Kohlmeyer, Eckel, Liebrich, Mai, Rahn, Morlock, Walter O., Walter F. (capt.), Schäfer.

Hungary:

Grosics, Buzansky, Lantos, Bozsik, Lorant, Zakarias, Czibor, Kocsis, Hidegkuti, Puskas (capt.), Toth J.

1958 World Cup

Pool 1

W. Germany	3	Argentina	1
N. Ireland	1	Czech.	0
W. Germany	2	Czech.	2
Argentina	3	N. Ireland	1
W. Germany	2	N. Ireland	2
Czech.	6	Argentina	1

Teams	P	W	D	L	F	A	Pts
W. Germany	3	1	2	0	7	5	4
Czech.	3	1	1	1	8	4	3
N. Ireland	3	1	1	1	4	5	3
Argentina	3	1	0	2	5	10	2

Play-off

N. Ireland	2	Czech.	1

Pool 2

France	7	Paraguay	3
Yugoslavia	1	Scotland	1
Yugoslavia	3	France	2
Paraguay	3	Scotland	2
France	2	Scotland	1
Yugoslavia	3	Paraguay	3

Teams	P	W	D	L	F	A	Pts
France	3	2	0	1	11	7	4
Yugoslavia	3	1	2	0	7	6	4
Paraguay	3	1	1	1	9	12	3
Scotland	3	0	1	2	4	6	1

Pool 3

Sweden	3	Mexico	0
Hungary	1	Wales	1
Wales	1	Mexico	1
Sweden	2	Hungary	1
Sweden	0	Wales	0
Hungary	4	Mexico	0

Teams	P	W	D	L	F	A	Pts
Sweden	3	2	1	0	5	1	5
Hungary	3	1	1	1	6	3	3
Wales	3	0	3	0	2	2	3
Mexico	3	0	1	2	1	8	1

Play-off

Wales	2	Hungary	1

Pool 4

England	2	Soviet Union	2
Brazil	3	Austria	0
England	0	Brazil	0
Soviet Union	2	Austria	0
Brazil	2	Soviet Union	0
England	2	Austria	2

Teams	P	W	D	L	F	A	Pts
Brazil	3	2	1	0	5	0	5
England	3	0	3	0	4	4	3
Soviet Union	3	1	1	1	4	4	3
Austria	3	0	1	2	2	7	1

Play-off

Soviet Union	1	England	0

Quarter-finals

France	4	N. Ireland	0
W. Germany	1	Yugoslavia	0
Sweden	2	Soviet Union	0
Brazil	1	Wales	0

Third place match

France	6	W. Germany	3

Semi-finals

Brazil	5	France	2
Sweden	3	W. Germany	1

Final

Brazil	(2)5	Sweden	(1)2
Vava (2),		Liedholm	
Pele (2), Zagallo		Simonsson	

Brazil: Gilmar, Santos D., Santos N., Zito, Bellini (capt.), Orlando, Garrincha, Didi, Vava, Pele, Zagalo.

Sweden: Svensson, Bergmark, Axbom, Boerjesson, Gustavsson, Parling, Hamrin, Gren, Simonsson, Liedholm (capt.), Skoglund.

Leading scorers

13 Fontaine (France); 6 Pele (Brazil), Rahn (W. Germany); 5 Vava (Brazil), McParland (N. Ireland).

1962 World Cup

Group 1

Uruguay	2	Colombia	1
Soviet Union	2	Yugoslavia	0
Yugoslavia	3	Uruguay	1
Soviet Union	4	Colombia	4
Soviet Union	2	Uruguay	1
Yugoslavia	5	Colombia	0

Teams	P	W	D	L	F	A	Pts
Soviet Union	3	2	1	0	8	5	5
Yugoslavia	3	2	0	1	8	3	4
Uruguay	3	1	0	2	4	6	2
Colombia	3	0	1	2	5	11	1

Group 2

Chile	3	Switzerland	1
W. Germany	0	Italy	0
Chile	2	Italy	0
W. Germany	2	Switzerland	1
W. Germany	2	Chile	0
Italy	3	Switzerland	0

Teams	P	W	D	L	F	A	Pts
W. Germany	3	2	1	0	4	1	5
Chile	3	2	0	1	5	3	4
Italy	3	1	1	1	3	2	3
Switzerland	3	0	0	3	2	8	0

Group 3

Brazil	2	Mexico	0
Czech.	1	Spain	0
Brazil	0	Czech.	0
Spain	1	Mexico	0
Brazil	2	Spain	1
Mexico	3	Czech.	1

Teams	P	W	D	L	F	A	Pts
Brazil	3	2	1	0	4	1	5
Czech.	3	1	1	1	2	3	3
Mexico	3	1	0	2	2	3	2
Spain	3	1	0	2	2	3	2

Group 4

Argentina	1	Bulgaria	0
Hungary	2	England	1
England	3	Argentina	1
Hungary	6	Bulgaria	1
Argentina	0	Hungary	0
England	0	Bulgaria	0

Teams	P	W	D	L	F	A	Pts
Hungary	3	2	1	0	8	2	5
England	3	1	1	1	4	3	3
Argentina	3	1	1	1	2	3	3
Bulgaria	3	0	1	2	1	7	1

Quarter-finals

Yugoslavia	1	W. Germany	0
Brazil	3	England	1
Chile	2	Soviet Union	1
Czech.	1	Hungary	0

Third place match

Chile	1	Yugoslavia	0

Leading scorers

5 , Jerkovic (Yugoslavia); 4 Garrincha (Brazil), Vava (Brazil), Sanchez L. (Chile), Albert (Hungary), Ivanov V. (USSR); 3 Amarildo (Brazil), Scherer (Czechoslovakia), Galic (Yugoslavia), Tichy (Hungary).

Semi-finals

Brazil	4	Chile	2
Czech.	3	Yugoslavia	1

Final

Brazil	(1)3	Czech.	(1)1
Amarildo, Zito, Vava		*Masopust*	

Brazil: Gilmar, Santos D., Mauro (capt.), Zozimo, Santos N., Zito, Didi, Garrincha, Vava, Amarildo, Zagalo.

Czechoslovakia: Schroiff, Tichy, Novak (capt.), Pluskal, Popluhar, Masopust, Pospichal, Scherer, Kvasniak, Kadraba, Jelinek.

1966 World Cup

Group 1

England	0	Uruguay	0
France	1	Mexico	1
Uruguay	2	France	1
England	2	Mexico	0
Uruguay	0	Mexico	0
England	2	France	0

Teams	P	W	D	L	F	A	Pts
England	3	2	1	0	4	0	5
Uruguay	3	1	2	0	2	1	4
Mexico	3	0	2	1	1	3	2
France	3	0	1	2	2	5	1

Group 2

W. Germany	5	Switzerland	0
Argentina	2	Spain	1
Spain	2	Switzerland	1
Argentina	0	W. Germany	0
Argentina	2	Switzerland	0
W. Germany	2	Spain	1

Teams	P	W	D	L	F	A	Pts
W. Germany	3	2	1	0	7	1	5
Argentina	3	2	1	0	4	1	5
Spain	3	1	0	2	4	5	2
Switzerland	3	0	0	3	1	9	0

Group 3

Brazil	2	Bulgaria	0
Portugal	3	Hungary	1
Hungary	3	Brazil	1
Portugal	3	Bulgaria	0
Portugal	3	Brazil	1
Hungary	3	Bulgaria	1

Teams	P	W	D	L	F	A	Pts
Portugal	3	3	0	0	9	2	6
Hungary	3	2	0	1	7	5	4
Brazil	3	1	0	2	4	6	2
Bulgaria	3	0	0	3	1	8	0

Group 4

Soviet Union	3	North Korea	0
Italy	2	Chile	0
Chile	1	North Korea	1
Soviet Union	1	Italy	0
North Korea	1	Italy	0
Soviet Union	2	Chile	1

Teams	P	W	D	L	F	A	Pts
Soviet Union	3	3	0	0	6	1	6
North Korea	3	1	1	1	2	4	3
Italy	3	1	0	2	2	2	2
Chile	3	0	1	2	2	5	1

Quarter-finals

England	1	Argentina	0
W. Germany	4	Uruguay	0
Portugal	5	North Korea	3
Soviet Union	2	Hungary	1

Third place match

Portugal	2	Soviet Union	1

Leading scorers

9 Eusebio (Portugal); 5 Haller (West Germany); 4 Beckenbauer (West Germany), Hurst (England), Bene (Hungary), Porkujan (USSR).

Semi-finals

W. Germany	2	Soviet Union	1
England	2	Portugal	1

Final

England	(1)4	W. Germany (1)2*
Hurst (3), Peters		Haller, Weber

England: Banks, Cohen, Wilson, Stiles, Charlton J., Moore (capt.), Ball, Hurst, Hunt, Charlton R., Peters.

West Germany: Tilkowski, Höttges, Schülz, Weber, Schnellinger, Haller, Beckenbauer, Overath, Seeler (capt.), Held, Emmerich.

1970 World Cup

Group 1

Mexico	0	Soviet Union	0
Belgium	3	El Salvador	0
Soviet Union	4	Belgium	1
Mexico	4	El Salvador	0
Soviet Union	2	El Salvador	0
Mexico	1	Belgium	0

Teams	P	W	D	L	F	A	Pts
Soviet Union	3	2	1	0	6	1	5
Mexico	3	2	1	0	5	0	5
Belgium	3	1	0	2	4	5	2
El Salvador	3	0	0	3	0	9	0

Group 2

Uruguay	2	Israel	0
Italy	1	Sweden	0
Uruguay	0	Italy	0
Sweden	1	Israel	1
Sweden	1	Uruguay	0
Italy	0	Israel	0

Teams	P	W	D	L	F	A	Pts
Italy	3	1	2	0	1	0	4
Uruguay	3	1	1	1	2	1	3
Sweden	3	1	1	1	2	2	3
Israel	3	0	2	1	1	3	2

Group 3

England	1	Romania	0
Brazil	4	Czech.	1
Romania	2	Czech.	1
Brazil	1	England	0
Brazil	3	Romania	2
England	1	Czech.	0

Teams	P	W	D	L	F	A	Pts
Brazil	3	3	0	0	8	3	6
England	3	2	0	1	2	1	4
Romania	3	1	0	2	4	5	2
Czech.	3	0	0	3	2	7	0

Group 4

Peru	3	Bulgaria	2
W. Germany	2	Morocco	1
Peru	3	Morocco	0
W. Germany	5	Bulgaria	2
W. Germany	3	Peru	1
Morocco	1	Bulgaria	1

Teams	P	W	D	L	F	A	Pts
W. Germany	3	3	0	0	10	4	6
Peru	3	2	0	1	7	5	4
Bulgaria	3	0	1	2	5	9	1
Morocco	3	0	1	2	2	6	1

Quarter-finals

W. Germany	3	England	2*
Brazil	4	Peru	2
Italy	4	Mexico	1
Uruguay	1	Soviet Union	0

Third place match

W. Germany	1	Uruguay	0

Brazil: Felix, Carlos Alberto (capt.), Brito, Piazza, Everaldo, Clodoaldo, Gerson, Jairzinho, Tostao, Pele, Rivelino.

Italy: Albertosi, Cera, Burgnich, Bertini (Juliano), Rosato, Facchetti (capt.), Domenghini, Mazzola, De Sisti, Boninsegna (Rivera), Riva.

Semi-finals

Italy	4	W. Germany	3*
Brazil	3	Uruguay	1

Final

Brazil	4	Italy	1
Pele, Gerson,		*Boninsegna*	
Jairzinho,			
Carlos Alberto			

Leading scorers

9 Müller (West Germany); 7 Jairzinho (Brazil); 4 Pele (Brazil), Cubillas (Peru), Byscevietz (USSR), Seeler (West Germany).

1974 World Cup

Group 1

W. Germany	1	Chile	0
E. Germany	2	Australia	0
W. Germany	3	Australia	0
E. Germany	1	Chile	1
E. Germany	1	W. Germany	0
Chile	0	Australia	0

Teams	P	W	D	L	F	A	Pts
E. Germany	3	2	1	0	4	1	5
W. Germany	3	2	0	1	4	1	4
Chile	3	0	2	1	1	2	1
Australia	3	0	1	2	0	5	1

Group 2

Brazil	0	Yugoslavia	0
Scotland	2	Zaire	0
Brazil	0	Scotland	0
Yugoslavia	9	Zaire	0
Scotland	1	Yugoslavia	1
Brazil	3	Zaire	0

Teams	P	W	D	L	F	A	Pts
Yugoslavia	3	1	2	0	10	1	4
Brazil	3	1	2	0	3	0	4
Scotland	3	1	2	0	3	1	4
Zaire	3	0	0	3	0	14	0

Group 3

Holland	2	Uruguay	0
Sweden	0	Bulgaria	0
Holland	0	Sweden	0
Bulgaria	1	Uruguay	1
Holland	4	Bulgaria	1
Sweden	3	Uruguay	0

Teams	P	W	D	L	F	A	Pts
Holland	3	2	1	0	6	1	5
Sweden	3	1	2	0	3	0	4
Bulgaria	3	0	2	1	2	5	2
Uruguay	3	0	1	2	1	6	1

Group 4

Italy	3	Haiti	1
Poland	3	Argentina	2
Italy	1	Argentina	1
Poland	7	Haiti	0
Argentina	4	Haiti	1
Poland	2	Italy	1

Teams	P	W	D	L	F	A	Pts
Poland	3	3	0	0	12	3	6
Argentina	3	1	1	1	7	5	3
Italy	3	1	1	1	5	4	3
Haiti	3	0	0	3	2	14	0

Group A

Brazil	1	E. Germany	0
Holland	4	Argentina	0
Holland	2	E. Germany	0
Brazil	2	Argentina	1
Holland	2	Brazil	0
Argentina	1	E. Germany	1

Teams	P	W	D	L	F	A	Pts
Holland	3	3	0	0	8	0	6
Brazil	3	2	0	1	3	3	4
E. Germany	3	0	1	2	1	4	1
Argentina	3	0	1	2	2	7	1

Group B

Poland	1	Sweden	0
W. Germany	2	Yugoslavia	0
Poland	2	Yugoslavia	1
W. Germany	4	Sweden	2
Sweden	2	Yugoslavia	1
W. Germany	1	Poland	0

Teams	P	W	D	L	F	A	Pts
W. Germany	3	3	0	0	7	2	6
Poland	3	2	0	1	3	2	4
Sweden	3	1	0	2	4	6	2
Yugoslavia	3	0	0	3	2	6	0

Third place match

Poland	1	Brazil	0

Final

W. Germany	(2)2	Holland	(1)1*

Breitner (pen),
Müller

Neeskens (pen)

Leading scorers

7 Lato (Poland); 5 Neeskens (Holland), Szarmach (Poland).

1978 World Cup

Group 1

Argentina	2	Hungary	1
Italy	2	France	1
Argentina	2	France	1
Italy	3	Hungary	1
Italy	1	Argentina	0
France	3	Hungary	1

Teams	P	W	D	L	F	A	Pts
Italy	3	3	0	0	6	2	6
Argentina	3	2	0	1	4	3	4
France	3	1	0	2	5	5	2
Hungary	3	0	0	3	3	8	0

Group 2

W. Germany	0	Poland	0
Tunisia	3	Mexico	1
Poland	1	Tunisia	0
W. Germany	6	Mexico	0
Poland	3	Mexico	1
W. Germany	0	Tunisia	0

Teams	P	W	D	L	F	A	Pts
Poland	3	2	1	0	4	1	5
W. Germany	3	1	2	0	6	0	4
Tunisia	3	1	1	1	3	2	3
Mexico	3	0	0	3	2	12	0

Group 3

Austria	2	Spain	1
Sweden	1	Brazil	1
Austria	1	Sweden	0
Brazil	0	Spain	0
Spain	1	Sweden	0
Brazil	1	Austria	0

Teams	P	W	D	L	F	A	Pts
Austria	3	2	0	1	3	2	4
Brazil	3	1	2	0	2	1	4
Spain	3	1	1	1	2	2	3
Sweden	3	0	1	2	1	3	1

Group 4

Peru	3	Scotland	1
Holland	3	Iran	1
Scotland	1	Iran	1
Holland	0	Peru	0
Peru	4	Iran	1
Scotland	3	Holland	2

Teams	P	W	D	L	F	A	Pts
Peru	3	2	1	0	7	2	5
Holland	3	1	1	1	5	3	3
Scotland	3	1	1	1	5	6	3
Iran	3	0	1	2	2	8	1

Group A

Italy	0	W. Germany	0
Holland	5	Austria	1
Italy	1	Austria	0
Austria	3	W. Germany	2
Holland	2	Italy	1
Holland	2	W. Germany	2

Teams	P	W	D	L	F	A	Pts
Holland	3	2	1	0	9	4	5
Italy	3	1	1	1	2	2	3
W. Germany	3	0	2	1	4	5	2
Austria	3	1	0	2	4	8	2

Group B

Argentina	2	Poland	0
Brazil	3	Peru	0
Argentina	0	Brazil	0
Poland	1	Peru	0
Brazil	3	Poland	1
Argentina	6	Peru	0

Teams	P	W	D	L	F	A	Pts
Argentina	3	2	1	0	8	0	5
Brazil	3	2	1	0	6	1	5
Poland	3	1	0	2	2	5	2
Peru	3	0	0	3	0	10	0

Third place match

Brazil	2	Italy	1

Final

Argentina	(1)3	Holland	(0)1*
Kempes (2), Bertoni		*Nanninga*	

Leading scorers

6 Kempes (Argentina); 5 Rensenbrink (Holland), Cubillas (Peru).

1982 World Cup

Group 1

Italy	0	Poland	0
Peru	0	Cameroon	0
Italy	1	Peru	1
Poland	0	Cameroon	0
Poland	5	Peru	1
Italy	1	Cameroon	1

Teams	P	W	D	L	F	A	Pts
Poland	3	1	2	0	5	1	4
Italy	3	0	3	0	2	2	3
Cameroon	3	0	3	0	1	1	3
Peru	3	0	2	1	2	6	2

Group 2

Algeria	2	W. Germany	1
Austria	1	Chile	0
W. Germany	4	Chile	1
Austria	2	Algeria	1
Algeria	3	Chile	2
W. Germany	1	Austria	0

Teams	P	W	D	L	F	A	Pts
W. Germany	3	2	0	1	6	3	4
Austria	3	2	0	1	3	1	4
Algeria	3	2	0	1	5	5	4
Chile	3	0	0	3	3	8	0

Group 3

Belgium	1	Argentina	0
Hungary	10	El Salvador	1
Argentina	4	Hungary	1
Belgium	1	El Salvador	0
Belgium	1	Hungary	1
Argentina	2	El Salvador	0

Teams	P	W	D	L	F	A	Pts
Belgium	3	2	1	0	3	1	5
Argentina	3	2	0	1	6	2	4
Hungary	3	1	1	1	12	6	3
El Salvador	3	0	0	3	1	13	3

Group 4

England	3	France	1
Czech.	1	Kuwait	1
England	2	Czech.	0
France	4	Kuwait	1
France	1	Czech.	1
England	1	Kuwait	0

Teams	P	W	D	L	F	A	Pts
England	3	3	0	0	6	1	6
France	3	1	1	1	6	5	3
Czech.	3	0	2	1	2	4	2
Kuwait	3	0	1	2	2	6	1

Group 5

Spain	1	Honduras	1
N. Ireland	0	Yugoslavia	0
Spain	2	Yugoslavia	1
N. Ireland	1	Honduras	1
Yugoslavia	1	Honduras	0
N. Ireland	1	Spain	0

Teams	P	W	D	L	F	A	Pts
N. Ireland	3	1	2	0	2	1	4
Spain	3	1	1	1	3	3	3
Yugoslavia	3	1	1	1	2	2	3
Honduras	3	0	2	1	2	3	2

Group 6

Brazil	2	Soviet Union	1
Scotland	5	New Zealand	2
Brazil	4	Scotland	1
Soviet Union	3	New Zealand	0
Scotland	2	Soviet Union	2
Brazil	4	New Zealand	0

Teams	P	W	D	L	F	A	Pts
Brazil	3	3	0	0	10	2	6
Soviet Union	3	1	1	1	6	4	3
Scotland	3	1	1	1	8	8	3
New Zealand	3	0	0	3	2	12	0

Group A

Poland	3	Belgium	0
Soviet Union	1	Belgium	0
Soviet Union	0	Poland	0

Teams	P	W	D	L	F	A	Pts
Poland	2	1	1	0	3	0	3
Soviet Union	2	1	1	0	1	0	3
Belgium	2	0	0	2	0	4	0

Group B

W. Germany	0	England	0
W. Germany	2	Spain	1
England	0	Spain	0

Teams	P	W	D	L	F	A	Pts
W. Germany	2	1	1	0	2	1	3
England	2	0	2	0	0	0	2
Spain	2	0	1	1	1	2	1

Group C

Italy	2	Argentina	1
Brazil	3	Argentina	1
Italy	3	Brazil	2

Teams	P	W	D	L	F	A	Pts
Italy	2	2	0	0	5	3	4
Brazil	2	1	0	1	5	4	2
Argentina	2	0	0	2	2	5	0

Group D

France	1	Austria	0
N. Ireland	2	Austria	2
France	4	N. Ireland	1

Teams	P	W	D	L	F	A	Pts
France	2	2	0	0	5	1	4
Austria	2	0	1	1	2	3	1
N. Ireland	2	0	1	1	3	6	1

Semi-finals

Italy	2	Poland	0
W. Germany	3	France	3*

(West Germany won 5–4 on penalties)

Third place match

Poland	3	France	2

Leading scorers

6 Rossi (Italy); 5 Rummenigge (West Germany); 4 Zico (Brazil), Boniek (Poland).

Final

Italy	(0)3	W. Germany	(0)1

Rossi, Tardelli, Altobelli — *Breitner*

Italy: Zoff (capt.), Bergomi, Cabrini, Collovati, Scirea, Gentile, Oriale, Tardelli, Conti, Graziani (Altobelli; Causio), Rossi.

West Germany: Schumacher, Kaltz, Förster K., Stielike, Förster B., Breitner, Dremmler (Hrubesch), Littbarski, Briegel, Fischer (Müller, H.), Rummenigge (capt.).

1986 World Cup

Group A

Bulgaria	1	Italy	1
Argentina	3	South Korea	1
Italy	1	Argentina	1
Bulgaria	1	South Korea	1
Argentina	2	Bulgaria	0
Italy	3	South Korea	2

Teams	P	W	D	L	F	A	Pts
Argentina	3	2	1	0	6	2	5
Italy	3	1	2	0	5	4	4
Bulgaria	3	0	2	1	2	4	2
South Korea	3	0	1	2	4	7	1

Group B

Mexico	2	Belgium	1
Paraguay	1	Iraq	0
Mexico	1	Paraguay	1
Belgium	2	Iraq	1
Paraguay	2	Belgium	2
Mexico	1	Iraq	0

Teams	P	W	D	L	F	A	Pts
Mexico	3	2	1	0	4	2	5
Paraguay	3	1	2	0	4	3	4
Belgium	3	1	1	1	5	5	4
Iraq	3	0	0	3	1	4	0

Group C

Soviet Union	6	Hungary	0
France	1	Canada	0
Soviet Union	1	France	1
Hungary	2	Canada	0
France	3	Hungary	0
Soviet Union	2	Canada	0

Teams	P	W	D	L	F	A	Pts
Soviet Union	3	2	1	0	9	1	5
France	3	2	1	0	5	1	5
Hungary	3	1	0	2	2	9	2
Canada	3	0	0	3	0	5	0

Group D

Brazil	1	Spain	0
N. Ireland	1	Algeria	1
Spain	2	N. Ireland	1
Brazil	1	Algeria	0
Spain	3	Algeria	0
Brazil	3	N. Ireland	0

Teams	P	W	D	L	F	A	Pts
Brazil	3	3	0	0	5	0	6
Spain	3	2	0	1	5	2	4
N. Ireland	3	0	1	2	2	6	1
Algeria	3	0	1	2	1	5	1

Group E

W. Germany	1	Uruguay	1
Denmark	1	Scotland	0
Denmark	6	Uruguay	1
W. Germany	2	Scotland	1
Scotland	0	Uruguay	0
Denmark	2	W. Germany	0

Teams	P	W	D	L	F	A	Pts
Denmark	3	3	0	0	9	1	6
W. Germany	3	1	1	1	3	4	3
Uruguay	3	0	2	1	2	7	2
Scotland	3	0	1	3	1	3	1

Group F

Morocco	0	Poland	0
Portugal	1	England	0
England	0	Morocco	0
Poland	1	Portugal	0
England	3	Poland	0
Morocco	3	Portugal	1

Teams	P	W	D	L	F	A	Pts
Morocco	3	1	2	0	3	1	4
England	3	1	1	1	3	1	3
Poland	3	1	1	1	3	3	3
Portugal	3	1	0	2	2	4	2

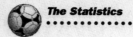

The Statistics

Second round
Knock-out phase comprising the top two teams from each group plus the four best third-placed teams.

Mexico	2	Bulgaria	0
Belgium	4	Soviet Union	3*
Brazil	4	Poland	0
Argentina	1	Uruguay	0
France	2	Italy	0
W. Germany	1	Morocco	0
England	3	Paraguay	0
Spain	5	Denmark	1

Quarter-finals

France	1	Brazil	1*

(France won 4–3 on pens)

W. Germany	0	Mexico	0*

(W. Germany won 4–1 on pens)

Argentina	2	England	1
Spain	1	Belgium	1*

(Belgium won 5–4 on pens)

Third place match

France	4	Belgium	2

Semi-finals

Argentina	2	Belgium	0
W. Germany	2	France	0

Final

Argentina	(1)3	W. Germany	(0)2
Brown, Valdano,		*Rummenigge,*	
Burruchaga		*Völler*	

Argentina: Pumpido, Cuciuffo, Olarticoechea, Ruggeri, Brown, Giusti, Burruchaga (Trobbiani), Batista, Valdano, Maradona (capt.), Enrique.

West Germany: Schumacher, Berthold, Briegel, Jakobs, Förster K., Eder, Brehme, Matthäus, Allofs (Völler), Magath (Hoeness, D.), Rummenigge (capt.).

Leading scorers
6 Lineker (England); 5 Butragueno (Spain), Careca (Brazil), Maradona (Argentina); 4 Altobelli (Italy), Belanov (USSR), Elkjaer (Denmark), Valdano (Argentina).

1990 World Cup

Group A

Italy	1	Austria	0
Czech.	5	USA	1
Italy	1	USA	0
Czech.	1	Austria	0
Italy	2	Czech.	0
Austria	2	USA	1

Group B

Cameroon	1	Argentina	0
Romania	2	Soviet Union	0
Argentina	2	Soviet Union	0
Cameroon	2	Romania	1
Argentina	1	Romania	1
Soviet Union	4	Cameroon	0

Group C

Brazil	2	Sweden	1
Costa Rica	1	Scotland	0
Brazil	1	Costa Rica	0
Scotland	2	Sweden	1
Brazil	1	Scotland	0
Costa Rica	2	Sweden	1

Group D

Colombia	2	UAE	0
W. Germany	4	Yugoslavia	1
Yugoslavia	1	Colombia	0
W. Germany	5	UAE	1
W. Germany	1	Colombia	1
Yugoslavia	4	UAE	1

Group E

Belgium	2	South Korea	0
Uruguay	0	Spain	0
Belgium	3	Uruguay	1
Spain	3	South Korea	1
Spain	2	Belgium	1
Uruguay	1	South Korea	0

Group F

England	1	Rep. Ireland	1
Holland	1	Egypt	1
England	0	Holland	0
Egypt	0	Rep. Ireland	0
England	1	Egypt	0
Holland	1	Rep. Ireland	1

Teams	P	W	D	L	F	A	Pts
Italy	3	3	0	0	4	0	6
Czech.	3	2	0	1	6	3	4
Austria	3	1	0	2	2	3	2
USA	3	0	0	3	2	8	0

Teams	P	W	D	L	F	A	Pts
Cameroon	3	2	0	1	3	5	4
Romania	3	1	1	1	4	3	3
Argentina	3	1	1	1	3	2	3
Soviet Union	3	1	0	2	4	4	2

Teams	P	W	D	L	F	A	Pts
Brazil	3	3	0	0	4	1	6
Costa Rica	3	2	0	1	3	2	4
Scotland	3	1	0	2	2	3	2
Sweden	3	0	0	3	3	6	0

Teams	P	W	D	L	F	A	Pts
W.Germany	3	2	1	0	10	3	5
Yugoslavia	3	2	0	1	6	5	4
Colombia	3	1	1	1	3	2	3
UAE	3	0	0	3	2	11	0

Teams	P	W	D	L	F	A	Pts
Spain	3	2	1	0	5	2	5
Belgium	3	2	0	1	6	3	4
Uruguay	3	1	1	1	2	3	3
South. Korea	3	0	0	3	1	6	0

Teams	P	W	D	L	F	A	Pts
England	3	1	2	0	2	1	4
Rep. Ireland	3	0	3	0	2	2	3
Holland	3	0	3	0	2	2	3
Egypt	3	0	2	1	1	2	2

Second phase

Knock-out phase comprising the top two teams from each group plus the four best third-placed teams

Cameroon	2	Colombia	1*
Czech.	4	Costa Rica	1
Argentina	1	Brazil	0
W. Germany	2	Holland	1
Rep. of Ireland	0	Romania	0*

(Rep. of Ireland won 5–4 on penalties)

Italy	2	Uruguay	0
Yugoslavia	2	Spain	1*
England	1	Belgium	0*

Quarter-finals

Argentina	0	Yugoslavia	0*

(Argentina won 3–2 on penalties)

Italy	1	Rep. of Ireland	0
W. Germany	1	Czech.	0
England	3	Cameroon	2*

Semi-finals

Argentina	1	Italy	1*

(Argentina won 4–3 on penalties)

W. Germany	1	England	1*

(West Germany won 4–3 on penalties)

Third place match

Italy	2	England	1

Final

W. Germany	(0)1	Argentina	(0)0

Brehme (pen)

West Germany: Illgner, Berthold (Reuter), Kohler, Augenthaler, Buchwald, Brehme, Littbarski, Hässler, Matthäus (capt.), Völler, Klinsmann.

Argentina: Goycochea, Lorenzo, Serrizuela, Sensini, Ruggeri (Monzon), Simon, Basualdo, Burruchaga (Calderon), Maradona (capt.), Troglio, Dezotti.

Leading scorers

6 Schillaci (Italy); 5 Skuhravy (Czechoslovakia); 4 Michel (Spain), Milla (Cameroon), Matthäus (West Germany), Lineker (England).

The Statistics

1994 World Cup

Group A

USA	1	Switzerland	1
Colombia	1	Romania	3
USA	2	Colombia	1
Romania	1	Switzerland	4
USA	0	Romania	1
Switzerland	0	Colombia	2

Teams	P	W	D	L	F	A	Pts
Romania	3	2	0	1	5	5	6
Switzerland	3	1	1	1	5	4	4
USA	3	1	1	1	3	3	4
Colombia	3	1	0	2	4	5	3

Group B

Cameroon	2	Sweden	2
Brazil	2	Russia	0
Brazil	3	Cameroon	0
Sweden	3	Russia	1
Russia	6	Cameroon	1
Brazil	1	Sweden	1

Teams	P	W	D	L	F	A	Pts
Brazil	3	2	1	0	6	1	7
Sweden	3	1	2	0	6	4	5
Russia	3	1	0	2	7	6	3
Cameroon	3	0	1	2	11	1	1

Group C

Germany	1	Bolivia	0
Spain	2	South Korea	2
Germany	1	Spain	1
South Korea	0	Bolivia	0
Bolivia	1	Spain	3
Germany	3	South Korea	2

Teams	P	W	D	L	F	A	Pts
Germany	3	2	1	0	5	3	7
Spain	3	1	2	0	6	4	5
South Korea	3	0	2	1	4	5	2
Bolivia	3	0	1	2	1	4	1

Group D

Argentina	4	Greece	0
Nigeria	3	Bulgaria	0
Argentina	2	Nigeria	1
Bulgaria	4	Greece	0
Greece	0	Nigeria	2
Argentina	0	Bulgaria	2

Teams	P	W	D	L	F	A	Pts
Nigeria	3	2	0	1	6	2	6
Bulgaria	3	2	0	1	6	3	6
Argentina	3	2	0	1	6	3	6
Greece	3	0	0	3	10	1	0

Group E

Italy	0	Rep. of Ireland	1
Norway	1	Mexico	0
Italy	1	Norway	0
Mexico	2	Rep. of Ireland	1
Rep. of Ireland	0	Norway	0
Italy	1	Mexico	1

Teams	P	W	D	L	F	A	Pts
Mexico	3	1	1	1	3	3	4
Rep. of Ireland	3	1	1	1	2	2	4
Italy	3	1	1	1	2	2	4
Norway	3	1	1	1	1	1	4

Group F

Belgium	1	Morocco	0
Holland	2	Saudi Arabia	1
Belgium	1	Holland	0
Saudi Arabia	2	Morocco	1
Morocco	1	Holland	2
Belgium	0	Saudi Arabia	1

Teams	P	W	D	L	F	A	Pts
Holland	3	2	0	1	4	3	6
Saudi Arabia	3	2	0	1	4	3	6
Belgium	3	2	0	1	2	1	6
Morocco	3	0	0	3	2	5	0

Second phase

Germany	3	Belgium	2
Spain	3	Switzerland	0
Saudi Arabia	1	Sweden	3
Romania	3	Argentina	2
Holland	2	Rep. of Ireland	0
Brazil	1	USA	0
Nigeria	1	Italy	2*
Mexico	1	Bulgaria	1*

(Bulgaria won 3–1 on penalties)

Quarter-finals

Italy	2	Spain	1
Holland	2	Brazil	3
Germany	1	Bulgaria	2
Sweden	2	Romania	2*

(Sweden won 5–4 on penalties)

Semi-finals

Brazil	1	Sweden	0
Italy	2	Bulgaria	1

Third place match

Sweden	4	Bulgaria	0

Final

Brazil	0	Italy	0*

(Brazil won 3–2 on penalties)

Brazil:

Taffarel, Jorginho (Cafu 20), Aldair, Marcio Santos, Branco, Mazinho (Viola 106), Dunga (capt.), Mauro Silva, Zinho, Romario, Bebeto.

Italy:

Pagliuca, Mussi (Apolloni 34), Maldini, Baresi (capt.), Benarrivo, Berti, Albertini, Baggio, D., (Evani 94), Donadoni, Baggio, R., Massaro.

Leading scorers

6 Salenko (Russia), Stoichkov (Bulgaria);
5 Andersson, K. (Sweden), Baggio, R. (Italy), Klinsmann (Germany), Romario (Brazil); 4 Batistuta (Argentina), Dahlin (Sweden), Raducioiu (Romania)

1998 World Cup

Group A

Brazil	2	Scotland	1
Morocco	2	Norway	2
Brazil	3	Morocco	0
Scotland	1	Norway	1
Brazil	1	Norway	2
Scotland	0	Morocco	3

Group B

Italy	2	Chile	2
Austria	1	Cameroon	1
Chile	1	Austria	1
Italy	3	Cameroon	0
Chile	1	Cameroon	1
Italy	2	Austria	1

Group C

Saudi Arabia	0	Denmark	1
France	3	South Africa	0
France	4	Saudi Arabia	0
South Africa	1	Denmark	1
France	2	Denmark	1
South Africa	2	Saudi Arabia	2

Group D

Paraguay	0	Bulgaria	0
Spain	2	Nigeria	3
Nigeria	1	Bulgaria	0
Spain	0	Paraguay	0
Nigeria	1	Paraguay	3
Spain	6	Bulgaria	1

Group E

South Korea	1	Mexico	3
Holland	0	Belgium	0
Belgium	2	Mexico	2
Holland	5	South Korea	0
Belgium	1	South Korea	1
Holland	2	Mexico	2

Group F

Germany	2	US	0
Yugoslavia	1	Iran	0
Germany	2	Yugoslavia	2
US	1	Iran	2
Germany	2	Iran	0
US	0	Yugoslavia	1

Group G

England	2	Tunisia	0
Romania	1	Columbia	0
Columbia	1	Tunisia	0
Romania	2	England	1
Romania	1	Tunisia	1
England	2	Columbia	0

Group H

Argentina	1	Japan	0
Croatia	3	Jamaica	1
Japan	0	Croatia	1
Argentina	5	Jamaica	0
Argentina	1	Croatia	0
Japan	1	Jamaica	2

Teams	P	W	D	L	F	A	Pts
Brazil	3	2	0	1	6	3	6
Norway	3	1	3	0	5	4	5
Morocco	3	1	1	1	5	5	4
Scotland	3	0	1	2	2	6	1

Teams	P	W	D	L	F	A	Pts
Italy	3	2	1	0	7	3	7
Chile	3	0	3	0	4	4	3
Austria	3	0	2	1	3	4	2
Cameroon	3	0	2	1	2	5	2

Teams	P	W	D	L	F	A	Pts
France	3	3	0	0	9	1	9
Denmark	3	1	1	1	3	3	4
South Africa	3	0	2	1	3	6	2
Saudi Arabia	3	0	1	2	2	7	1

Teams	P	W	D	L	F	A	Pts
Nigeria	3	2	0	1	5	5	6
Paraguay	3	1	2	0	3	1	5
Spain	3	1	1	1	8	4	4
Bulgaria	3	0	1	2	1	7	1

Teams	P	W	D	L	F	A	Pts
Holland	3	1	2	0	7	2	5
Mexico	3	1	2	0	7	5	5
Belgium	3	0	3	0	3	3	3
South Korea	3	0	1	2	2	9	1

Teams	P	W	D	L	F	A	Pts
Germany	3	2	1	0	6	2	7
Yugoslavia	3	2	1	0	4	2	7
Iran	3	1	0	2	2	4	3
US	3	0	0	3	1	5	0

Teams	P	W	D	L	F	A	Pts
Romania	3	2	1	0	4	2	7
England	3	2	0	1	5	2	6
Columbia	3	1	0	2	1	3	3
Tunisia	3	0	1	2	1	4	1

Teams	P	W	D	L	F	A	Pts
Argentina	3	3	0	0	7	0	9
Croatia	3	2	0	1	4	2	6
Jamaica	3	1	0	2	3	9	3
Japan	3	0	0	3	1	5	0

Second phase

Italy	1	Norway	0
Brazil	4	Chile	1
France	1	Paraguay	0

(France won with Golden Goal)

Nigeria	1	Denmark	4
Germany	2	Mexico	1
Holland	2	Yugoslavia	1
Romania	0	Croatia	1
Argentina	2	England	2

(Argentina won 4–3 on penalties)

Quarter-finals

Italy	0	France	0

(France won 4–3 on penalties)

Brazil	3	Denmark	2
Holland	2	Argentina	1
Germany	0	Croatia	3

Semi-finals

Brazil	1	Holland	1

(Brazil won 4–2 on penalties)

France	2	Croatia	1

Third place match

Holland	1	Croatia	2

Final

France	(2)3	Brazil	(0)0

Zidane (2), Petit

France: Barthez, Thuram, Leboeuf, Desailly, Lizarazu, Karembeu (Boghossian), Deschamps (capt), Petit, Zidane, Djorkaeff (Vieira), Guivar'ch (Dugarry).

Brazil: Taffarel, Cafu, Junior Baiano, Aldair, Roberto Carlos, Dunga (capt), Cesar Sampaio (Edmundo), Leonardo (Denilson), Rivaldo, Bebeto, Ronaldo.

Leading scorers: 6 Suker (Croatia); 5 Vieri (Italy), Batistuta (Argentina); 4 Salas (Chile), Hernandez (Mexico)

FIFA Under-20 World Championship

Finalists

1977

Soviet Union	2	Mexico	2

(Soviet Union won 9–8 on penalties)

1979

Argentina	3	Soviet Union	1

1981

W. Germany	4	Qatar	0

1983

Brazil	1	Argentina	0

1985

Brazil	1	Spain	0

1987

Yugoslavia	1	W. Germany	1

(Yugoslavia won 5–4 on penalties)

1989

Portugal	2	Nigeria	0

1991

Portugal	0	Brazil	0

(Portugal won 4–2 on penalties)

1993

Brazil	2	Ghana	1

1995

Argentina	2	Brazil	0

1997

Argentina	2	Uruguay	1

Women's World Championship

Finalists

1991

USA	2	Norway	1

1995

Norway	2	Germany	0

Copa America (South American Championship)

Winners

1910 Buenos Aires:
1st   Argentina
2nd   Uruguay*

1916 Buenos Aires:
1st   Uruguay
2nd   Argentina*

1917 Montevideo:
1st   Uruguay
2nd   Argentina

1919 Rio de Janeiro (play-off):

Brazil	1	Uruguay	0

Friedenreich
Att: 28,000

1920 Vina del Mar:
1st   Uruguay
2nd   Argentina

1921 Buenos Aires:
1st   Argentina
2nd   Brazil

1922 Rio de Janeiro (play-off):

Brazil	3	Paraguay	1

Formiga (2), Neco   Rivas G.
Att: 20,000

1923 Montevideo:
1st   Uruguay
2nd   Argentina

1924 Montevideo:
1st   Uruguay
2nd   Argentina

1925 Buenos Aires:
1st   Argentina
2nd   Brazil

1926 Santiago:
1st   Uruguay
2nd   Argentina

1927 Lima:
1st   Argentina
2nd   Uruguay

1929 Buenos Aires:
1st   Argentina
2nd   Paraguay

1935 Lima:
1st   Uruguay
2nd   Argentina*

1937 Buenos Aires (play-off):

Argentina	2	Brazil	0

De la Mata (2)

1939 Lima:
1st Peru
2nd Uruguay

1941 Santiago:
1st Argentina
2nd Uruguay*

1942 Montevideo:
1st Uruguay
2nd Argentina

1945 Santiago:
1st Argentina
2nd Brazil*

1946 Buenos Aires:
1st Argentina
2nd Brazil*

1947 Guayaquil:
1st Argentina
2nd Paraguay

1949 Rio de Janeiro (play-off):

Brazil	7	Paraguay	0

Ademir Menezes (3),
Tesourinha (2),
Jair R. Pinto (2)
Att: 55,000

1953 Lima (play-off):

Paraguay	3	Brazil	2

Lopez A., Gavilan,   *Baltazar (2)*
Fernandez
Att: 35,000

1955 Santiago:
1st Argentina
2nd Chile

1956 Montevideo:
1st Uruguay
2nd Chile*

1957 Lima:
1st Argentina
2nd Brazil

1959 Buenos Aires:
1st Argentina
2nd Brazil*

1959 Guayaquil:
1st Uruguay
2nd Argentina

1963 Bolivia:
1st Bolivia
2nd Paraguay

1967 Montevideo:
1st Uruguay
2nd Argentina

1975 Bogota (1st leg):

Colombia	1	Peru	0

Castro P.
Att: 50,000

1975 Lima (2nd leg):

Peru	2	Colombia	0

Oblitas, Ramirez O. Att: 50,000

1975 Caracas (play-off):

Peru	1	Colombia	0

Sotil
Att: 30,000

1979 Asuncion (1st leg):

Paraguay	3	Chile	0

Romero C. (2),
Morel M.

1979 Santiago (2nd leg):

Chile	1	Paraguay	0

Rivas
Att: 55,000

1979 Buenos Aires (play-off):

Paraguay	0	Chile	0

Att: 6,000
(Paraguay won on goal difference)

1983 Montevideo (1st leg):

Uruguay	2	Brazil	0

Francescoli, Diogo
Att: 65,000

1983 Salvador (2nd leg):

Brazil	1	Uruguay	1

Jorginho   *Aguilera*
Att: 95,000

1987 Buenos Aires:

Uruguay	1	Chile	0

Bengoechea
Att: 35,000

1989 Brazil:
1st Brazil
2nd Uruguay

1991 Chile:
1st Argentina
2nd Brazil

1993 Guayaquil:

Argentina	2	Mexico	1

Batistuta (2)   *Galindo (pen)*
Att: 40,000

1995 Montevideo:

Uruguay	1	Brazil	1

Bengoechea 48   *Tulio 30*
Att: 58,000
(Uruguay won 5–3 on pens)

1997 La Paz:

Brazil	3	Bolivia	1

Edmundo 37,   *Irwin Sanchez 45*
Ronaldo 79,
Ze Roberto 90
Att: 45,000

Notes:
Details of final matches or championship play-offs have been given where applicable. For all other tournaments, played on a league basis, only the first and second nationshave been listed.

* unofficial "extraordinarios" tournaments

FIFA Confederations Cup

Winners

1997

Brazil	6	Australia	0

European Championship

Winners

1960:
Soviet Union	2	Yugoslavia	1
Metreveli,		*Galic*	
Ponedelnik			

Att: 18,000 *(Paris)*

1964:
Spain	2	Soviet Union	1
Pereda, Marcelino		*Khusainov*	

Att: 105,000 *(Madrid, Bernabéu)*

1968:
Italy	1	Yugoslavia	1
Domenghini		*Dzajic*	

Att: 85,000 *(Rome)*

1968 replay:
Italy	2	*Yugoslavia*	0
Riva, Anastasi			

Att: 85,000 *(Rome)*

1972:
W. Germany	3	Soviet Union	0
Müller G. (2), Wimmer			

Att: 65,000 *(Brussels)*

1976:
Czech.	2	W. Germany	2*
Svehlik, Dobias		*Müller D.,*	
		Holzenbein	

(Czechoslovakia won 5–4 on penalties)
Att: 45,000 *(Belgrade)*

1980:
W. Germany	2	Belgium	1
Hrubesch (2)		*Vandereycken*	

Att: 48,000 *(Rome)*

1984:
France	2	Spain	0
Platini, Bellone			

Att: 47,000 *(Paris)*

1988:
Holland	2	Soviet Union	0
Gullit, Van Basten			

Att: 72,000 *(Munich)*

1992:
Denmark	2	Germany	0
Jensen, Vilfort			

Att: 37,000 *(Gothenburg)*

1996:
Germany	2	Czech Rep.	1
Bierhoff (2)		*Berger (pen)*	

Att: 73,611 *(Wembley)*
Germany won on golden goals rule

European Under-21 Championship

Winners

1978	Yugoslavia
1980	Soviet Union
1982	England
1984	England
1986	Spain
1988	France
1990	Soviet Union
1992	Italy
1994	Portugal
1996	Italy

European Youth Championship

Winners

1948	England
1949	France
1950	Austria
1951	Yugoslavia
1952	Spain
1953	Hungary
1954	Spain
1957	Austria
1958	Italy
1959	Bulgaria
1960	Hungary
1961	Portugal
1962	Romania
1963	England

1964	England
1965	East Germany
1966	Soviet Union/Italy
1967	Soviet Union
1968	Czechoslovakia
1969	Bulgaria
1970	East Germany
1971	England
1972	England
1973	England
1974	Bulgaria
1975	England
1976	Soviet Union
1977	Belgium
1978	Soviet Union
1979	Yugoslavia
1980	England
1981	West Germany
1982	Scotland
1983	France
1984	Hungary
1986	East Germany
1988	Soviet Union
1990	Soviet Union
1992	Turkey
1993	England
1994	Portugal
1995	Spain
1996	France
1997	France

African Nations Cup

Finalists

1957:

Egypt	4	Ethiopia	0

El Diba (4)
Att: 20,000 *(Khartoum)*

1959:

1st   Egypt
2nd   Sudan *(in Cairo)*

1962:

Ethiopia	4	Egypt	2*

Girma,   *Badawi 2*
Menguitsou (2),
Italo
Att: 50,000 *(Addis Ababa)*

1963:

Ghana	3	Sudan	0

Aggrey-Fynn,
Mfum (2)   Att: 80,000 *(Accra)*

1965:

Ghana	3	Tunisia	2*

Odoi (2), Kofi   *Chetali, Chaibi*
Att: 50,000 *(Tunis)*

1968:

Congo Kinshasa	1	Ghana	0

Kalala
Att: 80,000 *(Accra)*

1970:

Sudan	1	Ghana	0

El Issed
Att: 12,000 *(Khartoum)*

1972:

Congo	3	Mali	2

M'Bono (2), M'Pele   *Diakhite, Traore M.*
Att: 20,000 *(Yaounde)*

1974:

Zaire	2	Zambia	2*

Ndaye (2)   *Kaushi, Sinyangwe*
Att: 15,000 *(Cairo)*

1974 replay:

Zaire	2	Zambia	0

Ndaye (2)
Att: 1,000 *(Cairo)*

1976:

1st   Morocco
2nd   Guinea
(in Addis Ababa)

1978:

Ghana	2	Uganda	0

Afriye (2)
Att: 40,000 *(Accra)*

1980:

Nigeria	3	Algeria	0

Odegbami (2), Lawal
Att: 80,000 *(Lagos)*

1982:

Ghana	1	Libya	1*

Al Hassan   *Beshari*
(Ghana won 7–6 on penalties)
Att: 50,000 *(Tripoli)*

1984:

Cameroon	3	Nigeria	0

Ndjeya, Abega,
Ebongue
Att: 50,000 *(Abidjan)*

1986:

Egypt	0	Cameroon	0*

(Egypt won 5–4 on penalties)
Att: 100,000 *(Cairo)*

1988:

Cameroon	1	Nigeria	0

Kunde
Att: 50,000 *(Casablanca)*

1990:

Algeria	1	Nigeria	0

Oudjani

1992:

Ivory Coast	0	Ghana	0*

(Ghana won 11–10 on penalties.)
Att: 60,000 *(Dakar)*

1994:

Nigeria	2	Zambia	1
Amunike (2)		*Litana*	

Att: 25,000 *(Tunis)*

1996:

South Africa	2	Tunisia	0
Williams (2)			

Att: 80,000 *(Johannesburg)*

Asian Cup

Winners

1956:

South Korea	2	Israel	1

1960:

South Korea	3	Israel	0

1964:

Israel	2	India	0

1968:

Iran	3	Burma	1

1972:

Iran	2	South Korea	1

1976:

Iran	1	Kuwait	0

1980:

Kuwait 3		South Korea	0

1984:

Saudi Arabia	2	China	0

1988:

Saudi Arabia	0	South Korea	0

(Saudi Arabia won 4–3 on penalties)

1992:

Japan	1	Saudi Arabia	0

1996:

Saudi Arabia	0	U.A.E.	0

(Saudi Arabia won 4–2 on penalties)

Asian Games

Winners

1951

India	1	Iran	0

1954

Taiwan 5		South Korea	2

1958

Taiwan	3	South Korea	2

1962

India	2	South Korea	1

1966

Burma 1		Iran	0

1970

Burma	0	South Korea	0

1974

Iran	1	Israel	0

1978

North Korea	0	South Korea	0

1982

Iraq	1	Kuwait	0

1986

South Korea	2	Saudi Arabia	0

1990

Iran	0	North Korea	0

(Iran won 4–1 on penalties)

1994

Uzbekistan	4	China	2

Note:
The trophy was shared in 1970 and 1978

CONCACAF Championship

Winners

1941	Costa Rica
1943	El Salvador
1946	Costa Rica
1948	Costa Rica
1951	Panama
1953	Costa Rica
1955	Costa Rica
1957	Haiti
1960	Costa Rica
1961	Costa Rica
1963	Costa Rica
1965	Mexico
1967	Guatemala
1969	Costa Rica
1971	Mexico
1973	Haiti
1977	Mexico
1981	Honduras
1985	Canada
1989	Costa Rica
1991	USA
1993	Mexico
1996	Mexico

World Club Cup

Finalists

1960 Montevideo:

Peñarol	0	Real Madrid	0

Att: 75,000

Madrid:

Real Madrid	5	Peñarol	1
Puskas (2),		*Borges*	
Di Stefano, Herrera,			
Gento			

Att: 125,000

1961 Lisbon:

Benfica	1	Peñarol	0
Coluna			

Att: 50,000

Montevideo:

Peñarol	5	Benfica	0
Sasia, Joya (2),			
Spencer (2)			

Att: 56,000

Montevideo (play-off):

Peñarol	2	Benfica	1
Sasia (2)		*Eusebio*	

Att: 62,000

1962 Rio de Janeiro:

Santos	3	Benfica	2
Pele (2), Coutinho		*Santana (2)*	

Att: 90,000

Lisbon:

Benfica	2	Santos	5
Eusebio, Santana		*Pele (3), Coutinho,*	
		Pepe	

Att: 75,000

1963 Milan:

Milan	4	Santos	2
Trapattoni,		*Pele (2)*	
Amarildo (2), Mora			

Att: 80,000

Rio de Janeiro:

Santos	4	Milan	2
Pepe (2), Almir,		*Altafini, Mora*	
Lima			

Att: 150,000

Rio de Janeiro (play-off):

Santos	1	Milan	0
Dalmo			

Att: 121,000

1964 Avellanada:

Independiente	1	Internazionale	0
Rodriguez			

Att: 70,000

Milan:

Internazionale	2	Independiente	0
Mazzola, Corso			

Milan (play-off):

Internazionale	1	Independiente	0*
Corso			

Att: 45,000

1965 Milan:

Internazionale	3	Independiente	0
Peiro, Mazzola (2)			

Att: 70,000

Avellanada:

Independiente	0	Internazionale	0

Att: 70,000

1966 Montevideo:

Peñarol	2	Real Madrid	0
Spencer (2)			

Att: 70,000

Madrid:

Real Madrid	0	Peñarol	2
		Rocha, Spencer	

Att: 70,000

1967 Glasgow:

Celtic	1	Racing Club	0
McNeill			

Att: 103,000

Avellanada:

Racing Club	2	Celtic	1
Raffo, Cardenas		*Gemmell*	

Att: 80,000

Montevideo (play-off):

Racing Club	1	Celtic	0
Cardenas			

Att: 65,000

1968 Buenos Aires:

Estudiantes	1	Man. United	0
Conigliaro			

Att: 65,000

Manchester:

Manchester Utd	1	Estudiantes	1
Morgan		*Veron*	

Att: 60,000

1969 Milan:

Milan	3	Estudiantes	0
Sormani (2), Combin			

Att: 80,000

Buenos Aires:

Estudiantes	2	Milan	1
Conigliaro,		*Rivera*	
Aguirre-Suarez			

Att: 65,000
Milan won 4–2 on aggregate

1970 Buenos Aires:

Estudiantes	2	Feyenoord	2
Echecopar, Veron		*Van Hanegem,*	
		Kindvall	

Att: 65,000

Rotterdam:

Feyenoord	1	Estudiantes	0
Van Deale			

Att: 70,000 *Feyenoord won 3–2 on aggregate*

1971 Athens:

Panathinaikos	1	Nacional (Uru) 1
Filakouris		*Artime*

Att: 60,000

Montevideo:

Nacional	2	Panathinaikos	1
Artime (2)		*Filakouris*

Att: 70,000
Nacional won 3–2 on aggregate

1972 Avellanada:

Independiente	1	Ajax	1
Sa		*Cruyff*

Att: 65,000

Amsterdam:

Ajax	3	Independiente	0
Neeskens, Rep (2)		

Att: 60,000
Ajax won 4–1 on aggregate

1973 Rome (single match):

Independiente	1	Juventus	0
Bochini 40		

Att: 35,000

1974 Buenos Aires:

Independiente	1	Atlético Madrid	0
Balbuena 33		

Att: 60,000

Madrid:

Atlético Madrid	2	Independiente	0
Irureta 21, Ayala 86		

Att: 45,000
Atlético won 2–1 on aggregate

1975 not played

1976 Munich:

Bayern Munich	2	Cruzeiro	0
Müller, Kapellmann		

Att: 22,000

Belo Horizonte:

Cruzeiro	0	Bayern Munich	0

Att: 114,000
Bayern won 2–0 on aggregate

1977 Buenos Aires:

Boca Juniors	2	Mönchengladbach 2
Mastrangelo, Ribolzi		*Hannes, Bonhof*

Att: 50,000

Karlsruhe:

Mönchengladbach	0	Boca Juniors	3
		Zanabria, Mastrangelo, Salinas

Att: 21,000
Boca Juniors won 5–2 on aggregate

1978 not played

1979 Malmö:

Malmö	0	Olimpia	1
		Isasi

Asuncion:

Olimpia	2	Malmö	1
Solalinde, Michelagnoli		*Earlandsson*

Att: 35,000
Olimpia won 3–1 on aggregate

1980 Tokyo:

Nacional (Uru)	1	Nottm. Forest	0
Victorino		

Att: 62,000

1981 Tokyo:

Flamengo	3	Liverpool	0
Nunes (2), Adilio		

Att: 62,000

1982 Tokyo:

Peñarol	2	Aston Villa	0
Jair, Charrua		

Att: 62,000

1983 Tokyo:

Gremio	2	Hamburg SV	1
Renato (2)		*Schroder*

Att: 62,000

1984 Tokyo:

Independiente	1	Liverpool	0
Percudani		

Att: 62,000

1985 Tokyo:

Juventus	2	Argentinos Juniors	2*
Platini, Laudrup M.		*Ereros, Castro*

Att: 62,000
Juventus won 4–2 on penalties

1986 Tokyo:

River Plate	1	Steaua Bucharest	0
Alzamendi		

Att: 62,000

1987 Tokyo:

FC Porto	2	Peñarol	1*
Gomes, Madjer		*Viera*

Att: 45,000

1988 Tokyo:

Nacional (Uru)	2	PSV Eindhoven	2*
Ostolaza (2)		*Romario, Koeman, R.*

Att: 62,000
Nacional won 7–6 on penalties

1989 Tokyo:

Milan	1	Nacional (Col)	0
Evani		

Att: 62,000

1990 Tokyo:

Milan	3	Olimpia	0
Rijkaard (2), Stroppa		

Att: 60,000

1991 Tokyo:

Red Star Belgrade	3`	Colo Colo	0

Jugovic (2), Pancev
Att: 60,000

1992 Tokyo:

São Paulo	2	Barcelona	1

Rai (2) — *Stoichkov*
Att: 80,000

1993 Tokyo:

São Paulo	3	Milan	2

Palinha, Cerezo, Müller — *Massaro, Papin*
Att: 52,000

1994 Tokyo:

Velez Sarsfield	2	Milan	0

Trott, Abad
Att: 65,000

1995 Tokyo:

Ajax	0	Gremio	0

Att: 62,000
Ajax won 4–3 on penalties

1996 Tokyo:

Juventus	1	River Plate	0

Del Piero
Att: 55,000

1997 Tokyo:

B. Dortmund	2	Cruzeiro	0

Zorc, Herrlich
Att: 60,000

Note:

From 1960 to 1979 the World Club Cup was decided on points, not goal difference. Since 1980 it has been a one-off match in Tokyo

Copa Libertadores (South American Club Cup)

Finalists
1960 Montevideo:

Peñarol	1	Olimpia	0

Spencer
Att: 80,000

Asuncion:

Olimpia	1	Peñarol	1

Recalde — *Cubilla*
Att: 35,000

Winners:
Peñarol

1961 Montevideo:

Peñarol	1	Palmeiras	0

Spencer
Att: 50,000

São Paulo:

Palmeiras	1	Peñarol	1

Nardo — *Sasia*
Att: 40,000

Winners:
Peñarol

1962 Montevideo:

Peñarol	1	Santos	2

Spencer — *Coutinho (2)*
Att: 50,000

Santos	2	Peñarol	3

Dorval, Mengalvio — *Spencer, Sasia (2)*

Play-off – Buenos Aires:

Santos	3	Peñarol	0

Coutinho, Pele (2)
Att: 36,000

1963 Rio de Janeiro:

Santos	3	Boca Juniors	2

Coutinho 2, Lima — *Sanfilippo (2)*
Att: 55,000

Buenos Aires:

Boca Juniors	1	Santos	2

Sanfilippo — *Coutinho, Pele*
Att: 50,000

Winners:
Santos

1964 Montevideo:

Nacional (Uru)	0	Independiente	0

Att: 75,000

Avellaneda:

Independiente	1	Nacional (Uru)	0

Rodriguez
Att: 60,000

Winners:
Independiente

1965 Avellaneda:

Independiente	1	Peñarol	0

Bernao
Att: 55,000

Peñarol	3	Independiente	1

Goncalvez, Reznik, Rocha — *De la Mata*
Att: 65,000

Play-off – Santiago:

Independiente	4	Peñarol	1

Acevedo, Bernao, Avallay, Mura — *Joya*
Att: 25,000

1966 Montevideo:

Peñarol	2	River Plate	0

Abaddie, Joya
Att: 49,000

Buenos Aires:

River Plate	3	Peñarol	2

Onega, E., Onega, D.,
Sarnari
Att: 60,000.

Play-off – Santiago:

Peñarol	4	River Plate	2

Spencer (2), Rocha,   *Onega, D., Solari*
Abbadie
Att: 39,000

1967 Avellaneda:

Racing Club	0	Nacional (Uru)	0

Att: 54,000

Montevideo:

Nacional (Uru)	0	Racing Club	0

Att: 54,000

Play-off – Santiago:

Racing Club	2	Nacional (Uru)	1

Cardozo, Raffo   *Esparrago*
Att: 25,000

1968 La Plata:

Estudiantes	2	Palmeiras	1

Veron, Flores   *Servillio*
Att: 40,000

Sao Paulo:

Palmeiras	3	Estudiantes	1

Tupazinho (2),   *Veron*
Reinaldo
Att: 75,000

Play-off – Montevideo:

Estudiantes	2	Palmeiras	0

Ribaudo, Veron
Att: 30,000

1969 Montevideo:

Nacional (Uru)	0	Estudiantes	1
		Flores 66	

Att: 50,000

La Plata:

Estudiantes	2	Nacional (Uru)	0

Flores 31,
Conigliaro 37
Att: 30,000

Winners:
Estudiantes

1970 La Plata:

Estudiantes	1	Peñarol	0

Togneri 87
Att: 36,000

Montevideo:

Peñarol	0	Estudiantes	0

Att: 50,000

Winners:
Estudiantes

1971 La Plata:

Estudiantes	1	Nacional (Uru)	0

Romeo
Att: 32,000

Nacional (Uru)	1	Estudiantes	0

Masnik 17
Att: 62,000

Play-off – Lima:

Nacional (Uru)	2	Estudiantes	0

Esparrago 22,
Artime 65
Att: 42,000

1972 Lima:

Universitario	0	Independiente	0

Att: 45,000

Avellaneda:

Independiente	2	Universitario	1

Maglioni (2)   *Rojas*
Att: 65,000

1973 Avellaneda:

Independiente	1	Colo Colo	1

Mendoza 75   *Sa o.g. 71*
Att: 65,000

Santiago:

Colo Colo	0	Independiente	0

Att: 77,000

Play-off – Montevideo:

Independiente 2		Colo Colo	1

Mendoza 25,   *Caszely 39*
Giachello 107
Att: 45,000

1974 São Paulo:

Sao Paulo	2	Independiente	1

Rocha 48,   *Saggioratto 28*
Mirandinha 50
Att: 51,000

Avellaneda:

Independiente	2	São Paulo	0

Bochini 34,
Balbuena 48
Att: 48,000

Play-off – Santiago:

Independiente 1		São Paulo	0

Pavoni 37
Att: 27,000

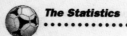

1975 Santiago:

Union Espanola	1	Independiente	0
Ahumada 87			
Att: 43,000			

Avellaneda:

Independiente	3	Union Espanola	1
Rojas 1, Pavoni 58,		*Las Heras*	
Bertoni 83			
Att: 52,000			

Play-off – Asuncion:

Independiente	2	Union Espanola	0
Ruiz Moreno 29,			
Bertoni 65			
Att: 45,000			

1976 Belo Horizonte:

Cruzeiro	4	River Plate	1
Nelinho, Palinha 2,		*Mas*	
Waldo			
Att: 58,000			

Buenos Aires:

River Plate	2	Cruzeiro	1
Lopez, J., Gonzalez		*Palinha*	
Att: 45,000			

Play-off – Santiago:

Cruzeiro	3	River Plate	2
Nelinho, Reinaldo,		*Mas, Urquiza*	
Joazinho			
Att: 35,000			

1977 Buenos Aires:

Boca Juniors	1	Cruzeiro	0
Veglio 3			
Att: 50,000			
Cruzeiro	1	Boca Juniors	0
Nelinho 76			
Att: 55,000			

Play-off – Montevideo:

Boca Juniors	0	Cruzeiro	0
Att: 45,000			

(Cruzerio won 5–4 on penalties)

1978 Cali:

Deportivo Cali	0	Boca Juniors	0

Buenos Aires:

Boca Juniors	4	Deportivo Cali	0
Perotti 15, 85,			
Mastrangelo 60,			
Salinas 71			

Winners:

Boca Juniors

1979 Asuncion:

Olimpia	2	Boca Juniors	0
Aquino 3, Piazza.		Att: 45,000	

Buenos Aires:

Boca Juniors	0	Olimpia	0
Att: 50,000			

Winners:

Olimpia

1980 Porto Alegre:

Inter PA (Brz)	0	Nacional (Uru)	0
Att: 80,000			

Montevideo:

Nacional (Uru)	1	Inter PA	0
Victorino 35			
Att: 75,000			

Winners:

Nacional

1981 Rio de Janeiro:

Flamengo	2	Cobreloa	1
Zico 12, 30		*Merello 65*	
Att: 114,000			

Santiago:

Cobreloa	1	Flamengo	0
Merello 79			
Att: 61,000			

Play-off – Montevideo:

Flamengo	2	Cobreloa	0
Zico 18, 79			
Att: 35,000			

1982 Montevideo:

Peñarol	0	Cobreloa	0
Att: 70,000			

Santiago:

Cobreloa	0	Peñarol	1
		Morena 89	
Att: 70,000			

Winners:

Peñarol

1983 Montevideo:

Peñarol	1	Gremio	1
Morena 35		*Tita 12*	
Att: 65,000			

Porto Alegre:

Gremio	2	Penarol	1
Caio 9, Cesar 87		*Morena 70*	
Att: 75,000			

Winners:

Gremio

1984 Porto Alegre:

Gremio	0	Independiente	1
		Burruchaga 24	
Att: 55,000			

Avellaneda:

Independiente	0	Gremio	0

Winners:
Independiente

1985 Buenos Aires:

Argentinos Juniors	1	America Cali	0

Comisso 40
Att: 50,000

Cali:

America Cali	1	Argentinos Juniors	0

Ortiz 3
Att: 50,000

Play-off – Asuncion:

Argentinos Juniors	1	America Cali	1

Comizzo 37 *Gareca 42*
Att: 35,000
Argentinos Juniors won 5–4 on penalties

1986 Cali:

America Cali	1	River Plate	2

Cabanas 47 *Funes 22, Alonso 25*
Att: 55,000

Buenos Aires:

River Plate	1	America Cali	0

Funes 70
Att: 85,000

Winners:
River Plate

1987 Cali:

America Cali	2	Peñarol	0

Bataglia, Cabanas
Att: 45,000

Montevideo:

Peñarol	2	America Cali	1

Aguirre 58, Villar 86 *Cabanas 19*
Att: 70,000

Play-off – Santiago:

Peñarol	1	America Cali	0

Aguirre 119
Att: 30,000

1988 Rosario:

Newell's Old Boys	1	Nacional (Uru)	0

Gabrich 60
Att: 45,000

Montevideo:

Nacional (Uru)	3	Newell's Old Boys	0

Vargas 10, Ostolaza 30, De Leon 81
Att: 75,000
Nacional won 3–1 on aggregate

1989 Asuncion:

Olimpia	2	Atlético Nacional	0

Bobadilla 36, Sanabria 60
Att: 50,000

Bogota:

Atlético Nacional	2	Olimpia	0

Mano og 46, Usurriaga 64
Att: 50,000
Atlético won 5–4 on penalties, aggregate 2–2

1990 Asuncion:

Olimpia	2	Barcelona	0

Amarilla 47, Samaniego 65
Att: 35,000

Guayaquil:

Barcelona	1	Olimpia	1

Trobbiani 61 *Amarilla 80*
Att: 55,000
Olimpia won 3–1 on aggregate

1991 Asuncion:

Olimpia	0	Colo Colo	0

Att: 48,000

Santiago:

Colo Colo	3	Olimpia	0

Perez 13, 18, Herrera 85
Att: 64,000
Colo Colo won 3–0 on aggregate.

1992 Rosario:

Newell's Old Boys	1	São Paulo	0

Berizzo 38
Att: 45,000

São Paulo:

São Paulo	1	Newell's OBs	0

Rai 65
Att: 105,000
São Paulo won 3–2 on penalties, 1–1 aggregate

1993 São Paulo:

São Paulo	5	Catolica	1

Lopez, o.g. Dinho, Gilmar, Rai, Muller *Almada*
Att: 99,000

Santiago:

Catolica	2	São Paulo	0

Lunari, Almada
Att: 50,000
São Paulo won 5–3 on aggregate

1994 Buenos Aires:

Velez Sarsfield	1	Sao Paulo	0

Asad

Att: 48,000

São Paulo:

São Paulo	1	Velez Sarsfield	0

Muller

Velez Sarsfield won 5–3 on penalties,
1–1 aggregate

1995 Porto Alegre:

Gremio	3	Atlético Nacional	1

Marulanda o.g.,   Angel
Jardel, Paulo,
Nunes

Att: 50,000

Medellin:

Atlético Nacional	1	Gremio	1

Aristizabal   Dinho (pen)

Att: 52,000

Gremio won 4–2 on aggregate

1996 Cali:

America	1	River Plate	0

De Avila

Att: 55,000

Buenos Aires:

River Plate	2	America	0

Crespo (2)

Att: 68,000

River Plate won 2–1 on aggregate

1997 Lima:

Sporting Cristal	0	Cruzeiro	0

Att: 45,000

Belo Horizonte:

Cruzeiro	1	Sporting Cristal 0

Elivelton 75

Att: 65,000

Cruzeiro won 1–0 on aggregate

South American Recopa

Winners

1988	Nacional
1989	Boca Juniors
1990	Olimpia
1991	Colo Colo
1992	São Paulo
1993	São Paulo
1994	São Paulo
1995	Independiente
1996	Gremio
1997	Lanus

South American Super Cup

Winners

1988	Racing Club
1989	Boca Juniors
1990	Olimpia
1991	Cruzeiro
1992	Cruzeiro
1993	Botafogo
1994	Independiente
1995	Independiente
1996	Velez Sarsfield
1997	River Plate

European Champions Club Cup (now UEFA Champions League)

Finalists

1956 Paris:
Real Madrid 4 Stade de Reims 3
Di Stefano, Rial (2), *Leblond, Templin,*
Marquitos *Hidalgo*
Att: 38,000

1957 Madrid:
Real Madrid 2 Fiorentina 0
Di Stefano, Gento
Att: 124,000

1958 Brussels:
Real Madrid 3 Milan 2*
Di Stefano, Rial, *Schiaffino, Grillo*
Gento
Att: 67,000

1959 Stuttgart:
Real Madrid 2 Stade de Reims 0
Mateos, Di Stefano
Att: 80,000

1960 Glasgow:
Real Madrid 7 Eintracht 3
Di Stefano (3), *Kress, Stein (2)*
Puskas (4)
Att: 127,621

1961 Berne:
Benfica 3 Barcelona 2
Ramallets o.g., Coluna (2) *Kocsis, Czibor*
Att: 33,000

1962 Amsterdam:
Benfica 5 Real Madrid 3
Aguas, Cavem, *Puskas (3)*
Coluna, Eusebio (2)
Att: 68,000

1963 Wembley:
Milan 2 Benfica 1
Altafini (2) *Eusebio*
Att: 45,000

1964 Vienna:
Internazionale 3 Real Madrid 1
Mazzola (2), Milani *Felo*
Att: 72,000

1965 Milan:
Internazionale 1 Benfica 0
Jair
Att: 80,000

1966 Brussels:
Real Madrid 2 Partizan Belgrade 1
Amancio, Serena *Vasovic*
Att: 55,000

1967 Lisbon:
Celtic 2 Internazionale 1
Gemmell, Chalmers *Mazzola*
Att: 55,000

1968 Wembley:
Man. United 4 Benfica 1*
Charlton (2), Best, *Graca*
Kidd
Att: 100,000

1969 Madrid:
Milan 4 Ajax 1
Prati (3), Sormani *Vasovic*
Att: 50,000

1970 Milan:
Feyenoord 2 Celtic 1*
Israel, Kindvall *Gemmell*
Att: 53,187

1971 Wembley:
Ajax 2 Panathinaikos 0
Van Dijk, Haan
Att: 90,000

1972 Rotterdam:
Ajax 2 Internazionale 0
Cruyff (2)
Att: 61,000

1973 Belgrade:
Ajax 1 Juventus 0
Rep
Att: 93,500

1974 Brussels:
Bayern Munich 1 Atlético Madrid 1*
Schwartzenbeck *Luis*
Att: 65,000

Brussels (replay):
Bayern Munich 4 Atlético Madrid 0
Hoeness (2),
Müller (2)
Att: 23,000

1975 Paris:
Bayern Munich 2 Leeds United 0
Roth, Müller
Att: 48,000

1976 Glasgow:
Bayern Munich 1 St Etienne 0
Roth
Att: 54,684

1977 Rome:
Liverpool 3 Borussia
Mönchengladbach 1
McDermott, *Simonsen*
Smith, Neal *Att: 57, 000*

The Statistics

1978 Wembley:

| Liverpool | 1 | Club Brugge | 0 |

Dalglish
Att: 92,000

1979 Munich:

| Nottm Forest | 1 | Malmö | 0 |

Francis
Att: 57,500

1980 Madrid:

| Nottm Forest | 1 | Hamburg | 0 |

Robertson
Att: 51,000

1981 Paris:

| Liverpool | 1 | Real Madrid | 0 |

Kennedy A.
Att: 48,360

1982 Rotterdam:

| Aston Villa | 1 | Bayern Munich | 0 |

Withe
Att: 46,000

1983 Athens:

| Hamburg | 1 | Juventus | 0 |

Magath
Att: 80,000

1984 Rome:

| Liverpool | 1 | AS Roma | 1* |

Neal *Pruzzo*
Att: 69,693
Liverpool won 4–2 on penalties

1985 Brussels:

| Juventus | 1 | Liverpool | 0 |

Platini
Att: 58,000

1986 Seville:

| Steaua Bucharest | 0 | Barcelona | 0* |

Att: 70,000
Steaua won 2–0 on penalties

1987 Vienna:

| FC Porto | 2 | Bayern Munich | 1 |

Madjer, Juary *Kogl*
Att: 56,000

1988 Stuttgart:

| PSV Eindhoven | 0 | Benfica | 0* |

Att: 55,000
PSV won 6–5 on penalties

1989 Barcelona:

| Milan | 4 | Steaua Bucharest | 0 |

Gullit (2), Van Basten (2)
Att: 97,000

1990 Vienna:

| Milan | 1 | Benfica | 0 |

Rijkaard
Att: 56,000

1991 Bari:

| Red Star Belgrade | 0 | Marseille | 0* |

Att: 50,000
Red Star won 5–3 on penalties

1992 Wembley:

| Barcelona | 1 | Sampdoria | 0* |

Koeman, R.
Att: 74,000

1993 Munich:

| Marseille | 1 | Milan | 0 |

Boli
Att: 72, 300

1994 Athens:

| Milan | 4 | Barcelona | 0 |

*Massaro (2),
Savicevic, Desailly*
Att: 76,000

1995 Vienna:

| Ajax | 1 | Milan | 0 |

Kluivert
Att 49,000

1996 Rome:

| Juventus | 1 | Ajax | 1 |

Ravanelli *Litmanen*
Att: 67,000
Juventus won 4–2 on penalties

1997 Munich:

| Borussia Dortmund | 3 | Juventus | 1 |

Riedle (2), Ricken *Del Piero*
Att: 55,000

1998 Amsterdam:

| Real Madrid | 3 | Juventus | 0 |

Mijatovic
Att: 47,500

European Cup-Winners' Cup

Finalists

1961 Glasgow:

| Rangers | 0 | Fiorentina | 2 |

Milani (2)
Att: 80,000

Florence:

| Fiorentina | 2 | Rangers | 1 |

Milani, Hamrin *Scott*
Att: 50,000
Fiorentina won 4–1 on aggregate

1962 Glasgow:

| Atlético Madrid | 1 | Fiorentina | 1* |

Peiro *Hamrin*
Att: 30,000

Stuttgart (replay):

| Atlético Madrid | 3 | Fiorentina | 0 |

*Jones, Mendonca,
Peiro*
Att: 39,000

1963 Rotterdam:

Tottenham	5	Atlético Madrid	1
Greaves (2), White, Dyson (2)		*Collar*	
		Att: 50,000	

1964 Brussels:

Sporting Lisbon	3	MTK Budapest	3*
Mascaranhas, Figueiredo (2)		*Sandor (2), Kuti*	
Att: 4,000			

Antwerp (replay):

Sporting Lisbon	1	MTK Budapest	0
Morais			
Att: 14,000			

1965 Wembley:

West Ham	2	TSV Munich	0
Sealey (2)			
Att: 98,000			

1966 Glasgow:

B. Dortmund	2	Liverpool	1*
Held, Libuda		*Hunt*	
Att: 42,000			

1967 Nuremberg:

Bayern Munich	1	Rangers	0*
Roth			
Att: 70,000			

1968 Rotterdam:

Milan	2	Hamburg SV	0
Hamrin (2)			
Att: 54,000			

1969 Basle:

Slovan Bratislava	3	Barcelona	2
Cvetler, Hrivnak, Jan Capkovic		*Zaldua, Rexach*	
Att: 40,000			

1970 Vienna:

Man. City	2	Gornik Zabrze	1
Young, Lee		*Oslizlo*	
Att: 10,000			

1971 Athens:

Chelsea	1	Real Madrid	1*
Osgood		*Zoco*	
Att: 42,000			

Athens (replay):

Chelsea	2	Real Madrid	1
Dempsey, Osgood		*Fleitas*	
Att: 24,000			

1972 Barcelona:

Rangers	3	Dynamo Moscow	2
Stein, Johnston (2)		*Estrekov, Makovikov*	
Att: 35,000			

1973 Salonika:

Milan	1	Leeds United	0
Chiarugi			
Att: 45,000			

1974 Rotterdam:

FC Magdeburg	2	Milan	0
o.g., Seguin		Att: 5,000	

1975 Basle:

Kiev Dynamo	3	Ferencvaros	0
Onischenko (2), Blokhin			
Att: 13,000			

1976 Brussels:

Anderlecht	4	West Ham	2
Rensenbrink (2), Van der Elst (2)		*Holland, Robson*	
Att: 58,000			

1977 Amsterdam:

Hamburg SV	2	Anderlecht	0
Volkert, Magath			
Att: 65,000			

1978 Paris:

Anderlecht	4	FK Austria	0
Rensenbrink (2), Van Binst (2)			
Att: 48,679			

1979 Basle:

Barcelona	4	Fortuna Düsseldorf	3*
Sanchez, Asensi, Rexach, Krankl		*Allofs K., Seel (2)*	
Att: 58,000			

1980 Brussels:

Valencia	0	Arsenal	0*
Att: 40,000			

Valencia won 5–4 on penalties

1981 Düsseldorf:

Dynamo Tbilisi	2	Carl Zeiss Jena	1
Gutsayev, Daraselia		*Hoppe*	
Att: 9,000			

1982 Barcelona:

Barcelona	2	Standard Liège	1
Simonsen, Quini		*Vandermissen*	
Att: 100,000			

1983 Gothenburg:

Aberdeen	2	Real Madrid	1*
Black, Hewitt		*Juanito*	
Att: 17,804			

1984 Basle:

Juventus	2	FC Porto	1
Vignola, Boniek		*Sousa*	
Att: 60,000			

1985 Rotterdam:

Everton	3	Rapid Vienna	1
Gray, Steven, Sheedy		*Krankl*	
Att: 50,000			

1986 Lyons:

Dynamo Kiev	3	Atlético Madrid	0
Zavarov, Blokhin, Yevtushenko		*Att: 57,000*	

1987 Athens:

| Ajax | 1 | Lokomotiv Leipzig | 0 |

Van Basten
Att: 35,000

1988 Strasbourg:

| Mechelen | 1 | Ajax | 0 |

De Boer
Att: 39,446

1989 Berne:

| Barcelona | 2 | Sampdoria | 0 |

Salinas, Recarte
Att: 45,000

1990 Gothenburg:

| Sampdoria | 2 | Anderlecht | 0* |

Vialli (2)
Att: 20,103

1991 Rotterdam:

| Man. United | 2 | Barcelona | 1 |

Hughes (2) · *Koeman*
Att: 42,000

1992 Lisbon:

| Werder Bremen | 2 | Monaco | 0 |

Allofs K., Rufer
Att: 16,000

1993 Wembley:

| Parma | 3 | Antwerp | 1 |

Minotti, Melli, Cuoghi · *Severeyns*
Att: 37,393

1994 Copenhagen:

| Arsenal | 1 | Parma | 0 |

Smith
Att: 33,765

1995 Paris:

| Zaragoza | 2 | Arsenal | 1 |

Esnaider, Nayim · *Hartson*
Att: 48,000

1996 Brussels:

| PSG | 1 | Rapid Vienna | 0 |

N'Gotty
Att: 37,500

1997 Rotterdam:

| Barcelona | 1 | PSG | 0 |

Ronaldo
Att: 50,000

1998 Stockholm:

| Chelsea | 1 | Stuttgart | 0 |

Zola
Att: 30,216

UEFA/Fairs Cup

Finalists

Inter-cities Industrial Fairs Cup
1958:

| London Select XI | 2 | Barcelona | 2 |

Greaves, Langley · *Tejada, Martinez 43*

| Barcelona | 6 | London Select XI | 0 |

Suarez (2), Evaristo (2), Martinez, Verges 63
Att: 62,000
Barcelona won 8–2 on aggregate

1960:

| Birmingham City | 0 | Barcelona | 0 |

Att: 40,000

| Barcelona | 4 | Birmingham City | 1 |

Martinez 3, Czibor (2), Coll · *Hooper*
Att: 70,000
Barcelona won 4–1 on aggregate

1961:

| Birmingham City | 2 | Roma | 2 |

Hellawell, Orritt · *Manfredini (2)*
Att: 21,000

| Roma | 2 | Birmingham City | 0 |

o.g, Pestrin
Att: 60,000
Roma won 4–2 on aggregate

1962:

| Valencia | 6 | Barcelona | 2 |

Yosu (2), Guillot (3), Nunez · *Kocsis (2)*
Att: 65,000

| Barcelona | 1 | Valencia | 1 |

Kocsis · *Guillot*
Att: 60,000
Valencia won 7–3 on aggregate

1963:

| Dinamo Zagreb | 1 | Valencia | 2 |

Zambata · *Waldo,Urtiaga*
Att: 40,000

| Valencia | 2 | Dinamo Zagreb | 0 |

Manio, Nunez
Att: 55,000
Valencia won 4–1 on aggregate

1964:

Zaragoza	2	Valencia	1
Villa, Marcelino		*Urtiaga 42*	

Att: 50,000 (in Barcelona)

1965:

Ferençvaros	1	Juventus	0
Fenyvesi			

Att: 25,000 (in Turin)

1966:

Barcelona	0	Zaragoza	1
Canario			

Att: 35,000

Zaragoza	2	Barcelona	4*
Marcelino (2)		*Pujol (3), Zaballa*	

Att: 70,000
Barcelona won 4–3 on aggregate

1967:

Dinamo Zagreb	2	Leeds	0
Cercek (2)			

Att: 40,000

Leeds	0	Dinamo Zagreb	0

Att: 35,000
Dinamo Zagreb won 2–0 on aggregate

1968:

Leeds	1	Ferençvaros	0
Jones			

Att: 25,000

Ferençvaros	0	Leeds	0

Att: 76,000
Leeds won 1–0 on aggregate

1969:

Newcastle	3	Ujpest Dozsa	0
Moncur (2), Scott			

Att: 60,000

Ujpest Dozsa	2	Newcastle	3
Bene, Gorocs		*Moncur, Arentoft, Foggon*	

Att: 37,000
Newcastle won 6–2 on aggregate

1970:

Anderlecht	3	Arsenal	1
Devrindt, Mulder (2)		*Kennedy*	

Att: 37,000

Arsenal	3	Anderlecht	0
Kelly, Radford, Sammels			

Att: 51,000
Arsenal won 4–3 on aggregate

1971:

Juventus	2	Leeds Utd	2
Bettega, Capello		*Madeley, Bates*	

Att: 65,000

Leeds Utd	1	Juventus	1
Clark		*Anastasi*	

Att: 42,000
Leeds Utd won on away goals, 3–3 aggregate

UEFA Cup

Finalists

1972:

Wolverhampton	1	Tottenham	2
McCalliog		*Chivers (2)*	

Att: 38,000

Tottenham	1	Wolverhampton	1
Mullery		*Wagstaffe*	

Att: 54,000
Tottenham won 3–2 on aggregate

1973:

Liverpool	0	Borussia Mg	0

abandoned after 27minutes – rain
Replay:

Liverpool	3	Borussia Mg	0
Keegan (2), Lloyd			

Att: 41,000

Borussia Mg	2	Liverpool	0
Heynckes (2)			

Att: 35,000
Liverpool won 3–2 on aggregate

1974:

Tottenham	2	Feyenoord	2
England , Van Daele o.g.		*Van Hanegem, De Jong*	

Att: 46,000

Feyenoord	2	Tottenham	0
Rijsbergen, Ressel			

Att: 59,000
Feyenoord won 4–2 on aggregate

1975:

Borussia Mg	0	Twente Enschede	0

Att: 42,000 (in Dusseldorf)

Twente Enschede	1	Borussia Mg	5
Drost		*Simonsen (2), Heynckes (3)*	

Att: 21,000
Borussia won 5–1 on aggregate

1976:

Liverpool	3	Club Brugge	2
Kennedy, Case, Keegan		*Lambert, Cools* Att: 49,000	

Club Brugge 1 Liverpool 1
Lambert *Keegan*
Att: 32,000
Liverpool won 4–3 on aggregate

1977:

Juventus 1 Athletic Bilbao 0
Tardelli
Att: 75,000
Athletic Bilbao 2 Juventus 1
Churruca, Carlos *Bettega*
Att: 43,000
Juventus won on away goals rule, 2–2 aggregate

1978:

Bastia 0 PSV Eindhoven 0
Att: 15,000
PSV Eindhoven 3 Bastia 0
Van der Kerkhof, W. ,
Deijkers,
Van der Kuijlen
Att: 27,000
PSV won 3–0 on aggregate

1979:

Red Star Belgrade 1 Borussia Mg 1
Sestic *Jurisic o.g.*
Att: 87,000
Borussia Mg 1 Red Star Belgrade 0
Simonsen
Att: 45,000 (in Dusseldorf)
Borussia Mg won 2–1 on aggregate

1980:

Borussia Mg 3 Eintracht
Frankfurt 2
Kulik (3) *Karger, Holzenbein*
Att: 25,000
Eintracht Frankfurt 1 Borussia Mg 0
Schaub
Att: 59,000
Eintracht Frankfurt won on away goals, 3–3
aggregate

1981:

Ipswich Town 3 AZ67 Alkmaar 0
Wark, Thijssen,
Mariner 56
Att: 27,000

AZ67 Alkmaar 4 Ipswich Town 2
Welzl, Metgod, *Thijssen, Wark*
Tol, Jonker
Att: 28,000
Ipswich won 5–4 on aggregate

1982:

IFK Gothenburg 1 Hamburg SV 0
Tord Holmgren
Att: 42,000
Hamburg SV 0 IFK Gothenburg 3
Corneliusson, Nilsson,
Fredriksson
Att: 60,000
IFK won 4–0 on aggregate

1983:

Anderlecht 1 Benfica 0
Brylle
Att: 55,000
Benfica 1 Anderlecht 1
Sheu *Lozano*
Att: 80,000
Anderlecht won 2–1 on aggregate

1984:

Anderlecht 1 Tottenham 1
Olsen *Miller*
Att: 35,000
Tottenham 1 Anderlecht 1*
Roberts *Czerniatynski*
Att: 46,000.
Tottenham won 4–3 on penalties, 2–2 aggregate

1985:

Videoton 0 Real Madrid 3
Michel, Santillana,
Valdano
Att: 30,000 (in Szekesfehervar)
Real Madrid 0 Videoton 1
Majer
Att: 90,000
Real Madrid won 3–1 on aggregate

1986:

Real Madrid 5 FC Köln 1
Sanchez, Gordillo *Allofs*
Valdano (2), Santillana
Att: 85,000
FC Köln 2 Real Madrid 0
Bein, Geilenkirche
Att: 15,000 (in West Berlin)
Real Madrid won 5–3 on aggregate

1987:

IFK Gothenburg 1 Dundee United 0
Pettersson
Att: 50,000
Dundee United 1 IFK Gothenburg 1
Clark *Nilsson L.*
Att: 21,000
IFK won 2–1 on aggregate

1988:

Espanol	3	Bayer Leverkusen	0

Losada (2), Soler
Att: 42,000 (in Barcelona)

Bayer Leverkusen 3		Espanol	0*

Tita, Gotz, Cha
Att: 22,000
Leverkusen won 3–2 on penalties, agg 3–3 aggregate

1989:

Napoli	2	VfB Stuttgart	1

Maradona, Careca *Gaudino*
Att: 83,000

VfB Stuttgart	3	Napoli	3

Klinsmann , *Alemao, Ferrera,*
De Napoli o.g., *Careca*
Schmaler O.
Att: 67,000
Napoli won 5–4 on aggregate

1990:

Juventus	3	Fiorentina	1

Galia, Casiraghi, *Buso*
De Agostini
Att: 45,000

Fiorentina	0	Juventus	0

Att: 32,000 (in Avellino)
Juventus won 3–1 on aggregate

1991:

Internazionale	2	Roma	0

Matthaus, Berti
Att: 75,000

Roma	1	Internazionale	0

Rizzitelli
Att: 71,000
Internazionale won 2–1 on aggregate

1992:

Torino	2	Ajax	2

Casagrande (2) *Jonk, Pettersson*
Att: 65,000

Ajax	0	Torino	0

Att: 42,000
Ajax won on away goals, 2–2 aggregate

1993:

Borussia Dortmund 1		Juventus	3

Rummenigge *Baggio, D.,*
  Baggio, R. (2)
Att: 37,000

Juventus	3	B. Dortmund	0

Baggio D. (2),
Moller
Att: 60,000
Juventus won 6–1 on aggregate

1994:

Austria Salzburg	0	Internazionale	1

  Berti
Att: 47,000

Internazionale	1	Austria Salzburg	0

Jonk
Att: 80,000
Internazionale won 2–0 on aggregate

1995:

Parma	1	Juventus	0

Baggio D.
Att: 22,000

Juventus	1	Parma	1

Vialli *Baggio D.*
Att: 80,000
Parma won 2–1 on aggregate

1996:

Bayern Munich	2	Bordeaux	0

Helmer, Scholl
Att: 62,500

Bordeaux	1	Bayern Munich	3

Dutuel *Scholl, Kostadinov,*
  Klinsmann
Att: 36,000
Bayern Munich won 5–1 on aggregate

1997:

Schalke	1	Internazionale	0

Wilmots
Att: 56,824

Internazionale	1	Schalke	0*

Zamorano
Att: 81,675
Schalke won 4–1 on penalties, 1–1 aggregate

1998: (one match only: Paris)

Internazionale	3	Lazio	0

Zamorano, Zanetti,
Ronaldo
Att: 45,000

European Super Cup

Winners

1972	Ajax
1973	Ajax
1974	not contested
1975	Kiev Dynamo
1976	Anderlecht
1977	Liverpool
1978	Anderlecht
1979	Nottingham Forest
1980	Valencia
1981	not contested
1982	Aston Villa
1983	Aberdeen
1984	Juventus
1985	not contested
1986	Steaua Bucharest
1987	FC Porto
1988	Mechelen
1989	Milan
1990	Milan
1991	Manchester Utd
1992	Barcelona
1993	Parma
1994	Milan
1995	Ajax
1996	Juventus

African Champions Cup

Winners

1964	Oryx Douala (Cameroon)
1965	not held
1966	Stade Abidjan (Ivory Coast)
1967	TP Englebert (Zaire)
1968	TP Englebert (Zaire)
1969	Al Ismaili (Egypt)
1970	Asante Kotoko (Ghana)
1971	Canon Yaounde (Cameroon)
1972	Hafia Conakry (Ghana)
1973	AS Vita Kinshasa (Zaire)
1974	CARA Brazzaville (Congo)
1975	Hafia Conakry (Ghana)
1976	MC Algiers (Algeria)
1977	Hafia Conakry (Ghana)
1978	Canon Yaounde (Cameroon)
1979	Union Douala (Cameroon)
1980	Canon Yaounde (Cameroon)
1981	JE Tizi-Ouzou (Algeria)
1982	Al Ahly (Egypt)
1983	Asante Kotoko (Ghana)
1984	Zamalek (Egypt)
1985	FAR Rabat (Morocco)
1986	Zamalek (Egypt)
1987	Al Ahly (Egypt)
1988	EP Setif (Algeria)
1989	Raja Casablanca (Morocco)
1990	JS Kabylie (Algeria)
1991	Club Africain (Algeria)
1992	Wydad Casablanca (Morocco)
1993	Zamalek (Egypt)
1994	Esperance (Tunisia)
1995	Orlando Pirates (South Africa)
1996	Zamalek (Egypt)
1997	Raja Casablanca (Morocco)

African Cup-Winners' Cup

Winners

1975	Tonnerre Yaounde (Cameroon)
1976	Shooting Stars (Nigeria)
1977	Enugu Rangers (Nigeria)
1978	Horoya Conakry (Guinea)
1979	Canon Yaounde (Cameroon)
1980	TP Mazembe (Zaire)
1981	Union Douala (Cameroon)
1982	Al Mokaoulum (Egypt)
1983	Al Mokaoulum (Egypt)
1984	Al Ahly (Egypt)
1985	Al Ahly (Egypt)
1986	Al Ahly (Egypt)
1987	Gor Mahia (Kenya)
1988	CA Bizerte (Tunisia)
1989	Al Merreikh (Sudan)
1990	BCC Lions (Nigeria)
1991	Power Dynamos (Zambia)
1992	Africa Sports (Ivory Coast)
1993	Al Ahly (Egypt)
1994	Daring Club (Zaire)
1995	J S Kabyle (Algeria)
1996	Arab Contractors (Egypt)
1997	Etoile Sahel (Tunisia)

CAF Cup

Winners

1992	Shooting Stars (Nigeria)
1993	Stella Abidjan (Ivory Coast)
1994	Bendel Insurance (Nigeria)
1995	Etoile Sahel (Tunisia)
1996	Kawkab (Morocco)
1997	Esperance (Tunisia)

CONCACAF Champions Cup

Winners

1962	Guadalajara CD (Mexico)
1963	Racing Club (Haiti)
1964	Not completed
1965	Not completed
1966	Not held
1967	Alianza (El Salvador)
1968	Toluca (Mex)
1969	Cruz Azul (Mex)
1970	Cruz Azul, Mex (North), Deportivo Saprissa (Central), Transvaal, Sur (Caribbean)
1971	Cruz Azul (Mex)
1972	Olimpia (Honduras)
1973	Transvaal (Surinam)
1974	Municipal (Guatemala)
1975	Atlético Espanol (Mex)
1976	Aguila (El Salvador)
1977	America (Mex)
1978	Univ Guadalajara, Mex (North), Comunicaciones (Central), Defence Force, Trin (Caribbean)
1979	Deportivo FAS (El Salvador)
1980	UNAM (Mex)
1981	Transvaal (Surinam)
1982	UNAM (Mex)
1983	Atlante (Mex)
1984	Violette (Haiti
1985	Defence Force (Trinidad)
1986	LD Alajuelense (Costa Rica)
1987	America (Mex)
1988	Olimpia (Hond)
1989	UNAM (Mex)
1990	America (Mex)
1991	Puebla (Mex)
1992	America (Mex)
1993	Deportivo Saprissa (CR)
1994	Cartagines (CR)
1995	Dep Saprissa (CR)

Inter-American Cup

Winners

1968	Estudiantes (Arg)
1971	Nacional (Uru)
1972	Independiente (Arg)
1973	Independiente (Arg)
1974	Independiente (Arg)
1976	Independiente (Arg)
1977	America (Mex)
1979	Olimpia (Hon)
1980	UNAM (Mex)
1985	Argentinos Juniors (Arg)
1986	River Plate (Arg)
1988	Nacional (Uru)
1989	Atlético Nacional (Col)
1990	America (Mex)
1992	Colo Colo (Chile)
1993	Un Catolica (Chile)
1994	Velez Sarsfield (Arg)

ENGLAND
Football League

Winners

Season	Champions	Pts	Runners-up	Pts
1888–89	Preston NE	40	Aston Villa	29
1889–90	Preston NE	33	Everton	31
1890–91	Everton	29	Preston NE	27
1891–92	Sunderland	42	Preston NE	37

First Division

Winners

Season	Champions	Pts	Runners-up	Pts
1892–93	Sunderland	48	Preston NE	37
1893–94	Aston Villa	44	Sunderland	38
1894–95	Sunderland	47	Everton	42
1895–96	Aston Villa	45	Derby County	41
1896–97	Aston Villa	47	Sheffield Utd	36
1897–98	Sheffield Utd	42	Sunderland	37
1898–99	Aston Villa	45	Liverpool	43
1899–00	Aston Villa	50	Sheffield Utd	48
1900–01	Liverpool	45	Sunderland	43
1901–02	Sunderland	44	Everton	41
1902–03	Sheffield Wed	42	Aston Villa	41
1903–04	Sheffield Wed	47	Manchester C	44
1904–05	Newcastle Utd	48	Everton	47
1905–06	Liverpool	51	Preston NE	47
1906–07	Newcastle Utd	51	Bristol City	48
1907–08	Manchester Utd	52	Aston Villa*	43
1908–09	Newcastle Utd	53	Everton	46
1909–10	Aston Villa	53	Liverpool	48
1910–11	Manchester Utd	52	Aston Villa	51
1911–12	Blackburn R	49	Everton	46
1912–13	Sunderland	54	Aston Villa	50
1913–14	Blackburn R	51	Aston Villa	44
1914–15	Everton	46	Oldham Ath	45
1919–20	WBA	60	Burnley	51
1920–21	Burnley	59	Manchester C	54
1921–22	Liverpool	57	Tottenham H	51
1922–23	Liverpool	60	Sunderland	54
1923–24	Huddersfield T*	57	Cardiff C	57
1924–25	Huddersfield T	58	WBA	56
1925–26	Huddersfield T	57	Arsenal	52
1926–27	Newcastle Utd	56	Huddersfield T	51
1927–28	Everton	53	Huddersfield T	51
1928–29	Sheffield Wed	52	Leicester C	51
1929–30	Sheffield Wed	60	Derby County	50
1930–31	Arsenal	66	Aston Villa	59
1931–32	Everton	56	Arsenal	54
1932–33	Arsenal	58	Aston Villa	54
1933–34	Arsenal	59	Huddersfield T	56
1934–35	Arsenal	58	Sunderland	54
1935–36	Sunderland	56	Derby County	48
1936–37	Manchester C	57	Charlton Ath	54
1937–38	Arsenal	52	Wolves	51
1938–39	Everton	59	Wolves	55
1946–47	Liverpool	57	Manchester Utd*	56
1947–48	Arsenal	59	Manchester Utd*	52
1948–49	Portsmouth	58	Manchester Utd*	53
1949–50	Portsmouth*	53	Wolves	53
1950–51	Tottenham H	60	Manchester Utd	56
1951–52	Manchester Utd	57	Tottenham H	53
1952–53	Arsenal*	54	Preston NE	54
1953–54	Wolves	57	WBA	53
1954–55	Chelsea	52	Wolves	48
1955–56	Manchester Utd	60	Blackpool*	49
1956–57	Manchester Utd	64	Tottenham H*	56
1957–58	Wolves	64	Preston NE	59
1958–59	Wolves	61	Manchester Utd	55
1959–60	Burnley	55	Wolves	54
1960–61	Tottenham H	66	Sheffield Wed	58
1961–62	Ipswich T	56	Burnley	53
1962–63	Everton	61	Tottenham H	55
1963–64	Liverpool	57	Manchester Utd	53
1964–65	Manchester Utd*	61	Leeds Utd	61
1965–66	Liverpool	61	Leeds Utd*	55
1966–67	Manchester Utd	60	Nottm Forest*	56
1967–68	Manchester C	58	Manchester Utd	56
1968–69	Leeds Utd	67	Liverpool	61
1969–70	Everton	66	Leeds Utd	57
1970–71	Arsenal	65	Leeds Utd	64
1971–72	Derby County	58	Leeds Utd*	57
1972–73	Liverpool	60	Arsenal	57
1973–74	Leeds Utd	62	Liverpool	57
1974–75	Derby County	53	Liverpool*	51
1975–76	Liverpool	60	QPR	59
1976–77	Liverpool	57	Manchester C	56
1977–78	Nottm Forest	64	Liverpool	57
1978–79	Liverpool	68	Nottm Forest	60
1979–80	Liverpool	60	Manchester Utd	58
1980–81	Aston Villa	60	Ipswich T	56
1981–82	Liverpool	87	Ipswich T	83
1982–83	Liverpool	82	Watford	71
1983–84	Liverpool	80	Southampton	77
1984–85	Everton	90	Liverpool*	77
1985–86	Liverpool	88	Everton	86
1986–87	Everton	86	Liverpool	77
1987–88	Liverpool	90	Manchester Utd	81
1988–89	Arsenal*	76	Liverpool	76
1989–90	Liverpool	79	Aston Villa	70
1990–91	Arsenal+	83	Liverpool	76
1991–92	Leeds Utd	82	Manchester Utd	78

Notes: * Position decided by goal average or goal difference, + 2 points deducted.

FA Premier League

Winners

Season	Champions	Pts	Runners-up	Pts
1992–93	Manchester Utd	84	Aston Villa	74
1993–94	Manchester Utd	92	Blackburn R	84
1994–95	Blackburn R	89	Manchester Utd	88
1995–96	Manchester Utd	82	Newcastle Utd	78
1996–97	Manchester Utd	75	Newcastle Utd	68
1997–98	Arsenal	78	Manchester Utd	77

Football League Cup

Winners

Year	Winners	Runners-up	Result
1961	Aston Villa	Rotherham Utd	0–2, 3–0*
1962	Norwich C	Rochdale	3–0, 1–0
1963	Birmingham C	Aston Villa	3–1, 0–0
1964	Leicester C	Stoke C	1–1, 3–2
1965	Chelsea	Leicester C	3–2, 0–0
1966	WBA	West Ham Utd	1–2, 4–1
1967+	QPR	WBA	3–2
1968	Leeds Utd	Arsenal	1–0
1969	Swindon T	Arsenal	3–1*
1970	Manchester C	WBA	2–1*
1971	Tottenham H	Aston Villa	2–0
1972	Stoke C	Chelsea	2–1
1973	Tottenham H	Norwich C	1–0
1974	Wolves	Manchester C	2–1
1975	Aston Villa	Norwich C	1–0
1976	Manchester C	Newcastle Utd	2–1
1977	Aston Villa	Everton	0–0*, 1–1*, 3–2*
1978	Nottm Forest	Liverpool	0–0*, 1–0
1979	Nottm Forest	Southampton	3–2
1980	Wolves	Nottm Forest	1–0
1981	Liverpool	West Ham Utd	1–1*, 2–1
1982	Liverpool	Tottenham H	3–1*
1983	Liverpool	Manchester Utd	2–1*
1984	Liverpool	Everton	0–0*, 1–0
1985	Norwich C	Sunderland	1–0
1986	Oxford Utd	QPR	3–0
1987	Arsenal	Liverpool	2–1
1988	Luton Town	Arsenal	3–2
1989	Nottm Forest	Luton Town	3–1
1990	Nottm Forest	Oldham Ath	1–0
1991	Sheffield Wed	Manchester Utd	1–0
1992	Man.Utd	Nottm Forest	1–0
1993	Arsenal	Sheffield Wed	2–1

1994	Aston Villa	Manchester Utd	3–1
1995	Liverpool	Bolton Wanderers	2–1
1996	Aston Villa	Leeds Utd	3–0
1997	Leicester City	Middlesbrough	1–1*, 1–0*
1998	Chelsea	Middlesbrough	2–0

Notes: * After extra time, + One-leg Final from this year

FA Cup

Winners

Year	Winners	Runners-up	Result
1872	Wanderers	Royal Engineers	1–0
1873	Wanderers	Oxford University	2–0
1874	Oxford Univ.	Royal Engineers	2–0
1875	Royal Eng.	Old Etonians	1–1*, 2–0
1876	Wanderers	Old Etonians	0–0*, 3–0
1877	Wanderers	Oxford University	2–0*
1878+	Wanderers	Royal Engineers	3–1
1879	Old Etonians	Clapham Rovers	1–0
1880	Clapham R.	Oxford University	1–0
1881	Old Carthus.	Old Etonians	3–0
1882	Old Etonians	Blackburn R	1–0
1883	Blackburn Oly.	Old Etonians	2–1*
1884	Blackburn R	Queens Park Glasgow	2–1
1885	Blackburn R	Queens Park Glasgow	2–0
1886	Blackburn R	WBA	0–0*, 2–0
1887	Aston Villa	WBA	2–0
1888	WBA	Preston NE	2–1
1889	Preston NE	Wolves	3–0
1890	Blackburn R	Sheffield Wed	6–1
1891	Blackburn R	Notts County	3–1
1892	WBA	Aston Villa	3–0
1893	Wolves	Everton	1–0
1894	Notts County	Bolton W	4–1
1895	Aston Villa	WBA	1–0
1896	Sheffield Wed	Wolves	2–1
1897	Aston Villa	Everton	3–2
1898	Nottm Forest	Derby County	3–1
1899	Sheffield Utd	Derby County	4–1
1900	Bury	Southampton	4–0
1901	Tottenham H	Sheffield Utd	2–2*, 3–1
1902	Sheffield Utd	Southampton	1–1*, 2–1
1903	Bury	Derby County	6–0
1904	Manchester C	Bolton W	1–0
1905	Aston Villa	Newcastle Utd	2–0
1906	Everton	Newcastle Utd	1–0
1907	Sheffield Wed	Everton	2–1
1908	Wolves	Newcastle Utd	3–1
1909	Manchester Utd	Bristol C	1–0
1910	Newcastle Utd	Barnsley	1–1*, 2–0
1911	Bradford C	Newcastle Utd	0–0*, 1–0
1912	Barnsley	WBA	0–0*, 1–0

1913	Aston Villa	Sunderland	1–0
1914	Burnley	Liverpool	1–0
1915	Sheffield Utd	Chelsea	3–0
1920	Aston Villa	Huddersfield T	1–0*
1921	Tottenham H	Wolves	1–0
1922	Huddersfield T	Preston NE	1–0
1923	Bolton W	West Ham Utd	2–0
1924	Newcastle Utd	Aston Villa	2–0
1925	Sheffield Utd	Cardiff C	1–0
1926	Bolton W	Manchester C	1–0
1927	Cardiff C	Arsenal	1–0
1928	Blackburn R	Huddersfield T	3–1
1929	Bolton W	Portsmouth	2–0
1930	Arsenal	Huddersfield T	2–0
1931	WBA	Birmingham C	2–1
1932	Newcastle Utd	Arsenal	2–1
1933	Everton	Manchester C	3–0
1934	Manchester C	Portsmouth	2–1
1935	Sheffield Wed	WBA	4–2
1936	Arsenal	Sheffield Utd	1–0
1937	Sunderland	Preston NE	3–1
1938	Preston NE	Huddersfield T	1–0*
1939	Portsmouth	Wolves	4–1
1946	Derby County	Charlton Ath	4–1*
1947	Charlton Ath	Burnley	1–0*
1948	Manchester U.	Blackpool	4–2
1949	Wolves	Leicester C	3–1
1950	Arsenal	Liverpool	2–0
1951	Newcastle U.	Blackpool	2–0
1952	Newcastle U.	Arsenal	1–0
1953	Blackpool	Bolton W	4–3
1954	WBA	Preston NE	3–2
1955	Newcastle U.	Manchester C	3–1
1956	Manchester C	Birmingham C	3–1
1957	Aston Villa	Manchester Utd	2–1
1958	Bolton W	Manchester Utd	2–0
1959	Nottm Forest	Luton T	2–1
1960	Wolves	Blackburn R	3–0
1961	Tottenham H	Leicester C	2–0
1962	Tottenham H	Burnley	3–1
1963	Man. Utd	Leicester C	3–1
1964	West Ham Utd	Preston NE	3–2
1965	Liverpool	Leeds Utd	2–1*
1966	Everton	Sheffield Wed	3–2
1967	Tottenham H	Chelsea	2–1
1968	WBA	Everton	1–0*
1969	Manchester C	Leicester C	1–0
1970	Chelsea	Leeds Utd	2–2*, 2–1*
1971	Arsenal	Liverpool	2–1*
1972	Leeds Utd	Arsenal	1–0
1973	Sunderland	Leeds Utd	1–0
1974	Liverpool	Newcastle Utd	3–0
1975	West Ham Utd	Fulham	2–0
1976	Southampton	Man. Utd	1–0
1977	Man. Utd	Liverpool	2–1
1978	Ipswich T	Arsenal	1–0

1979	Arsenal	Man. Utd	3–2
1980	West Ham Utd	Arsenal	1–0
1981	Tottenham H	Manchester C	1–1*, 3–2
1982	Tottenham H	QPR	1–1*, 1–0
1983	Man. Utd	Brighton & HA	2–2*, 4–0
1984	Everton	Watford	2–0
1985	Man. Utd	Everton	1–0*
1986	Liverpool	Everton	3–1
1987	Coventry C	Tottenham H	3–2*
1988	Wimbledon	Liverpool	1–0
1989	Liverpool	Everton	3–2*
1990	Man. Utd	Crystal Palace	3–3*, 1–0
1991	Tottenham H	Nottm Forest	2–1*
1992	Liverpool	Sunderland	2–0
1993	Arsenal	Sheffield Wed	1–1*, 2–1*
1994	Man. Utd	Chelsea	4–0
1995	Everton	Manchester Utd	1–0
1996	Man. Utd	Liverpool	1–0
1997	Chelsea	Middlesbrough	2–0
1998	Arsenal	Newcastle Utd	2–0

Notes: * After extra time;   + Cup won outright but restored to the FA

England Internationals 1872–99

Results

Date	Opponents	Venue	Score
30/11/72	Scotland	Glasgow	0–0
8/3/73	Scotland	Kennington Oval	4–2
7/3/74	Scotland	Glasgow	1–2
6/3/75	Scotland	Kennington Oval	2–2
4/3/76	Scotland	Glasgow	0–3
3/3/77	Scotland	Kennington Oval	1–3
2/3/78	Scotland	Glasgow	2–7
18/1/79	Wales	Kennington Oval	2–1
5/4/79	Scotland	Kennington Oval	5–4
13/3/80	Scotland	Glasgow	4–5
15/3/80	Wales	Wrexham	3–2
26/2/81	Wales	Blackburn	0–1
12/3/81	Scotland	Kennington Oval	1–6
18/2/82	Ireland	Belfast	13–0
11/3/82	Scotland	Glasgow	1–5
13/3/82	Wales	Wrexham	3–5
3/2/83	Wales	Kennington Oval	5–0
24/2/83	Ireland	Aigburth	7–0
10/3/83	Scotland	Sheffield	2–3
25/2/84	Ireland	Belfast	8–1
15/3/84	Scotland	Glasgow	0–1
17/3/84	Wales	Wrexham	4–0

28/2/85	Ireland	Manchester	4–0
4/3/85	Wales	Blackburn	1–1
21/3/85	Scotland	Kennington Oval	1–1
3/3/86	Ireland	Belfast	6–1
29/3/86	Wales	Wrexham	3–1
31/3/86	Scotland	Glasgow	1–1
5/2/87	Ireland	Sheffield	7–0
26/2/87	Wales	Kennington Oval	4–0
19/3/87	Scotland	Blackburn	2–3
4/2/88	Wales	Crewe	5–1
17/3/88	Scotland	Glasgow	5–0
31/3/88	Ireland	Belfast	5–1
23/2/89	Wales	Stoke	4–1
2/3/89	Ireland	Everton	6–1
13/4/89	Scotland	Kennington Oval	2–3
15/3/90	Wales	Wrexham	3–1
15/3/90	Ireland	Belfast	9–1
5/4/90	Scotland	Glasgow	1–1
7/3/91	Wales	Sunderland	4–1
7/3/91	Ireland	Wolverhampton	6–1
6/4/91	Scotland	Blackburn	2–1
5/3/92	Wales	Wrexham	2–0
5/3/92	Ireland	Belfast	2–0
2/4/92	Scotland	Glasgow	4–1
25/2/93	Ireland	Birmingham	6–1
13/3/93	Wales	Stoke	6–0
1/4/93	Scotland	Richmond	5–2
1/3/94	Ireland	Belfast	2–2
12/3/94	Wales	Wrexham	5–1
7/4/94	Scotland	Glasgow	2–2
9/3/95	Ireland	Derby	9–0
18/3/95	Wales	Queen's Club, London	1–1
6/4/95	Scotland	Goodison Park	3–0
7/3/96	Ireland	Belfast	2–0
16/3/96	Wales	Cardiff	9–1
4/4/96	Scotland	Glasgow	1–2
20/2/97	Ireland	Nottingham	6–0
29/3/97	Wales	Sheffield	4–0
3/4/97	Scotland	Crystal Palace	1–2
5/3/98	Ireland	Belfast	3–2
28/3/98	Wales	Wrexham	3–0
2/4/98	Scotland	Glasgow	3–1
18/2/99	Ireland	Sunderland	13–2
20/3/99	Wales	Bristol	4–0
8/4/99	Scotland	Birmingham	2–1

1900–29

Results

Date	Opponents	Venue	Score
17/3/00	Ireland	Dublin	2–0
26/3/00	Wales	Cardiff	1–1
7/4/00	Scotland	Glasgow	1–4
9/3/01	Ireland	Southampton	3–0
18/3/01	Wales	Newcastle	6–0
30/3/01	Scotland	Crystal Palace	2–2
3/3/02	Wales	Wrexham	0–0
22/3/02	Ireland	Belfast	1–0
3/5/02	Scotland	Birmingham	2–2
14/2/03	Ireland	Wolverhampton	4–0
2/3/03	Wales	Portsmouth	2–1
4/4/03	Scotland	Sheffield	1–2
29/2/04	Wales	Wrexham	2–2
12/3/04	Ireland	Belfast	3–1
9/4/04	Scotland	Glasgow	1–0
25/2/05	Ireland	Middlesbrough	1–1
27/3/05	Wales	Anfield	3–1
1/4/05	Scotland	Crystal Palace	1–0
17/2/06	Ireland	Belfast	5–0
19/3/06	Wales	Cardiff	1–0
7/4/06	Scotland	Glasgow	1–2
16/2/07	Ireland	Goodison Park	1–0
18/3/07	Wales	Fulham	1–1
6/4/07	Scotland	Newcastle	1–1
15/2/08	Ireland	Belfast	3–1
16/3/08	Wales	Wrexham	7–1
4/4/08	Scotland	Glasgow	1–1
6/6/08	Austria	Vienna	6–1
8/6/08	Austria	Vienna	11–1
10/6/08	Hungary	Budapest	7–0
13/6/08	Bohemia	Prague	4–0
13/2/09	Ireland	Bradford Park Av.	4–0
15/3/09	Wales	Nottingham	2–0
3/4/09	Scotland	Crystal Palace	2–0
29/5/09	Hungary	Budapest	4–2
31/5/09	Hungary	Budapest	8–2
1/6/09	Austria	Vienna	8–1
12/2/10	Ireland	Belfast	1–1
14/3/10	Wales	Cardiff	1–0
2/4/10	Scotland	Glasgow	0–2
11/2/11	Ireland	Derby	2–1
13/3/11	Wales	Millwall	3–0
1/4/11	Scotland	Goodison Park	1–1
10/2/12	Ireland	Dublin	6–1
11/3/12	Wales	Wrexham	2–0
23/3/12	Scotland	Glasgow	1–1
15/2/13	Ireland	Belfast	1–2
17/3/13	Wales	Bristol	4–3
5/4/13	Scotland	Stamford Bridge	1–0
14/2/14	Ireland	Middlesbrough	0–3

The Statistics

16/3/14	Wales	Cardiff	2–0
4/4/14	Scotland	Glasgow	1–3
25/10/19	Ireland	Belfast	1–1
15/3/20	Wales	Highbury	1–2
10/4/20	Scotland	Sheffield	5–4
23/10/20	Ireland	Sunderland	2–0
14/3/21	Wales	Cardiff	0–0
9/4/21	Scotland	Glasgow	0–3
21/5/21	Belgium	Brussels	2–0
22/10/21	Ireland	Belfast	1–1
13/3/22	Wales	Anfield	1–0
8/4/22	Scotland	Birmingham	0–1
21/10/22	Ireland	West Bromwich	2–0
5/3/23	Wales	Cardiff	2–2
19/3/23	Belgium	Highbury	6–1
14/4/23	Scotland	Glasgow	2–2
10/5/23	France	Paris	4–1
21/5/23	Sweden	Stockholm	4–2
24/5/23	Sweden	Stockholm	3–1
20/10/23	Ireland	Belfast	1–2
1/11/23	Belgium	Antwerp	2–2
3/3/24	Wales	Blackburn	1–2
12/4/24	Scotland	Wembley	1–1
17/5/24	France	Paris	3–1
22/10/24	Ireland	Anfield	3–1
8/12/24	Belgium	West Bromwich	4–0
28/2/25	Wales	Swansea	2–1
4/4/25	Scotland	Glasgow	0–2
21/5/25	France	Paris	3–2
24/10/25	Ireland	Belfast	0–0
1/3/26	Wales	Selhurst Park	1–3
17/4/26	Scotland	Manchester	0–1
24/4/26	Belgium	Antwerp	5–3
20/10/26	Ireland	Anfield	3–3
12/2/27	Wales	Wrexham	3–3
2/4/27	Scotland	Glasgow	2–1
11/5/27	Belgium	Brussels	9–1
21/5/27	Luxembourg	Luxembourg	5–2
26/5/27	France	Paris	6–0
22/10/27	Ireland	Belfast	0–2
28/11/27	Wales	Burnley	1–2
31/3/28	Scotland	Wembley	1–5
17/5/28	France	Paris	5–1
19/5/28	Belgium	Antwerp	3–1
22/10/28	Ireland	Anfield	2–1
17/11/28	Wales	Swansea	3–2
13/4/29	Scotland	Glasgow	0–1
9/5/29	France	Paris	4–1
11/5/29	Belgium	Brussels	5–1
15/5/29	Spain	Madrid	3–4
19/10/29	Ireland	Belfast	3–0
20/11/29	Wales	Stamford Bridge	6–0

1930–39

Results

Date	Opponents	Venue	Score
5/4/30	Scotland	Wembley	5–2
10/5/30	Germany	Berlin	3–3
14/5/30	Austria	Vienna	0–0
20/10/30	Ireland	Sheffield	5–1
22/11/30	Wales	Wrexham	4–0
28/3/31	Scotland	Glasgow	0–2
14/5/31	France	Paris	2–5
16/5/31	Belgium	Brussels	4–1
17/10/31	Ireland	Belfast	6–2
18/11/31	Wales	Anfield	3–1
9/12/31	Spain	Highbury	7–1
9/4/32	Scotland	Wembley	3–0
17/10/32	Ireland	Blackpool	1–0
16/11/32	Wales	Wrexham	0–0
7/12/32	Austria	Stamford Bridge	4–3
1/4/33	Scotland	Glasgow	1–2
13/5/33	Italy	Rome	1–1
20/5/33	Switzerland	Berne	4–0
14/10/33	Ireland	Belfast	3–0
15/11/33	Wales	Newcastle	1–2
6/12/33	France	White Hart Lane	4–1
14/4/34	Scotland	Wembley	3–0
10/5/34	Hungary	Budapest	1–2
16/5/34	Czechoslovakia	Prague	1–2
29/9/34	Wales	Cardiff	4–0
14/11/34	Italy	Highbury	3–2
6/2/35	Ireland	Goodison Park	2–1
6/4/35	Scotland	Glasgow	0–2
18/5/35	Holland	Amsterdam	1–0
19/10/35	Ireland	Belfast	3–1
4/12/35	Germany	White Hart Lane	3–0
5/2/36	Wales	Wolverhampton	1–2
4/4/36	Scotland	Wembley	1–1
6/5/36	Austria	Vienna	1–2
9/5/36	Belgium	Brussels	2–3
17/10/36	Wales	Cardiff	1–2
18/11/36	Ireland	Stoke	3–1
2/12/36	Hungary	Highbury	6–2
17/4/37	Scotland	Glasgow	1–3
14/5/37	Norway	Oslo	6–0
17/5/37	Sweden	Stockholm	4–0
20/5/37	Finland	Helsinki	8–0
23/10/37	Ireland	Belfast	5–1
17/11/37	Wales	Middlesbrough	2–1
1/12/37	Czechoslovakia	White Hart Lane	5–4
9/4/38	Scotland	Wembley	0–1
14/5/38	Germany	Berlin	6–3
21/5/38	Switzerland	Zurich	1–2
26/5/38	France	Paris	4–2
22/10/38	Wales	Cardiff	2–4

26/10/38	FIFA	Highbury	3–0
9/11/38	Norway	Newcastle	4–0
16/11/38	Ireland	Manchester	7–0
15/4/39	Scotland	Glasgow	2–1
13/5/39	Italy	Milan	2–2
18/5/39	Yugoslavia	Belgrade	1–2
24/5/39	Romania	Bucharest	2–0

1940–49

Results

Date	Opponents	Venue	Score
28/9/46	N. Ireland	Belfast	7–2
30/9/46	Rep. of Ireland	Dublin	1–0
19/10/46	Wales	Maine Road	3–0
27/11/46	Holland	Huddersfield	8–2
12/4/47	Scotland	Wembley	1–1
3/5/47	France	Highbury	3–0
18/5/47	Switzerland	Zurich	0–1
27/5/47	Portugal	Lisbon	10–0
21/9/47	Belgium	Brussels	5–2
18/10/47	Wales	Cardiff	3–0
5/11/47	N Ireland	Goodison Park	2–2
19/11/47	Sweden	Highbury	4–2
10/4/48	Scotland	Glasgow	2–0
16/5/48	Italy	Turin	4–0
26/9/48	Denmark	Copenhagen	0–0
9/10/48	N. Ireland	Belfast	6–2
10/11/48	Wales	Villa Park	1–0
1/12/48	Switzerland	Highbury	6–0
9/4/48	Scotland	Wembley	1–3
13/5/49	Sweden	Stockholm	1–3
18/5/49	Norway	Oslo	4–1
22/5/49	France	Paris	3–1
21/9/49	Rep. of Ireland	Goodison Park	0–2
15/10/49	Wales	Cardiff (WCQ)	4–1
16/11/49	N. Ireland	Maine Road(WCQ)	9–2
30/11/49	Italy	White Hart Lane	2–0

1950

Results

Date	Opponents	Venue	Score
15/4	Scotland	Glasgow (WCQ)	1–0
14/5	Portugal	Lisbon	5–3
18/5	Belgium	Brussels	4–1
15/6	Chile	Rio de Janeiro (WCF)	2–0
29/6	USA	Belo Horizonte (WCF)	0–1
2/7	Spain	Rio de Janeiro (WCF)	0–1
7/10	N. Ireland	Belfast	4–1
15/11	Wales	Sunderland	4–2
22/11	Yugoslavia	Highbury	2–2

1951

Results

Date	Opponents	Venue	Score
14/4	Scotland	Wembley	2–3
9/5	Argentina	Wembley	2–1
9/5	Portugal	Goodison Park	5–2
3/10	France	Highbury	2–2
20/10	Wales	Cardiff	1–1
14/11	N. Ireland	Villa Park	2–0
28/11	Austria	Wembley	2–2

1952

Results

Date	Opponents	Venue	Score
5/4	Scotland	Glasgow	2–1
18/5	Italy	Florence	1–1
25/5	Austria	Vienna	3–2
28/5	Switzerland	Zurich	3–0
4/10	N. Ireland	Belfast	2–2
12/11	Wales	Wembley	5–2
26/11	Belgium	Wembley	5–0

1953

Results

Date	Opponents	Venue	Score
18/4	Scotland	Wembley	2–2
17/5	Argentina	Buenos Aires	0–0
	(abandoned after 21 minutes, rain)		
24/5	Chile	Santiago	2–1
31/5	Uruguay	Montevideo	1–2
8/6	USA	New York	6–3
10/10	Wales	Cardiff (WCQ)	4–1
21/10	Rest of Europe	Wembley	4–4
11/11	N. Ireland	Goodison Pk (WCQ)	3–1
25/11	Hungary	Wembley	3–6

1954

Results

Date	Opponents	Venue	Score
3/4	Scotland	Glasgow (WCQ)	4–2
16/5	Yugoslavia	Belgrade	0–1
23/5	Hungary	Budapest	1–7
17/6	Belgium	Basle (WCF)	4–4*
20/6	Switzerland	Berne (WCF)	2–0
26/6	Uruguay	Basle (WCF)	2–4
2/10	N. Ireland	Belfast	2–0
10/11	Wales	Wembley	3–2
1/12	W. Germany	Wembley	3–1

1955

Results

Date	Opponents	Venue	Score
2/4	Scotland	Wembley	7–2
18/5	France	Paris	0–1
18/5	Spain	Madrid	1–1
22/5	Portugal	Oporto	1–3
2/10	Denmark	Copenhagen	5–1
22/10	Wales	Cardiff	1–1
2/11	N. Ireland	Wembley	3–0
30/11	Spain	Wembley	4–1

1956

Results

Date	Opponents	Venue	Score
14/4	Scotland	Glasgow	1–1
9/5	Brazil	Wembley	4–2
16/5	Sweden	Stockholm	0–0
20/5	Finland	Helsinki	5–1
26/5	West Germany	Berlin	3–1
6/10	N. Ireland	Belfast	1–1
14/11	Wales	Wembley	3–1
28/11	Yugoslavia	Wembley	3–0
5/12	Denmark (WCQ)	Wolverhampton	5–2

1957

Results

Date	Opponents	Venue	Score
6/4	Scotland	Wembley	2–
8/5	Rep. of Ireland	Wembley (WCQ)	5–
15/5	Denmark	Copenhagen (WCQ)	4–
19/5	Rep. of Ireland	Dublin (WCQ)	1–
19/10	Wales	Cardiff	4–
6/11	N. Ireland	Wembley	2–
27/11	France	Wembley	4–

1958

Results

Date	Opponents	Venue	Score
19/4	Scotland	Glasgow	4–
7/5	Portugal	Wembley	2–
11/5	Yugoslavia	Belgrade	0–
18/5	USSR	Moscow	1–
8/6	USSR	Gothenburg (WCF)	2–
11/6	Brazil	Gothenburg (WCF)	0–
15/6	Austria	Boras (WCF)	2–
17/6	USSR	Gothenburg (WCF)	0–
4/10	N. Ireland	Belfast	3–
22/10	USSR	Wembley	5–
26/11	Wales	Villa Park	2–

1959

Results

Date	Opponents	Venue	Score
11/4	Scotland	Wembley	1–0
6/5	Italy	Wembley	2–2
13/5	Brazil	Rio de Janeiro	0–2
17/5	Peru	Lima	1–4
24/5	Mexico	Mexico City	1–2
28/5	USA	Los Angeles	8–1
17/10	Wales	Cardiff	1–1
28/10	Sweden	Wembley	2–3
18/11	N. Ireland	Wembley	2–1

1960

Results

Date	Opponents	Venue	Score
19/4	Scotland	Glasgow	1–1
11/5	Yugoslavia	Wembley	3–3
15/5	Spain	Madrid	0–3
22/5	Hungary	Budapest	0–2
8/10	N. Ireland	Belfast	5–2
19/10	Luxembourg	Luxembourg (WCQ)	9–0
26/10	Spain	Wembley	4–2
23/11	Wales	Wembley	5–1

1961

Results

Date	Opponents	Venue	Score
15/4	Scotland	Wembley	9–3
10/5	Mexico	Wembley	8–0
21/5	Portugal	Lisbon (WCQ)	1–1
24/5	Italy	Rome	3–2
27/5	Austria	Vienna	1–3
28/9	Luxembourg	Highbury (WCQ)	4–1
14/10	Wales	Cardiff	1–1
25/10	Portugal	Wembley (WCQ)	2–0
22–11	N. Ireland	Wembley	1–1

1962

Results

Date	Opponents	Venue	Score
4/4	Austria	Wembley	3–1
14/4	Scotland	Glasgow	0–2
9/5	Switzerland	Wembley	3–1
20/5	Peru	Lima	4–0
31/5	Hungary	Rancagua (WCF)	1–2
2/6	Argentina	Rancagua (WCF)	3–1
7/6	Bulgaria	Rancagua (WCF)	0–0
10/6	Brazil	Vina del Mar (WCF)	1–3
3/10	France	Hillsborough (ECQ)	1–1
20/10	N. Ireland	Belfast	3–1
21/11	Wales	Wembley	4–0

1963

Results

Date	Opponents	Venue	Score
27/2	France	Paris (ECQ)	2–5
6/4	Scotland	Wembley	1–2
8/5	Brazil	Wembley	1–1
20/5	Czechoslovakia	Bratislava	4–2
2/6	E. Germany	Leipzig	2–1
5/6	Switzerland	Basle	8–1
12/10	Wales	Cardiff	4–0
23/10	Rest of World	Wembley	2–1
20/11	N. Ireland	Wembley	8–3

1964

Results

Date	Opponents	Venue	Score
11/4	Scotland	Glasgow	0–1
6/5	Uruguay	Wembley	2–1
17/5	Portugal	Lisbon	4–3
24/5	Rep. of Ireland	Dublin	3–1
27/5	USA	New York	10–0
30/5	Brazil	Rio de Janeiro	1–5
4/6	Portugal	São Paulo	1–1
6/6	Argentina	Rio de Janeiro	0–1
3/10	N. Ireland	Belfast	4–3
21/10	Belgium	Wembley	2–2
18/11	Wales	Wembley	2–1
9/12	Holland	Amsterdam	1–1

1965

Results

Date	Opponents	Venue	Score
10/4	Scotland	Wembley	2–2
5/5	Hungary	Wembley	1–0
9/5	Yugoslavia	Belgrade	1–1
12/5	W. Germany	Nuremberg	1–0
16/5	Sweden	Gothenburg	2–1
2/10	Wales	Cardiff	0–0
20/10	Austria	Wembley	2–3
10/11	N. Ireland	Wembley	2–1
8/12	Spain	Madrid	2–0

1966

Results

Date	Opponents	Venue	Score
5/1	Poland	Anfield	1–1
23/2	W. Germany	Wembley	1–0
2/4	Scotland	Glasgow	4–3
4/5	Yugoslavia	Wembley	2–0
26/6	Finland	Helsinki	3–0
29/6	Norway	Oslo	6–1
3/7	Denmark	Copenhagen	2–0
5/7	Poland	Chorzow	1–0
11/7	Uruguay	Wembley (WCF)	0–0
16/7	Mexico	Wembley (WCF)	2–0
20/7	France	Wembley (WCF)	2–0
23/7	Argentina	Wembley (WCF)	1–0
26/7	Portugal	Wembley (WCF)	2–1
30/7	W. Germany	Wembley (WCF)	4–2*
22/10	N. Ireland	Belfast (ECQ)	2–0
2/11	Czechoslovakia	Wembley	0–0
16/11	Wales	Wembley (ECQ)	5–1

1967

Results

Date	Opponents	Venue	Score
15/4	Scotland	Wembley (ECQ)	2–3
24/5	Spain	Wembley	2–0
27/5	Austria	Vienna	1–0
21/10	Wales	Cardiff (ECQ)	3–0
22/11	N. Ireland	Wembley (ECQ)	2–0
6/12	USSR	Wembley	2–2

1968

Results

Date	Opponents	Venue	Score
24/2	Scotland	Glasgow (ECQ)	1–1
3/4	Spain	Wembley (ECQ)	1–0
8/5	Spain	Madrid (ECQ)	2–1
22/5	Sweden	Wembley	3–1
1/6	W. Germany	Hanover	0–1
5/6	Yugoslavia	Florence (ECF)	0–1
8/6	USSR	Rome (ECF)	2–0
6/11	Romania	Bucharest	0–0
11/12	Bulgaria	Wembley	1–1

1969

Results

Date	Opponents	Venue	Score
15/1	Romania	Wembley	1–1
12/3	France	Wembley	5–0
3/5	N. Ireland	Belfast	3–1
7/5	Wales	Wembley	2–1
10/5	Scotland	Wembley	4–1
1/6	Mexico	Mexico City	0–0
8/6	Uruguay	Montevideo	2–1
12/6	Brazil	Rio de Janeiro	1–2
5/11	Holland	Amsterdam	1–0
10/12	Portugal	Wembley	1–0

1970

Results

Date	Opponents	Venue	Score
14/1	Holland	Wembley	0–0
25/2	Belgium	Brussels	3–1
18/4	Wales	Cardiff	1–1
21/4	N Ireland	Wembley	3–1
25/4	Scotland	Glasgow	0–0
20/5	Colombia	Bogota	4–0
24/5	Ecuador	Quito	2–0
2/6	Romania	Guadalajara (WCF)	1–0
7/6	Brazil	Guadalajara (WCF)	0–1
11/6	Czechoslovakia	Guadalajara (WCF)	1–0
14/6	W. Germany	Leon (WCF)	2–3*
25/11	E. Germany	Wembley	3–1

1971

Results

Date	Opponents	Venue	Score
3/2	Malta	Valletta (ECQ)	1–0
21/4	Greece	Wembley (ECQ)	4–0
12/5	Malta	Wembley (ECQ)	5–0
15/5	N. Ireland	Belfast	1–0
19/5	Wales	Wembley	0–0
22/5	Scotland	Wembley	3–1
13/10	Switzerland	Basle (ECQ)	3–2
10/11	Switzerland	Wembley (ECQ)	1–1
1/12	Greece	Athens (ECQ)	2–0

1972

Results

Date	Opponents	Venue	Score
29/4	W. Germany	Wembley (ECQ)	1–3
13/5	W. Germany	Berlin (ECQ)	0–0
20/5	Wales	Cardiff	3–0
23/5	N. Ireland	Wembley	0–1
27/5	Scotland	Glasgow	1–0
11/10	Yugoslavia	Wembley	1–11
5/11	Wales	Cardiff (WCQ)	1–0

1973

Results

Date	Opponents	Venue	Score
24/1	Wales	Wembley (WCQ)	1–1
14/2	Scotland	Glasgow	5–0
12/5	N. Ireland	Anfield	2–1
15/5	Wales	Wembley	3–0
19/5	Scotland	Wembley	1–0
27/5	Czechoslovakia	Prague	1–1
6/6	Poland	Chorzow (WCQ)	0–2
10/6	USSR	Moscow	2–1
14/6	Italy	Turin	0–2
26/9	Austria	Wembley	7–0
17/10	Poland	Wembley (WCQ)	1–1
14/11	Italy	Wembley	0–1

1974

Results

Date	Opponents	Venue	Score
3/4	Portugal	Lisbon	0–0
11/5	Wales	Cardiff	2–0
15/5	N. Ireland	Wembley	1–0
18/5	Scotland	Glasgow	0–2
22/5	Argentina	Wembley	2–2
29/5	E. Germany	Leipzig	1–1
1/6	Bulgaria	Sofia	1–0
5/6	Yugoslavia	Belgrade	2–2
30/10	Czechoslovakia	Wembley (ECQ)	3–0
20/11	Portugal	Wembley (ECQ)	0–0

1975

Results

Date	Opponents	Venue	Score
12/3	W. Germany	Wembley	2–0
16/4	Cyprus	Wembley (ECQ)	5–0
11/5	Cyprus	Limassol (ECQ)	1–0
17/5	N. Ireland	Belfast	0–0
21/5	Wales	Wembley	2–2
24/5	Scotland	Wembley	5–1
3/9	Switzerland	Basle	2–1
30/10	Czechoslovakia	Bratislava (ECQ)	1–2
19/11	Portugal	Lisbon (ECQ)	1–1

1976

Results

Date	Opponents	Venue	Score
24/3	Wales	Wrexham	2–1
8/5	Wales	Cardiff	1–0
11/5	N. Ireland	Wembley	4–0
15/5	Scotland	Glasgow	1–2
23/5	Brazil	Los Angeles	0–1
28/5	Italy	New York	3–2
13/6	Finland	Helsinki (WCQ)	4–1
8/9	Rep. of Ireland	Wembley	1–1
13/10	Finland	Wembley (WCQ)	2–1
17/11	Italy	Rome (WCQ)	0–2

1977

Results

Date	Opponents	Venue	Score
9/2	Holland	Wembley	0–2
30/3	Luxembourg	Wembley (WCQ)	5–0
28/5	N. Ireland	Belfast	2–1
31/5	Wales	Wembley	0–1
4/6	Scotland	Wembley	1–2
8/6	Brazil	Rio de Janeiro	0–0
12/6	Argentina	Buenos Aires	1–1
15/6	Uruguay	Montevideo	0–0
7/9	Switzerland	Wembley	0–0
12/10	Luxembourg	Luxembourg (WCQ)	2–0
16/11	Italy	Wembley (WCQ)	2–0

1978

Results

Date	Opponents	Venue	Score
22/2	W. Germany	Munich	1–2
19/4	Brazil	Wembley	1–1
13/5	Wales	Cardiff	3–1
16/5	N. Ireland	Wembley	1–0
20/5	Scotland	Glasgow	1–0
24/5	Hungary	Wembley	4–1
20/9	Denmark	Copenhagen (ECQ)	4–3
25/10	Rep. of Ireland	Dublin (ECQ)	1–1
29/11	Czechoslovakia	Wembley	1–0

1979

Results

Date	Opponents	Venue	Score
7/2	N. Ireland	Wembley (ECQ)	4–0
19/5	N. Ireland	Belfast	2–0
23/5	Wales	Wembley	0–0
26/5	Scotland	Wembley	3–1
6/6	Bulgaria	Sofia (ECQ)	3–0
10/6	Sweden	Stockholm	0–0
13/6	Austria	Vienna	3–4
12/9	Denmark	Wembley (ECQ)	1–0
17/10	N. Ireland	Belfast (ECQ)	5–1
22/11	Bulgaria	Wembley (ECQ)	2–0

1980

Results

Date	Opponents	Venue	Score
6/2	Rep. of Ireland	Wembley (ECQ)	2–0
26/3	Spain	Barcelona	2–0
13/5	Argentina	Wembley	3–1
17/5	Wales	Wrexham	1–4
20/5	N. Ireland	Wembley	1–1
24/5	Scotland	Glasgow	2–0
31/5	Australia	Sydney	2–1
12/6	Belgium	Turin (ECF)	1–1
15/6	Italy	Turin (ECF)	0–1
18/6	Spain	Naples (ECF)	2–1
10/9	Norway	Wembley (WCQ)	4–0
15/10	Romania	Bucharest (WCQ)	1–2
19/11	Switzerland	Wembley (WCQ)	2–1

1981

Results

Date	Opponents	Venue	Score
25/3	Spain	Wembley	1–2
29/4	Romania	Wembley (WCQ)	0–0
12/5	Brazil	Wembley	0–1
20/5	Wales	Wembley	0–0
23/5	Scotland	Wembley	0–1
30/5	Switzerland	Basle (WCQ)	1–2
6/6	Hungary	Budapest (WCQ)	3–1
9/9	Norway	Oslo (WCQ)	1–2
18/11	Hungary	Wembley (WCQ)	1–0

1982

Results

Date	Opponents	Venue	Score
23/2	N. Ireland	Wembley	4–0
25/5	Holland	Wembley	2–0
29/5	Scotland	Glasgow	1–0
2/6	Iceland	Reykjavik	1–1
3/6	Finland	Helsinki	4–1
16/6	France	Bilbao (WCF)	3–1
20/6	Czechoslovakia	Bilbao (WCF)	2–0
25/6	Kuwait	Bilbao (WCF)	1–0
29/6	W. Germany	Madrid (WCF)	0–0
5/7	Spain	Madrid (WCF)	0–0
22/9	Denmark	Copenhagen (ECQ)	2–2

13/10	W. Germany	Wembley	1–2
17/11	Greece	Salonika (ECQ)	3–0
15/12	Luxembourg	Wembley (ECQ)	9–0

16/6	USA	Los Angeles	5–0
11/9	Romania	Wembley (WCQ)	1–1
16/10	Turkey	Wembley (WCQ)	5–0
13/11	N. Ireland	Wembley (WCQ)	0–0

1983

Results

Date	Opponents	Venue	Score
23/2	Wales	Wembley	2–1
30/3	Greece	Wembley (ECQ)	0–0
27/4	Hungary	Wembley (ECQ)	2–0
28/5	N. Ireland	Belfast	0–0
1/6	Scotland	Wembley	2–0
12/6	Australia	Sydney	0–0
15/6	Australia	Brisbane	1–0
19/6	Australia	Melbourne	1–1
21/9	Denmark	Wembley (ECQ)	0–1
12/10	Hungary	Budapest (ECQ)	3–0
16/11	Luxembourg	Luxembourg (ECQ)	4–0

1984

Results

Date	Opponents	Venue	Score
29/2	France	Paris	0–2
4/4	N. Ireland	Wembley	1–0
2/5	Wales	Wrexham	0–1
26/5	Scotland	Glasgow	1–1
2/6	USSR	Wembley	0–2
10/6	Brazil	Rio de Janeiro	2–0
13/6	Uruguay	Montevideo	0–2
17/6	Chile	Santiago	0–0
12/9	E. Germany	Wembley	1–0
17/10	Finland	Wembley (WCQ)	5–0
14/11	Turkey	Istanbul (WCQ)	8–0

1985

Results

Date	Opponents	Venue	Score
27/2	N. Ireland	Belfast (WCQ)	1–0
26/3	Rep. of Ireland	Wembley	2–1
1/5	Romania	Bucharest (WCQ)	0–0
22/5	Finland	Helsinki (WCQ)	1–1
25/5	Scotland	Glasgow	0–1
6/6	Italy	Mexico City	1–2
9/6	Mexico	Mexico City	0–1
12/6	W. Germany	Mexico City	3–0

1986

Results

Date	Opponents	Venue	Score
29/1	Egypt	Cairo	4–0
26/2	Israel	Ramat Gan	2–1
26/3	USSR	Tblisi	1–0
23/4	Scotland	Wembley	2–1
17/5	Mexico	Los Angeles	3–0
24/5	Canada	Burnaby	1–0
3/6	Portugal	Monterrey (WCF)	0–1
6/6	Morocco	Monterrey (WCF)	0–0
11/6	Poland	Monterrey (WCF)	3–0
18/6	Paraguay	Mexico City (WCF)	3–0
22/6	Argentina	Mexico City (WCF)	1–2
10/9	Sweden	Stockholm	0–1
15/10	N. Ireland	Wembley (ECQ)	3–0
12/11	Yugoslavia	Wembley (ECQ)	2–0

1987

Results

Date	Opponents	Venue	Score
10/2	Spain	Madrid	4–2
1/4	N. Ireland	Belfast (ECQ)	2–0
29/4	Turkey	Izmir (ECQ)	0–0
19/5	Brazil	Wembley	1–1
23/5	Scotland	Glasgow	0–0
9/9	W. Germany	Düsseldorf	1–3
14/10	Turkey	Wembley (ECQ)	8–0
11/11	Yugoslavia	Belgrade (ECQ)	4–1

1988

Results

Date	Opponents	Venue	Score
17/2	Israel	Tel Aviv	0–0
23/3	Holland	Wembley	2–2
27/4	Hungary	Budapest	0–0
21/5	Scotland	Wembley	1–0
24/5	Colombia	Wembley	1–1
28/5	Switzerland	Lausanne	1–0

12/6	Rep. of Ireland	Stuttgart (ECF)	0–1
15/6	Holland	Düsseldorf (ECF)	1–3
18/6	USSR	Frankfurt (ECF)	1–3
14/9	Denmark	Wembley	1–0
19/10	Sweden	Wembley (WCQ)	0–0
16/11	Saudi Arabia	Riyadh	1–1

1989

Results

Date	Opponents	Venue	Score
8/2	Greece	Athens	2–1
8/3	Albania	Tirana (WCQ)	2–0
26/4	Albania	Wembley (WCQ)	5–0
23/5	Chile	Wembley	0–0
27/5	Scotland	Glasgow	2–0
3/6	Poland	Wembley (WCQ)	3–0
7/6	Denmark	Copenhagen	1–1
6/9	Sweden	Stockholm (WCQ)	0–0
11/10	Poland	Katowice (WCQ)	0–0
15/11	Italy	Wembley	0–0
13/12	Yugoslavia	Wembley	2–1

1990

Results

Date	Opponents	Venue	Score
28/3	Brazil	Wembley	1–0
25/4	Czechoslovakia	Wembley	4–2
15/5	Denmark	Wembley	1–0
22/5	Uruguay	Wembley	1–2
2/6	Tunisia	Tunis	1–1
11/6	Rep. of Ireland	Cagliari (WCF)	1–1
16/6	Holland	Cagliari (WCF)	0–0
21/6	Egypt	Cagliari (WCF)	1–0
26/6	Belgium	Bologna (WCF)	1–0
1/7	Cameroon	Naples (WCF)	3–2
4/7	W. Germany	Turin (WCF)	1–1*
	(England lost 3–4 on penalties)		
7/7	Italy	Bari (WCF)	1–2
12/9	Hungary	Wembley	1–0
17/10	Poland	Wembley (ECQ)	2–0
14/11	Rep. of Ireland	Dublin (ECQ)	1–1

1991

Results

Date	Opponents	Venue	Score
6/2	Cameroon	Wembley	2–0
27/3	Rep. of Ireland	Wembley (ECQ)	1–1
1/5	Turkey	Izmir (ECQ)	1–0
21/5	USSR	Wembley	3–1
25/5	Argentina	Wembley	2–2
1/6	Australia	Sydney	1–0
3/6	New Zealand	Auckland	1–0
8/6	New Zealand	Wellington	2–0
12/6	Malaysia	Kuala Lumpur	4–2
11/9	Germany	Wembley	0–1
16/10	Turkey	Wembley (ECQ)	1–0
13/11	Poland	Poznan (ECQ)	1–1

1992

Results

Date	Opponents	Venue	Score
19/2	France	Wembley	2–0
25/3	Czechoslovakia	Prague	2–2
29/4	CIS	Moscow	2–2
12/5	Hungary	Budapest	1–0
17/5	Brazil	Wembley	1–1
3/6	Finland	Helsinki	2–1
11/6	Denmark	Malmö (ECF)	0–0
14/6	France	Malmö (ECF)	0–0
17/6	Sweden	Stockholm (ECF)	1–2
9/9	Spain	Santander	0–1
14/10	Norway	Wembley (WCQ)	1–1
18/11	Turkey	Wembley (WCQ)	4–0

1993

Results

Date	Opponents	Venue	Score
17/2	San Marino	Wembley (WCQ)	6–0
31/3	Turkey	Izmir (WCQ)	2–0
28/4	Holland	Wembley (WCQ)	2–2
29/5	Poland	Katowice (WCQ)	1–1
2/6	Norway	Oslo (WCQ)	0–2
9/6	USA	Boston (USC)	0–2
13/6	Brazil	Washington (USC)	1–1
19/6	Germany	Detroit (USC)	1–2
8/9	Poland	Wembley (WCQ)	3–0
13/10	Holland	Rotterdam (WCQ)	0–2
17/11	San Marino	Bologna (WCQ)	7–1

1994

Results

Date	Opponents	Venue	Score
9/3	Denmark	Wembley	1–0
17/5	Greece	Wembley	5–0
22/5	Norway	Wembley	0–0
7/9	USA	Wembley	2–0
16/11	Nigeria	Wembley	1–0

1995

Results

Date	Opponents	Venue	Score
15/2	Rep. of Ireland	Dublin	0–1
	(abandoned after 21 minutes, crowd trouble)		
29/3	Uruguay	Wembley	0–0
3/6	Japan	Wembley (UT)	2–1
8/6	Sweden	Leeds (UT)	3–3
11/6	Brazil	Wembley (UT)	1–3
6/9	Colombia	Wembley	0–0
11/10	Norway	Oslo	0–0
15/11	Switzerland	Wembley	3–1
12/12	Portugal	Wembley	1–1

1996

Results

Date	Opponents	Venue	Score
27/3	Bulgaria	Wembley	1–0
24/4	Croatia	Wembley	0–0
18/5	Hungary	Wembley	3–0
23/5	China	Beijing	3–0
8/6	Switzerland	Wembley (ECF)	1–1
15/6	Scotland	Wembley (ECF)	2–0
18/6	Holland	Wembley (ECF)	4–1
22/6	Spain	Wembley (ECF)	0–0
	(England won 4–2 on penalties)		
26/6	Germany	Wembley (ECF)	1–1
	(England lost 5–6 on penalties)		
1/9	Moldova	Chisinau (WCQ)	3–0
9/10	Poland	Wembley (WCQ)	2–1
9/11	Georgia	Tbilisi (WCQ)	2–0

1997

Results

Date	Opponents	Venue	Score
12/2	Italy	Wembley (WCQ)	0–1
29/3	Mexico	Wembley	2–0
30/4	Georgia	Wembley (WCQ)	2–0
24/5	South Africa	Old Trafford	2–1
31/5	Poland	Chorzow (WCQ)	2–0
4/6	Italy	Nantes (TdF)	2–0
7/6	France	Montpellier (TdF)	1–0
10/6	Brazil	Paris (TdF)	0–1
10/9	Moldova	Wembley (WCQ)	4–0
11/10	Italy	Rome (WCQ)	0–0
15/11	Cameroon	Wembley	2–0

1998

Results

Date	Opponents	Venue	Score
11/2	Chile	Wembley	0–2
25/3	Switzerland	Basle	1–1
22/4	Portugal	Wembley	3–0
23/5	Saudi Arabia	Wembley	0–0
27/5	Morocco	Casablanca	2–0
29/5	Belgium	Casablanca	0–0
	(Belgium won 4–3 on penalties)		
15/6	Tunisia	Marseilles (WCF)	2–0
22/6	Romania	Toulouse (WCF)	1–2
26/6	Columbia	Lens (WCF)	2–0
30/6	Argentina	St Etienne (WCF)	2–2
	(Argentina won 4–3 on penalties)		

SCOTLAND

Scottish League First Division

Winners

Season	Champions	Pts	Runners-up	Pts
1890–91	Dumbarton	29	Rangers	29 +
1891–92	Dumbarton	37	Rangers	35
1892–93	Celtic	29	Rangers	28
1893–94	Celtic	29	Hearts	26
1894–95	Hearts	31	Celtic	26
1895–96	Celtic	30	Rangers	26
1896–97	Hearts	28	Hibernian	26
1897–98	Celtic	33	Rangers	29
1898–99	Rangers	36	Hearts	26
1899–00	Rangers	32	Celtic	25
1900–01	Rangers	35	Celtic	29
1901–02	Rangers	28	Celtic	26
1902–03	Hibernian	37	Dundee	31
1903–04	Third Lanark	43	Hearts	39
1904–05	Celtic	41	Rangers	41+
1905–06	Celtic	49	Hearts	43
1906–07	Celtic	55	Dundee	48
1907–08	Celtic	55	Falkirk	51
1908–09	Celtic	51	Dundee	50
1909–10	Celtic	54	Falkirk	52
1910–11	Rangers	52	Aberdeen	48
1911–12	Rangers	51	Celtic	45
1912–13	Rangers	53	Celtic	49
1913–14	Celtic	65	Rangers	59
1914–15	Celtic	65	Hearts	61
1915–16	Celtic	67	Rangers	56
1916–17	Celtic	64	Morton	54
1917–18	Rangers	56	Celtic	55
1918–19	Celtic	58	Rangers	57
1919–20	Rangers	71	Celtic	68
1920–21	Rangers	76	Celtic	66
1921–22	Celtic	67	Rangers	66
1922–23	Rangers	55	Airdrieonians	50
1923–24	Rangers	59	Airdrieonians	50
1924–25	Rangers	60	Airdrieonians	57
1925–26	Celtic	58	Airdrieonians*	50
1926–27	Rangers	56	Motherwell	51
1927–28	Rangers	60	Celtic*	55
1928–29	Rangers	67	Celtic	51
1929–30	Rangers	60	Motherwell	55
1930–31	Rangers	60	Celtic	58
1931–32	Motherwell	66	Rangers	61
1932–33	Rangers	62	Motherwell	59
1933–34	Rangers	66	Motherwell	62
1934–35	Rangers	55	Celtic	52
1935–36	Celtic	66	Rangers*	61
1936–37	Rangers	61	Aberdeen	54
1937–38	Celtic	61	Hearts	58
1938–39	Rangers	59	Celtic	48
1946–47	Rangers	46	Hibernian	44
1947–48	Hibernian	48	Rangers	46
1948–49	Rangers	46	Dundee	45
1949–50	Rangers	50	Hibernian	49
1950–51	Hibernian	48	Rangers*	38
1951–52	Hibernian	45	Rangers	41
1952–53	Rangers*	43	Hibernian	43
1953–54	Celtic	43	Hearts	38
1954–55	Aberdeen	49	Celtic	46
1955–56	Rangers	52	Aberdeen	46
1956–57	Rangers	55	Hearts	53
1957–58	Hearts	62	Rangers	49
1958–59	Rangers	50	Hearts	48
1959–60	Hearts	54	Kilmarnock	50
1960–61	Rangers	51	Kilmarnock	50
1961–62	Dundee	54	Rangers	51
1962–63	Rangers	57	Kilmarnock	48
1963–64	Rangers	55	Kilmarnock	49
1964–65	Kilmarnock*	50	Hearts	50
1965–66	Celtic	57	Rangers	55
1966–67	Celtic	58	Rangers	55
1967–68	Celtic	63	Rangers	61
1968–69	Celtic	54	Rangers	49
1969–70	Celtic	57	Rangers	45
1970–71	Celtic	56	Aberdeen	54
1971–72	Celtic	60	Aberdeen	50
1972–73	Celtic	57	Rangers	56
1973–74	Celtic	53	Hibernian	49
1974–75	Rangers	56	Hibernian	49

Premier Division

Winners

Season	Champions	Pts	Runners-up	Pts
1975–76	Rangers	54	Celtic	48
1976–77	Celtic	55	Rangers	46
1977–78	Rangers	55	Aberdeen	53
1978–79	Celtic	48	Rangers	45
1979–80	Aberdeen	48	Celtic	47
1980–81	Celtic	56	Aberdeen	49
1981–82	Celtic	55	Aberdeen	53
1982–83	Dundee Utd	56	Celtic*	55
1983–84	Aberdeen	57	Celtic	50
1984–85	Aberdeen	59	Celtic	52
1985–86	Celtic*	50	Hearts	50
1986–87	Rangers	69	Celtic	63
1987–88	Celtic	72	Hearts	62
1988–89	Rangers	56	Aberdeen	50
1989–90	Rangers	51	Aberdeen*	44
1990–91	Rangers	55	Aberdeen	53

1991–92	Rangers	72	Hearts	63
1992–93	Rangers	73	Aberdeen	64
1993–94	Rangers	58	Aberdeen	55
1994–95	Rangers	69	Motherwell	54
1995–96	Rangers	87	Celtic	83
1996–97	Rangers	80	Celtic	75
1997–98	Celtic	74	Rangers	72

Notes: * On goal average/difference;
+ Championship held jointly

Scottish League Cup

Finalists

Season	Winners	Runners-up	Score
1946–47	Rangers	Aberdeen	4–0
1947–48	East Fife	Falkirk	0–0, 4–1
1948–49	Rangers	Raith Rovers	2–0
1949–50	East Fife	Dunfermline A.	3–0
1950–51	Motherwell	Hibernian	3–0
1951–52	Dundee	Rangers	3–2
1952–53	Dundee	Kilmarnock	2–0
1953–54	East Fife	Partick T.	3–2
1954–55	Hearts	Motherwell	4–2
1955–56	Aberdeen	St Mirren	2–1
1956–57	Celtic	Partick T.	0–0, 3–0
1957–58	Celtic	Rangers	7–1
1958–59	Hearts	Partick T.	5–1
1959–60	Hearts	Third Lanark	2–1
1960–61	Rangers	Kilmarnock	2–0
1961–62	Rangers	Hearts	1–1, 3–1
1962–63	Hearts	Kilmarnock	1–0
1963–64	Rangers	Morton	5–0
1964–65	Rangers	Celtic	2–1
1965–66	Celtic	Rangers	2–1
1966–67	Celtic	Rangers	1–0
1967–68	Celtic	Dundee	5–3
1968–69	Celtic	Hibernian	6–2
1969–70	Celtic	St Johnstone	1–0
1970–71	Rangers	Celtic	1–0
1971–72	Partick T.	Celtic	4–1
1972–73	Hibernian	Celtic	2–1
1973–74	Dundee	Celtic	1–0
1974–75	Celtic	Hibernian	6–3
1975–76	Rangers	Celtic	1–0
1976–77	Aberdeen	Celtic	2–1
1977–78	Rangers	Celtic	2–1
1978–79	Rangers	Aberdeen	2–1
1979–80	Dundee Utd	Aberdeen	0–0, 3–0
1980–81	Dundee Utd	Dundee	3–0
1981–82	Rangers	Dundee Utd	2–1
1982–83	Celtic	Rangers	2–1
1983–84	Rangers	Celtic	3–2

1984–85	Rangers	Dundee Utd	1–0
1985–86	Aberdeen	Hibernian	3–0
1986–87	Rangers	Celtic	2–1
1987–88	Rangers	Aberdeen	3–3
	Rangers won 5–3 on penalties		
1988–89	Rangers	Aberdeen	3–2
1989–90	Aberdeen	Rangers	2–1
1990–91	Rangers	Celtic	2–1
1991–92	Hibernian	Dunfermline A.	2–0
1992–93	Rangers	Aberdeen	2–1
1993–94	Rangers	Hibernian	2–1
1994–95	Raith Rovers	Celtic	0–0
	(Raith Rovers won 6–5 on penalties)		
1995–96	Aberdeen	Dundee	2–0
1996–97	Rangers	Hearts	4–3
1997–98	Celtic	Dundee Utd	2–0

Scottish FA Cup

Finalist

Year	Winners	Runners-up	Score
1874	Queen's Park	Clydesdale	2–0
1875	Queen's Park	Renton	3–0
1876	Queen's Park	Third Lanark	1–1, 2–0
1877	Vale of Leven	Rangers	0–0, 1–1, 3–2
1878	Vale of Leven	Third Lanark	1–0
1879	Vale of Leven	Rangers	
	Rangers failed to appear for replay after 1–1 draw. Vale awarded Cup		
1880	Queen's Park	Thornlibank	3–0
1881	Queen's Park	Dumbarton	3–1
1882	Queen's Park	Dumbarton	2–2, 4–1
1883	Dumbarton	Vale of Leven	2–2, 2–1
1884	Queen's Park	Vale of Leven	
	Vale of Leven failed to appear. Queen's Park awarded Cup		
1885	Renton	Vale of Leven	0–0, 3–1
1886	Queen's Park	Renton	3–1
1887	Hibernian	Dumbarton	2–1
1888	Renton	Cambuslang	6–1
1889	Third Lanark	Celtic	3–0+, 2–1
	+Replay ordered because of playing conditions in the first game		
1890	Queen's Park	Vale of Leven	1–1, 2–1
1891	Hearts	Dumbarton	1–0
1892	Celtic	Queen's Park	5–1
	After mutually protested game which Celtic won 1–0		
1893	Queen's Park	Celtic	2–1
1894	Rangers	Celtic	3–1
1895	St Bernard's	Renton	2–1
1896	Hearts	Hibernian	3–1
1897	Rangers	Dumbarton	5–1
1898	Rangers	Kilmarnock	2–0
1899	Celtic	Rangers	2–0

1900	Celtic	Queen's Park	4–3
1901	Hearts	Celtic	4–3
1902	Hibernian	Celtic	1–0
1903	Rangers	Hearts	1–1, 0–0, 2–0
1904	Celtic	Rangers	3–2
1905	Third Lanark	Rangers	0–0, 3–1
1906	Hearts	Third Lanark	1–0
1907	Celtic	Hearts	3–0
1908	Celtic	St Mirren	5–1
1909	Celtic	Rangers	2–2, 1–1

Owing to riot, the cup was withheld after two drawn games

1910	Dundee	Clyde	2–2, 0–0, 2–1
1911	Celtic	Hamilton A.	0–0, 2–0
1912	Celtic	Clyde	2–0
1913	Falkirk	Raith R.	2–0
1914	Celtic	Hibernian	0–0, 4–1
1920	Kilmarnock	Albion R.	3–2
1921	Partick T.	Rangers	1–0
1922	Morton	Rangers	1–0
1923	Celtic	Hibernian	1–0
1924	Airdrieonians	Hibernian	2–0
1925	Celtic	Dundee	2–1
1926	St Mirren	Celtic	2–0
1927	Celtic	East Fife	3–1
1928	Rangers	Celtic	4–0
1929	Kilmarnock	Rangers	2–0
1930	Rangers	Partick T.	0–0, 2–1
1931	Celtic	Motherwell	2–2, 4–2
1932	Rangers	Kilmarnock	1–1, 3–0
1933	Celtic	Motherwell	1–0
1934	Rangers	St Mirren	5–0
1935	Rangers	Hamilton A.	2–1
1936	Rangers	Third Lanark	1–0
1937	Celtic	Aberdeen	2–1
1938	East Fife	Kilmarnock	1–1, 4–2
1939	Clyde	Motherwell	4–0
1947	Aberdeen	Hibernian	2–1
1948	Rangers	Morton	1–1, 1–0
1949	Rangers	Clyde	4–1
1950	Rangers	East Fife	3–0
1951	Celtic	Motherwell	1–0
1952	Motherwell	Dundee	4–0
1953	Rangers	Aberdeen	1–1, 1–0
1954	Celtic	Aberdeen	2–1
1955	Clyde	Celtic	1–1, 1–0
1956	Hearts	Celtic	3–1
1957	Falkirk	Kilmarnock	1–1, 2–1
1958	Clyde	Hibernian	1–0
1959	St Mirren	Aberdeen	3–1
1960	Rangers	Kilmarnock	2–0
1961	Dunfermline A.	Celtic	0–0, 2–0
1962	Rangers	St Mirren	2–0
1963	Rangers	Celtic	1–1, 3–0
1964	Rangers	Dundee	3–1
1965	Celtic	Dunfermline A.	3–2

1966	Rangers	Celtic	0–0, 1–0
1967	Celtic	Aberdeen	2–0
1968	Dunfermline A.	Hearts	3–1
1969	Celtic	Rangers	4–0
1970	Aberdeen	Celtic	3–1
1971	Celtic	Rangers	1–1, 2–1
1972	Celtic	Hibernian	6–1
1973	Rangers	Celtic	3–2
1974	Celtic	Dundee Utd	3–0
1975	Celtic	Airdrieonians	3–1
1976	Rangers	Hearts	3–1
1977	Celtic	Rangers	1–0
1978	Rangers	Aberdeen	2–1
1979	Rangers	Hibernian	0–0, 0–0, 3–2
1980	Celtic	Rangers	1–0
1981	Rangers	Dundee Utd	0–0, 4–1
1982	Aberdeen	Rangers	4–1*
1983	Aberdeen	Rangers	1–0*
1984	Aberdeen	Celtic	2–1*
1985	Celtic	Dundee Utd	2–1
1986	Aberdeen	Hearts	3–0
1987	St Mirren	Dundee Utd	1–0 *
1988	Celtic	Dundee Utd	2–1
1989	Celtic	Rangers	1–0
1990	Aberdeen	Celtic	0–0*

(Aberdeen won 9–8 on penalties)

1991	Motherwell	Dundee Utd	4–3*
1992	Rangers	Airdrieonians	2–1
1993	Rangers	Aberdeen	2–1
1994	Dundee Utd	Rangers	1–0
1995	Celtic	Airdrieonians	1–0
1996	Rangers	Hearts	5–1
1997	Kilmarnock	Falkirk	1–0
1998	Hearts	Rangers	2–1

Scotland Internationals 1872–99

Results

Date	Opponents	Venue	Score
30/11/72	England	Glasgow	0–0
8/3/73	England	London	2–4
7/3/74	England	Glasgow	2–1
6/3/75	England	London	2–2
4/3/76	England	Glasgow	3–0
25/3/76	Wales	Glasgow	4–0
3/3/77	England	London	3–1
5/3/77	Wales	Wrexham	2–0
2/3/78	England	Glasgow	7–2

23/3/78	Wales	Glasgow	9–0
7/4/79	Wales	Wrexham	3–0
5/4/79	England	London	4–5
13/3/80	England	Glasgow	5–4
27/3/80	Wales	Glasgow	5–1
12/3/81	England	London	6–1
14/3/81	Wales	Wrexham	5–1
11/3/82	England	Glasgow	5–1
25/3/82	Wales	Glasgow	5–0
10/3/83	England	Sheffield	3–2
12/3/83	Wales	Wrexham	3–0
26/1/84	Ireland	Belfast	5–0
15/3/84	England	Glasgow	1–0
29/3/84	Wales	Glasgow	4–1
14/3/85	Ireland	Glasgow	8–2
21/3/85	England	London	1–1
23/3/85	Wales	Wrexham	8–1
20/3/86	Ireland	Belfast	7–2
31/3/86	England	Glasgow	1–1
10/4/86	Wales	Glasgow	4–4
19/2/87	Ireland	Glasgow	4–1
19/3/87	England	Blackburn	3–2
21/3/87	Wales	Wrexham	2–0
10/3/88	Wales	Edinburgh	5–1
17/3/88	England	Glasgow	0–5
24/3/88	Ireland	Belfast	10–2
9/3/89	Ireland	Glasgow	7–0
13/4/89	England	London	3–2
15/4/89	Wales	Wrexham	0–0
22/3/90	Wales	Glasgow	5–0
29/3/90	Ireland	Belfast	4–1
5/4/90	England	Glasgow	1–1
21/3/91	Wales	Wrexham	4–3
28/3/91	Ireland	Glasgow	2–1
6/4/91	England	Blackburn	1–2
19/3/92	Ireland	Belfast	3–2
26/3/92	Wales	Edinburgh	6–1
2/4/92	England	Glasgow	1–4
18/3/93	Wales	Wrexham	8–0
25/3/93	Ireland	Glasgow	6–1
1/4/93	England	Richmond	2–5
24/3/94	Wales	Kilmarnock	5–2
31/3/94	Ireland	Belfast	2–1
7/4/94	England	Glasgow	2–2
23/3/95	Wales	Wrexham	2–2
30/3/95	Ireland	Glasgow	3–1
6/4/95	England	Liverpool	0–3
21/3/96	Wales	Dundee	4–0
28/3/96	Ireland	Belfast	3–3
4/4/96	England	Glasgow	2–1
20/3/97	Wales	Wrexham	2–2
27/3/97	Ireland	Glasgow	5–1
3/4/97	England	London	2–1
19/3/98	Wales	Motherwell	5–2
26/3/98	Ireland	Belfast	3–0
2/4/98	England	Glasgow	1–3

18/3/99	Wales	Wrexham	6–0
25/3/99	Ireland	Glasgow	9–1
8/4/99	England	Birmingham	1–2

1900–09

Results

Date	Opponents	Venue	Score
3/2/00	Wales	Aberdeen	5–2
3/3/00	Ireland	Belfast	3–0
7/4/00	England	Glasgow	4–1
23/2/01	Ireland	Glasgow	11–0
2/3/01	Wales	Wrexham	1–1
30/3/01	England	London	2–2
1/3/02	Ireland	Belfast	5–1
15/3/02	Wales	Greenock	5–1
3/5/02	England	Birmingham	2–2
9/3/03	Wales	Cardiff	1–0
21/3/03	Ireland	Glasgow	0–2
4/4/03	England	Sheffield	2–1
12/3/04	Wales	Dundee	1–1
26/3/04	Ireland	Dublin	1–1
9/4/04	England	Glasgow	0–1
6/3/05	Wales	Wrexham	1–3
18/3/05	Ireland	Glasgow	4–0
1/4/05	England	London	0–1
3/3/06	Wales	Edinburgh	0–2
17/3/06	Ireland	Dublin	1–0
7/4/06	England	Glasgow	2–1
4/3/07	Wales	Wrexham	0–1
16/3/07	Ireland	Glasgow	3–0
6/4/07	England	Newcastle	1–1
7/3/08	Wales	Dundee	2–1
14/3/08	Ireland	Dublin	5–0
4/4/08	England	Glasgow	1–1
1/3/09	Wales	Wrexham	2–3
15/3/09	Ireland	Glasgow	5–0
3/4/09	England	London	0–2

1910–14

Results

Date	Opponents	Venue	Score
5/3/10	Wales	Kilmarnock	1–0
19/3/10	Ireland	Belfast	0–1
2/4/10	England	Glasgow	2–0
6/3/11	Wales	Cardiff	2–2
18/3/11	Ireland	Glasgow	2–0
1/4/11	England	Liverpool	1–1
2/3/12	Wales	Edinburgh	1–0
16/3/12	Ireland	Belfast	4–1
23/3/12	England	Glasgow	1–1
3/3/13	Wales	Wrexham	0–0
15/3/13	Ireland	Dublin	2–1
5/4/13	England	Stamford Bridge	0–1
28/2/14	Wales	Glasgow	0–0
14/3/14	Ireland	Belfast	1–1
4/4/14	England	Glasgow	3–1

1920–29

Results

Date	Opponents	Venue	Score
26/2/20	Wales	Cardiff	1–1
13/3/20	Ireland	Glasgow	3–0
10/4/20	England	Sheffield	4–5
12/2/21	Wales	Aberdeen	2–1
26/2/21	Ireland	Belfast	2–0
9/4/21	England	Glasgow	3–0
4/2/22	Wales	Wrexham	1–2
4/3/22	Ireland	Glasgow	2–1
8/4/22	England	Birmingham	1–0
3/3/23	Ireland	Belfast	1–0
17/3/23	Wales	Glasgow	2–0
14/4/23	England	Glasgow	2–2
16/2/24	Wales	Cardiff	0–2
1/3/24	Ireland	Glasgow	2–0
12/4/24	England	Wembley	1–1
14/2/25	Wales	Edinburgh	3–1
28/2/25	Ireland	Belfast	3–0
4/4/25	England	Glasgow	2–0
31/10/25	Wales	Cardiff	3–0
27/2/26	Ireland	Glasgow	4–0
17/4/26	England	Manchester	1–0
30/10/26	Wales	Glasgow	3–0
26/2/27	Ireland	Belfast	2–0
2/4/27	England	Glasgow	1–2
29/10/27	Wales	Wrexham	2–2

25/2/28	Ireland	Glasgow	0–1
31/3/28	England	Wembley	5–1
27/10/28	Wales	Glasgow	4–2
23/2/29	Ireland	Belfast	7–3
13/4/29	England	Glasgow	1–0
26/5/29	Norway	Bergen	7–3
1/6/29	Germany	Berlin	1–1
4/6/29	Holland	Amsterdam	2–0
26/10/29	Wales	Cardiff	4–2

1930–39

Results

Date	Opponents	Venue	Score
22/2/30	Ireland	Glasgow	3–1
5/4/30	England	Wembley	2–5
18/5/30	France	Paris	2–0
25/10/30	Wales	Glasgow	1–1
21/2/31	Ireland	Belfast	0–0
28/3/31	England	Glasgow	2–0
16/5/31	Austria	Vienna	0–5
20/5/31	Italy	Rome	0–3
24/5/31	Switzerland	Geneva	3–2
19/9/31	Ireland	Glasgow	3–1
31/10/31	Wales	Wrexham	3–2
9/4/32	England	Wembley	0–3
8/5/32	France	Paris	3–1
19/9/32	Ireland	Belfast	4–0
26/10/32	Wales	Edinburgh	2–5
1/4/33	England	Glasgow	2–1
16/9/33	Ireland	Glasgow	1–2
4/10/33	Wales	Cardiff	2–3
29/11/33	Austria	Glasgow	2–2
14/4/34	England	Wembley	0–3
20/10/34	Ireland	Belfast	1–2
21/11/34	Wales	Aberdeen	3–2
6/4/35	England	Glasgow	2–0
5/10/35	Wales	Cardiff	1–1
13/11/35	Ireland	Edinburgh	2–1
4/4/36	England	Wembley	1–1
14/10/36	Germany	Glasgow	2–0
31/10/36	Ireland	Belfast	3–1
2/12/36	Wales	Dundee	1–2
17/4/37	England	Glasgow	3–1
9/5/37	Austria	Vienna	1–1
22/5/37	Czechoslovakia	Prague	3–1
30/10/37	Wales	Cardiff	1–2
10/11/37	Ireland	Aberdeen	1–1
8/12/37	Czechoslovakia	Glasgow	5–0
9/4/38	England	Wembley	1–0
21/5/38	Holland	Amsterdam	3–1

Date	Opponents	Venue	Score
8/10/38	Ireland	Belfast	2–0
9/11/38	Wales	Edinburgh	3–2
7/12/38	Hungary	Glasgow	3–1
15/4/39	England	Glasgow	1–2

1940–49

Results

Date	Opponents	Venue	Score
19/10/46	Wales	Wrexham	1–3
27/11/46	N. Ireland	Glasgow	0–0
12/4/47	England	Wembley	1–1
18/5/47	Belgium	Brussels	1–2
24/5/47	Luxembourg	Luxembourg	6–0
4/10/47	N. Ireland	Belfast	0–2
12/11/47	Wales	Glasgow	1–2
10/4/48	England	Glasgow	0–2
28/4/48	Belgium	Glasgow	2–0
17/5/48	Switzerland	Berne	1–2
23/5/48	France	Paris	0–3
23/10/48	Wales	Cardiff	3–1
17/11/48	N. Ireland	Glasgow	3–2
9/4/49	England	Wembley	3–1
27/4/49	France	Glasgow	2–0
1/10/49	N. Ireland	Belfast (WCQ)	8–2
9/11/49	Wales	Glasgow (WCQ)	2–0

1950–59

Results

Date	Opponents	Venue	Score
15/4/50	England	Glasgow (WCQ)	0–1
26/4/50	Switzerland	Glasgow	3–1
25/5/50	Portugal	Lisbon	2–2
27/5/50	France	Paris	1–0
21/10/50	Wales	Cardiff	3–1
1/11/50	N. Ireland	Glasgow	6–1
13/12/50	Austria	Glasgow	0–1
14/4/51	England	Wembley	3–2
12/5/51	Denmark	Glasgow	3–1
16/5/51	France	Glasgow	1–0
20/5/51	Belgium	Brussels	5–0
27/5/51	Austria	Vienna	0–4
6/10/51	N. Ireland	Belfast	3–0
28/11/51	Wales	Glasgow	0–1
5/4/52	England	Glasgow	1–2
30/4/52	USA	Glasgow	6–0
25/5/52	Denmark	Copenhagen	2–1
30/5/52	Sweden	Stockholm	1–3
15/10/52	Wales	Cardiff	2–1
5/11/52	N. Ireland	Glasgow	1–1
18/4/53	England	Wembley	2–2
6/5/53	Sweden	Glasgow	1–2
3/10/53	N. Ireland	Belfast (WCQ)	3–1
4/11/53	Wales	Glasgow (WCQ)	3–3
3/4/54	England	Glasgow (WCQ)	2–4
5/5/54	Norway	Glasgow	1–0
19/5/54	Norway	Oslo	1–1
25/5/54	Finland	Helsinki	2–1
16/6/54	Austria	Zurich (WCF)	0–1
19/6/54	Uruguay	Basle (WCF)	0–7
16/10/54	Wales	Cardiff	1–0
3/11/54	N. Ireland	Glasgow	2–2
8/12/54	Hungary	Glasgow	2–4
2/4/55	England	Wembley	2–7
16/5/55	Portugal	Glasgow	3–0
15/5/55	Yugoslavia	Belgrade	2–2
19/5/55	Austria	Vienna	4–1
29/5/55	Hungary	Budapest	1–3
8/10/55	N. Ireland	Belfast	1–2
9/11/55	Wales	Glasgow	2–0
14/4/56	England	Glasgow	1–1
2/5/56	Austria	Glasgow	1–1
20/10/56	Wales	Cardiff	2–2
7/11/56	N. Ireland	Glasgow	1–0
21/11/56	Yugoslavia	Glasgow	2–0
6/4/57	England	Wembley	1–2
8/5/57	Spain	Glasgow (WCQ)	4–2
19/5/57	Switzerland	Basle (WCQ)	2–1
22/5/57	W Germany	Stuttgart	3–1
26/5/57	Spain	Madrid (WCQ)	1–4
5/10/57	N. Ireland	Belfast	1–1
6/11/57	Switzerland	Glasgow (WCQ)	3–2
13/11/57	Wales	Glasgow	1–1
19/4/58	England	Glasgow	0–4
7/5/58	Hungary	Glasgow	1–1
1/6/58	Poland	Warsaw	2–1
8/6/58	Yugoslavia	Vasteras (WCF)	1–1
11/6/58	Paraguay	Norrköping (WCF)	2–3
15/6/58	France	Örebro (WCF)	1–2
18/10/58	Wales	Cardiff	3–0
5/11/58	N. Ireland	Glasgow	2–2
11/4/59	England	Wembley	0–1
6/5/59	W. Germany	Glasgow	3–2
27/5/59	Holland	Amsterdam	2–1
3/6/59	Portugal	Lisbon	0–1
3/10/59	N. Ireland	Belfast	4–0
14/11/59	Wales	Glasgow	1–1

1960

Results

Date	Opponents	Venue	Score
9/4	England	Glasgow	1–1
4/5	Poland	Glasgow	2–3
29/5	Austria	Vienna	1–4
5/6	Hungary	Budapest	3–3
8/6	Turkey	Ankara	2–4
22/10	Wales	Cardiff	0–2
9/11	N. Ireland	Glasgow	5–2

1961

Results

Date	Opponents	Venue	Score
15/4	England	Wembley	3–9
3/5	Rep. of Ireland	Glasgow (WCQ)	4–1
7/5	Rep. of Ireland	Dublin (WCQ)	3–0
14/5	Czechoslovakia	Bratislava (WCQ)	0–4
26/9	Czechoslovakia	Glasgow (WCQ)	3–2
7/10	N. Ireland	Belfast	6–1
8/11	Wales	Glasgow	2–0
29/11	Czechoslovakia	Brussels (WCQ)	2–4

1962

Results

Date	Opponents	Venue	Score
14/4	England	Glasgow	2–0
2/5	Uruguay	Glasgow	2–3
20/10	Wales	Cardiff	3–2
7/11	N. Ireland	Glasgow	5–1

1963

Results

Date	Opponents	Venue	F–A
6/4	England	Wembley	2–1
8/5	Austria	Glasgow	4–1
4/6	Norway	Bergen	3–4
9/6	Rep. of Ireland	Dublin	0–1
13/6	Spain	Madrid	6–2
12/10	N. Ireland	Belfast	1–2
7/11	Norway	Glasgow	6–1
20/11	Wales	Glasgow	2–1

1964

Results

Date	Opponents	Venue	Score
11/4	England	Glasgow	1–0
12/5	W. Germany	Hanover	2–2
3/10	Wales	Cardiff	2–3
21/10	Finland	Glasgow (WCQ)	3–1
25/11	N. Ireland	Glasgow	3–2

1965

Results

Date	Opponents	Venue	Score
10/4	England	Wembley	2–2
8/5	Spain	Glasgow	0–0
23/5	Poland	Chorzow (WCQ)	1–1
27/5	Finland	Helsinki (WCQ)	2–1
2/10	N. Ireland	Belfast	2–3
13/10	Poland	Glasgow (WCQ)	1–2
9/11	Italy	Glasgow (WCQ)	1–0
24/11	Wales	Glasgow	4–1
7/12	Italy	Naples (WCQ)	0–3

1966

Results

Date	Opponents	Venue	Score
2/4	England	Glasgow	3–4
11/5	Holland	Glasgow	0–3
18/6	Portugal	Glasgow	0–1
25/6	Brazil	Glasgow	1–1
22/10	Wales	Cardiff (ECQ)	1–1
16/11	N. Ireland	Glasgow (ECQ)	2–1

1967

Results

Date	Opponents	Venue	Score
15/4	England	Wembley (ECQ)	3–2
10/5	USSR	Glasgow	0–2
21/10	N. Ireland	Belfast (ECQ)	0–1
22/11	Wales	Glasgow (ECQ)	3–2

1968

Results

Date	Opponents	Venue	Score
24/2	England	Glasgow (ECQ)	1–1
30/5	Holland	Amsterdam	0–0
16/10	Denmark	Copenhagen	1–0
6/11	Austria	Glasgow (WCQ)	2–1
11/12	Cyprus	Nicosia (WCQ)	5–0

1969

Results

Date	Opponents	Venue	Score
16/4	W. Germany	Glasgow (WCQ)	1–1
3/5	Wales	Wrexham	5–3
6/5	N. Ireland	Glasgow (ECQ)	1–1
10/5	England	Wembley	1–4
12/5	Cyprus	Glasgow (WCQ)	8–0

21/9	Rep. of Ireland	Dublin	1–1
22/10	W. Germany	Hamburg (WCQ)	2–3
5/11	Austria	Vienna (WCQ)	0–2

1970

Results

Date	Opponents	Venue	Score
18/4	N. Ireland	Belfast	1–0
22/4	Wales	Glasgow	0–0
25/4	England	Glasgow	0–0
11/11	Denmark	Glasgow (ECQ)	1–0

1971

Results

Date	Opponents	Venue	Score
3/2	Belgium	Liège (ECQ)	0–3
21/4	Portugal	Lisbon (ECQ)	0–2
15/5	Wales	Cardiff	0–0
18/5	N. Ireland	Glasgow	0–1
22/5	England	Wembley	1–3
9/6	Denmark	Copenhagen (ECQ)	0–1
14/6	USSR	Moscow	0–1
13/10	Portugal	Glasgow (ECQ)	2–1
10/11	Belgium	Aberdeen (ECQ)	1–0
1/12	Holland	Rotterdam	1–2

1972

Results

Date	Opponents	Venue	Score
26/4	Peru	Glasgow	2–0
20/5	N. Ireland	Glasgow	2–0
24/5	Wales	Glasgow	1–0
27/5	England	Glasgow	0–1
29/6	Yugoslavia	Belo Horizonte	2–2
2/7	Czechoslovakia	Porto Alegre	0–0
5/7	Brazil	Rio de Janeiro	0–1
18/10	Denmark	Copenhagen (WCQ)	4–1
15/11	Denmark	Glasgow (WCQ)	2–0

1973

Results

Date	Opponents	Venue	Score
14/2	England	Glasgow	0–5
12/5	Wales	Wrexham	2–0
16/5	N. Ireland	Glasgow	1–2
19/5	England	Wembley	0–1
22/6	Switzerland	Berne	0–1
30/6	Brazil	Glasgow	0–1
26/9	Czechoslovakia	Glasgow (WCQ)	2–1
17/10	Czechoslovakia	Bratislava (WCQ)	0–1
14/11	W Germany	Glasgow	1–1

1974

Results

Date	Opponents	Venue	Score
27/3	W. Germany	Frankfurt	1–2
11/5	N. Ireland	Glasgow	0–1
14/5	Wales	Glasgow	2–0
18/5	England	Glasgow	2–0
2/6	Belgium	Brussels	1–2
6/6	Norway	Oslo	2–1
14/6	Zaire	Dortmund (WCF)	2–0
18/6	Brazil	Frankfurt (WCF)	0–0
22/6	Yugoslavia	Frankfurt (WCF)	1–1
30/10	E. Germany	Glasgow	3–0
20/11	Spain	Glasgow (ECQ)	1–2

1975

Results

Date	Opponents	Venue	Score
5/2	Spain	Valencia (ECQ)	1–1
16/4	Sweden	Gothenburg	1–1
13/5	Portugal	Glasgow	1–0
17/5	Wales	Cardiff	2–2
20/5	N. Ireland	Glasgow	3–0
24/5	England	Wembley	1–5
1/6	Romania	Bucharest (ECQ)	1–1
3/9	Denmark	Copenhagen (ECQ)	1–0
29/10	Denmark	Glasgow (ECQ)	3–1
17/12	Romania	Glasgow (ECQ)	1–1

1976

Results

Date	Opponents	Venue	Score
7/4	Switzerland	Glasgow	1–0
6/5	Wales	Glasgow	3–1
8/5	N. Ireland	Glasgow	3–0
15/5	England	Glasgow	2–1
8/9	Finalsnd	Glasgow	6–0
13/10	Czechoslovakia	Prague (WCQ)	0–2
17/11	Wales	Glasgow (WCQ)	1–0

1977

Results

Date	Opponents	Venue	Score
27/4	Sweden	Glasgow	3–1
28/5	Wales	Wrexham	0–0
1/6	N. Ireland	Glasgow	3–0
4/6	England	Wembley	2–0
15/6	Chile	Santiago	4–2
18/6	Argentina	Buenos Aires	1–1
23/6	Brazil	Rio de Janeiro	0–2
7/9	E. Germany	E Berlin	0–1
21/9	Czechoslovakia	Glasgow (WCQ)	3–1
12/10	Wales	Liverpool (WCQ)	2–0

1978

Results

Date	Opponents	Venue	Score
22/2	Bulgaria	Glasgow	2–1
13/5	N. Ireland	Glasgow	1–1
17/5	Wales	Glasgow	1–1
20/5	England	Glasgow	0–1
3/6	Peru	Cordoba (WCF)	1–3
7/6	Iran	Cordoba (WCF)	1–1
11/6	Holland	Mendoza (WCF)	3–2
20/9	Austria	Vienna (ECQ)	2–3
25/10	Norway	Glasgow (ECQ)	3–2
29/11	Portugal	Lisbon (ECQ)	0–1

1979

Results

Date	Opponents	Venue	Score
19/5	Wales	Cardiff	0–3
22/5	N. Ireland	Glasgow	1–0
26/5	England	Wembley	1–3
2/6	Argentina	Glasgow	1–3
7/6	Norway	Oslo (ECQ)	4–0
12/9	Peru	Glasgow	1–1
17/10	Austria	Glasgow (ECQ)	1–1
21/11	Belgium	Brussels (ECQ)	0–2
19/12	Belgium	Glasgow (ECQ)	1–3

1980

Results

Date	Opponents	Venue	Score
26/3	Portugal	Glasgow (ECQ)	4–1
16/5	N. Ireland	Belfast	0–1
21/5	Wales	Glasgow	1–0
24/5	England	Glasgow	0–2
28/5	Poland	Poznan	0–1
31/5	Hungary	Budapest	1–3
10/9	Sweden	Stockholm (WCQ)	1–0
15/10	Portugal	Glasgow (WCQ)	0–0

1981

Results

Date	Opponents	Venue	Score
25/2	Israel	Tel Aviv (WCQ)	1–0
25/3	N. Ireland	Glasgow (WCQ)	1–1
28/4	Israel	Glasgow (WCQ)	3–1
16/5	Wales	Swansea	0–2
19/5	N. Ireland	Glasgow	2–0
23/5	England	Wembley	1–0
9/9	Sweden	Glasgow (WCQ)	2–0
14/10	N. Ireland	Belfast (WCQ)	0–0
18/11	Portugal	Lisbon (WCQ)	1–2

1982

Results

Date	Opponents	Venue	Score
24/2	Spain	Valencia	0–3
23/3	Holland	Glasgow	2–1
28/4	N. Ireland	Belfast	1–1
24/5	Wales	Glasgow	1–0
29/5	England	Glasgow	0–1
15/6	New Zealand	Malaga WCF)	5–2
18/6	Brazil	Seville (WCF)	1–4
22/6	USSR	Malaga (WCF)	2–2
13/10	E. Germany	Glasgow ECQ)	2–0
17/11	Switzerland	Berne (ECQ)	0–2
15/12	Belgium	Brussels (ECQ)	2–3

1983

Results

Date	Opponents	Venue	Score
30/3	Switzerland	Glasgow (ECQ)	2–2
24/5	N. Ireland	Glasgow	0–0
28/5	Wales	Cardiff	2–0
1/6	England	Wembley	0–2
12/6	Canada	Vancouver	2–0
16/6	Canada	Edmonton	3–0
20/6	Canada	Toronto	2–0
21/9	Uruguay	Glasgow	2–0
12/10	Belgium	Glasgow (ECQ)	1–1
16/11	E. Germany	Halle (ECQ)	1–2
13/12	N. Ireland	Belfast	0–2

1984

Results

Date	Opponents	Venue	Score
28/2	Wales	Glasgow	2–1
26/5	England	Glasgow	1–1
1/6	France	Marseille	0–2
12/9	Yugoslavia	Glasgow	6–1
17/10	Iceland	Glasgow (WCQ)	3–0
14/11	Spain	Glasgow (WCQ)	3–1

1985

Results

Date	Opponents	Venue	Score
27/2	Spain	Seville (WCQ)	0–1
27/3	Wales	Glasgow (WCQ)	0–1
25/5	England	Glasgow	1–0
28/5	Iceland	Reykjavik (WCQ)	1–0
10/9	Wales	Cardiff (WCQ)	1–1
16/10	E. Germany	Glasgow	0–0
20/11	Australia	Glasgow (WCQ)	2–0
4/12	Australia	Melbourne (WCQ)	0–0

1986

Results

Date	Opponents	Venue	Score
28/1	Israel	Tel Aviv	1–0
26/3	Romania	Glasgow	3–0
23/4	England	Wembley	1–2
29/4	Holland	Eindhoven	0–0
4/6	Denmark	Nezahualcoyot (WCF)	0–1
8/6	W. Germany	Queretaro (WCF)	1–2
13/6	Uruguay	Nezahualcoyot (WCF)	0–0
10/9	Bulgaria	Glasgow (ECQ)	0–0
15/10	Rep. of Ireland	Dublin (ECQ)	0–0
12/11	Luxembourg	Glasgow (ECQ)	3–0

1987

Results

Date	Opponents	Venue	Score
18/2	Rep. of Ireland	Glasgow (ECQ)	0–1
1/4	Belgium	Brussels (ECQ)	1–4
6/5	Brazil	Glasgow	0–2
23/5	England	Glasgow	0–0
9/9	Hungary	Glasgow	2–0
14/10	Belgium	Glasgow (ECQ)	2–0
11/11	Bulgaria	Sofia (ECQ)	1–0
2/12	Luxembourg	Esch (ECQ)	0–0

1988

Results

Date	Opponents	Venue	Score
17/2	Saudi Arabia	Riyadh	2–2
22/3	Malta	Valletta	1–1
27/4	Spain	Madrid	0–0
17/5	Colombia	Glasgow	0–0
21/5	England	Wembley	0–1
14/9	Norway	Oslo (WCQ)	2–1
19/10	Yugoslavia	Glasgow (WCQ)	1–1
22/12	Italy	Perugia	0–2

1989

Results

Date	Opponents	Venue	Score
8/2	Cyprus	Limassol (WCQ)	3–2
8/3	France	Glasgow (WCQ)	2–0
26/4	Cyprus	Glasgow (WCQ)	2–1
27/5	England	Glagow	0–2
30/5	Chile	Glasgow	2–0
6/9	Yugoslavia	Zagreb (WCQ)	1–3
11/10	France	Paris (WCQ)	0–3
15/11	Norway	Glasgow (WCQ)	1–1

1990

Results

Date	Opponents	Venue	Score
28/3	Argentina	Glasgow	1–0
25/4	E. Germany	Glasgow	0–1
19/5	Poland	Glasgow	1–1
28/5	Malta	Valletta	2–1
11/6	Costa Rica	Genoa (WCF)	0–1
16/6	Sweden	Genoa (WCF)	2–1
20/6	Brazil	Turin (WCF)	0–1
12/9	Romania	Glasgow (ECQ)	2–1
17/10	Switzerland	Glasgow (ECQ)	2–1
14/11	Bulgaria	Sofia (ECQ)	1–1

1991

Results

Date	Opponents	Venue	Score
6/2	USSR	Glasgow	0–1
27/3	Bulgaria	Glasgow (ECQ)	1–1
1/5	San Marino	Serravalle (ECQ)	2–0
11/9	Switzerland	Berne (ECQ)	2–2
16/10	Romania	Bucharest (ECQ)	0–1
13/11	San Marino	Glasgow (ECQ)	4–0

1992

Results

Date	Opponents	Venue	Score
25/3	Finland	Glasgow	1–1
17/5	USA	Denver	1–0
21/5	Canada	Toronto	3–1
3/6	Norway	Oslo	0–0
12/6	Holland	Gothenburg (ECF)	0–1
15/6	Germany	Gothenburg (ECF)	0–2
18/6	CIS	Norrkoping (ECF)	3–0
9/9	Switzerland	Berne (WCQ)	1–3
14/10	Portugal	Glasgow (WCQ)	0–0
18/11	Italy	Glasgow (WCQ)	0–0

1993

Results

Date	Opponents	Venue	Score
17/2	Malta	Glasgow (WCQ)	3–0
24/3	Germany	Glasgow	0–1
28/4	Portugal	Lisbon (WCQ)	0–5
19/5	Estonia	Tallinn (WCQ)	3–0
2/6	Estonia	Aberdeen (WCQ)	3–1
8/9	Switzerland	Glasgow (WCQ)	1–1
13/10	Italy	Rome (WCQ)	1–3
17/11	Malta	Sliema (WCQ)	2–0

1994

Results

Date	Opponents	Venue	Score
23/3	Holland	Glasgow	0–1
20/4	Austria	Vienna	–1
27/5	Holland	Utrecht	1–3
7/9	Finland	Helsinki (ECQ)	2–0
12/10	Faroe Islands	Glasgow (ECQ)	5–1
16/11	Russia	Glasgow (ECQ)	1–1
19/12	Greece	Athens (ECQ)	0–1

1995

Results

Date	Opponents	Venue	Score
29/3	Russia	Moscow (ECQ)	0–0
26/4	San Marino	Serravalle (ECQ)	2–0
21/5	Japan	Hiroshima	0–0
24/5	Ecuador	Toyama, Japan	2–1
7/6	Faroe Islands	Toftir (ECQ)	2–0
16/8	Greece	Glasgow (ECQ)	1–0
6/9	Finland	Glasgow (ECQ)	1–0
11/10	Sweden	Stockholm	0–2
15/11	San Marino	Glasgow (ECQ)	5–0

1996

Results

Date	Opponents	Venue	Score
27/3	Australia	Glasgow	1–0
24/4	Denmark	Copenhagen	0–2
26/5	USA	New Britain, Conn	1–2
29/5	Colombia	Miami	0–1
10/6	Holland	Birmingham (ECF)	0–0
15/6	England	Wembley (ECF)	0–2
18/6	Switzerland	Birmingham (ECF)	1–0

The Statistics

1997

Results

Date	Opponents	Venue	Score
11/2	Estonia	Monaco (WCQ)	0–0
29/3	Estonia	Kilmarnock (WCQ)	2–0
2/4	Austria	Glasgow (WCQ)	2–0
30/4	Sweden	Gothenburg (WCQ)	1–2
27/5	Wales	Kilmarnock	0–1
1/6	Malta	Valletta	3–2
8/6	Belarus	Minsk (WCQ)	1–0
7/9	Belarus	Aberdeen (WCQ)	4–1
11/10	Latvia	Glasgow (WCQ)	2–0
12/11	France	Saint-Etienne	1–2

1998

Results

Date	Opponents	Venue	Score
25/3	Denmark	Glasgow	0–1
22/4	Finland	Edinburgh	1–1
23/5	Columbia	New Jersey	2–2
30/5	USA	Washington	0–0
10/6	Brazil	Paris (WCF)	1–2
16/6	Norway	Bordeaux (WCF)	1–1
23/6	Morocco	St Etienne (WCF)	0–3

WALES
League of Wales

Winners

1993	Cwmbran Town
1994	Bangor City
1995	Bangor City
1996	Barry Town
1997	Barry Town
1998	Barry Town

League of Wales Cup

Finalists

Year	Winners	Runners-up	Score
1993	Caersws	Afan Lido	Penalties
1994	Afan Lido	Bangor City	1–0
1995	Llansantffraid	Ton Pentre	2–1
1996	Connah's Quay	Ebbw Vale	1–0
1997	Barry Town	Bangor City	2–2
(Barry Town won 4–2 on penalties)			

Welsh Cup Finals

Finalists

Year	Winners	Runners-up	Score
1878	Wrexham	Druids	1–0
1879	Newtown	Wrexham	1–0
1880	Druids	Ruthin	2–1
1881	Druids	Newtown White Stars	2–0
1882	Druids	Northwich	2–1
1883	Wrexham	Druids	1–0
1884	Oswestry	Druids	3–2
1885	Druids	Oswestry	2–0
1886	Druids	Newtown	5–0
1887	Chirk	Davenham	4–2
1888	Chirk	Newtown	5–0
1889	Bangor City	Northwich	2–1
1890	Chirk	Wrexham	1–0
1891	Shrewsbury T.	Wrexham	5–2
1892	Chirk	Westminster R.	2–1
1893	Wrexham	Chirk	2–1
1894	Chirk	Westminster R.	2–0
1895	Newtown	Wrexham	3–2

1896	Bangor Town	Wrexham	3–1
1897	Wrexham	Newtown	2–0
1898	Druids	Wrexham	1–1, 2–1
1899	Druids	Wrexham	2–2, 1–0
1900	Aberystwyth	Druids	3–0
1901	Oswestry	Druids	1–0
1902	Wellington	Wrexham	1–0
1903	Wrexham	Aberaman	8–0
1904	Druids	Aberdare	3–2
1905	Wrexham	Aberdare	3–0
1906	Wellington	Whitchurch	3–2
1907	Oswestry	Whitchurch	2–0
1908	Chester	Connah's Quay	3–1
1909	Wrexham	Chester	1–0
1910	Wrexham	Chester	2–1
1911	Wrexham	Connah's Quay	6–1
1912	Cardiff City	Pontypridd	0–0, 3–0
1913	Swansea	Pontypridd	0–0, 1–0
1914	Wrexham	Llanelly	1–1, 3–0
1915	Wrexham	Swansea	0–0, 1–0
1920	Cardiff City	Wrexham	2–1
1921	Wrexham	Pontypridd	1–1, 3–1
1922	Cardiff City	Ton Pentre	2–0
1923	Cardiff City	Aberdare	3–2
1924	Wrexham	Merthyr	2–2, 1–0
1925	Wrexham	Flint	3–1
1926	Ebbw Vale	Swansea	3–2
1927	Cardiff C	Rhyl	0–0, 4–2
1928	Cardiff C	Bangor	2–0
1929	Connah's Quay	Cardiff City	3–0
1930	Cardiff City	Rhyl	0–0, 4–2
1931	Wrexham	Shrewsbury Town	7–0
1932	Swansea	Wrexham	1–1, 2–0
1933	Chester	Wrexham	2–0
1934	Bristol City	Tranmere R.	1–1, 3–0
1935	Tranmere R.	Chester	1–0
1936	Crewe	Chester	2–0
1937	Crewe	Rhyl	1–1, 3–1
1938	Shrewsbury	Swansea	2–1
1939	S. Liverpool	Cardiff City	2–1
1940	Welling Town	Swansea	4–0
1947	Chester	Merthyr Tydfil	0–0, 5–1
1948	Lovells Ath.	Shrewsbury Town	3–0
1949	Merthyr Tydfil	Swansea T	2–0
1950	Swansea Town	Wrexham	4–1
1951	Merthyr Tydfil	Cardiff C	1–1, 3–2
1952	Rhyl	Merthyr Tydfil	4–3
1953	Rhyl	Chester	2–1
1954	Flint T Utd	Chester	2–0
1955	Barry T	Chester	1–1, 4–3
1956	Cardiff City	Swansea Town	3–2
1957	Wrexham	Swansea Town	2–1
1958	Wrexham	Chester	1–1, 2–0
1959	Cardiff City	Lovells Ath.	2–0
1960	Wrexham	Cardiff City	0–0, 1–0
1961	Swansea Town	Bangor City	3–1

1962	Bangor City	Wrexham	3–1
1963	Borough Utd	Newport County	2–1 *
1964	Cardiff City	Bangor City	5–3 *
1965	Cardiff City	Wrexham	8–2 *
1966	Swansea Town	Chester	2–1
1967	Cardiff City	Wrexham	2–1 *
1968	Cardiff City	Hereford Utd	6–1 *
1969	Cardiff City	Swansea T	5–1 *
1970	Cardiff City	Chester	5–0
1971	Cardiff City	Wrexham	4–1 *
1972	Wrexham	Cardiff City	3–2 *
1973	Cardiff City	Bangor City	5–1 *
1974	Cardiff City	Stourbridge	2–0 *
1975	Wrexham	Cardiff City	5–2 *
1976	Cardiff City	Hereford Utd	6–5 *
1977	Shrewsbury T.	Cardiff City	4–2 *
1978	Wrexham	Bangor City	3–1 *
1979	Shrewsbury T.	Wrexham	2–1 *
1980	Newport C.	Shrewsbury .T	5–1 *
1981	Swansea City	Hereford Utd	2–1 *
1982	Swansea City	Cardiff City	2–1 *
1983	Swansea City	Wrexham	4–1 *
1984	Shrewsbury T.	Wrexham	2–0 *
1985	Shrewsbury T.	Bangor City	5–1 *
1986	Kidderminster H.	Wrexham	1–1, 2–1
1987	Merthyr Tydfil	Newport Co.	2–2, 1–0
1988	Cardiff City	Wrexham	1–0
1989	Swansea City	Kidderminster H.	5–0
1990	Hereford United	Wrexham	2–1
1991	Swansea City	Wrexham	2–0
1992	Cardiff City	Hednesford Town	1–0
1993	Cardiff City	Rhyl	5–0
1994	Barry Town	Cardiff City	2–1
1995	Wrexham	Cardiff City	2–1
1996	Llansantffraid	Barry Town	3–3
	(Llansantffraid won 3–2 on penalties)		
1997	Barry Town	Cwmbran Town	2–1
1997	Bangor City	Connah's Quay	1–1
	(Bangor City won 4–2 on penalties)		

* Aggregate score

Welsh Internationals 1876–99

Results

Date	Opponents	Venue	Score
25/3/76	Scotland	Glasgow	0–4
5/3/77	Scotland	Wrexham	0–2
23/3/78	Scotland	Glasgow	0–9
18/1/79	England	The Oval, London	1–2

7/4/79	Scotland	Wrexham	0–3
15/3/80	England	Wrexham	2–3
27/3/80	Scotland	Glasgow	1–5
26/2/81	England	Blackburn	1–0
14/3/81	Scotland	Wrexham	1–5
25/2/82	Ireland	Wrexham	7–1
15/3/82	England	Wrexham	5–3
25/3/82	Scotland	Glasgow	0–5
3/2/83	England	The Oval, London	0–5
12/3/83	Scotland	Wrexham	0–3
17/3/83	Ireland	Belfast	1–1
9/2/84	Ireland	Wrexham	6–0
17/3/84	England	Wrexham	0–4
29/3/84	Scotland	Glasgow	1–4
14/3/85	England	Blackburn	1–1
23/3/85	Scotland	Wrexham	1–8
11/4/85	Ireland	Belfast	8–2
27/2/86	Ireland	Wrexham	5–0
29/3/86	England	Wrexham	1–3
10/4/86	Scotland	Glasgow	1–4
26/2/87	England	The Oval, London	0–4
12/3/87	Ireland	Belfast	1–4
21/3/87	Scotland	Wrexham	0–2
4/2/88	England	Crewe	1–5
3/3/88	Ireland	Wrexham	11–0
10/3/88	Scotland	Edinburgh	1–5
23/2/89	England	Stoke	1–4
15/4/89	Scotland	Wrexham	0–0
27/4/89	Ireland	Belfast	3–1
8/2/90	Ireland	Shrewsbury	5–2
15/3/90	England	Wrexham	1–3
22/3/90	Scotland	Glasgow	0–5
7/2/91	Ireland	Belfast	2–7
7/3/91	England	Sunderland	1–4
21/3/91	Scotland	Wrexham	3–4
27/2/92	Ireland	Bangor	1–1
5/3/92	England	Wrexham	0–2
26/3/92	Scotland	Edinburgh	1–6
13/3/93	England	Stoke-on-Trent	0–6
18/3/93	Scotland	Wrexham	0–8
5/4/93	Ireland	Belfast	3–4
24/2/94	Ireland	Swansea	4–1
12/3/94	England	Wrexham	1–5
24/3/94	Scotland	Kilmarnock	2–5
16/3/95	Ireland	Belfast	2–2
18/3/95	England	Queen's Club, London	1–1
23/3/95	Scotland	Wrexham	2–2
29/2/96	Ireland	Wrexham	6–1
16/3/96	England	Cardiff	1–9
21/3/96	Scotland	Dundee	0–4
6/3/97	Ireland	Belfast	3–4
20/3/97	Scotland	Wrexham	2–2
29/3/97	England	Sheffield	0–4
19/2/98	Ireland	Llandudno	0–1
19/3/98	Scotland	Motherwell	2–5
28/3/98	England	Wrexham	0–3
4/3/99	Ireland	Belfast	0–1
18/3/99	Scotland	Wrexham	0–6
20/3/99	England	Bristol	0–4

1900–19

Results

Date	Opponents	Venue	Score
3/2/00	Scotland	Aberdeen	2–5
24/2/00	Ireland	Llandudno	2–0
26/3/00	England	Cardiff	1–1
2/3/01	Scotland	Wrexham	1–1
18/3/01	England	Newcastle	0–6
23/3/01	Ireland	Belfast	1–0
22/2/02	Ireland	Cardiff	0–3
3/3/02	England	Wrexham	0–0
15/3/02	Scotland	Greenock	1–5
2/3/03	England	Portsmouth	1–2
9/3/03	Scotland	Cardiff	0–1
28/3/03	Ireland	Belfast	0–2
29/2/04	England	Wrexham	2–2
12/3/04	Scotland	Dundee	1–1
21/3/04	Ireland	Bangor	0–1
6/3/05	Scotland	Wrexham	3–1
27/3/05	England	Liverpool	1–5
8/4/05	Ireland	Belfast	2–2
3/3/06	Scotland	Edinburgh	2–0
19/3/06	England	Cardiff	0–1
2/4/06	Ireland	Wrexham	4–4
23/2/07	Ireland	Belfast	3–2
4/3/07	Scotland	Wrexham	1–0
18/3/07	England	Fulham	1–1
7/3/08	Scotland	Dundee	1–2
16/3/08	England	Wrexham	1–7
11/4/08	Ireland	Aberdare	0–1
1/3/09	Scotland	Wrexham	3–2
15/3/09	England	Nottingham	0–2
20/3/09	Ireland	Belfast	3–2
5/3/10	Scotland	Kilmarnock	0–1
14/3/10	England	Cardiff	0–1
11/4/10	Ireland	Wrexham	4–1
28/1/11	Ireland	Belfast	2–1
6/3/11	Scotland	Cardiff	2–2
13/3/11	England	Millwall	0–3
2/3/12	Scotland	Edinburgh	0–1
11/3/12	England	Wrexham	0–2
13/4/12	Ireland	Cardiff	2–3
18/1/13	Ireland	Belfast	1–0
3/3/13	Scotland	Wrexham	0–0
17/3/13	England	Bristol	3–4
19/1/14	Ireland	Wrexham	1–2
28/2/14	Scotland	Glasgow	0–0
16/3/14	England	Cardiff	0–2

1920–29

Results

Date	Opponents	Venue	Score
14/2/20	Ireland	Belfast	2–2
26/2/20	Scotland	Cardiff	1–1
15/3/20	England	Highbury	2–1
12/2/21	Scotland	Aberdeen	1–2
16/3/21	England	Cardiff	0–0
9/4/21	Ireland	Swansea	2–1
4/2/22	Scotland	Wrexham	2–1
13/3/22	England	Liverpool	0–1
1/4/22	Ireland	Belfast	1–1
5/3/23	England	Cardiff	2–2
17/3/23	Scotland	Glasgow	0–2
14/4/23	Ireland	Wrexham	0–3
16/2/24	Scotland	Cardiff	2–0
3/3/24	England	Blackburn	2–1
15/3/24	Ireland	Belfast	1–0
14/2/25	Scotland	Edinburgh	1–3
28/2/25	England	Swansea	1–2
18/4/25	Ireland	Wrexham	0–0
31/10/25	Scotland	Cardiff	0–3
13/2/26	Ireland	Belfast	0–3
1/3/26	England	Crystal Palace	3–1
30/10/26	Scotland	Glasgow	0–3
14/2/27	England	Wrexham	3–3
9/4/27	Ireland	Cardiff	2–2
29/10/27	Scotland	Wrexham	2–2
28/11/27	England	Burnley	2–1
4/2/28	Ireland	Belfast	2–1
27/10/28	Scotland	Glasgow	2–4
17/11/28	England	Swansea	2–3
2/2/29	Ireland	Wrexham	2–2
26/10/29	Scotland	Cardiff	2–4
20/11/29	England	Stamford Bridge	0–6

1930–39

Results

Date	Opponents	Venue	Score
1/2/30	Ireland	Belfast	0–7
25/10/30	Scotland	Glasgow	1–1
22/11/30	England	Wrexham	0–4
22/4/31	Ireland	Wrexham	3–2
31/10/31	Scotland	Wrexham	2–3
18/11/31	England	Liverpool	1–3
5/12/31	Ireland	Belfast	0–4
26/10/32	Scotland	Edinburgh	5–2
16/11/32	England	Wrexham	0–0
7/12/32	Ireland	Wrexham	4–1
25/5/33	France	Paris	1–1
4/10/33	Scotland	Cardiff	3–2
4/11/33	Ireland	Belfast	1–1
15/11/33	England	Newcastle	2–1
29/9/34	England	Cardiff	0–4
21/11/34	Scotland	Aberdeen	2–3
27/3/35	Ireland	Wrexham	3–1
5/10/35	Scotland	Cardiff	1–1
5/2/36	England	Wolverhampton	2–1
11/3/36	Ireland	Belfast	2–3
17/10/36	England	Cardiff	2–1
2/12/36	Scotland	Dundee	2–1
17/3/37	Ireland	Wrexham	4–1
30/10/37	Scotland	Cardiff	2–1
17/11/37	England	Middlesbrough	1–2
16/3/38	Ireland	Belfast	0–1
22/10/38	England	Cardiff	4–2
9/11/38	Scotland	Edinburgh	2–3
15/3/39	Ireland	Wrexham	3–1
20/5/39	France	Paris	1–2

1940–49

Results

Date	Opponents	Venue	Score
19/10/46	Scotland	Wrexham	3–1
13/11/46	England	Manchester	0–3
16/4/47	N. Ireland	Belfast	1–2
18/10/47	England	Cardiff	0–3
12/11/47	Scotland	Glasgow	2–1
10/3/48	N. Ireland	Wrexham	2–0
23/10/48	Scotland	Cardiff	1–3
10/11/48	England	Villa Park	0–1
9/3/49	N. Ireland	Belfast	2–0
15/5/49	Portugal	Lisbon	2–3
23/5/49	Belgium	Liège	1–3
26/5/49	Switzerland	Berne	0–4
15/10/49	England	Cardiff (WCQ)	1–4
9/11/49	Scotland	Glasgow (WCQ)	0–2
23/11/49	Belgium	Cardiff	5–1

1950–59

Results

Date	Opponents	Venue	Score
8/3/50	N. Ireland	Wrexham (WCQ)	0–0
21/10/50	Scotland	Cardiff	1–3
15/11/50	England	Sunderland	2–4
7/3/51	N. Ireland	Belfast	2–1
12/5/51	Portugal	Cardiff	2–1
16/5/51	Switzerland	Wrexham	3–2
20/10/51	England	Cardiff	1–1
20/11/51	Scotland	Glasgow	1–0
5/12/51	Rest of UK	Cardiff	3–2
19/3/52	N. Ireland	Swansea	3–0
18/10/52	Scotland	Cardiff	1–2
12/11/52	England	Wembley	2–5
15/4/53	N. Ireland	Belfast	3–2
14/5/53	France	Paris	1–6
21/5/53	Yugoslavia	Belgrade	2–5
10/10/53	England	Cardiff (WCQ)	1–4
4/11/53	Scotland	Glasgow (WCQ)	3–3
31/3/54	N. Ireland	Wrexham (WCQ)	1–2
9/5/54	Austria	Vienna (ECQ)	0–2
22/9/54	Yugoslavia	Cardiff	1–3
16/10/54	Scotland	Cardiff	0–1
10/11/54	England	Wembley	2–3
20/4/55	N. Ireland	Belfast	3–2
22/10/55	England	Cardiff	2–1
9/11/55	Scotland	Glasgow	0–2
23/11/55	Austria	Wrexham (ECQ)	1–2
11/4/56	N. Ireland	Cardiff	1–1
20/10/56	Scotland	Cardiff	2–2
14/11/56	England	Wembley	1–3
10/4/57	N. Ireland	Belfast	0–0
1/5/57	Czechoslovakia	Cardiff (WCQ)	1–0
19/5/57	E. Germany	Leipzig (WCQ)	1–2
26/5/57	Czechoslovakia	Prague (WCQ)	0–2
25/9/57	E. Germany	Cardiff (WCQ)	4–1
19/10/57	England	Cardiff	0–4
13/11/57	Scotland	Glasgow	1–1
15/1/58	Israel	Tel Aviv (WCQ)	2–0
5/2/58	Israel	Cardiff (WCQ)	2–0
16/4/58	N. Ireland	Cardiff	1–1
8/6/58	Hungary	Sandviken (WCF)	1–1
11/6/58	Mexico	Stockholm (WCF)	1–1
15/6/58	Sweden	Stockholm (WCF)	0–0
17/6/58	Hungary	Stockholm (WCF)	2–1
19/6/58	Brazil	Gothenburg (WCF)	0–1
18/10/58	Scotland	Cardiff	0–3
26/11/58	England	Villa Park	2–2
22/4/59	N. Ireland	Belfast	1–4
17/10/59	England	Cardiff	1–1
4/11/59	Scotland	Glasgow	1–1

1960–69

Results

Date	Opponents	Venue	Score
6/4/60	N. Ireland	Wrexham	3–2
28/9/60	Rep. of Ireland	Dublin	3–2
22/10/60	Scotland	Cardiff	2–0
23/11/60	England	Wembley	1–5
12/4/61	N. Ireland	Belfast	5–1
19/4/61	Spain	Cardiff (WCQ)	1–2
18/5/61	Spain	Madrid (WCQ)	1–1
28/5/61	Hungary	Budapest	2–3
14/10/61	England	Cardiff	1–1
8/11/61	Scotland	Glasgow	0–2
11/4/62	N. Ireland	Cardiff	4–0
12/5/62	Brazil	Rio de Janeiro	1–3
16/5/62	Brazil	São Paulo	1–3
22/5/62	Mexico	Mexico City	1–2
20/10/62	Scotland	Cardiff	2–3
7/11/62	Hungary	Budapest (ECQ)	1–3
21/11/62	England	Wembley	0–4
20/3/63	Hungary	Cardiff (ECQ)	1–1
3/4/63	N. Ireland	Belfast	4–1
12/10/63	England	Cardiff	0–4
20/11/63	Scotland	Glasgow	1–2
15/4/64	N. Ireland	Swansea	2–3
3/10/64	Scotland	Cardiff	3–2
21/10/64	Denmark	Copenhagen (WCQ)	0–1
18/11/64	England	Wembley	1–2
9/12/64	Greece	Athens (WCQ)	0–2
17/2/65	Greece	Cardiff (WCQ)	4–1
31/3/65	N. Ireland	Belfast	5–0
1/5/65	Italy	Florence	1–4
30/5/65	USSR	Moscow (WCQ)	1–2
2/10/65	England	Cardiff	0–0
27/10/65	USSR	Cardiff (WCQ)	2–1
24/11/65	Scotland	Glasgow (ECQ)	1–4
1/12/65	Denmark	Wrexham (WCQ)	4–2
30/3/66	N. Ireland	Cardiff	1–4
14/5/66	Brazil	Rio de Janeiro	1–3
18/5/66	Brazil	Belo Horizonte	0–1
22/5/66	Chile	Santiago	0–2
22/10/66	Scotland	Cardiff (ECQ)	1–1
16/11/66	England	Wembley (ECQ)	1–5
12/4/67	N. Ireland	Belfast (ECQ)	0–0
21/10/67	England	Cardiff (ECQ)	0–3
22/11/67	Scotland	Glasgow	2–3
28/2/68	N. Ireland	Wrexham (ECQ)	2–0
8/5/68	W. Germany	Cardiff	1–1
23/10/68	Italy	Cardiff (WCQ)	0–1
26/3/69	W. Germany	Frankfurt	1–1
16/4/69	E. Germany	Dresden (WCQ)	1–2
3/5/69	Scotland	Wrexham	3–5
7/5/69	England	Wembley	1–2

10/5/69	N. Ireland	Belfast	0–0
28/7/69	Rest of UK	Cardiff	0–1
22/10/69	E Germany	Cardiff (WCQ)	1–3
4/11/69	Italy	Rome (WCQ)	1–4

1970

Results

Date	Opponents	Venue	Score
18/4	England	Cardiff	1–1
22/4	Scotland	Glasgow	0–0
25/4	N. Ireland	Swansea	1–0
11/11	Romania	Cardiff (ECQ)	0–0

1971

Results

Date	Opponents	Venue	Score
21/4	Czechoslovakia	Swansea (ECQ)	1–3
15/5	Scotland	Cardiff	0–0
18/5	England	Wembley	0–0
22/5	N. Ireland	Belfast	0–1
26/5	Finland	Helsinki (ECQ)	1–0
13/10	Finland	Swansea (ECQ)	3–0
27/10	Czechoslovakia	Prague (ECQ)	0–1
24/11	Romania	Bucharest (ECQ)	0–2

1972

Results

Date	Opponents	Venue	Score
20/5	England	Cardiff	0–3
24/5	Scotland	Glasgow	0–1
27/5	N. Ireland	Wrexham	0–0
15/11	England	Cardiff (WCQ)	0–1

1973

Results

Date	Opponents	Venue	Score
24/1	England	Wembley (WCQ)	1–1
28/3	Poland	Cardiff (WCQ)	2–0
12/5	Scotland	Wrexham	0–2
15/5	England	Wembley	0–3
19/5	N. Ireland	Liverpool	0–1
26/9	Poland	Chorzow (WCQ)	0–3

1974

Results

Date	Opponents	Venue	Score
11/5	England	Cardiff	0–2
14/5	Scotland	Glasgow	0–2
18/5	N. Ireland	Wrexham	1–0
4/9	Austria	Vienna (ECQ)	1–2
30/10	Hungary	Cardiff (ECQ)	2–0
20/11	Luxembourg	Swansea (ECQ)	5–0

1975

Results

Date	Opponents	Venue	Score
16/4	Hungary	Budapest (ECQ)	2–1
1/5	Luxembourg	Luxembourg (ECQ)	3–1
17/5	Scotland	Cardiff	2–2
21/5	England	Wembley	2–2
23/5	N. Ireland	Belfast	0–1
19/11	Austria	Wrexham (ECQ)	1–0

1976

Results

Date	Opponents	Venue	Score
24/3	England	Wrexham	1–2
24/4	Yugoslavia	Zagreb (ECQ)	0–2
6/5	Scotland	Glasgow	1–3
8/5	England	Cardiff	0–1
14/5	N. Ireland	Swansea	1–0
22/5	Yugoslavia	Cardiff (ECQ)	1–1
6/10	W. Germany	Cardiff	0–2
17/11	Scotland	Glasgow (WCQ)	0–1

1977

Results

Date	Opponents	Venue	Score
30/3	Czechoslovakia	Wrexham (WCQ)	3–0
28/5	Scotland	Wrexham	0–0
31/5	England	Wembley	1–0
3/6	N. Ireland	Belfast	1–1
6/9	Kuwait	Wrexham	0–0
20/9	Kuwait	Kuwait	0–0
12/10	Scotland	Liverpool (WCQ)	0–2
16/11	Czechoslovakia	Prague (WCQ)	0–1
14/12	W. Germany	Dortmund	1–1

1978

Results

Date	Opponents	Venue	Score
18/4	Iran	Teheran	1–0
13/5	England	Cardiff	1–3
17/5	Scotland	Glasgow	1–1
19/5	N. Ireland	Wrexham	1–0
25/10	Malta	Wrexham (ECQ)	7–0
29/11	Turkey	Wrexham (ECQ)	1–0

1979

Results

Date	Opponents	Venue	Score
2/5	W. Germany	Wrexham (ECQ)	0–2
19/5	Scotland	Cardiff	3–0
23/5	England	Wembley	0–0
25/5	N. Ireland	Belfast	1–1
2/6	Malta	Valetta (ECQ)	2–0
11/9	Rep. of Ireland	Swansea	2–1
17/10	W. Germany	Cologne (ECQ)	1–5
21/11	Turkey	Izmir (ECQ)	0–1

1980

Results

Date	Opponents	Venue	Score
17/5	England	Wrexham	4–1
21/5	Scotland	Glasgow	0–1
23/5	N. Ireland	Cardiff	0–1
2/6	Iceland	Reykjavik (WCQ)	4–0
15/10	Turkey	Cardiff (WCQ)	4–0
19/11	Czechoslovakia	Cardiff (WCQ)	1–0

1981

Results

Date	Opponents	Venue	Score
24/2	Rep. of Ireland	Dublin	3–1
25/3	Turkey	Ankara (WCQ)	1–0
16/5	Scotland	Swansea	2–0
20/5	England	Wembley	0–0
30/5	USSR	Wrexham (WCQ)	0–0
9/9	Czechoslovakia	Prague (WCQ)	0–2
14/10	Iceland	Swansea (WCQ)	2–2
18/11	USSR	Tbilisi (WCQ)	0–3

1982

Results

Date	Opponents	Venue	Score
24/3	Spain	Valencia	1–1
27/4	England	Cardiff	0–1
24/5	Scotland	Glasgow	0–1
27/5	N. Ireland	Wrexham	3–0
2/6	France	Toulouse	1–0
22/9	Norway	Swansea (ECQ)	1–0
15/12	Yugoslavia	Titograd (ECQ)	4–4

1983

Results

Date	Opponents	Venue	Score
23/2	England	Wembley	1–2
27/4	Bulgaria	Wrexham (ECQ)	1–0
28/5	Scotland	Cardiff	0–2
31/5	N. Ireland	Belfast	1–0
12/6	Brazil	Cardiff	1–1
21/9	Norway	Oslo (ECQ)	0–0
12/10	Romania	Wrexham	5–0
16/11	Bulgaria	Sofia (ECQ)	0–1
14/12	Yugoslavia	Cardiff (ECQ)	1–1

1984

Results

Date	Opponents	Venue	Score
28/2	Scotland	Glasgow	1–2
2/5	England	Wrexham	1–0
22/5	N. Ireland	Swansea	1–1
6/6	Norway	Trondheim	0–1
10/6	Israel	Tel Aviv	0–0
12/9	Iceland	Reykjavik (WCQ)	0–1
17/10	Spain	Seville (WCQ)	0–3
14/11	Iceland	Cardiff (WCQ)	2–1

1985

Results

Date	Opponents	Venue	Score
26/2	Norway	Wrexham	1–1
27/3	Scotland	Glasgow (WCQ)	1–0
30/4	Spain	Wrexham (WCQ)	3–0
5/6	Norway	Bergen	2–4
10/9	Scotland	Cardiff (WCQ)	1–1
16/10	Hungary	Cardiff	0–3

1986

Results

Date	Opponents	Venue	Score
25/2	Saudi Arabia	Dhahran	2–1
26/3	Rep. of Ireland	Dublin	1–0
21/4	Uruguay	Cardiff	0–0
10/5	Canada	Toronto	0–2
20/5	Canada	Vancouver	3–0
10/9	Finland	Helsinki (ECQ)	1–1

1987

Results

Date	Opponents	Venue	Score
18/2	USSR	Swansea	0–0
1/4	Finland	Wrexham (ECQ)	4–0
29/4	Czechoslovakia	Wrexham (ECQ)	1–1
9/9	Denmark	Cardiff (ECQ)	1–0
14/10	Denmark	Copenhagen (ECQ)	0–1
11/11	Czechoslovakia	Prague (ECQ)	0–2

1988

Results

Date	Opponents	Venue	Score
23/3	Yugoslavia	Swansea	1–2
27/4	Sweden	Stockholm	1–4
1/6	Malta	Valletta	3–2
4/6	Italy	Brescia	1–0
14/9	Holland	Amsterdam (WCQ)	0–1
19/10	Finland	Swansea (WCQ)	2–2

1989

Results

Date	Opponents	Venue	Score
8/2	Israel	Tel Aviv	3–3
26/4	Sweden	Wrexham	0–2
31/5	W. Germany	Cardiff (WCQ)	0–0
6/9	Finland	Helsinki (WCQ)	0–1
11/10	Holland	Wrexham (WCQ)	1–2
15/11	W. Germany	Cologne (WCQ)	1–2

1990

Results

Date	Opponents	Venue	Score
28/3	Rep. of Ireland	Dublin	0–1
25/4	Sweden	Stockholm	2–4
20/5	Costa Rica	Cardiff	1–0
1/9	Denmark	Copenhagen	0–1
17/10	Belgium	Cardiff(ECQ)	3–1
14/11	Luxembourg	Luxembourg (ECQ)	1–0

1991

Results

Date	Opponents	Venue	Score
6/2	Rep. of Ireland	Wrexham	0–3
27/3	Belgium	Brussels (ECQ)	1–1
1/5	Iceland	Cardiff	1–0
29/5	Poland	Radom	0–0
5/6	W. Germany	Cardiff (ECQ)	1–0
11/9	Brazil	Cardiff	1–0
16/10	W. Germany	Nüremberg (ECQ)	1–4
13/11	Luxembourg	Cardiff (ECQ)	1–0

1992

Results

Date	Opponents	Venue	Score
19/2	Rep. of Ireland	Dublin	1–0
29/4	Austria	Vienna	1–1
20/5	Romania	Bucharest (WCQ)	1–5
30/5	Holland	Utrecht	0–4
3/6	Argentina	Tokyo	0–1
7/6	Japan	Matsuyama	1–0
9/9	Faroes	Cardiff (WCQ)	6–0
14/10	Cyprus	Limassol (WCQ)	1–0
18/11	Belgium	Brussels (WCQ)	0–2

1993

Results

Date	Opponents	Venue	Score
17/2	Rep. of Ireland	Dublin	1–2
31/3	Belgium	Cardiff (WCQ)	2–0
28/4	Czechoslovakia	Ostrava (WCQ)	1–1
6/6	Faroes	Toftir (WCQ)	3–0
8/9	RCS*	Cardiff (WCQ)	2–2
13/10	Cyprus	Cardiff (WCQ)	2–0
17/11	Romania	Cardiff (WCQ)	1–2

* Representation of Czechs & Slovaks (was Czechoslovakia).

1994

Results

Date	Opponents	Venue	Score
9/3	Norway	Cardiff	1–3
20/4	Sweden	Wrexham	0–2
23/5	Estonia	Tallinn	2–1
7/9	Albania	Cardiff (ECQ)	2–0
12/10	Moldova	Chisinau (ECQ)	2–3
16/11	Georgia	Tbilisi (ECQ)	0–5
14/12	Bulgaria	Cardiff (ECQ)	0–3

1995

Results

Date	Opponents	Venue	Score
29/3	Bulgaria	Sofia (ECQ)	1–3
26/4	Germany	Düsseldorf (ECQ)	1–1
7/6	Georgia	Cardiff (ECQ)	0–1
6/9	Moldova	Cardiff (ECQ)	1–0
11/10	Germany	Cardiff (ECQ)	1–2
15/11	Albania	Tirana (ECQ)	1–1

1996

Results

Date	Opponents	Venue	Score
24/1	Italy	Terni	0–3
24/4	Switzerland	Lugano	0–2
2/6	San Marino	Serravalle (WCQ)	5–0
31/8	San Marino	Cardiff (WCQ)	6–0
5/10	Holland	Cardiff	1–3
9/11	Holland	Eindhoven (WCQ)	1–7
14/12	Turkey	Cardiff (WCQ)	0–0

1997

Results

Date	Opponents	Venue	Score
11/2	Rep of Ireland	Cardiff	0–0
29/3	Belgium	Cardiff (WCQ)	1–2
27/5	Scotland	Kilmarnock	1–0
20/8	Turkey	Istanbul (WCQ)	4–6
11/10	Belgium	Brussels (WCQ)	2–3
11/11	Brazil	Brasilia (WCQ)	0–3

1998

Results

Date	Opponents	Venue	Score
25/3	Jamaica	Cardiff	0–0

NORTHERN IRELAND

League Champions

Winners

1891	Linfield
1892	Linfield
1893	Linfield
1894	Glentoran
1895	Linfield
1896	Distillery
1897	Glentoran
1898	Glenfield
1899	Distillery
1900	Belfast Celtic
1901	Distillery
1902	Linfield
1903	Distillery
1904	Linfield
1905	Glentoran
1906	Cliftonville/ Distillery
1907	Linfield
1908	Linfield
1909	Linfield
1910	Cliftonville
1911	Linfield
1912	Glentoran
1913	Glentoran
1914	Linfield
1915	Belfast Celtic
1920	Belfast Celtic
1921	Glentoran
1922	Linfield
1923	Linfield
1924	Queen's Isl.
1925	Glentoran
1926	Belfast Celtic
1927	Belfast Celtic
1928	Belfast Celtic
1929	Belfast Celtic
1930	Linfield
1931	Glentoran
1932	Linfield
1933	Belfast Celtic
1934	Linfield
1935	Linfield
1936	Belfast Celtic
1937	Belfast Celtic
1938	Belfast Celtic
1939	Belfast Celtic
1940	Belfast Celtic
1948	Belfast Celtic
1949	Linfield
1950	Linfield
1951	Glentoran
1952	Glenavon
1953	Glentoran
1954	Linfield
1955	Linfield
1956	Linfield
1957	Glentoran
1958	Ards
1959	Linfield
1960	Glenavon
1961	Linfield
1962	Linfield
1963	Distillery
1964	Glentoran
1965	Derry City
1966	Linfield
1967	Glentoran
1968	Glentoran
1969	Linfield
1970	Glentoran
1971	Linfield
1972	Glentoran
1973	Crusaders
1974	Coleraine
1975	Linfield
1976	Crusaders
1977	Glentoran
1978	Linfield
1979	Linfield
1980	Linfield
1981	Linfield
1982	Linfield
1983	Linfield
1984	Linfield
1985	Linfield
1986	Linfield
1987	Linfield
1988	Glentoran
1989	Linfield
1990	Portadown
1991	Portadown
1992	Glentoran
1993	Linfield
1994	Linfield
1995	Crusaders
1996	Portadown
1997	Crusaders
1998	Cliftonville

Irish Cup Finals

Finalists

Year	Winners	Runners-up	Score
1881	Moyola Park	Cliftonville	1–0
1882	Queen's Island	Cliftonville	2–1
1883	Cliftonville	Ulster	5–0
1884	Distillery	Ulster	5–0
1885	Distillery	Limavady	2–0
1886	Distillery	Limavady	1–0
1887	Ulster	Cliftonville	3–1
1888	Cliftonville	Distillery	2–1
1889	Distillery	YMCA	5–4
1890	Gordon	Cliftonville	2–2, 3–0
1891	Linfield	Ulster	4–2
1892	Linfield	The Black Watch	7–0
1893	Linfield	Cliftonville	5–1
1894	Distillery	Linfield	2–2, 3–2
1895	Linfield	Bohemians	10–1
1896	Distillery	Glentoran	3–1
1897	Cliftonville	Sherwood	3–1
1898	Linfield	St Columbs Hall	2–0
1899	Linfield	Glentoran	1–0
1900	Cliftonville	Bohemians	2–1
1901	Cliftonville	Freebooters, Dublin	1–0
1902	Linfield	Distillery	5–1
1903	Distillery	Bohemians	3–1
1904	Linfield	Derry Celtic	5–0
1905	Distillery	Shelbourne	3–0
1906	Shelbourne	Belfast Celtic	2–0
1907	Cliftonville	Shelbourne	0–0, 1–0
1908	Bohemians	Shelbourne	1–1, 3–1
1909	Cliftonville	Bohemians	0–0, 2–1
1910	Distillery	Cliftonville	1–0
1911	Shelbourne	Bohemians	0–0, 2–1
1912	*Not played: Linfield awarded cup*		
1913	Linfield	Glentoran	2–0
1914	Glentoran	Linfield	3–1
1915	Linfield	Belfast Celtic	1–0
1916	Linfield	Glentoran	1–0
1917	Glentoran	Belfast Celtic	2–0
1918	Belfast Celtic	Linfield	0–0, 0–0, 2–0
1919	Linfield	Glentoran	1–1, 0–0, 2–1
1920	*Not played: Shelbourne awarded cup*		
1921	Glentoran	Glenavon	2–0

1922	Linfield	Glenavon	2–0
1923	Linfield	Glentoran	2–0
1924	Queen's Island	Willowfield	1–0
1925	Distillery	Glentoran	2–1
1926	Belfast Celtic	Linfield	3–2
1927	Ards	Cliftonville	3–2
1928	Willowfield	Larne	1–0
1929	Ballymena Utd	Belfast Celtic	2–1
1930	Linfield	Ballymena United	4–3
1931	Linfield	Ballymena United	3–0
1932	Glentoran	Linfield	2–1
1933	Glentoran	Distillery	1–1, 1–1, 3–1
1934	Linfield	Cliftonville	5–0
1935	Glentoran	Larne	0–0, 0–0, 1–0
1936	Linfield	Derry City	0–0, 2–1
1937	Belfast Celtic	Linfield	3–0
1938	Belfast Celtic	Bangor	0–0, 2–0
1939	Linfield	Ballymena Utd	2–0
1940	Ballymena Utd	Glenavon	2–0
1941	Belfast Celtic	Linfield	1–0
1942	Linfield	Glentoran	3–1
1943	Belfast Celtic	Glentoran	1–0
1944	Belfast Celtic	Linfield	3–1
1945	Linfield	Glentoran	4–2
1946	Linfield	Distillery	3–0
1947	Belfast Celtic	Glentoran	1–0
1948	Linfield	Coleraine	3–0
1949	Derry City	Glentoran	3–1
1950	Linfield	Distillery	2–1
1951	Glentoran	Ballymena Utd	3–1
1952	Ards	Glentoran	1–0
1953	Linfield	Coleraine	5–0
1954	Derry City	Glentoran	1–0
1955	Dundela	Glenavon	3–0
1956	Distillery	Glentoran	1–0
1957	Glenavon	Derry City	2–0
1958	Ballymena Utd	Linfield	2–0
1959	Glenavon	Ballymena Utd	2–0
1960	Linfield	Ards	5–1
1961	Glenavon	Linfield	5–1
1962	Linfield	Portadown	4–0
1963	Linfield	Distillery	2–1
1964	Derry City	Glentoran	2–0
1965	Coleraine	Glenavon	2–1
1966	Glentoran	Linfield	2–0
1967	Crusaders	Glentoran	3–1
1968	Crusaders	Linfield	2–0
1969	Ards	Distillery	4–2
1970	Linfield	Ballymena Utd	2–1
1971	Distillery	Derry City	3–0
1972	Coleraine	Portadown	2–1
1973	Glentoran	Linfield	3–2
1974	Ards	Ballymena Utd	2–1
1975	Coleraine	Linfield	1–1, 0–0, 1–0
1976	Carrick Rangers	Linfield	2–1
1977	Coleraine	Linfield	4–1

1978	Linfield	Ballymena Utd	3–1
1979	Cliftonville	Portadown	3–2
1980	Linfield	Crusaders	2–0
1981	Ballymena Utd	Glenavon	1–0
1982	Linfield	Coleraine	2–1
1983	Glentoran	Linfield	1–1, 2–1
1984	Ballymena Utd	Carrick Rangers	4–1
1985	Glentoran	Linfield	1–1, 1–0
1986	Glentoran	Coleraine	2–1
1987	Glentoran	Larne	1–0
1988	Glentoran	Glenavon	1–0
1989	Ballymena Utd	Larne	1–0
1990	Glentoran	Portadown	3–0
1991	Portadown	Glenavon	2–1
1992	Glenavon	Linfield	2–1
1993	Bangor	Ards	1–1, 1–1, 1–0
1994	Linfield	Bangor	2–0
1995	Linfield	Carrick Rangers	3–1
1996	Glentoran	Glenavon	1–0
1997	Glenavon	Cliftonville	1–0
1998	Glentoran	Glenavon	1–0

Northern Ireland Internationals 1882–1899

Results

Date	Opponents	Venue	Score
18/2/82	England	Belfast	0–13
25/2/82	Wales	Wrexham	1–7
24/2/83	England	Liverpool	0–7
17/3/83	Wales	Belfast	1–1
26/1/84	Scotland	Belfast	0–5
9/2/84	Wales	Wrexham	0–6
23/2/84	England	Belfast	1–8
28/2/85	England	Manchester	0–4
14/3/85	Scotland	Glasgow	2–8
11/4/85	Wales	Belfast	2–8
27/2/86	Wales	Wrexham	0–5
13/3/86	England	Belfast	1–6
20/3/86	Scotland	Belfast	2–7
5/2/87	England	Sheffield	0–7
19/2/87	Scotland	Glasgow	1–4
12/3/87	Wales	Belfast	4–1
3/3/88	Wales	Wrexham	0–11
24/3/88	Scotland	Belfast	2–10
7/4/88	England	Belfast	1–5
2/3/89	England	Liverpool	1–6
9/3/89	Scotland	Glasgow	0–7
27/4/89	Wales	Belfast	1–3

8/2/90	Wales	Shrewsbury	2–5
15/3/90	England	Belfast	1–9
29/3/90	Scotland	Belfast	1–4
7/2/91	Wales	Belfast	7–2
7/3/91	England	Wolverhampton	1–6
28/3/91	Scotland	Glasgow	1–2
27/2/92	Wales	Bangor	1–1
5/3/92	England	Belfast	0–2
19/3/92	Scotland	Belfast	2–3
25/2/93	England	Birmingham	1–6
25/3/93	Scotland	Glasgow	1–6
5/4/93	Wales	Belfast	4–3
24/2/94	Wales	Swansea	1–4
3/3/94	England	Belfast	2–2
31/3/94	Scotland	Belfast	1–2
9/3/95	England	Derby	0–9
16/3/95	Wales	Belfast	2–2
30/3/95	Scotland	Glasgow	1–3
29/2/96	Wales	Wrexham	1–6
7/3/96	England	Belfast	0–2
28/3/96	Scotland	Belfast	3–3
20/2/97	England	Nottingham	0–6
6/3/97	Wales	Belfast	4–3
27/3/97	Scotland	Glasgow	1–5
19/2/98	Wales	Llandudno	1–0
5/3/98	England	Belfast	2–3
26/3/98	Scotland	Belfast	0–3
18/2/99	England	Sunderland	2–13
4/3/99	Wales	Belfast	1–0
25/3/99	Scotland	Glasgow	1–9

1900–09

Results

Date	Opponents	Venue	Score
24/2/00	Wales	Llandudno	0–2
3/3/00	Scotland	Belfast	0–3
17/3/00	England	Dublin	0–2
23/2/01	Scotland	Glasgow	0–11
9/3/01	England	Southampton	0–3
23/3/01	Wales	Belfast	0–1
22/2/02	Wales	Cardiff	3–0
1/3/02	Scotland	Belfast	1–3
22/3/02	England	Belfast	0–1
14/2/03	England	Wolverhampton	0–4
21/3/03	Scotland	Glasgow	2–0
28/3/03	Wales	Belfast	2–0
12/3/04	England	Belfast	1–3
21/3/04	Wales	Bangor	1–0
26/3/04	Scotland	Dublin	1–1
25/2/05	England	Middlesbrough	1–1

18/3/05	Scotland	Glasgow	0–4
8/4/05	Wales	Belfast	2–2
17/2/06	England	Belfast	0–5
17/3/06	Scotland	Dublin	0–1
2/4/06	Wales	Wrexham	4–4
16/2/07	England	Liverpool	0–1
23/2/07	Wales	Belfast	3–2
16/3/07	Scotland	Glasgow	0–3
15/2/08	England	Belfast	1–3
14/3/08	Scotland	Dublin	0–5
11/4/08	Wales	Aberdare	1–0
13/2/09	England	Bradford	0–4
15/3/09	Scotland	Glasgow	0–5
20/3/09	Wales	Belfast	2–3

1910–19

Results

Date	Opponents	Venue	Score
12/2/10	England	Belfast	1–1
19/3/10	Scotland	Belfast	1–0
11/4/10	Wales	Wrexham	1–4
28/1/11	Wales	Belfast	1–2
11/2/11	England	Derby	1–2
18/3/11	Scotland	Glasgow	0–2
10/2/12	England	Dublin	1–6
16/3/12	Scotland	Belfast	1–4
13/4/12	Wales	Cardiff	3–2
18/1/13	Wales	Belfast	0–1
15/2/13	England	Belfast	2–1
15/3/13	Scotland	Dublin	1–2
19/1/14	Wales	Wrexham	2–1
14/2/14	England	Middlesbrough	3–0
14/3/14	Scotland	Belfast	1–1
25/10/19	England	Belfast	1–1

1920–29

Results

Date	Opponents	Venue	Score
14/2/20	Wales	Belfast	2–2
13/3/20	Scotland	Glasgow	0–3
23/10/20	England	Sunderland	0–2
26/2/21	Scotland	Belfast	0–2
9/4/21	Wales	Swansea	1–2

Date	Opponents	Venue	Score
22/10/21	England	Belfast	1–1
4/3/22	Scotland	Glasgow	1–2
1/4/22	Wales	Belfast	1–1
21/10/22	England	West Bromwich	0–2
3/3/23	Scotland	Belfast	0–1
14/4/23	Wales	Wrexham	3–0
20/10/23	England	Belfast	2–1
1/3/24	Scotland	Glasgow	0–2
15/3/24	Wales	Belfast	0–1
22/10/24	England	Liverpool	1–3
28/2/25	Scotland	Belfast	0–3
18/4/25	Wales	Wrexham	0–0
24/10/25	England	Belfast	0–0
13/2/26	Scotland	Belfast	3–0
27/2/26	Scotland	Glasgow	0–4
20/10/26	England	Liverpool	3–3
26/2/27	Scotland	Belfast	0–2
19/4/27	Wales	Cardiff	2–2
22/10/27	England	Belfast	2–0
4/2/28	Wales	Belfast	1–2
25/2/28	Scotland	Glasgow	1–0
22/10/28	England	Liverpool	1–2
2/2/29	Wales	Wrexham	2–2
23/2/29	Scotland	Belfast	3–7
19/10/29	England	Belfast	0–3

1930–39

Results

Date	Opponents	Venue	Score
1/2/30	Wales	Belfast	0–7
22/2/30	Scotland	Glasgow	1–3
20/10/30	England	Sheffield	1–5
21/2/31	Scotland	Belfast	0–0
22/4/31	Wales	Wrexham	2–3
19/9/31	Scotland	Glasgow	1–3
17/10/31	England	Belfast	2–6
5/12/31	Wales	Belfast	4–0
12/9/32	Scotland	Belfast	0–4
17/10/32	England	Blackpool	0–1
7/12/32	Wales	Wrexham	1–4
16/9/33	Scotland	Glasgow	2–1
14/10/33	England	Belfast	0–3
4/11/33	Wales	Belfast	1–1
20/10/34	Scotland	Belfast	2–1
6/2/35	England	Liverpool	1–2
27/3/35	Wales	Wrexham	1–3
19/10/35	England	Belfast	1–3
13/11/35	Scotland	Edinburgh	1–2
11/3/36	Wales	Belfast	3–2
31/10/36	Scotland	Belfast	1–3

Date	Opponents	Venue	Score
18/11/36	England	Stoke-on-Trent	1–3
17/3/37	Wales	Wrexham	1–4
23/10/37	England	Belfast	1–5
10/11/37	Scotland	Aberdeen	1–1
16/3/38	Wales	Belfast	1–0
8/11/38	Scotland	Belfast	0–2
16/11/38	England	Manchester	0–7
15/3/39	Wales	Wrexham	1–3

1940–49

Results

Date	Opponents	Venue	Score
28/9/40	England	Belfast	2–7
27/11/40	Scotland	Glasgow	0–0
16/4/47	Wales	Belfast	2–1
4/10/47	Scotland	Belfast	2–0
5/11/47	England	Everton	2–2
10/3/48	Wales	Wrexham	0–2
9/10/48	England	Belfast	2–6
17/11/48	Scotland	Glasgow	2–3
9/3/49	Wales	Belfast	0–2
1/10/49	Scotland	Belfast (WCQ)	2–8
6/11/49	England	Manchester (WCQ)	2–9

1950–59

Results

Date	Opponents	Venue	Score
8/3/50	Wales	Wrexham (WCQ)	0–0
7/10/50	England	Belfast	1–4
1/11/50	Scotland	Glasgow	1–6
7/3/51	Wales	Belfast	1–2
12/5/51	France	Belfast	2–2
6/10/51	Scotland	Belfast	0–3
20/11/51	England	Villa Park	0–2
19/3/52	Wales	Swansea	0–3
4/10/52	England	Belfast	2–2
5/11/52	Scotland	Glasgow	1–1
11/11/52	France	Paris	1–3
15/4/53	Wales	Belfast (WCQ)	2–3
3/10/53	Scotland	Belfast (WCQ)	1–3
11/11/53	England	Everton (WCQ)	1–3

Date	Opponent	Venue	Score
2/10/54	England	Belfast	0–2
3/11/54	Scotland	Glasgow	2–2
20/4/55	Wales	Belfast	2–3
8/10/55	Scotland	Belfast	2–1
2/11/55	England	Wembley	0–3
11/4/56	Wales	Cardiff	1–1
6/10/56	England	Belfast	1–1
7/11/56	Scotland	Glasgow	0–1
16/1/57	Portugal	Lisbon (WCQ)	1–1
10/4/57	Wales	Belfast	0–0
25/4/57	Italy	Rome (WCQ)	0–1
1/5/57	Portugal	Belfast (WCQ)	3–0
5/10/57	Scotland	Belfast	1–1
6/11/57	England	Wembley	3–2
4/12/57	Italy	Belfast	2–2
15/1/58	Italy	Belfast (WCQ)	2–1
16/4/58	Wales	Cardiff	1–1
11/6/58	Argentina	Halmstad (WCF)	1–3
15/6/58	West Germany	Malmö	2–2
17/6/58	Czechoslovakia	Malmö (WCF)	2–1
19/6/58	France	Norrkoping (WCF)	0–4
4/10/58	England	Belfast	3–3
8/10/58	Czechoslovakia	Halmstad (WCF)	1–0
15/10/58	Spain	Madrid	2–6
5/11/58	Scotland	Glasgow	2–2
22/4/59	Wales	Belfast	4–1
3/10/59	Scotland	Belfast	0–4
18/11/59	England	Wembley	1–2

1960–69

Results

Date	Opponents	Venue	Score
6/4/60	Wales	Wrexham	2–3
8/10/60	England	Belfast	2–5
26/10/60	W. Germany	Belfast (WCQ)	3–4
9/11/60	Scotland	Glasgow	2–5
12/4/61	Wales	Belfast	1–5
25/4/61	Italy	Bologna	2–3
3/5/61	Greece	Athens (WCQ)	1–2
10/5/61	W. Germany	Berlin (WCQ)	1–2
7/10/61	Scotland	Belfast	1–6
17/10/61	Greece	Belfast (WCQ)	2–0
22/11/61	England	Wembley	1–1
11/4/62	Wales	Cardiff	0–4
9/5/62	Holland	Rotterdam	0–4
10/10/62	Poland	Katowice (WCQ)	2–0
20/10/62	England	Belfast	1–3
7/11/62	Scotland	Glasgow	1–5
28/11/62	Poland	Belfast (WCQ)	2–0

Date	Opponent	Venue	Score
3/4/63	Wales	Belfast	1–4
30/5/63	Spain	Bilbao	1–1
12/10/63	Scotland	Belfast	2–1
30/10/63	Spain	Belfast	0–1
20/11/63	England	Wembley	3–8
15/4/64	Wales	Swansea	3–2
29/4/64	Uruguay	Belfast	3–0
3/10/64	England	Belfast	3–4
14/10/64	Switzerland	Belfast (WCQ)	1–0
14/11/64	Switzerland	Lausanne (WCQ)	1–2
25/11/64	Scotland	Glasgow	2–3
17/3/65	Holland	Belfast (WCQ)	2–1
31/3/65	Wales	Belfast	0–5
7/4/65	Holland	Rotterdam (WCQ)	0–0
7/5/65	Albania	Belfast (WCQ)	4–1
2/10/65	Scotland	Belfast	3–2
10/11/65	England	Wembley	1–2
24/11/65	Albania	Tirana (WCQ)	1–1
30/3/66	Wales	Cardiff	4–1
7/5/66	W. Germany	Belfast	0–2
22/6/66	Mexico	Belfast	4–1
22/10/66	England	Belfast (ECQ)	0–2
16/11/66	Scotland	Glasgow	1–2
12/4/67	Wales	Belfast (ECQ)	0–0
21/10/67	Scotland	Belfast	1–0
22/11/67	England	Wembley (ECQ)	0–2
28/2/68	Wales	Wrexham (ECQ)	0–2
10/9/68	Israel	Jaffa	3–2
23/10/68	Turkey	Belfast (WCQ)	4–1
11/12/68	Turkey	Istanbul (WCQ)	3–0
3/5/69	England	Belfast	1–3
6/5/69	Scotland	Glasgow	1–1
10/5/69	Wales	Belfast	0–0
10/9/69	USSR	Belfast (WCQ)	0–0
22/10/69	USSR	Moscow (WCQ)	0–2

1970

Results

Date	Opponents	Venue	Score
18/4	Scotland	Belfast	0–1
21/4	England	Wembley	1–3
25/4	Wales	Swansea	0–1
11/11	Spain	Seville (ECQ)	0–3

1971

Results

Date	Opponents	Venue	F–A
3/2	Cyprus	Nicosia (ECQ)	3–0
21/4	Cyprus	Belfast (ECQ)	5–0
15/5	England	Belfast	0–1
18/5	Scotland	Glasgow	1–0
22/5	Wales	Belfast	1–0
22/9	USSR	Moscow (ECQ)	0–1
13/10	USSR	Belfast (ECQ)	1–1

1972

Results

Date	Opponents	Venue	Score
16/2	Spain	Hull (ECQ)	1–1
20/5	Scotland	Glasgow	0–2
23/5	England	Wembley	1–0
27/5	Wales	Wrexham	0–0
18/10	Bulgaria	Sofia (WCQ)	0–3

1973

Results

Date	Opponents	Venue	Score
14/2	Cyprus	Nicosia (WCQ)	0–1
28/3	Portugal	Coventry (WCQ)	1–1
8/5	Cyprus	London (WCQ)	3–0
12/5	England	Liverpool	1–2
16/5	Scotland	Glasgow	2–1
19/5	Wales	Liverpool	1–0
26/9	Bulgaria	Hillsborough (WCQ)	0–0
14/11	Portugal	Lisbon (WCQ)	1–1

1974

Results

Date	Opponents	Venue	Score
11/5	Scotland	Glasgow	1–0
15/5	England	Wembley	0–1
18/5	Wales	Wrexham	0–1
4/9	Norway	Oslo (ECQ)	1–2
30/10	Sweden	Solna (ECQ)	2–0

1975

Results

Date	Opponents	Venue	Score
16/3	Yugoslavia	Belfast (ECQ)	1–0
17/5	England	Belfast	0–0
20/5	Scotland	Glasgow	0–3
23/5	Wales	Belfast	1–0
3/9	Sweden	Belfast (ECQ)	1–2
29/10	Norway	Belfast (ECQ)	3–0
19/11	Yugoslavia	Belgrade (ECQ)	0–1

1976

Results

Date	Opponents	Venue	Score
24/3	Israel	Tel Aviv	1–1
8/5	Scotland	Glasgow	0–3
11/5	England	Wembley	0–4
14/5	Wales	Swansea	0–1
13/10	Holland	Rotterdam (WCQ)	2–2
10/11	Belgium	Liège (WCQ)	0–2

1977

Results

Date	Opponents	Venue	Score
27/4	W. Germany	Cologne	0–5
28/5	England	Belfast	1–2
1/6	Scotland	Glasgow	0–2
3/6	Wales	Belfast	1–1
11/6	Iceland	Reykjavik (WCQ)	0–1
21/9	Iceland	Belfast (WCQ)	2–0
12/10	Holland	Belfast (WCQ)	0–1
16/11	Belgium	Belfast (WCQ)	3–0

1978

Results

Date	Opponents	Venue	Score
13/5	Scotland	Glasgow	1–1
16/5	England	Wembley	0–1
19/5	Wales	Wrexham	0–1
20/9	Rep. of Ireland	Dublin (ECQ)	0–0
25/10	Denmark	Belfast (ECQ)	2–1
29/11	Bulgaria	Sofia (ECQ)	2–0

1979

Results

Date	Opponents	Venue	Score
7/2	England	Wembley (ECQ)	0–4
2/5	Bulgaria	Belfast (ECQ)	2–0
19/5	England	Belfast	0–2
22/5	Scotland	Glasgow	0–1
25/5	Wales	Belfast	1–1
6/6	Denmark	Copenhagen (ECQ)	0–4
17/10	England	Belfast (ECQ)	1–5
21/11	Rep. of Ireland	Belfast (ECQ)	1–0

1980

Results

Date	Opponents	Venue	Score
26/3	Israel	Tel Aviv (WCQ)	0–0
16/5	Scotland	Belfast	1–0
20/5	England	Wembley	1–1
23/5	Wales	Cardiff	1–0
11/6	Australia	Sydney	2–1
15/6	Australia	Melbourne	1–1
18/6	Australia	Adelaide	2–1
15/10	Sweden	Belfast (WCQ)	3–0
19/11	Portugal	Lisbon (WCQ)	0–1

1981

Results

Date	Opponents	Venue	Score
25/3	Scotland	Glasgow (WCQ)	1–1
29/4	Portugal	Belfast (WCQ)	1–0
19/5	Scotland	Glasgow	0–2
3/6	Sweden	Stockholm (WCQ)	0–1
14/10	Scotland	Belfast (WCQ)	0–0
18/11	Israel	Belfast (WCQ)	1–0

1982

Results

Date	Opponents	Venue	Score
23/2	England	Wembley	0–4
24/3	France	Paris	0–4
28/4	Scotland	Belfast	1–1
27/5	Wales	Wrexham	0–3
17/6	Yugoslavia	Zaragoza (WCF)	0–0
21/6	Honduras	Zaragoza (WCF)	1–1
25/6	Spain	Valencia (WCF)	1–0
1/7	Austria	Madrid (WCF)	2–2
4/7	France	Madrid (WCF)	1–4
13/10	Austria	Vienna (ECQ)	0–2
17/11	W. Germany	Belfast (ECQ)	1–0
15/12	Albania	Tirana (ECQ)	0–0

1983

Results

Date	*Opponents*	*Venue*	*Score*
30/3	Turkey	Belfast (ECQ)	2–1
27/4	Albania	Belfast (ECQ)	1–0
24/5	Scotland	Glasgow (ECQ)	0–0
28/5	England	Belfast	0–0
31/5	Wales	Belfast	0–1
21/9	Austria	Belfast (ECQ)	3–1
12/10	Turkey	Ankara (ECQ)	0–1
16/11	W. Germany	Hamburg (ECQ)	1–0
13/12	Scotland	Belfast	2–0

1984

Results

Date	*Opponents*	*Venue*	*Score*
4/4	England	Wembley	0–1
22/5	Wales	Swansea	1–1
27/5	Finland	Pori (WCQ)	0–1
12/9	Romania	Belfast (WCQ)	3–2
16/10	Israel	Belfast	3–0
14/11	Finland	Belfast (WCQ)	2–1

1985

Results

Date	*Opponents*	*Venue*	*Score*
27/2	England	Belfast (WCQ)	0–1
27/3	Spain	Palma	0–0
1/5	Turkey	Belfast (WCQ)	2–0
11/9	Turkey	Izmir (WCQ)	0–0
16/10	Romania	Bucharest (WCQ)	1–0
13/11	England	Wembley (WCQ)	0–0

1986

Results

Date	*Opponents*	*Venue*	*Score*
26/2	France	Paris	0–0
26/3	Denmark	Belfast	1–1
23/4	Morocco	Belfast	2–1
3/6	Algeria	Guadalajara (WCF)	1–1
7/6	Spain	Guadalajara (WCF)	1–2
12/6	Brazil	Guadalajara (WCF)	0–3
15/10	England	Wembley (ECQ)	0–3
12/11	Turkey	Izmir (ECQ)	0–0

1987

Results

Date	*Opponents*	*Venue*	*Score*
18/2	Israel	Tel Aviv	1–1
1/4	England	Belfast (ECQ)	0–2
29/4	Yugoslavia	Belfast (ECQ)	1–2
14/10	Yugoslavia	Sarajevo (ECQ)	0–3
11/11	Turkey	Belfast (ECQ)	1–0

1988

Results

Date	*Opponents*	*Venue*	*Score*
17/2	Greece	Athens	2–3
23/3	Poland	Belfast	1–1
27/4	France	Belfast	0–0
21/5	Malta	Belfast (WCQ)	3–0
14/9	Rep. of Ireland	Belfast (WCQ)	0–0
19/10	Hungary	Budapest (WCQ)	0–1
21/12	Spain	Seville (WCQ)	0–4

1989

Results

Date	Opponents	Venue	Score
8/2	Spain	Belfast (WCQ)	0–2
26/4	Malta	Valletta (WCQ)	2–0
26/5	Chile	Belfast	0–1
6/9	Hungary	Belfast (WCQ)	1–2
11/10	Rep. of Ireland	Dublin (WCQ)	0–3

1990

Results

Date	Opponents	Venue	Score
27/3	Norway	Belfast	2–3
18/5	Uruguay	Belfast	1–0
12/9	Yugoslavia	Belfast (ECQ)	0–2
17/10	Denmark	Belfast (ECQ)	1–1
14/11	Austria	Vienna (ECQ)	0–0

1991

Results

Date	Opponents	Venue	Score
5/2	Poland	Belfast	3–1
27/3	Yugoslavia	Belgrade (ECQ)	1–4
1/5	Faeroes	Belfast (ECQ)	1–1
11/9	Faeroes	Landsrona (ECQ)	5–0
16/10	Austria	Belfast (ECQ)	2–1
13/11	Denmark	Odense (ECQ)	1–2

1992

Results

Date	Opponents	Venue	Score
28/4	Lithuania	Belfast (WCQ)	2–2
2/6	Germany	Bremen	1–1
9/9	Albania	Belfast (WCQ)	3–0
14/10	Spain	Belfast (WCQ)	0–0
18/11	Denmark	Belfast (WCQ)	0–1

1993

Results

Date	Opponents	Venue	Score
17/2	Albania	Tirana (WCQ)	2–1
31/3	Rep of Ireland	Dublin (WCQ)	0–3
28/4	Spain	Seville (WCQ)	1–3
25/5	Lithuania	Vilnius (WCQ)	1–0
2/6	Latvia	Riga (WCQ)	2–1
8/9	Latvia	Belfast (WCQ)	2–0
13/10	Denmark	Copenhagen (WCQ)	0–1
17/11	Rep of Ireland	Belfast (WCQ)	1–1

1994

Results

Date	Opponents	Venue	Score
20/4	Liechtenstein	Belfast (ECQ)	4–1
3/6	Colombia	Boston	0–2
12/6	Mexico	Miami	0–3
7/9	Portugal	Belfast (ECQ)	1–2
12/10	Austria	Vienna (ECQ)	2–1
16/11	Rep of Ireland	Belfast (ECQ)	0–4

1995

Results

Date	Opponents	Venue	Score
29/3	Rep of Ireland	Dublin (ECQ)	1–1
26/4	Latvia	Riga (ECQ)	1–0
22/5	Canada	Edmonton	0–2
25/5	Chile	Edmonton	1–2
7/6	Latvia	Belfast (ECQ)	1–2
3/9	Portugal	Lisbon (ECQ)	1–1
11/10	Liechtenstein	Eschen (ECQ)	4–0
15/11	Austria	Belfast (ECQ)	5–3

1998

Results

Date	Opponents	Venue	Score
25/3	Slovakia	Belfast	1–0
22/4	Switzerland	Belfast	1–0

1996

Results

Date	Opponents	Venue	Score
27/3	Norway	Belfast	0–2
24/4	Sweden	Belfast	1–2
29/5	Germany	Belfast	1–1
31/8	Ukraine	Belfast (WCQ)	0–1
5/10	Armenia	Belfast (WCQ)	1–1
9/11	Germany	Nüremburg (WCQ)	1–1
14/12	Albania	Belfast (WCQ)	2–0

1997

Results

Date	Opponents	Venue	Score
29/3	Portugal	Belfast (WCQ)	0–0
2/4	Ukraine	Kiev (WCQ)	1–2
30/4	Armenia	Yerevan (WCQ)	0–0
21/5	Thailand	Bangkok	0–0
2/8	Germany	Belfast (WCQ)	1–3
10/9	Albania	Zurich (WCQ)	0–1
11/10	Portugal	Lisbon (WCQ)	0–1

REPUBLIC OF IRELAND

International results 1926–59

Date	Opponents	Venue	Score
21/3/26	Italy	Turin	0–3
23/4/27	Italy	Dublin	1–2
12/2/28	Belgium	Liège	4–2
30/4/29	Belgium	Dublin	4–0
11/5/30	Belgium	Brussels	3–1
26/4/31	Spain	Barcelona	1–1
13/12/31	Spain	Dublin	0–5
8/5/32	Holland	Amsterdam	2–0
25/2/34	Belgium	Dublin (WCQ)	4–4
8/4/34	Holland	Amsterdam (WCQ)	2–5
15/12/34	Hungary	Dublin	2–4
5/5/35	Switzerland	Basle	0–1
8/5/35	Germany	Dortmund	1–3
8/12/35	Holland	Dublin	3–5
17/3/36	Switzerland	Dublin	1–0
3/5/36	Hungary	Budapest	3–3
9/5/36	Luxembourg	Luxembourg	5–1
17/10/36	Germany	Dublin	5–2
6/12/36	Hungary	Dublin	2–3
17/5/37	Switzerland	Berne	1–0
23/5/37	France	Paris	2–0
10/10/37	Norway	Oslo (WCQ)	2–3
7/11/37	Norway	Dublin (WCQ)	3–3
18/5/38	Czechoslovakia	Prague	2–2
22/5/38	Poland	Warsaw	0–6
18/9/38	Switzerland	Dublin	4–0
13/11/38	Poland	Dublin	3–2
19/3/39	Hungary	Cork	2–2
18/5/39	Hungary	Budapest	2–2
23/5/39	Germany	Bremen	1–1
16/6/46	Portugal	Lisbon	1–3
23/6/46	Spain	Madrid	1–0
30/9/46	England	Dublin	0–1
2/3/47	Spain	Dublin	3–2
4/5/47	Portugal	Dublin	0–2
23/5/48	Portugal	Lisbon	0–2
30/5/48	Spain	Barcelona	1–2
5/12/48	Switzerland	Dublin	0–1
24/4/49	Belgium	Dublin	0–2
22/5/49	Portugal	Dublin	1–0
2/6/49	Sweden	Stockholm (WCQ)	1–3
12/6/49	Spain	Dublin	1–4
8/9/49	Finland	Dublin (WCQ)	3–0
21/9/49	England	Everton	2–0
9/10/49	Finland	Helsinki (WCQ)	1–1
13/11/49	Sweden	Dublin (WCQ)	1–3
10/5/50	Belgium	Brussels	1–5
26/11/50	Norway	Dublin	2–2
13/5/51	Argentina	Dublin	0–1
30/5/51	Norway	Oslo	3–2
17/10/51	W Germany	Dublin	3–2
4/5/52	W Germany	Cologne	0–3
7/5/52	Austria	Vienna	0–6
1/6/52	Spain	Madrid	0–6
25/3/53	Austria	Dublin	4–0
4/10/53	France	Dublin (WCQ)	3–5
28/10/53	Luxembourg	Dublin (WCQ)	4–0
25/11/53	France	Paris (WCQ)	0–1
7/3/54	Luxembourg	Luxembourg (WCQ)	1–0
8/11/54	Norway	Dublin	2–1
1/5/55	Holland	Dublin	1–0
25/5/55	Norway	Oslo	3–1
28/5/55	W Germany	Hamburg	1–2
19/9/55	Yugoslavia	Dublin	1–4
27/11/55	Spain	Dublin	2–2
10/5/56	Holland	Rotterdam	4–1
3/10/56	Denmark	Dublin (WCQ)	2–1
25/11/56	W Germany	Dublin	3–0
8/5/57	England	Wembley (WCQ)	1–5
19/5/57	England	Dublin (WCQ)	1–1
2/10/57	Denmark	Copenhagen (WCQ)	2–0
14/3/58	Austria	Vienna	1–3
11/5/58	Poland	Katowice	2–2
5/10/58	Poland	Dublin	2–2
5/4/59	Czechoslovakia	Dublin (ECQ)	2–0
10/5/59	Czechoslovakia	Bratislava (ECQ)	0–4
1/11/59	Sweden	Dublin	3–2

1960–69

Results

Date	Opponents	Venue	Score
30/3/60	Chile	Dublin	2–0
11/5/60	W Germany	Düsseldorf	1–0
18/5/60	Sweden	Malmö	1–4
28/9/60	Wales	Dublin	2–3
6/11/60	Norway	Dublin	3–1
3/5/61	Scotland	Glasgow (WCQ)	1–4
7/5/61	Scotland	Dublin (WCQ)	0–3
8/10/61	Czechoslovakia	Dublin (WCQ)	1–3
29/10/61	Czechoslovakia	Prague (WCQ)	1–7
8/4/62	Austria	Dublin	2–3
12/8/62	Iceland	Dublin (ECQ)	4–2
2/9/62	Iceland	Reykjavik (ECQ)	1–1
9/6/63	Scotland	Dublin	1–0
25/9/63	Austria	Vienna (ECQ)	0–0
13/10/63	Austria	Dublin (ECQ)	3–2

Date	Opponents	Venue	Score
11/3/64	Spain	Seville (ECQ)	1–5
8/4/64	Spain	Dublin (ECQ)	0–2
10/5/64	Poland	Cracow	1–3
13/5/64	Norway	Oslo	4–1
24/5/64	England	Dublin	1–3
25/10/64	Poland	Dublin	3–2
24/3/65	Belgium	Dublin	0–2
5/5/65	Spain	Dublin (WCQ)	1–0
27/10/65	Spain	Seville (WCQ)	1–4
10/11/65	Spain	Paris (WCQ)	0–1
4/5/66	W Germany	Dublin	0–4
22/5/66	Austria	Vienna	0–1
25/5/66	Belgium	Liège	3–2
23/10/66	Spain	Dublin (ECQ)	0–0
16/11/66	Turkey	Dublin (ECQ)	2–1
7/12/66	Spain	Valencia (ECQ)	0–2
22/2/67	Turkey	Ankara (ECQ)	1–2
21/5/67	Czechoslovakia	Dublin (ECQ)	0–2
22/11/67	Czechoslovakia	Prague (ECQ)	2–1
15/5/68	Poland	Dublin	2–2
30/10/68	Poland	Katowice	0–1
10/11/68	Austria	Dublin	2–2
4/12/68	Denmark	Dublin (WCQ)	1–1
	(abandoned after 51 minutes)		
4/5/69	Czechoslovakia	Dublin (WCQ)	1–2
27/5/69	Denmark	Copenhagen (WCQ)	0–2
8/6/69	Hungary	Dublin (WCQ)	1–2
21/9/69	Scotland	Dublin	1–1
7/10/69	Czechoslovakia	Prague (WCQ)	0–3
15/10/69	Denmark	Dublin (WCQ)	1–1
5/11/69	Hungary	Budapest (WCQ)	0–4

1970–89

Results

Date	Opponents	Venue	Score
6/5/70	Poland	Dublin	1–2
9/5/70	W Germany	Berlin	1–2
23/9/70	Poland	Dublin	0–2
14/10/70	Sweden	Dublin (ECQ)	1–1
28/10/70	Sweden	Malmö (ECQ)	0–1
8/12/71	Italy	Rome (ECQ)	0–3
10/5/71	Italy	Dublin (ECQ)	1–2
30/5/71	Austria	Dublin (ECQ)	1–4
10/10/71	Austria	Linz (ECQ)	0–6
18/6/72	Iran	Recife	2–1
19/6/72	Ecuador	Natal	3–2
21/6/72	Chile	Recife	1–2
25/6/72	Portugal	Recife	1–2
18/10/72	USSR	Dublin (WCQ)	1–2
15/11/72	France	Dublin (WCQ)	2–1
13/5/73	USSR	Moscow (WCQ)	0–1
16/5/73	Poland	Wroclaw	0–2
19/5/73	France	Paris (WCQ)	1–1
6/6/73	Norway	Oslo	1–1
21/10/73	Poland	Dublin	1–0
8/5/74	Uruguay	Montevideo	0–2
12/5/74	Chile	Santiago	2–1
30/10/74	USSR	Dublin (ECQ)	3–0
20/11/74	Turkey	Izmir (ECQ)	1–1
1/3/75	W Germany	Dublin	1–0 +
	(+ W Germany 'B' side)		
11/5/75	Switzerland	Dublin (ECQ)	2–1
18/5/75	USSR	Kiev (ECQ)	1–2
29/10/75	Turkey	Dublin (ECQ)	4–0
24/3/76	Norway	Dublin	3–0
26/5/76	Poland	Prosjan	2–0
8/9/76	England	Wembley	1–1
13/10/76	Turkey	Ankara	3–3
17/11/76	France	Paris (WCQ)	0–2
9/2/77	Spain	Dublin	0–1
30/3/77	France	Dublin (WCQ)	1–0
24/4/77	Poland	Dublin	0–0
1/6/77	Bulgaria	Sofia (WCQ)	1–2
12/10/77	Bulgaria	Dublin (WCQ)	0–0
5/4/78	Turkey	Dublin	4–2
12/4/78	Poland	Lodz	0–3
21/5/78	Norway	Oslo	0–0
24/5/78	Denmark	Copenhagen (ECQ)	3–3
20/9/78	N Ireland	Dublin (ECQ)	0–0
25/10/78	England	Dublin (ECQ)	1–1
2/5/79	Denmark	Dublin (ECQ)	2–0
19/5/79	Bulgaria	Sofia (ECQ)	0–1
22/5/79	W Germany	Dublin	1–3
11/9/79	Wales	Swansea	1–2
26/9/79	Czechoslovakia	Prague	1–4
17/10/79	Bulgaria	Dublin (ECQ)	3–0
29/10/79	USA	Dublin	3–2
21/11/79	N Ireland	Belfast (ECQ)	0–1
6/2/80	England	Wembley (ECQ)	0–2
26/3/80	Cyprus	Nicosia (WCQ)	3–2
30/4/80	Switzerland	Dublin	2–0
16/5/80	Argentina	Dublin	0–1
10/9/80	Holland	Dublin (WCQ)	2–1
15/10/80	Belgium	Dublin (WCQ)	1–1
28/10/80	France	Paris (WCQ)	0–2
19/11/80	Cyprus	Dublin (WCQ)	6–0
24/2/81	Wales	Dublin	1–3
25/3/81	Belgium	Brussels (WCQ)	0–1
29/4/81	Czechoslovakia	Dublin	3–1
21/5/81	W Germany	Bremen	0–3
	(W Germany 'B' side)		
23/5/81	Poland	Bydgoszcz	0–3
9/9/81	Holland	Rotterdam (WCQ)	2–2
14/10/81	France	Dublin (WCQ)	3–2
22/5/82	Chile	Santiago	0–1
27/5/82	Brazil	Vberlandia	0–7
30/5/82	Trinidad & Tobago	Port Of Spain	1–2
22/9/82	Holland	Rotterdam (ECQ)	1–2
17/11/82	Spain	Dublin (ECQ)	3–3

30/3/83	Malta	Valletta (ECQ)	1–0
27/4/83	Spain	Zaragoza (ECQ)	0–2
12/10/83	Holland	Dublin (ECQ)	2–3
16/11/83	Malta	Dublin (ECQ)	8–0
4/4/84	Israel	Tel Aviv	0–3
23/5/84	Poland	Dublin	0–0
3/6/84	China	Sapporo	1–0
8/8/84	Mexico	Dublin	0–0
12/9/84	USSR	Dublin (WCQ)	1–0
17/10/84	Norway	Oslo (WCQ)	0–1
14/11/84	Denmark	Copenhagen	0–3
5/2/85	Italy	Dublin	1–2
26/3/85	England	Wembley	1–2
1/5/85	Norway	Dublin (WCQ)	0–0
21/5/85	Israel	Tel Aviv	0–0
26/5/85	Spain	Cork (WCQ)	0–0
2/6/85	Switzerland	Dublin (WCQ)	3–0
11/9/85	Switzerland	Berne (WCQ)	0–0
16/10/85	USSR	Moscow (WCQ)	0–2
13/11/85	Denmark	Dublin (WCQ)	1–4
26/3/86	Wales	Dublin	0–1
23/4/86	Uruguay	Dublin	1–1
25/5/86	Iceland	Reykjvik	2–1
27/5/86	Czechoslovakia	Reykjvik	1–0
10/9/86	Belgium	Brussels (ECQ)	2–2
15/10/86	Scotland	Dublin (ECQ)	0–0
12/11/86	Poland	Warsaw	0–1
18/2/87	Scotland	Glasgow (ECQ)	1–0
1/4/87	Bulgaria	Sofia (ECQ)	1–2
29/4/87	Belgium	Dublin (ECQ)	0–0
23/5/87	Brazil	Dublin	1–0
28/5/87	Luxembourg	Luxembourg (ECQ)	2–0
9/9/87	Luxembourg	Dublin (ECQ)	2–1
14/10/87	Bulgaria	Dublin (ECQ)	2–0
10/11/87	Israel	Dublin	5–0
23/3/88	Romania	Dublin	2–0
27/4/88	Yugoslavia	Dublin	2–0
22/5/88	Poland	Dublin	3–1
1/6/88	Norway	Oslo	0–0
12/6/88	England	Stuggart (ECF)	1–0
15/6/88	USSR	Hanover (ECF)	1–1
18/6/88	Holland	Gelsenkirchen (ECF)	0–1
14/9/88	N Ireland	Belfast (WCQ)	0–0
19/10/88	Tunisia	Dublin	4–0
16/11/88	Spain	Seville (WCQ)	0–2
7/2/89	France	Dublin	0–0
8/3/89	Hungary	Budapest (WCQ)	0–0
26/4/89	Spain	Dublin (WCQ)	1–0
28/5/89	Malta	Dublin (WCQ)	2–0
4/6/89	Hungary	Dublin (WCQ)	2–0
6/9/89	W Germany	Dublin	1–1
11/10/89	N Ireland	Dublin (WCQ)	3–0
15/11/89	Malta	Valetta (WCQ)	2–0

1990

Results

Date	Opponents	Venue	Score
12/1	Morocco	Dublin	1–0
28/3	Wales	Dublin	1–0
25/4	USSR	Dublin	1–0
16/5	Finland	Dublin	1–1
27/5	Turkey	Izmir	0–0
3/6	Malta	Valetta	3–0
11/6	England	Cagliari (WCF)	1–1
17/6	Egypt	Palermo (WCF)	0–0
21/6	Holland	Palermo (WCF)	1–1
25/6	Romania	Genoa (WCF)	0–0
(Rep of Ireland won on penalties: 5–4)			
30/6	Italy	Rome (WCF)	0–1
17/10	Turkey	Dublin (ECQ)	5–0
14/11	England	Dublin (ECQ)	1–1

1991

Results

Date	Opponents	Venue	Score
6/2	Wales	Wrexham	3–0
27/3	England	Wembley (ECQ)	1–1
1/5	Poland	Dublin (ECQ)	0–0
22/5	Chile	Dublin	1–1
2/6	USA	Foxboro	1–1
11/9	Hungary	Gyor	2–1
16/10	Poland	Poznan (ECQ)	3–3
13/11	Turkey	Istanbul (ECQ)	3–1

1992

Results

Date	Opponents	Venue	Score
19/2	Wales	Dublin	0–1
25/3	Switzerland	Dublin	2–1
29/4	USA	Dublin	4–1
26/5	Albania	Dublin (WCQ)	2–0
30/5	USA	Washington	1–3
4/6	Italy	Foxboro	0–2
7/6	Portugal	Foxboro	2–0
9/9	Latvia	Dublin (WCQ)	4–0
14/10	Denmark	Copenhagen (WCQ)	0–0
18/11	Spain	Seville (WCQ)	0–0

1993

Results

Date	Opponents	Venue	Score
17/2	Wales	Dublin	2–1

31/3	N Ireland	Dublin (WCQ)	3–0
28/4	Denmark	Dublin (WCQ)	1–1
26/5	Albania	Tirana (WCQ)	2–1
2/6	Latvia	Riga (WCQ)	2–1
16/6	Lithuania	Vilnius (WCQ)	1–0
8/9	Lithuania	Dublin (WCQ)	2–0
13/10	Spain	Dublin (WCQ)	1–3
17/11	N Ireland	Belfast (WCQ)	1–1

1994

Results

Date	Opponents	Venue	Score
23/3	Russia	Dublin	0–0
20/4	Holland	Tilburg	1–0
24/5	Bolivia	Dublin	1–0
29/5	Germany	Hannover	2–0
4/6	Czech Republic	Dublin	1–3
18/6	Italy	New York (WCF)	1–0
24/6	Mexico	Orlando (WCF)	1–2
28/6	Norway	New York (WCF)	0–0
4/7	Holland	Orlando (WCF)	0–2
7/9	Latvia	Riga (ECQ)	3–0
12/10	Liechtenstein	Dublin (ECQ)	4–0
16/11	N Ireland	Belfast (ECQ)	4–0

1995

Results

Date	Opponents	Venue	Score
15/2	England	Dublin	1–0
	(abandoned after 21 minutes)		
29/3	N Ireland	Dublin (ECQ)	1–1
26/4	Portugal	Dublin (ECQ)	1–0
3/6	Liechtenstein	Vaduz (ECQ)	0–0
11/6	Austria	Dublin (ECQ)	1–3
6/9	Austria	Vienna (ECQ)	1–3
11/10	Latvia	Dublin (ECQ)	2–1
15/11	Portugal	Lisbon (ECQ)	0–3
13/12	Holland	Liverpool (ECQ)	0–2

1996

Results

Date	Opponents	Venue	Score
27/3	Russia	Dublin	0–2
24/4	Czech Republic	Prague	0–2
29/5	Portugal	Dublin	0–1
31/8	Liechtenstein	Vaduz (WCQ)	5–0
9/10	FYR Macedonia	Dublin (WCQ)	3–0
10/11	Iceland	Dublin (WCQ)	0–0

1997

Results

Date	Opponents	Venue	Score
11/2	Wales	Cardiff	0–0
2/4	FYR Macedonia	Skopje (WCQ)	2–3
30/4	Romania	Bucharest (WCQ)	0–1
21/5	Liechtenstein	Dublin (WCQ)	5–0
20/8	Lithuania	Dublin (WCQ)	0–0
10/9	Lithuania	Vilnius (WCQ)	2–1
11/10	Romania	Dublin (WCQ)	1–1
29/10	Belgium	Dublin (WCQ)	1–1
15/11	Belgium	Brussels (WCQ)	1–2

1998

Date	Opponents	Venue	Score
25/3	Czech Rep.	Olomouc	1–2
22/4	Argentina	Dublin	0–2
23/5	Mexico	Dublin	0–0

Football Records

A selection of the biggest and best, smallest and worst. From highes[ ] scores to highest attendance, look no further...

CLUB

Highest scores:

Arbroath 36, Bon Accord (Aberdeen) 0
(Scottish Cup 1st Round, September 12, 1885).
Dundee Harp 35, Aberdeen Rovers 0
(Scottish Cup 1st Round, September 12, 1885).
First–class match: Arbroath 36, Bon Accord 0
(Scottish Cup 1st Round, September 12, 1885).
International match: Ireland 0, England 13
(February 18, 1882).
FA Cup: Preston North End 26, Hyde United 0
(1st Round, October 15, 1887).
League Cup: West Ham United 10, Bury 0
(2nd Round, 1st Leg, October 25, 1983); Liverpool 10,
Fulham 0 (2nd Round, 1st Leg, September 23, 1986).

Record aggregates:

League Cup: Liverpool 13, Fulham 2
(10–0h, 3–2a), September 23–October 7, 1986).
West Ham United 12, Bury 1 (2–1a, 10–0h), October
4–25, 1983. Liverpool 11, Exeter City 0 (5–0h, 6–0a),
October 7–28, 1981.
Premier League: (Home) Manchester United 9,
Ipswich Town 0 (March 4, 1995). *(Away)* Sheffield
Wednesday 1, Nottingham Forest 7 (April 1, 1995).
First Division: (Home) WBA 12, Darwen 0 (April 4,
1892); Nottingham Forest 12, Leicester Fosse 0 (April
21, 1909). *(Away)* Newcastle United 1, Sunderland 9

(December 5, 1908); Cardiff City 1, Wolverhampton
Wanderers 9 (September 3, 1955).
Second Division: (Home) Newcastle United 13,
Newport County 0 (October 5, 1946). *(Away)* Burslem
PV 0, Sheffield United 10 (December 10, 1892).
Third Division: (Home) Gillingham 10, Chesterfield [ ]
(September 5, 1987).
(Away) Halifax Town 0, Fulham 8 (September 16, 1969)
Third Division South: (Home) Luton Town 12, Brist[ ]
Rovers 0 (April 13, 1936).
(Away) Northampton Town 0, Walsall 8 (February 2, 1947).
Third Division North: (Home) Stockport County 13,
Halifax Town 0 (January 6, 1934).
(Away) Accrington Stanley 0, Barnsley 9 (February 3, 1934[ ]
Fourth Division: (Home) Oldham Athletic 11,
Southport 0 (December 26, 1962). *(Away)* Crewe
Alexandra 1, Rotherham United 8 (September 8, 1973[ ]
Aggregate Third Division North: Tranmere Rovers
13, Oldham Athletic 4 (December 26, 1935).
Scottish Premier Division: (Home) Aberdeen 8,
Motherwell 0 (March 26, 1979). *(Away)* Hamilton
Academicals 0, Celtic 8 (November 5, 1988).
Scottish Division One: (Home) Celtic 11, Dundee 0
(October 26, 1895).
(Away) Airdrieonians 1, Hibernian 11 (October 24,
1950).
Scottish Division Two: (Home) Airdrieonians 15,
Dundee Wanderers 1 (December 1, 1894).
(Away) Alloa Athletic 0, Dundee 10 (March 8, 1947).

Internationals:

France 0, England 15 (Amateur match, 1906).

Ireland 0, England 13 (February 18, 1882).

Biggest England win at Wembley: England 9, Luxembourg 0 (European Championship qualifier, December 15, 1982). Scotland 11, Ireland 0 (February 23, 1901). Northern Ireland 7, Wales 0 (February 1, 1930). Wales 11, Ireland 0 (March 3, 1888). Republic of Ireland 8, Malta 0 (European Championship qualifier, November 16, 1983).

Record international defeats: Hungary 7, England 1 (May 23, 1954). England 9, Scotland 3 (April 15, 1961). Ireland 0, England 13 (February 18, 1882). Scotland 9, Wales 0 (March 23, 1878). Brazil 7, Republic of Ireland 0 (May 27, 1982).

World Cup qualifying round: Maldives 0, Iran 17 (June 2, 1997).

World Cup Finals: Hungary 10, El Salvador 1 (Spain, June 15, 1982). Hungary 9, South Korea 0 (Switzerland, June 17, 1954). Yugoslavia 9, Zaire 0 (West Germany, June 18, 1974).

League:

FA Premier League: Manchester United 9, Ipswich Town 0 (March 4, 1995).

Record away win: Sheffield Wednesday 1, Nottingham Forest 7 (April 1, 1995).

Football League (old 1st Division): Aston Villa 12, Accrington 2 (March 12, 1892). Tottenham Hotspur 10, Everton 4 (October 11, 1958; highest 1st Division aggregate this century). West Bromwich Albion 12, Darwen 0 (April 4, 1892). Nottingham Forest 12, Leicester Fosse 0 (April 12, 1909).

Record away win: Cardiff City 1, Wolverhampton Wanderers 9 (September 3, 1955).

New 1st Division: Bolton Wanderers 7, Swindon Town 0 (March 8, 1997).

Old 2nd Division: Manchester City 11, Lincoln City 3 (March 23, 1895). Newcastle United 13, Newport County 0 (October 5, 1946). Small Heath 12, Walsall Town Swifts 0 (December 17, 1892). Darwen 12, Walsall 0 (December 26, 1896). Small Heath 12, Doncaster Rovers 0 (April 11, 1903).

Record away win: Burslem Port Vale 0, Sheffield United 10 (December 10, 1892).

New 2nd Division: Hartlepool 1, Plymouth Argyle 8 (May 7, 1994).

Old 3rd Division: Gillingham 10, Chesterfield 0 (September 5, 1987). Tranmere Rovers 9, Accrington Stanley 0 (April 18, 1959). Brighton and Hove Albion 9, Southend United 1 (November 22, 1965). Brentford 9, Wrexham 0 (October 15, 1963).

Record away win: Halifax Town 0, Fulham 8 (September 16, 1969).

New 3rd Division: Torquay United 1, Scunthorpe United 8 (October 28, 1995).

3rd Division (North): Stockport County 13, Halifax Town 0 (January 6, 1934). Tranmere Rovers 13, Oldham Athletic 4 (December 26, 1935; highest Football League aggregate).

Record away win: Accrington Stanley 0, Barnsley 9 (February 3, 1934).

3rd Division (South): Luton Town 12, Bristol Rovers 0 (April 13, 1936). Gillingham 9, Exeter City 4 (January 7, 1951).

Record away win: Northampton Town 0, Walsall 8 (April 8, 1947).

Old 4th Division: Oldham Athletic 11, Southport 0 (December 26, 1962). Hartlepool United 10, Barrow 1 (April 4, 1959). Wrexham 10, Hartlepool United 1 (March 3, 1962).

Record away win: Crewe Alexandra 1, Rotherham United 8 (September 8, 1973).

Scottish Premier Division: Aberdeen 8, Motherwell 0 (March 26, 1979). Kilmarnock 1, Rangers 8 (September 6, 1980). Hamilton A. 0, Celtic 8 (November 5, 1988).

Record aggregate: Celtic 8, Hamilton A 3 (January 3, 1987).

Scottish League Division One: Celtic 11, Dundee 0 (October 26, 1895).

Record away win: Airdrie 1, Hibernian 11 (October 24, 1959).

Scottish League Division Two: Airdrieonians 15, Dundee Wanderers 1 (December 1, 1894).

Record British score this century: Stirling Albion 20, Selkirk 0 (Scottish Cup 1st Round, December 8, 1984).

Longest series of consecutive championships:
Three clubs have won the League Championship three years in succession: Huddersfield Town (1923–24, 1924–25, 1925–26), Arsenal (1932–33, 1933–34, 1934–35), and Liverpool (1981–82, 1982–83, 1983–84).
Both Celtic (1965–66, 1966–67, 1967–68, 1968–69, 1969–70, 1970–71, 1971–72, 1972–73, 1973–74) and Rangers (1988–89, 1989–90, 1990–91, 1991–92, 1992–93, 1993–94, 1994–95, 1995–96, 1996–97) have won the Scottish League Championship nine years in succession.

Most goals scored in a season:

Premier League: Newcastle United (82 goals, 42 games, 1993–94).

Division One: Aston Villa (128 goals, 42 games, 1930–31).

Division Two: Middlesbrough (122 goals, 42 games, 1926–27).

Division Three South: Millwall
(127 goals, 42 games, 1927–28).
Division Three North: Bradford City
(128 goals, 42 games, 1928–29).
Division Three: QPR (111 goals, 46 games,
1961–62).
Division Four: Peterborough United
(134 goals, 46 games, 1960–61).
Scottish Premier Division: Rangers
(101 goals, 44 games, 1991–92),
Dundee United (90 goals, 36 games, 1982–83),
Celtic (90 goals, 36 games, 1982–83).
Scottish Division One: Hearts
(132 goals, 34 games, 1957–58).
Scottish Division Two: Raith Rovers
(142 goals, 34 games, 1937–38).
New Division One: Dunfermline Athletic
(93 goals, 44 games, 1993–94),
Motherwell (93 goals, 39 games, 1981–82).
New Division Two: Ayr United
(95 goals, 39 games, 1987–88).
New Division Three: Forfar Athletic
(74 goals, 36 games, 1996–97).

Fewest goals scored in a season:

Premier League: Leeds United
(28 goals, 38 games, 1996–97).
(Minimum 42 games).
Division One: Stoke City
(24 goals, 42 games, 1984–85).
Division Two: Watford
(24 goals, 42 games, 1971–72);
Leyton Orient (30 goals, 46 games, 1994–95).
Division Three South: Crystal Palace
(33 goals, 42 games, 1950–51).
Division Three North: Crewe Alexandra
(32 goals, 42 games, 1923–24).
Division Three: Stockport County
(27 goals, 46 games, 1969–70).
Division Four: Crewe Alexandra
(29 goals, 46 games, 1981–82).
(Minimum 30 games).
Scottish Premier Division: Hamilton Academicals
(19 goals, 36 games, 1988–89);
Dunfermline Athletic (22 goals, 44 games, 1991–92).
Scottish Division One: Brechin City
(30 goals, 44 games, 1993–94);
Ayr United (20 goals, 34 games, 1966–67).
Scottish Division Two: Lochgelly United
(20 goals, 38 games, 1923–24).
New Division One: Stirling Albion
(18 goals, 39 games, 1980–81);
Dumbarton (23 goals, 36 games, 1995–96).

New Division Two: Berwick Rangers
(22 goals, 36 games, 1994–95).
New Division Three: Alloa Athletic
(26 goals, 36 games, 1995–96).

Most goals against in a season:

Premier League: Swindon Town
(100 goals, 42 games, 1993–94).
First Division: Blackpool
(125 goals, 42 games, 1930–31).
Second Division: Darwen
(141 goals, 34 games, 1898–99).
Third Division South: Merthyr Tydfil
(135 goals, 42 games, 1929–30).
Third Division North: Nelson
(136 goals, 42 games, 1927–28).
Third Division: Accrington Stanley
(123 goals, 46 games, 1959–60).
Fourth Division: Hartlepool United
(109 goals, 46 games, 1959–60).
Scottish Premier Division: Morton (100 goals, 44
games, 1987–88, and from 36 games, 1984–85).
Scottish Division One: Leith Athletic
(137 goals, 38 games, 1931–32).
Scottish Division Two: Edinburgh City
(146 goals, 38 games, 1931–32).
New Division One: Queen of the South
(99 goals, 39 games, 1988–89);
Cowdenbeath (109 goals, 44 games, 1992–93).
New Division Two: Meadowbank Thistle
(89 goals, 39 games, 1977–78).
New Division Three: Albion Rovers
(82 goals, 36 games, 1994–95).

Fewest goals against in a season:

Premier League: Arsenal (28 goals, 42 games, 1993–94);
Manchester United (28 goals, 42 games, 1994–95).
(Minimum 42 games).
First Division: Liverpool
(16 goals, 42 games, 1978–79).
Second Division: Manchester United
(23 goals, 42 games, 1924–25);
West Ham United (34 goals, 46 games, 1990–91).
Third Division South: Southampton
(21 goals, 42 games, 1921–22).
Third Division North: Port Vale
(21 goals, 46 games, 1953–54).
Third Division: Gillingham
(20 goals, 46 games, 1995–96).
Fourth Division: Lincoln City
(25 goals, 46 games, 1980–81).

(Minimum 30 games).
Scottish Premier Division: Rangers (19 goals, 36 games, 1989–90); Rangers (23 goals, 44 games, 1986–87); Celtic (23 goals, 44 games, 1987–88).
Scottish Division One: Celtic (14 goals, 38 games, 1913–14).
Scottish Division Two: Morton (20 goals, 38 games, 1966–67).
New Division One: St. Johnstone (23 goals, 36 games, 1996–97); Hibernian (24 goals, 39 games, 1980–81); Falkirk (32 goals, 44 games, 1993–94).
New Division Two: St. Johnstone (24 goals, 39 games, 1987–88); Stirling Albion (24 goals, 39 games, 1990–91).
New Division Three: Brechin City (21 goals, 36 games, 1995–96).

Most points in a season:

Two points for a win:
First Division: Liverpool (1978–79), 68 points from 42 matches.
Second Division: Tottenham Hotspur (1919–20), 70 points from 42 matches.
Third Division: Aston Villa (1971–72), 70 points from 46 matches.
Third Division South: Nottingham Forest (1950–51) and Bristol City (1954–55), 70 points from 46 matches.
Third Division North: Doncaster Rovers (1946–47), 72 points from 42 matches.
Fourth Division: Lincoln City (1975–76), 74 points from 46 matches.
Scottish Premier Division: Aberdeen (1984–85), 59 points from 36 matches; Rangers (1992–93), 73 points from 44 matches.
Scottish Division One: Rangers (1920–21), 76 points from 42 matches.
Scottish Division Two: Morton (1966–67), 69 points from 38 matches.
New Division One: St. Mirren (1976–77), 62 points from 39 matches; Falkirk (1993–94), 66 points from 44 matches.
New Division Two: Forfar Athletic (1983–84), 63 points from 39 matches.
Three points for a win:
Premier League: Manchester United (1993–94), 92 points from 42 matches.
Old First Division: Everton (1984–85), 90 points from 42 matches; Liverpool (1987–88), 90 points from 40 matches.
New First Division: Bolton Wanderers (1996–97), 98 points from 46 matches.
Old Second Division: Chelsea (1988–89), 99 points from 46 matches.

New Second Division: Stoke City (1992–93), 93 points from 46 matches.
Old Third Division: Bournemouth (1986–87), 97 points from 46 matches.
New Third Division: Carlisle United (1994–95), 91 points from 42 matches.
Fourth Division: Swindon Town (1985–86), 102 points from 46 matches.
Scottish Premier Division: Rangers (1995–96), 87 points from 36 matches.
Scottish Division One: St. Johnstone (1996–97), 80 points from 36 matches.
Scottish Division Two: Stirling Albion (1995–96), 81 points from 36 matches.
Scottish Division Three: Forfar Athletic (1994–95), 80 points from 36 matches.

Fewest points in a season:

Premier League: Ipswich Town (1994–95), 27 points from 42 matches.
(Minimum 34 games).
First Division: Stoke City (1984–85), 17 points from 42 matches.
Second Division: Doncaster Rovers (1904–05), 8 points from 34 matches; Loughborough Town (1899–1900), 8 points from 34 matches; Walsall (1988–89), 31 points from 46 matches.
Third Division: Rochdale (1973–74), 21 points from 46 matches; Cambridge United (1984–85), 21 points from 46 matches.
Third Division South: Merthyr Tydfil (1924–25, and 1929–30), 21 points from 42 matches; QPR (1925–26), 21 points from 42 matches.
Third Division North: Rochdale (1931–32), 11 points from 40 matches.
Fourth Division: Workington (1976–77), 19 points from 46 matches.
(Minimum 30 games).
Scottish Premier Division: St. Johnstone (1975–76), 11 points from 36 matches; Morton (1987–88), 16 points from 44 matches.
Scottish Division One: Stirling Albion (1954–55), 6 points from 30 matches.
Scottish Division Two: Edinburgh City (1936–37), 7 points from 34 matches.
New Division One: Queen of the South (1988–89), 10 points from 39 matches; Cowdenbeath (1992–93), 13 points from 44 matches.
New Division Two: Berwick Rangers (1987–88), 16 points from 39 matches; Stranraer (1987–88), 16 points from 39 matches.
New Division Three: Albion Rovers (1994–95), 18 points from 36 matches.

Most wins in a season:

Premier League: Manchester United (1993–94) and Blackburn Rovers (1994–95), 27 wins from 42 matches.

First Division: Tottenham Hotspur (1960–61), 31 wins from 42 matches.

Second Division: Tottenham Hotspur (1919–20), 32 wins from 42 matches.

Third Division South: Millwall (1927–28), Plymouth Argyle (1929–30) and Cardiff City (1946–47), 30 wins from 42 matches; Nottingham Forest (1950–51) and Bristol City (1954–55), 30 wins from 46 matches.

Third Division North: Doncaster Rovers (1946–47), 33 wins from 42 matches.

Third Division: Aston Villa (1971–72), 32 wins from 46 matches.

Fourth Division: Lincoln City (1975–76) and Swindon Town (1985–86), 32 wins from 46 matches.

Scottish Premier Division: Rangers (1995–96) and Aberdeen (1984–85), 27 wins from 36 matches; Rangers (1991–92 and 1992–93), 33 wins from 44 matches.

Scottish Division One: Rangers (1920–21), 35 wins from 42 matches.

Scottish Division Two: Morton (1966–67), 33 wins from 38 matches.

New Division One: Motherwell (1981–82), 26 wins from 39 matches.

New Division Two: Forfar Athletic (1983–84) and Ayr United (1987–88), 27 wins from 39 matches.

New Division Three: Forfar Athletic (1994–95), 25 wins from 36 matches.

Most home wins in a season: Five clubs have won every home League match in a season: Liverpool (14 games, in 1893–94), Bury (15, 1894–95), Sheffield Wednesday (17, 1899–1900) and Birmingham City (17, 1902–03), all in the old Second Division, and Brentford in Division Three South (21 games, 1929–30).

Undefeated sequences (at home): Liverpool went 85 competitive first–team games unbeaten at home between January 23, 1978 (2–3 v Birmingham) and January 31, 1981 (1–2 v Leicester), comprising 63 in the League, 9 in the League Cup, 7 in European competition and 6 in the FA Cup.

Millwall were unbeaten at home in the League for 59 consecutive matches from 1964–67.

Bradford Park Avenue hold the record for most consecutive home victories, winning 25 successive home games in Division Three North: the last 18 in 1926–27 and the first 7 the following season.

The longest run of home wins in the top division is 21 by Liverpool: the last 9 of 1971–72 and the first 12 of 1972–73.

Undefeated sequences (at home and away): Nottingham Forest went 42 League matches unbeaten, spanning the last 26 games of the 1977–78 season, and the first 16 of 1978–79, from November 1977 to the 2–0 defeat to Liverpool on December 9, 1978. The sequence comprised 21 wins and 21 draws.

In all competitions, Forest went 40 games unbeaten between March and December 1978, comprising 21 wins and 19 draws in 29 League matches, 6 League Cup, 4 European Cup and 1 Charity Shield.

Forest also hold the record unbeaten run in the Premiership, going 25 matches undefeated (15 wins, 10 draws), between February and November 1995, before losing 7–0 to Blackburn Rovers.

The longest unbeaten start to a League season is 29 matches, achieved by Leeds United (Division One, 1973–74: 19 wins, 10 draws, goals 51–16), and Liverpool (Division One, 1987–88: 22 wins, 7 draws, goals 67–13).

Burnley hold the record for the most consecutive League matches unbeaten in a season, with 30 First Division games between September 6, 1920 and March 25, 1921 (21 wins, 9 draws, goals 68–17).

Sequences without a win (at home): In the 1931–32 season, Rochdale went eight home League games without a win in the Third Division North. Between November 1958 and October 1959, Portsmouth drew 2 and lost 14 out of 16 consecutive home games.

Sequences without a win (at home and away): Cambridge United went 31 matches (21 lost, 10 drawn) without a League win in the 1983–84 season, between October 8 and April 23, on the way to finishing bottom of the Second Division.

The record for the most consecutive League defeats is held by Darwen in the 1898–99 Division One season. In Division Two in 1988–89, Walsall suffered 15 successive League defeats.

The longest non-winning start to a League season is 25 matches (4 draws, 21 defeats) by Newport County, Division Four (August 15, 1970 to January 9, 1971). Since then, the record is 16 games: Burnley (9 draws, 7 defeats in Division Two, 1979–80); Hull City (10 draws, 6 defeats in Division Two, 1989–90); Sheffield United (4 draws, 12 defeats in Division One, 1990–91). The worst start to a Premier League season was made by Swindon Town in 1993–94, who went 15 matches without a win (6 draws, 9 defeats).

The worst losing start to a League season was made by Manchester United, who suffered 12 consecutive defeats in Division One in 1930–31.

Most away wins in a season: Doncaster Rovers won 18 of the 21 League fixtures as Division Three North champions in 1946–47.

Fewest wins
in a season:

Premier League: Swindon Town (1993–94),
5 wins from 42 matches.

First Division: Stoke City (1889–90),
3 wins from 22 matches; Woolwich Arsenal (1912–13),
3 wins from 38 matches; Stoke City (1984–85), 3 wins
from 42 matches.

Second Division: Loughborough Town (1899–1900),
1 win from 34 matches.

Third Division South: Merthyr Tydfil (1929–30) and
QPR (1925–26), 6 wins from 42 matches.

Third Division North: Rochdale (1931–32),
4 wins from 40 matches.

Third Division: Rochdale (1931–32),
2 wins from 46 matches.

Fourth Division: Southport (1976–77),
3 wins from 46 matches.

Scottish Premier Division: St. Johnstone (1975–76)
and Kilmarnock (1982–83), 3 wins from 36 matches;
Morton (1987–88), 3 wins from 44 matches.

Scottish Division One: Vale of Leven (1891–92),
no wins from 22 matches.

Scottish Division Two: East Stirlingshire (1905–06),
1 win from 22 matches; Forfar Athletic (1974–75),
1 win from 38 matches.

New Division One: Queen of the South (1988–89),
2 wins from 39 matches; Cowdenbeath (1992–93), 3
wins from 44 matches.

New Division Two: Forfar Athletic (1975–76),
4 wins from 26 matches; Stranraer (1987–88), 4 wins
from 39 matches.

New Division Three: Albion Rovers (1994–95),
5 wins from 36 matches.

Most defeats
in a season:

Premier League: Ipswich Town (1994–95),
29 defeats in 42 matches.

First Division: Stoke City (1984–85),
31 defeats in 42 matches.

Second Division: Tranmere Rovers (1938–39),
31 defeats in 42 matches; Chester City (1992–93), 33
defeats in 46 matches.

Third Division South: Merthyr Tydfil (1924–25),
29 defeats in 42 matches; Walsall (1952–53 and
1953–54), 29 defeats in 46 matches.

Third Division North: Rochdale (1931–32),
33 defeats in 40 matches.

Third Division: Cambridge United (1984–85),
33 defeats in 46 matches.

Fourth Division: Newport County (1987–88),
33 defeats in 46 matches.

Scottish Premier Division: Morton (1984–85),
29 defeats in 36 matches.

Scottish Division One: St. Mirren (1920–21),
31 defeats in 42 matches.

Scottish Division Two: Brechin City (1962–63),
30 defeats on 36 matches; Lochgelly (1923–24), 30
defeats in 38 matches.

New Division One: Queen of the South (1988–89),
29 defeats in 39 matches; Dumbarton (1995–96), 31
defeats in 36 matches; Cowdenbeath (1992–93), 34
defeats in 44 matches.

New Division Two: Berwick Rangers (1987–88),
29 defeats in 39 matches.

New Division Three: Albion Rovers (1994–95),
28 defeats in 36 matches.

Fewest defeats
in a season:

Premier League: Manchester United (1993–94),
4 defeats in 42 matches.

First Division: Preston North End (1888–89),
no defeats in 22 matches; Arsenal (1990–91), 1 defeat
in 38 matches; Liverpool (1987–88), 2 defeats in 40
matches; Leeds United (1968–69), 2 defeats in 42
matches.

Second Division: Liverpool (1893–94), no defeats in
28 matches; Burnley (1897–98), 2 defeats in 30
matches; Bristol City (1905–06), 2 defeats in 38
matches; Leeds United (1963–64), 3 defeats in 42
matches; Chelsea (1988–89), 5 defeats in 46 matches.

Third Division: QPR (1966–67) and Bristol Rovers
(1989–90), 5 defeats in 46 matches.

Third Division South: Southampton (1921–22) and
Plymouth Argyle (1929–30), 4 defeats in 42 matches.

Third Division North: Port Vale (1953–54), 3 defeats
in 46 matches; Doncaster Rovers (1946–47) and
Wolverhampton Wanderers (1923–24), 3 defeats in 42
matches.

Fourth Division: Lincoln City (1975–76),
Sheffield United (1981–82), Bournemouth (1981–82),
4 defeats in 46 matches.

Scottish Premier Division: Rangers (1995–96),
3 defeats in 36 matches; Celtic (1987–88), 3 defeats in
44 matches.

Scottish Division One: Rangers (1898–99), no
defeats in 18 matches; Rangers (1920–21), 1 defeat in 42
matches.

Scottish Division Two: Clyde (1956–57),
Morton (1962–63) and St. Mirren (1967–68),
1 defeat in 36 matches.

New Division One: Partick Thistle (1975–76),
2 defeats in 26 matches; St. Mirren (1976–77), 2
defeats in 39 matches; Raith Rovers (1992–93) and
Falkirk (1993–94), 4 defeats in 44 matches.

New Division Two: Raith Rovers (1975–76), 1 defeat
in 26 matches; Clydebank (1975–76), 3 defeats in 26

matches; Forfar Athletic (1983–84) and Raith Rovers (1986–87), 3 defeats in 39 matches;
Livingston (1995–96), 6 defeats in 36 matches.
New Division Three: Forfar Athletic (1994–95) and Inverness C (1996–97), 6 defeats in 36 matches.

Most drawn games in a season:

Premier League: Manchester City (1993–94), Sheffield United (1993–94) and Southampton (1994–95), 18 draws in 42 matches.
First Division: Norwich City (1978–79), 23 draws in 42 matches.
Fourth Division: Exeter City (1986–87), 23 draws in 46 matches.
Scottish Premier Division: Aberdeen (1993–94), 21 draws in 44 matches.
New Division One: East Fife (1986–87), 21 draws in 44 matches.
Most Titles: Liverpool, 18 (1900–01, 1905–06, 1921–22, 1922–23, 1946–47, 1963–64, 1965–66, 1972–73, 1975–76, 1976–77, 1978–79, 1979–80, 1981–82, 1982–83, 1983–84, 1985–86, 1987–88, 1989–90).
Most Premier League Championships: Manchester United, 4 (1992–93, 1993–94, 1995–96, 1996–97).
Most Division Two titles: 6, by Leicester City (1924–25, 1936–37, 1953–54, 1956–57, 1970–71, 1979–80) and Manchester City (1898–99, 1902–03, 1909–10, 1927–28, 1946–47, 1965–66).
Most Division Three titles: 2, by Portsmouth (1961–62, 1982–83) and Oxford United (1967–68, 1983–84).
Most Division Four titles: 2, by Chesterfield (1969–70, 1984–85), Doncaster Rovers (1965–66, 1968–69) and Peterborough United (1960–61, 1973–74).
Most Division Three South titles: Bristol City, 3 (1922–23, 1926–27, 1954–55).
Most Division Three North titles: 3, by Barnsley (1933–34, 1938–39, 1954–55), Doncaster Rovers (1934–35, 1946–47, 1949–50) and Lincoln City (1931–32, 1947–48, 1951–52).
Most Scottish League Championships: Rangers, 47.
Most FA Cup victories: Manchester United, 9 (1909, 1948, 1963, 1977, 1983, 1985, 1990, 1994, 1996).
Most Scottish FA Cup victories: Celtic, 30.
Most League Cup victories: 5, by Aston Villa (1961, 1975, 1977, 1994 and 1996) and Liverpool (1981, 1982, 1983, 1984 and 1995).
Most Scottish League Cup victories: Rangers, 20.

INDIVIDUAL

Most goals in a game:

International: Sofus Nielsen (Denmark), 10 goals vs. France, at White City (Olympics, October 22, 1908); Gottfried Fuchs (Germany), 10 goals vs. Russia, in Stockholm (Olympics, July 1, 1912).
World Cup: Gary Cole (Australia), 7 goals vs. Fiji, (August 14, 1981); Karim Bagheri (Iran), 7 goals vs. Maldives, (June 2, 1997).
World Cup Final: Geoff Hurst (England), 3 goals vs. West Germany, 1966.
Major European Cup game: Lothar Emmerich (Borussia Dortmund), 6 goals vs. Floriana (Cup Winners' Cup, 1965).
Premier League: Andy Cole (Manchester United), 5 goals vs. Ipswich Town (March 4, 1995).
Old First Division: Ted Drake (Arsenal), 7 goals vs. Aston Villa (December 14, 1935); James Ross (Preston North End), 7 goals vs. Stoke City (October 6, 1888).
First Division: John Durnin (Oxford United), 4 goals vs. Luton Town (1992–93); Guy Whittingham (Portsmouth), 4 goals vs. Bristol Rovers (1992–93); Craig Russell (Sunderland), 4 goals vs. Millwall (1995–96).
Old Second Division: Tommy Briggs (Blackburn Rovers), 7 goals vs. Bristol Rovers (February 5, 1955); Neville Coleman (Stoke City), 7 goals vs. Lincoln City (away, February 23, 1957).
Second Division: Paul Barnes (Burnley), 5 goals v Stockport County (1996–97).
Third Division South: Joe Payne (Luton Town), 10 goals vs. Bristol Rovers (April 13, 1936).
Third Division North: Bunny Bell (Tranmere Rovers), 9 goals vs. Oldham Athletic (December 26, 1935).
Old Third Division: Steve Earle (Fulham), 5 goals vs. Halifax Town (September 16, 1969);
Barrie Thomas (Scunthorpe United), 5 goals vs. Luton Town (April 24, 1965);
Keith East (Swindon Town), 5 goals vs. Mansfield Town (November 20, 1965);
Alf Wood (Shrewsbury Town), 5 goals vs. Blackburn Rovers (October 2, 1971);
Tony Caldwell (Bolton Wanderers), 5 goals vs. Walsall (September 10, 1983);
Andy Jones (Port Vale), 5 goals vs. Newport County (May 4, 1987);
Steve Wilkinson (Mansfield Town), 5 goals vs. Birmingham City (April 3, 1990).
Third Division: Tony Naylor (Crewe Alexandra), 5 goals vs. Colchester United (1992–93); Steve Butler (Cambridge United), 5 goals vs. Exeter City (1993–94).
Fourth Division: Bert Lister (Oldham Athletic), 6 goals v Southport (December 26, 1962).
FA Cup: Ted MacDougall (Bournemouth), 9 goals vs.

Margate (1st Round, November 20, 1971).
FA Cup Final: Billy Townley (Blackburn Rovers), 3 goals vs. Sheffield Wednesday (Kennington Oval, 1890); Jimmy Logan (Notts County), 3 goals vs. Bolton Wanderers (Everton, 1894); Stan Mortensen (Blackpool), 3 goals vs. Bolton Wanderers (Wembley, 1953).
League Cup: Frankie Bunn (Oldham Athletic), 6 goals vs. Scarborough (October 25, 1989).
Scottish Premier Division: Paul Sturrock (Dundee United), 5 goals vs. Morton (November 17, 1984).
Scottish Division One: Jimmy McGrory (Celtic), 8 goals vs. Dunfermline Athletic (September 14, 1928).
Scottish Division Two: Owen McNally (Arthurlie), 8 goals vs. Armadale (October 1, 1927); Jim Dyet (King's Park), 8 goals vs. Forfar Athletic (January 2, 1930); John Calder (Morton), 8 goals vs. Raith Rovers (April 18, 1936); Norman Hayward (Raith Rovers), 8 goals vs. Brechin City (August 20, 1937).
Scottish Cup: John Petrie (Arbroath), 13 goals vs. Bon Accord (1st Round, September 12, 1885); Gerry Baker (St. Mirren), 10 goals vs. Glasgow University (1st Round, January 30, 1960); Joe Baker (Hibernian, Gerry's brother), 9 goals vs. Peebles Rovers (2nd Round, February 11, 1961).
Scottish League Cup: Jim Fraser (Ayr United), 5 goals vs. Dumbarton (August 13, 1952); Jim Forrest (Rangers), 5 goals vs. Stirling Albion (August 17, 1966).

Most League goals in a season:
Premier League: Andy Cole (Newcastle United, 1993–94), 34 goals in 40 matches; Alan Shearer (Blackburn Rovers, 1994–95), 34 goals in 42 matches.
Old First Division: Dixie Dean (Everton, 1927–28), 60 goals in 39 matches.
First Division: Guy Whittingham (Portsmouth, 1992–93), 42 goals in 46 matches.
Old Second Division: George Camsell (Middlesbrough, 1926–27), 59 goals in 37 matches.
Second Division: Jimmy Quinn (Reading, 1993–94), 35 goals in 46 matches.
Third Division South: Joe Payne (Luton Town, 1936–37), 55 goals in 39 matches.
Third Division North: Ted Harston (Mansfield Town, 1936–37), 55 goals in 41 matches.
Old Third Division: Derek Reeves (Southampton, 1959–60), 39 goals in 46 matches.
Third Division: Graeme Jones (Wigan Athletic, 1996–97), 31 goals in 40 matches.

Fourth Division: Terry Bly (Peterborough United, 1960–61), 52 goals in 46 matches.
FA Cup: J.D. Ross (Preston North End 1887–88) 20

goals in 9 matches. Sandy Brown (Tottenham Hotspur, 1900–01), 15 goals in 8 matches.
League Cup: Clive Allen (Tottenham Hotspur, 1986–87), 12 goals in 9 matches.
Scottish Premier Division: Brian McClair (Celtic, 1986–87), 35 goals.
Scottish Division One: William McFayden (Motherwell, 1931–32), 53 goals in 34 matches.
Scottish Division Two: Jim Smith (Ayr United, 1927–28), 66 goals in 38 matches.

Most League goals:
Football League:
Arthur Rowley

Club	Goals	Matches	Seasons
WBA	4	24	1946–48
Fulham	27	56	1948–50
Leicester City	251	303	1950–58
Shrewsbury Town	152	236	1958–65
Totals	**434**	**619**	

Scottish League:
Jimmy McGrory

Club	Goals	Matches	Seasons
Celtic	1	3	1922–23
Clydebank	13	30	1923–24
Celtic	396	375	1924–38
Totals	**410**	**408**	

Most League goals for one club:
349 – Dixie Dean (Everton, 1925–37).

Most FA Cup goals:
Pre-war: Henry Cursham, 48 (Notts County).
Post-war: Ian Rush, 43 (Chester, Liverpool and Newcastle United).
Most FA Cup final goals: 5, Ian Rush (Liverpool): 1986 (2), 1989 (2), 1992 (1).

Penalties:
Most in a season (individual): Francis Lee (Manchester City, 1971–72), 13 goals.
Most awarded in one game: Five – Crystal Palace (4: 1 scored, 3 missed) vs. Brighton and Hove Albion (1 scored), Division 2, 1988–89.
Most saved in a season: 8 out of 10, Paul Cooper (Ipswich Town, 1979–80).

Most League appearances
(750 + matches):

1005, Peter Shilton (286 Leicester City, 110 Stoke City, 202 Nottingham Forest, 188 Southampton, 175 Derby County, 34 Plymouth Argyle, 1 Bolton Wanderers, 9 Leyton Orient), 1966–97.

863, Tommy Hutchison (165 Blackpool, 314 Coventry City, 46 Manchester City, 92 Burnley, 178 Swansea City, 68 Alloa), 1965–91.

824, Terry Paine (713 Southampton, 111 Hereford United), 1957–77.

782, Robbie James (484 Swansea City, 48 Stoke City, 87 QPR, 23 Leicester City, 89 Bradford City, 51 Cardiff City).

777, Alan Oakes (565 Manchester City, 211 Chester City, 1 Port Vale), 1959–84.

771, John Burridge (27 Workington, 134 Blackpool, 65 Aston Villa, 6 Southend United (loan), 88 Crystal Palace, 39 QPR, 74 Wolverhampton Wanderers, 6 Derby County (loan), 109 Sheffield United, 62 Southampton, 67 Newcastle United, 65 Hibernian, 3 Scarborough, 4 Lincoln City, 3 Aberdeen, 3 Dumbarton, 3 Falkirk, 4 Manchester City, 3 Darlington, 6 Queen of the South), 1968–96.

770, John Trollope (all for Swindon Town), 1960–80 – record for one club.

764, Jimmy Dickson (all for Portsmouth), 1946–65.

761, Roy Sproson (all for Port Vale), 1950–72.

758, Ray Clemence (48 Scunthorpe United, 470 Liverpool, 240 Tottenham Hotspur), 1966–87.

758, Billy Bonds (95 Charlton Athletic, 663 West Ham United).

757, Pat Jennings (48 Watford, 472 Tottenham Hotspur, 237, Arsenal), 1963–86.

757, Frank Worthington (171 Huddersfield Town, 210 Leicester City, 84 Bolton Wanderers, 75 Birmingham City, 32 Leeds United, 195 Sunderland, 34 Southampton, 31 Brighton and Hove Albion, 59 Tranmere Rovers, 23 Preston North End, 19 Stockport County), 1966–88.

Consecutive: 401, Harold Bell (401 Tranmere Rovers; 459 in all games), 1946–55.

Most FA Cup appearances: 88, Ian Callaghan (79 Liverpool, 7 Swansea City, 2 Crewe Alexandra).

Most senior matches: 1390, Peter Shilton (1005 League, 86 FA Cup, 102 League Cup, 125 internationals, 13 Under-23s, 4 Football League XI, 20 European Cup, 7 Texaco Cup, 5 Simod Cup, 4 European Super Cup, 4 UEFA Cup, 3 Screen Sport Super Cup, 3 Zenith Data Systems Cup, 2 Autoglass Trophy, 2 Charity Shield, 2 Full Members' Cup, 1 Anglo–Italian Cup, 1 Football League play-offs, 1 World Club Championship).

Goalkeeping records:
Longest run without conceding a goal:

British record (all competitive games): Chris Woods (Rangers), in 1196 minutes from November 26, 1986, to January 31, 1987.

Football League: Steve Death (Reading), 1103 minutes from March 24 to August 18, 1979.

Youngest players:

Premier League: Neil Finn, 17 years 3 days, West Ham United vs. Manchester City, January 1, 1996.

Premier League scorer: Andy Turner, 17 years 166 days, Tottenham vs. Everton, September 5, 1992.

Football League: Albert Geldard, 15 years 158 days, Bradford Park Avenue vs. Millwall, Division Two, September 16, 1929. Ken Roberts, also 15 years 158 days, Wrexham vs. Bradford Park Avenue, Division Three North, September 1, 1951.

Football League scorer: Ronnie Dix, 15 years 180 days, Bristol Rovers vs. Norwich City, Division Three South, March 3, 1928.

First Division: Derek Forster, 15 years 158 days, Sunderland vs. Leicester City, August 22, 1984.

First Division scorer: Jason Dozzell, 16 years 57 days, as substitute, Ipswich Town vs. Coventry City, February 4, 1984.

First Division hat-tricks: Alan Shearer, 17 years 240 days, Southampton vs. Arsenal, March 9, 1988. Jimmy Greaves, 17 years 10 months, Chelsea vs. Portsmouth, December 25, 1957.

FA Cup (any round): Andy Awford, 15 years 88 days, as substitute, Worcester City vs. Boreham Wood, 3rd Qualifying Round, October 10, 1987.

FA Cup proper: Scott Endersby, 15 years 288 days, Kettering vs. Tilbury, 1st Round, November 26, 1977.

FA Cup Final: James Prinsep, 17 years 245 days, Clapham Rovers vs. Old Etonians, 1879.

FA Cup Final scorer: Norman Whiteside, 18 years 18 days, Manchester United vs. Brighton and Hove Albion, 1983.

FA Cup Final captain: David Nish, 21 years 212 days, Leicester City vs. Manchester City, 1969.

League Cup Final scorer: Norman Whiteside, 17 years 324 days, Man United vs. Liverpool, 1983.

League Cup Final captain: Barry Venison, 20 years 7 months 8 days, Sunderland vs. Norwich City, 1985.

Oldest players:

Football League: Neil McBain, 52 years 4 months, New Brighton vs. Hartlepool United, Division Three North, March 15, 1947 (McBain was New Brighton's

manager and had to play in an emergency).
First Division: Stanley Matthews, 50 years 5 days,
Stoke City vs. Fulham, February 6, 1965.
FA Cup Final: Walter Hampson, 41 years 8 months,
Newcastle United vs. Aston Villa, 1924.
FA Cup: Billy Meredith, 49 years 8 months, Man City
vs. Newcastle United, March 29, 1924.

Sendings-off:

Most in a season: 314 (League alone), 1994–95.
Most in a day: 15 (3 League, 12 FA Cup), November
20, 1982.
Most in the League in a day: 13, December 14,
1985.
Most in the League over a weekend: 15,
December 22–23, 1990.
FA Cup Final: Kevin Moran, Manchester United vs.
Everton, 1985.
Others at Wembley: Boris Stankovic, Yugoslavia vs.
Sweden (Olympics), 1948; Antonio Rattin, Argentina
vs. England (World Cup), 1966; Billy Bremner (Leeds
United) and Kevin Keegan (Liverpool), Charity Shield
1974; Gilbert Dresch, Luxembourg vs. England (World
Cup qualifier), 1977; Mike Henry, Sudbury Town vs.
Tamworth (FA Vase), 1989; Jason Cook, Colchester
United vs. Witton Albion (FA Vase), 1992; Lee Dixon,
Arsenal vs. Tottenham Hotspur (FA Cup semi-final),
1993; Peter Swan, Port Vale vs. WBA (play-offs), 1993;
Andrei Kanchelskis, Manchester United vs. Aston Villa
(Coca-Cola Cup Final), 1994); Michael Wallace and
Chris Beaumont (both Stockport County) vs. Burnley
(play-offs), 1994; Tetsuji Hashiratani, Japan vs.
England (Umbro Cup), 1995; Derek Ward, Northwich
Victoria vs. Macclesfield Town (FA Trophy), 1996;
Tony Rogers, Dagenham and Redbridge vs. Woking
(FA Trophy), 1997; Brian Statham, Brentford vs. Crewe
(play-offs), 1997.
Quickest: 19 seconds, Mark Smith, Crewe vs.
Darlington (away), Division Three (March 12, 1994).
Quickest in Premier League: 72 seconds, Tim
Flowers, Blackburn Rovers vs. Leeds United
(February 1, 1995).
Quickest in Division One: 85 seconds, Liam
O'Brien, Manchester United vs. Southampton,
(January 3, 1987).
Quickest in the FA Cup: 52 seconds, Ian
Culverhouse, Swindon Town vs. Everton (away), 3rd
Round (January 5, 1997).
Quickest in European competition: 90 seconds,
Sergei Dirkach, Dynamo Moscow vs. Ghent, UEFA
Cup 3rd Round, 2nd Leg (December 11, 1991).
Quickest in the World Cup: 55 seconds, Jose Batista,
Uruguay vs. Scotland (Neza, Mexico; June 13, 1986).
World record: 10 seconds, Giuseppe Lorenzo,
Bologna vs. Parma, Italian Serie A, December 9, 1990.
Most in one game: 4: Northampton Town (0) vs.

Hereford United (4), Division Three (November 11,
1992); Crewe Alexandra (2) vs. Bradford Park Avenue
(2), Division Three North (Janaury 8, 1955); Sheffield
United (1) vs. Portsmouth (3), Division Two (December
13, 1986); Port Vale (2) vs. Northampton Town (2),
Littlewoods Cup (August 18, 1987); Brentford (2) vs.
Mansfield Town (2), Division Three (December 12,
1987).
Most sendings-off in a career: 21 – Willie Johnston
(7 Rangers, 6 WBA, 4 Vancouver Whitecaps, 3 Hearts,
1 Scotland).

Record attendances:

Premier League: 55,314 – Manchester United vs.
Wimbledon, January 29, 1997.
Old First Division: 83,260 – Manchester United vs.
Arsenal (Maine Road), January 17, 1948.
First Division: 30,729 – Manchester City v Oldham
Athletic, March 8, 1997.
Old Second Division: 70,302 – Tottenham Hotspur
vs. Southampton, February 25, 1950.
Second Division: 18,674 – Bristol City vs. Bristol
Rovers, December 15, 1996.
Old Third Division: 49,309 – Sheffield Wednesday vs.
Sheffield United, December 26, 1979.
Third Division South: 51,621 – Cardiff City vs.
Bristol City, April 7, 1947.
Third Division North: 49,655 – Hull City vs.
Rotherham United, December 25, 1948.
Fourth Division: 37,774 – Crystal Palace vs.
Millwall, March 31, 1961.
Record Football League aggregate (season):
41,271,414 (1948–49) – 88 clubs.
Record Football League aggregate (single day):
1,269,934, December 27, 1949.
*Record average home League attendance for
season:* 57,758, Manchester United, 1967–68.
Last 1 million League crowd aggregate:
1,007,200, December 27, 1971.
Scottish League: 118,567 – Rangers vs. Celtic
(Ibrox Stadium), January 2, 1939.
FA Cup Final: 126,047 – Bolton Wanderers vs. West
Ham United (Wembley), April 28, 1923.
European Cup: 135,826 – Celtic vs. Leeds United
(semi-final at Hampden Park), April 15, 1970.
Scottish Cup: 146,433 – Celtic vs. Aberdeen
(Hampden Park), April 24, 1937.
Record cup-tie aggregate: 265,199, at two matches
between Rangers and Morton, Scottish Cup Final,
1947–48.
World Cup: 199,854 – Brazil v Uruguay (Maracana,
Rio), July 16, 1950.

Major Soccer Awards

FIFA World Footballer of the Year

1991	Lothar Matthäus (Germany)
1992	Marco Van Basten (Holland)
1993	Roberto Baggio (Italy)
1994	Romario (Brazil)
1995	George Weah (Liberia)
1996	Ronaldo (Brazil)

World Footballer of the Year (World Soccer magazine)

1982	Paolo Rossi (Juventus & Italy)
1983	Zico (Udinese & Brazil)
1984	Michel Platini (Juventus & France)
1985	Michel Platini (Juventus & France)
1986	Diego Maradona (Napoli & Argentina)
1987	Ruud Gullit (Milan & Holland)
1988	Marco Van Basten (Milan & Holland)
1989	Ruud Gullit (Milan & Holland)
1990	Lothar Matthäus (Internazionale & West Germany)
1991	Jean-Pierre Papin (Marseille & France)
1992	Marco Van Basten (Milan & Holland)
1993	Roberto Baggio (Juventus & Italy)
1994	Paolo Maldini (Milan & Italy)
1995	Gianluca Vialli (Juventus & Italy)
1996	Ronaldo (Barcelona & Brazil)
1997	Ronaldo (Barcelona, Inter Milan & Brazil)

European Footballer of the Year (France Football magazine)

1956	Stanley Matthews (Blackpool)
1957	Alfredo Di Stefano (Real Madrid)
1958	Raymond Kopa (Real Madrid)

1959	Alfredo Di Stefano (Real Madrid)		*1993*	Roberto Baggio (Juventus)
1960	Luis Suarez (Barcelona)		*1994*	Hristo Stoichkov (Barcelona)
1961	Omar Sivori (Juventus)		*1995*	George Weah (Milan)
1962	Josef Masopust (Dukla Prague)		*1996*	Matthias Sammer (B Dortmund)

1963 Lev Yashin (Moscow Dynamo)

1964 Denis Law (Manchester Utd)

South American Footballer of the Year

1965 Eusebio (Benfica)

1966 Bobby Charlton (Manchester U)

1967 Florian Albert (Ferencvaros)

1968 George Best (Manchester U)

1969 Gianni Rivera (Milan)

1970 Gerd Müller (Bayern Munich)

1971 Johan Cruyff (Ajax)

1972 Franz Beckenbauer (B Munich)

1973 Johan Cruyff (Barcelona)

1974 Johan Cruyff (Barcelona)

1975 Oleg Blokhin (Dynamo Kiev)

1976 Franz Beckenbauer (B Munich)

1977 Allan Simonsen (Borussia MG)

1978 Kevin Keegan (Hamburg)

1979 Kevin Keegan (Hamburg)

1980 Karl-Heinz Rumenigge (B Munich)

1981 Karl-Heinz Rumenigge (B Munich)

1982 Paolo Rossi (Juventus)

1983 Michel Platini (Juventus)

1984 Michel Platini (Juventus)

1985 Michel Platini (Juventus)

1986 Igor Belanov (Dynamo Kiev)

1987 Ruud Gullit (Milan)

1988 Marco Van Basten (Milan)

1989 Marco Van Basten (Milan)

1990 Lothar Matthäus (Inter)

1991 Jean-Pierre Papin (Marseilles)

1992 Marco Van Basten (Milan)

1971	Tostao (Brazil)
1972	Teofilio Cubillas (Peru)
1973	Pele (Brazil)
1974	Elias Figueroa (Chile)
1975	Elias Figueroa (Chile)
1976	Elias Figueroa (Chile)
1977	Zico (Brazil)
1978	Mario Kempes (Argentina)
1979	Diego Maradona (Argentina)
1980	Diego Maradona (Argentina)
1981	Zico (Brazil)
1982	Zico (Brazil)
1983	Socrates (Brazil)
1984	Enzo Francescoli (Uruguay)
1985	Romero (Brazil)
1986	Alzamendi (Uruguay)
1987	Carlos Valderrama (Colombia)
1988	Ruben Paz (Uruguay)
1989	Bebeto (Brazil)
1990	Raul Amarilla (Paraguay)
1991	Oscar Ruggeri (Argentina)
1992	Rai (Brazil)
1993	Carlos Valderrama (Colombia)
1994	Cafu (Brazil)
1995	Enzo Francescoli (Uruguay)
1996	Jose Luis Chilavert (Paraguay)

African Footballer of the Year (France Football magazine)

1970   Salif Keita (Mali)

1971   Ibrahim Sunday (Ghana)

1972   Cherif Souleymane (Guinea)

1973   Tshimen Bwanga (Zaïre)

1974   Paul Moukila (Congo)

1975   Ahmed Faras (Morocco)

1976   Roger Milla (Cameroon)

1977   Tarak Dhiab (Tunisia)

1978   Karim Abdoul Razak (Ghana)

1979   Thomas N'Kono (Cameroon)

1980   Manga Onguene (Cameroon)

1981   Lakhdar Belloumi (Algeria)

1982   Thomas N'Kono (Cameroon)

1983   Mahmoud Al Khatib (Egypt)

1984   Theophile Abega (Cameroon)

1985   Mohamed Timoumi (Morocco)

1986   Badou Zaki (Morocco)

1987   Rabah Madjer (Algeria)

1988   Kalusha Bwalya (Zambia)

1989   George Weah (Liberia)

1990   Roger Milla (Cameroon)

1991   Abedi Pele (Ghana)

1992   Abedi Pele (Ghana)

1993   Abedi Pele (Ghana)

1994   George Weah (Liberia)

1995   George Weah (Liberia)

1996   Nwankwo Kanu (Nigeria)

The African Confederation player of the year award has been awarded to:

1993   Rashidi Yekini (Nigeria)

1994   Emanuel Amunike (Nigeria)

1995   George Weah (Liberia)

1996   Nwankwo Kanu (Nigeria)

Asian Footballer of the Year

1990   Kim Joo-sung (South Korea)

1991   Kim Joo-sung (South Korea)

1992   no award

1993   Kazu Miura (Japan)

1994   Said Al-Owairan (Saudi Arabia)

1995   Masami Ihara (Japan)

1996   Khodad Azizi (Iran)

Oceania Footballer of the Year

1990   Robby Slater (Australia)

1991   Wynton Rufer (New Zealand)

1992   Wynton Rufer (New Zealand)

1993   Robby Slater (Australia)

1994   Aurelio Vidmar (Australia)

1995   Christian Karembeu (New Caledonia & France)

English Footballer of the Year (Football Writers' Association)

1948 Stanley Matthews (Blackpool)

1949 Johnny Carey (Manchester U)

1950 Joe Mercer (Arsenal)

1951 Harry Johnston (Blackpool)

1952 Billy Wright (Wolves)

1953 Nat Lofthouse (Bolton W)

1954 Tom Finney (Preston North End)

1955 Don Revie (Manchester C)

1956 Bert Trautmann (Manchester C)

1957 Tom Finney (Preston North End)

1958 Danny Blanchflower (Tottenham H)

1959 Syd Owen (Luton Town)

1960 Bill Slater (Wolverhampton W)

1961 Danny Blanchflower (Tottenham H)

1962 Jimmy Adamson (Burnley)

1963 Stanley Matthews (Stoke City)

1964 Bobby Moore (West Ham United)

1965 Bobby Collins (Leeds United)

1966 Bobby Charlton (Manchester U)

1967 Jackie Charlton (Leeds United)

1968 George Best (Manchester United)

1969 Dave Mackay (Derby County) and Tony Book (Manchester City)

1970 Billy Bremner (Leeds United)

1971 Frank McLintock (Arsenal)

1972 Gordon Banks (Stoke City)

1973 Pat Jennings (Tottenham H)

1974 Ian Callaghan (Liverpool)

1975 Alan Mullery (Fulham)

1976 Kevin Keegan (Liverpool)

1977 Emlyn Hughes (Liverpool)

1978 Kenny Burns (Nottingham Forest)

1979 Kenny Dalglish (Liverpool)

1980 Terry McDermott (Liverpool)

1981 Frans Thijssen (Ipswich Town)

1982 Steve Perryman (Tottenham H)

1983 Kenny Dalglish (Liverpool)

1984 Ian Rush (Liverpool)

1985 Neville Southall (Everton)

1986 Gary Lineker (Everton)

1987 Clive Allen (Tottenham H)

1988 John Barnes (Liverpool)

1989 Steve Nicol (Liverpool)

1990 John Barnes (Liverpool)

1991 Gordon Strachan (Leeds United)

1992 Gary Lineker (Tottenham H)

1993 Chris Waddle (Sheffield W)

1994 Alan Shearer (Blackburn Rovers)

1995 Jürgen Klinsmann (Tottenham H)

1996 Eric Cantona (Manchester U)

1997 Gianfranco Zola (Chelsea)

1998 Dennis Bergkamp (Arsenal)

Scottish Footballer of the Year

1965 Billy McNeill (Celtic)

1966 John Greig (Rangers)

1967 Ronnie Simpson (Celtic)

1968 Gordon Wallace (Raith Rovers)

1969 Bobby Murdoch (Celtic)

1970 Pat Stanton (Hibernian)

1971 Martin Buchan (Aberdeen)

1972 Dave Smith (Rangers)

1973	George Connelly (Celtic)	*1986*	Sandy Jardine (Hearts)
1974	Scotland World Cup squad	*1987*	Brian McClair (Celtic)
1975	Sandy Jardine (Rangers)	*1988*	Paul McStay (Celtic)
1976	John Greig (Rangers)	*1989*	Richard Gough (Rangers)
1977	Danny McGrain (Celtic)	*1990*	Alex McLeish (Aberdeen)
1978	Derek Johnstone (Rangers)	*1991*	Maurice Malpas (Dundee United)
1979	Andy Ritchie (Morton)	*1992*	Ally McCoist (Rangers)
1980	Gordon Strachan (Aberdeen)	*1993*	Andy Goram (Rangers)
1981	Alan Rough (Partick Thistle)	*1994*	Mark Hateley (Rangers)
1982	Paul Sturrock (Dundee United)	*1995*	Brian Laudrup (Rangers)
1983	Charlie Nicholas (Celtic)	*1996*	Paul Gascoigne (Rangers
1984	Willie Miller (Aberdeen)	*1997*	Brian Laudrup (Rangers)
1985	Hamish McAlpine (Dundee United)	*1998*	Craig Burley (Celtic)

Chronology

1848 First code of rules compiled at Cambridge University

1855 Sheffield FC, world's oldest club, formed

1862 Notts County, world's oldest league club, formed

1863 FA formed, Oct 26

1871 FA Cup inaugurated

1872 Size of ball fixed

1872 Scotland draw 0–0 with England in first official international, at West of Scotland cricket ground

1873 Scottish FA and Cup launched

1874 Shinguards introduced by Sam Weller Widdowson of Nottingham Forest and England

1875 Crossbar replaces tape

1876 FA of Wales formed

1878 Referee's whistle used for first time, at Nottingham Forest's ground

1878 Almost 20,000 people watch first floodlit match, between two Sheffield teams, with lighting provided by four lamps on 30ft wooden towers

1882 International Board formed

1883 Two-handed throw-in introduced

1885 Professionalism legalized

1888 Football League, brainchild of Aston Villa director, William McGregor, founded, and first matches played on Sept 8

1888 Scottish Cup winners Renton

beat English FA Cup winners West Bromwich for the "Championship of the World"

1889 Unbeaten Preston, "The Invincibles", become first club to win League and Cup double

1890 Scottish and Irish Leagues formed

1891 Goal nets and penalties introduced

1891 Referees and linesman replace umpires and referees

1892 Football League Second Division formed

1893 Genoa, oldest Italian League club, formed

1895 FA Cup, held by Aston Villa, stolen from Birmingham shop window and never seen again

1897 Players' Union formed

1897 Juventus formed

1898 Promotion and relegation introduced

1899 Barcelona formed

1901 Maximum wage rule in force

1901 Southern League Tottenham Hotspur become first professional club to take FA Cup south

1901 First 100,000 attendance (110,802) at Cup Final, venue Crystal Palace

1901 Argentina beat Uruguay 3–2 in first international between South American countries

1902 Ibrox Park disaster: 25 killed when part of new wooden stand collapses at Scotland vs. England match

1902 Real Madrid formed

1902 Austria beat Hungary 5–0 in Vienna, the first international between teams outside the home countries

1904 FIFA formed with seven members

1905 England join FIFA

1905: Goalkeepers ordered to stay on goal-line at penalties

1905 First £1,000 transfer: Alf Common, from Sunderland to Middlesbrough

1908 Transfer limit of £350 introduced in January, withdrawn in April

1908 UK beat Denmark to win first Olympic title, at Shepherds Bush

1908 England travel to Vienna to beat Austria 6–1 in their first international on foreign soil

1910 Argentina win the first South

American Championship

1919 League extended to 44 clubs

1920 Third Division South formed

1921 Third Division North formed

1923 Football pools introduced

1923 First Wembley FA Cup final: Bolton 2 West Ham 0

1924 First Wembley international: England 1 Scotland 1

1924 Goal can be scored direct from corner kick

1925 Offside rule change: a player needs two, not three, players between him and goal to stay onside

1926 Huddersfield complete first hat-trick of championships

1927 Hughie Ferguson's goal against Arsenal makes Cardiff first club to take FA Cup out of England

1928 The four home countries withdraw from FIFA

1928 Bill "Dixie" Dean scores 60 First Division goals, still a record

1929 Goalkeepers ordered to stay on goal-line until penalty is kicked

1930 Uruguay win first World Cup

1933 Numbered shirts worn in the FA cup final for first time, winners Everton wearing 1–11, Manchester City 12–22

1934 Sudden death of Arsenal manager Herbert Chapman on Jan 6

1936 Joe Payne's 10-goal record (Luton 12 Bristol Rovers 0)

1938 First live TV transmission of Cup Final (Preston 1 Huddersfield 0)

1939 Compulsory numbering of players in Football League

1939 All normal competitions suspended because of war

1946 British Associations rejoin FIFA

1946 33 killed and 500 injured as wall and crowd barriers collapse at Bolton vs. Stoke FA Cup tie

1947 First £20,000 transfer: Tommy Lawton, from Chelsea to Notts County

1949 England's first home defeat by a non-Home nation (0–2 vs. Republic of Ireland at Goodison Park, Liverpool)

1949 Entire Torino team wiped out when aircraft taking them home from Lisbon crashes near Turin

1950 League extended from 88 to 92

clubs

1950 England humbled 1–0 by US in World Cup group match, and world record crowd (203,500) see Uruguay beat Brazil 2–1 in the Final in Rio

1950 Scotland first beaten at home by foreign team (Austria, 1–0)

1951 White ball comes into use

1951 First official match under floodlights played at Highbury: between Arsenal and Hapoel Tel Aviv

1952 Newcastle become first to win successive FA Cup finals at Wembley

1953 Hungary beat England 6–3 at Wembley

1954 Hungary beat England 7–1 in Budapest

1955 First floodlit FA Cup tie (replay): Kidderminster vs. Brierley Hill Alliance

1956 First floodlit League match: Portsmouth vs. Newcastle

1956 Real Madrid, from an entry of 16 teams, win first European Cup

1956 South Korea defeat Israel to win first Asian Cup

1957 First African Nations Cup final: Egypt 4 Ethiopia 1

1958 Electrified pitch used by Everton to beat frost

1958 Munich air disaster kills 19, including eight Manchester United players

1958 English League restructured into four divisions

1958 Barcelona beat a London Select team 8–2 over two games to win first Inter City Fairs Cup

1959 Billy Wright of Wolves, first man to reach 100 caps for England, retires on 105

1960 FA recognizes Sunday football

1960 Football League Cup introduced

1960 European champions Real Madrid win first World Club Championship, beating South American champions Penarol over two legs

1960 Soviet Union win the first European Championship

1960 Penarol of Uruguay win first Copa Libertadores

1961 Tottenham complete first League and Cup double this century

1961 Maximum wage (£20) abolished

1961 First British £100-a-week wage paid to Johnny Haynes by Fulham

1961 Spurs pay £99,999 for striker Jimmy Greaves from Torino

1961 First £100,000 British transfer: Denis Law, from Manchester City to Torino

1961 Fiorentina beat Rangers 4–2 over two games to win first European Cup-winners' Cup

1961 Hapoel Tel Aviv defeat Selangor of Malaysia 2–1 to win first Asian Champions Cup

1962 Manchester United pay record £115,000 to bring Law back from Italy

1963 Tottenham beat Atletico Madrid 5–1 in Cup-winners' Cup Final to become first British club to win European trophy

1963 FA centenary

1963 First Pools Panel

1964 First televised Match of the Day (BBC 2, Liverpool 3 Arsenal 2, August 22)

1964 318 die and 500 injured in crowd riot over disallowed goal during Peru vs. Argentina Olympic tie in Lima

1964 Oryx Douala of Cameroon defeat Stade Malien of Mali 2–1 to win first African Champions Club Cup

1965 Ten Football League players jailed and banned for life for match-fixing

1965 Stanley Matthews knighted

1965 Substitutes allowed for injured players in League matches

1966 England win World Cup, beating West Germany 4–2 after extra time at Wembley

1967 Alf Ramsey, England manager, knighted

1967 Celtic beat Internazionale 2–1 to become first British winners of European Cup and complete unprecedented grand slam: European Cup, Scottish League, League Cup, Scottish Cup and Glasgow Cup

1967 First substitutes in Cup final (Chelsea vs. Tottenham), but neither is used

1968 74 die at Nunez, Buenos Aires, when panic breaks out during River Plate vs. Boca Juniors match

1968 Alan Mullery becomes first England player sent off, vs. Yugoslavia in European

Championship

1968 Manchester United become first English winners of European Cup beating Benfica 4–1 after extra time

1970 Brazil beat Italy 4–1 to capture World Cup for third time and win Jules Rimet trophy outright

1971 66 fans trampled to death and 100 injured in second Ibrox disaster, as they tumbled down stairway just before end of Rangers vs. Celtic New Year's Day game

1972 Fairs Cup becomes UEFA Cup and is won by Tottenham, who defeat Wolves 3–2 over two games

1974 League football played on Sunday for first time

1974 Last FA Amateur Cup Final

1974 Joao Havelange succeeds Sir Stanley Rous as FIFA president

1977 Liverpool win League Championship and European Cup

1978 Freedom of contract accepted for League players

1978 Liverpool first English club to win successive European Cups

1978 Ban on foreign players in English football lifted

1979 First all-British £500,000 transfer: David Mills, from Middlesbrough to West Bromwich

1979 First £1m British transfer: Trevor Francis, from Birmingham City to Nottingham Forest

1981 Tottenham win 100th Cup Final

1981 Liverpool win European Cup, becoming first British side to hold it three times

1981 Three points for a win introduced in Football League

1981 Record British transfer: Bryan Robson, from WBA to Manchester United for £1.5m

1981 QPR install first artificial pitch in English football

1982 340 fans crushed to death during Spartak Moscow vs. Haarlem UEFA Cup tie at Lenin Stadium

1982 Aston Villa become sixth consecutive English winners of European Cup

1982 Tottenham retain FA Cup, first time since Spurs in 1961–62

1982 League Cup becomes Milk Cup

1982 Italy defeat West Germany 3–1

in Madrid to complete third World Cup triumph

1983 Football League sponsored by Canon for three years

1984 Aberdeen take Scottish Cup for third successive season and win championship

1984 Liverpool win European Cup in penalty shoot-out and complete unique treble for an English club, with Milk Cup and League title

1984 Northern Ireland win last British Home Championship

1984 France win their first honour – the European Championship

1984 Britain's biggest score this century: Stirling Albion beat Selkirk 20–0 in Scottish Cup

1985 Bradford City fire disaster kills 56

1985 Kevin Moran (Manchester United) becomes first player sent off in Cup Final

1985 Heysel disaster: 39 die as a result of rioting at Liverpool vs. Juventus European Cup Final in Brussels. UEFA ban English clubs indefinitely from European competition

1986 Sir Stanley Rous dies, aged 91

1986 Wales FA move HQ from Wrexham to Cardiff after 110 years

1986 Luton ban all visiting supporters as a measure against hooliganism

1986 Two substitutes allowed in FA and League Cups

1987 Play-offs introduced for last promotion place; re-election abolished; automatic promotion for winners of Conference

1987 The 18-strong squad plus youth players and officials of Alianza Lima die in plane crash

1989 Hillsborough disaster: 95 crushed to death at Liverpool vs. Nottingham Forest FA Cup semi-final

1990 International Board amends offside law (player level no longer offside); FIFA make professional foul a sending-off offence

1990 English clubs (Manchester United and Aston Villa) restored to European competition

1990 Guiseppe Lorenzo of Bologna

creates world record by being sent off after 10 seconds for striking Parma opponent

1991 End of artificial pitches in Division One (Oldham and Luton)

1992 Premier League of 22 clubs launched; Football League reduced to 71 clubs in three divisions

1992 15 killed and 1,300 injured when temporary stand collapses at Bastia, Corsica, during Bastia vs. Marseille in French Cup semi-final

1993 Marseille are the first French team to win European Cup, but cannot defend their trophy following bribery scandal

1994 Manchester United win "double"

1994 Brazil become first country to win the World Cup on a penalty shoot-out, beating Italy after 0–0 draw

1996 Manchester United become first club to win English "double" twice

1996 English host the European Championship finals for the first time

1997 Manchester United win the Premier League to maintain their stranglehold on the English game

1997 Chelsea win the FA Cup with the fastest goal in FA Cup history by Roberto Di Matteo and win 2–0 against Middlesbrough (who were also the losers in the League Cup)

1998 Arsenal break the Manchester United monopoly on the way to winning the Double as they also beat Newcastle United 2–0 in the FA Cup final

1998 England crash out on penalties in the second round of the World Cup. Host-nation France go on to win the trophy for the first time beating Brazil 3–0 in the final